The
SECRET SOCIETY
of
MOSES

The
SECRET SOCIETY
of
MOSES

The Mosaic Bloodline
and a Conspiracy
Spanning Three Millennia

FLAVIO BARBIERO
TRANSLATED BY STEVE SMITH

Inner Traditions
Rochester, Vermont • Toronto, Canada

Inner Traditions
One Park Street
Rochester, Vermont 05767
www.InnerTraditions.com

Library of Congress Cataloging-in-Publication Data

Barbiero, Flavio.
  The secret society of Moses : the mosaic bloodline and a conspiracy spanning three
millennia / Flavio Barbiero ; translated by Steve Smith.
      p. cm.
  Includes bibliographical references and index.
  ISBN 978-1-59477-273-3 (pbk.)
  1. History—Religious aspects. 2. History—Philosophy. 3. Moses (Biblical leader)
I. Title.
  BL65.H5B37 2010
  222'.109—dc22

                                                                    2009036506

Printed and bound in the United States by Lake Book Manufacturing

10   9   8   7   6   5   4   3   2   1

Text design by Jon Desautels and layout by Priscilla Baker
This book was typeset in Garamond Premier Pro with Futura used as a display
typeface

To send correspondence to the author of this book, mail a first-class letter to the
author c/o Inner Traditions • Bear & Company, One Park Street, Rochester, VT
05767, and we will forward the communication.

CONTENTS

PREFACE

Today, at the beginning of the twenty-first century, no more than 30 percent of the world's population adheres to religions that have their origins and doctrinal foundations in the Bible.

In the last century, at the height of European colonial expansion, almost the whole world was owned and governed directly by this minority. Now colonialism in its purest and most iniquitous form has faded, but the power of the nations with Judeo-Christian roots over the rest of the world is perhaps just as strong as it was then, albeit exercised in ways that are more sophisticated and respectful of human rights. The inescapable conclusion is that today's world is dominated by the spiritual heirs of Moses, who must therefore be seen as one of the greatest protagonists in human history.

Without Moses there would have been no Jewish religion, and without the powerful unifying force of this religion, nothing would have distinguished the descendants of Israel from the myriad other peoples and tribes in the Middle East, which have left only ephemeral traces in history. Christianity would never have been born and the world today would be completely different.

When, in a remote corner of the Sinai desert, Moses gave his little tribe of nomadic shepherds the tablets of the Ten Commandments, he certainly did not imagine that he was laying the foundations of a religion that within a few millennia would dominate the whole planet.

Yet even if he had been able to foresee this, he surely could never have imagined that none other than the main beneficiaries of his spiritual inheritance, in the climactic moment of his triumph, would start to doubt whether he had ever existed. A strong modern scientific current, passing transversally through Jews, Christians, and nonbelievers, now casts doubt on the historicity of the first books of the Bible and the very existence of characters such as Abraham, Isaac, Jacob (the father of the people of Israel), and especially Moses, the true originator of it all.

How this conclusion was arrived at and why—whether by conviction, calculation, or something else—is not a theme with which this book intends to deal. It should be stated immediately, however, that this text starts from very different suppositions: from the profound conviction that Moses, as an individual figure, actually existed and that the events surrounding him are narrated in the Bible as their protagonists and eyewitnesses experienced, understood, and reported them; that there have certainly been interpolations and misrepresentations of the text, but not such as to question the historicity of the events narrated and of their protagonists.

There is therefore an immediate problem whose solution is the underlying theme of this book: that of the progeny of Moses. Muhammad left descendants that reign on all the Arab thrones. Buddha left descendants still respected and venerated in all those countries that adopted his doctrine. Throughout the world, thousands of people—the *cohanim*, the Jewish priestly class—declare themselves to be directly descended from the man whom the Bible presents as Moses's elder brother, Aaron.

And Moses? What happened to his line? Where are his descendants? Why does nobody today claim the greatest of the prophets among his or her ancestors? If Moses had descendants, in addition to his spiritual inheritance he must have left a material, genetic inheritance, and the genes transmitted directly from his seed should be found in the DNA of a great number of people today. Yet who are these people? Where are they? Why do we know nothing about them?

This book tries to answer these questions. By examining the information contained in the only truly "historical" document we have on the subject, the Bible, we discover a surprising quantity of precise and detailed information on Moses's family, allowing us to establish with certainty that he had descendants and to reconstruct the relevant events regarding his family in a thorough and reliable way for the whole historical period covered by the Bible. It is a riveting and surprising story that many, no doubt, will find disconcerting; but it is a true story, as far as what the Hebrew Scriptures tells us can be considered true.

It is a story that is not the fruit of simple conjecture or of more or less gratuitous inferences, but instead is the result of research. Step by step, it follows the movements of the family that Moses generated in the Sinai desert after his escape from Egypt. We follow his descendants first in the conquest of Palestine and then in the period of the Roman Empire and the rise of the West—through an infinite series of facts and historical documents that form an impressive and convergent sum of circumstantial evidence, concluding with the main proof, accepted today in every courtroom in the world: genetic verification. We will see, in fact, that a considerable percentage of the European population carries in its DNA a genetic inheritance directly transmitted by Moses.

Developed in this book is a thesis—not a theory—which finds its series of supporting arguments not in unpublished or secret documents of more-or-less proven authenticity (emerging as if by magic from some poorly explored archive), but instead in universally recognized historical texts that are accessible to everyone. Everybody can judge and evaluate the validity of the conclusions presented here by using only his or her own common sense. I am certain that in the end everyone will find this thesis if not exactly unassailable, then at least credible.

THE JUDAIC PRIESTLY LINE

My family origins are not obscure. We are of priestly descent. There are different foundations for nobility in every people, and the excellence of our line is confirmed by belonging to the priestly order.

In my case, my family descends not simply from priests, but from the first of the twenty-four priestly classes—itself a mark of distinction—and, within this class, from the most illustrious tribe. Further, on my mother's side I am related to the royal family: my mother is a granddaughter of Hasmoneus, who, for a long time, held the high priesthood and the realm of our people.

Thus did Josephus Flavius begin his autobiography, written in Rome in about AD 94, during the reign of the Emperor Domitian.

Two relevant pieces of information for our story are contained in these opening statements. The first is that the noble class of the Jewish people in Roman times consisted of the descendants of twenty-four branches of a priestly family who had returned to Jerusalem from Babylonian exile at the end of the fifth century BC, and who, under the patronage of Ezra, had stipulated a pact with each other for the reconstruction of the Temple and its management in the centuries to come (see 1 Chronicles 24:1–19).

The second relevant piece of information is that even the position of "royalty" fell at that time to the Jewish priestly line, and in particular to those lines that descended from the Hasmoneans, who, from 141 to 63 BC, had governed Jerusalem not only as high priests but also as kings,[1] expropriating from the descendants of David (assuming that they still existed) every right to the throne. The Jewish royal family in Roman times was descended from priests, and not from David.*

When Josephus Flavius wrote these words, however, the noble priestly class, of which he proudly declared himself a part, practically no longer existed. It had been wiped out twenty-five years earlier by Titus Flavius Vespasian, who, during the destruction of Jerusalem in AD 70, had killed thousands of priests.

Obviously, there were many survivors. In the Roman Empire there were numerous Judaic communities led by representatives of the priestly class, and the members of the priestly lines deported by Titus Flavius amounted to at least a few hundred. How many they were in total is difficult to say, but their numbers were certainly still quite high. Yet the realm of Judah, which had been their nation of origin, no longer existed by then. It was destroyed, as had been the main instrument of their power and the very reason for their existence: the Temple of Jerusalem.† In this way, the pact of alliance among the twenty-four priestly branches for the running of the Temple of Jerusalem—which, after their return from Babylon, had been the unifying factor of their line and the prime creator of its fortunes—also came to lose significance. It seemed that by now the priestly families had forever lost every power and noble prerogative and were destined, with time, to lose even their identity.

But Josephus Flavius had already conceived and put into action a

---

*Indeed, it is true that Herod—who was of Edomite origin and was made king of Judah by the Roman senate in 40 BC—in order to legitimize his position in the eyes of the Jewish people, was quick to marry Mariamme, the daughter of the Hasmonean Hyrcanus, the last king of Judah.

†When Titus destroyed the Temple, he had hundreds of priests executed on the pretext that their existence was no longer justified, because the Temple no longer existed.

plan of counterattack that not only would return the priestly line to its past splendors, but also aimed much higher. He had employed a strategy to ensure that the line, deprived of power and almost wiped out by Rome, would sooner or later take over not the fallen Palestine, but the Roman Empire itself, and would become its dominant class.

Given the circumstances, his plan might have appeared as an incredible utopia—even pure madness—but in hindsight, it seems so well devised and realistic that it could only be successful. His plan was worthy of the figure of great brilliance and limitless ambition that he was deemed to be. Despite the scant consideration given to him by modern historians, he is surely one of the most commanding figures in history. In fact, he might be considered equal in stature to his great ancestor, Moses. Yes, Moses: this is not a slip of the pen. The starting point of this book is, in fact, the demonstration that Josephus Flavius, and with him the whole Judaic priestly line, descended directly from Moses.

Yet, according to the universally recognized and accepted tradition, all the priests descended from Moses's brother Aaron. It is a tradition that was born at the time of Ezra—and as a result of Ezra's works. Since then, it has been continually reasserted with force and conviction, to the point of becoming an unquestioned truth that nobody has ever doubted, but it is a truth that is easy to disprove on the basis of the information provided by the Bible.

This is what we shall see in the coming chapters.

PART ONE

The Family of Moses

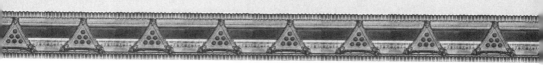

1

CENSORSHIP IN THE BIBLE REGARDING MOSES AND HIS DESCENDANTS

THE DEATH OF MOSES

It was a clear day at the beginning of April, when

> . . . Moses went up from the plains of Moab unto the mountain of
> Nebo, to the top of Pisgah, that [is] over against Jericho. And the
> Lord showed him all the land of Gilead, unto Dan, and all Naphtali,
> and the land of Ephraim, and Manasseh, and all the land of Judah,
> unto the utmost sea, and the south, and the plain of the valley of
> Jericho, the city of palm trees, unto Zoar. And the Lord said unto
> him, This [is] the land, which I sware unto Abraham, unto Isaac,
> and unto Jacob, saying, I will give it unto thy seed: I have caused
> thee to see [it] with thine eyes, but thou shalt not go over thither.
> So Moses the servant of the Lord died there in the land of Moab,
> according to the word of the Lord. And He buried him in a valley
> in the land of Moab, over against Bethpeor: but no man knoweth of
> his sepulchre unto this day.[1]

These six verses, for the most part extremely vague, recount one of the most important events in the whole Pentateuch: the last acts, death, and burial of the greatest of the prophets. Of this prophet, Deuteronomy tells us: "And there arose not a prophet since in Israel like unto Moses, whom the Lord knew face-to-face, in all the signs and the wonders, which the Lord sent him to do in the land of Egypt to Pharaoh, and to all his servants, and to all his land, and in all that mighty hand, and in all the great terror, which Moses shewed in the sight of all Israel."[2]

The scarcity of information provided by Deuteronomy regarding this episode is surprising and provokes many questions. At that time and in that part of the world, death and burial were the most important events in an individual's life—especially in the case of an important figure such as Moses. Why was the book's writer so reticent on this subject? Is it possible that this was all he knew about the death and burial of Moses?

The author of Deuteronomy appears extremely well informed about the events immediately prior to the prophet's death.[*] He does not miss a word of Moses's long speech in the valley of Moab. He describes the ceremony of the handover from Moses to Joshua in a precise and detailed way. Only when he arrives at the crux of the whole matter—at the moment of the funeral and burial—does he know nothing about it. It seems extremely unlikely—in fact, so incredible as to be astonishing.

One reasonable explanation for this strange silence is that those who had witnessed Moses's death and had taken care of his burial wanted to avoid providing information that might in some way have compromised the secret of the location of his tomb. Everything to do with Moses's death, then, had to remain secret. This is possible, though there may be room for other hypotheses.

---

[*]According to most exegetes, the book following Deuteronomy, Joshua, was written by the same author, who was therefore also fully informed on the events following the death of Moses.

What is certain, in any event, is that the Bible maintains the most rigorous silence on Moses's death and burial. In the account in Deuteronomy, the only figures present at Moses's demise and interment are himself and God: "Moses went up . . . unto the mountain of Nebo. . . . And the Lord shewed him all the land. . . . Moses . . . died there. . . . And He buried him in a valley." There is not the slightest mention of any attendants or those who took care of the burial.

This, not surprisingly, has sparked the imagination of religious exegetes, and contributed more than a little to giving the prophet the image, halfway between the human and the divine, that justifies any explanation of "supernatural" events surrounding him. Even his death and burial are seen by religious commentators as supernatural events. The Masoretic Text says that it is God himself who buries Moses. The explanations given for this are manifold and all equally unsatisfactory from a rational point of view. St. John Chrysostom, and with him a vast array of Christian commentators, held that in this way God wanted to prevent the Jews, who were inclined to idolatry, from making a superstitious cult out of Moses's mortal remains.

Others, however, think that Moses did not actually die, but rather that he was taken up into heaven as Enoch and Elijah had been in their time. This was a deep-rooted legend among the ancient Jews. The historian Josephus Flavius, for example, in *Antiquities of the Jews* (Book IV, chapter XIV), says, regarding the prophet's last moments: "Suddenly a cloud engulfed him, and took him to a nearby valley, far from prying eyes; in the holy books, however, he said about himself that he had died, for fear that, because of his extraordinary merits, it would be said that he had mutated into a God."

By reasoning in supernatural terms, anything becomes legitimate, but the fact is that Moses was a man of flesh and blood like everybody else, and his death is the main proof of this. Further, surely he was not alone on Nebo; somebody attended him in his last moments and somebody took care of his burial. Who? The first person who comes to mind is Joshua, his faithful companion since childhood, who had just been nominated supreme head of the Jewish people. Eleazar, son of his fraternal friend Aaron, was probably also present, but the people who absolutely had to be there were his two sons, Gershom and Eliezer.

One constant feature in reports of the deaths of biblical patriarchs is that they were invariably attended on the point of death and buried by their own sons. Abraham is buried by "his sons Isaac and Ishmael . . . in the cave of Machpelah, in the field of Ephron, the son of Zohar the Hittite, which is before Mamre" (Genesis 25:9). Isaac is buried by his sons Esau and Jacob (Genesis 35:29). Jacob's funeral is particularly solemn, and the whole of the second half of the last chapter of Genesis is dedicated to it. His corpse is embalmed in Egypt and then transported to Hebron and buried in the cavern of Mach Pelah by all his sons. Aaron too, who died a few months earlier than Moses and in analogous circumstances, on a mountaintop, is attended in his final moments and buried by his own son Eleazar (Numbers 20:29).

Yet what about Moses? Logic and tradition suggest that his sons attended him in his dying moments, officiated at his funeral, and buried him—but the Bible does not say so. This seems so strange that we might wonder whether there is a specific reason for this omission. Is the reticence of the account in Deuteronomy intended to shroud in mystery the circumstances of Moses's death and burial, or is its purpose to hide the fact that he had his sons with him?

This is not a gratuitous question. Everybody knows the enormous importance that family and progeny had for men of that epoch—especially in Jewish society. It is a concept that is reiterated continually in the Bible. Moses could not have escaped this rule. Yet in the last three books of the Pentateuch, Moses's family is never mentioned. It is completely canceled out, as if it had never existed. This is a huge omission, but it seems to have escaped the attention of the exegetes and students of the Bible, who appear, strangely, to attach no importance to it.

MOSES'S FAMILY

In all the works that discuss Moses there are interminable dissertations on his natural parents and even more so on his adoptive parents who, according to some traditions, were members of the family of the pharaoh. None of them, however, ever speaks about the family generated by Moses himself: his children and their descendants. It is a matter that seems subject to a rigorous taboo. We search in vain for information in the countless books that deal with Moses. There is no doubt that he had a wife and children, but what happened to them? Who wanted to erase them from the Bible, and why?

When Moses flees from Egypt, followed by an arrest warrant for having killed an Egyptian, he takes refuge in the country of the Midianites and is given hospitality by the priest Jethro. "And he gave Moses Zipporah his daughter. And she bare [him] a son, and he called his name Gershom: for he said, I have been a stranger in a strange land" (Exodus 2:22). Later, Zipporah gives him a second son, Eliezer.

When Moses returns to Egypt to organize the Exodus, according to Exodus 4:20, he takes his wife and children with him at least for part of the journey. Yet clearly either this information is not correct, or he subsequently sends them back to his father-in-law, Jethro, in the Sinai, because this is where they are at the moment of the Exodus. Chapter 18 of Exodus is dedicated entirely to Jethro's visit to Moses in Rephidim, near the Holy Mount, on which occasion Jethro brings back Moses's family:

> Then Jethro, Moses's father-in-law, took Zipporah, Moses's wife, after Moses had sent her back with her two sons. The name of the one [was] Gershom, for Moses said, "I have been an alien in a strange land," and the name of the other [was] Eliezer, "for the God of my father," [said Moses, "was] mine help, and delivered me from the sword of Pharaoh." And Jethro, Moses's father-in-law, came with Moses's sons and wife unto Moses in the wilderness, where he encamped at the mount of God. And he said unto Moses, "I thy father-in-law Jethro am come unto thee, and thy wife, and her two sons with her."[3]

This is the last time that Zipporah and Moses's two sons are mentioned in the Pentateuch. From this moment on, they seem to vanish into thin air. We can exclude the hypothesis that they returned to the country of Midian with Jethro. Exodus 18:27 says, "And Moses let his father-in-law depart; and he went his way into his own land." If Zipporah and her sons had gone with him, the account would have reported it.

That Zipporah and her two sons remain with Moses is also confirmed by a curious episode cited in Numbers 12. Chronologically, the Jethro episode is placed at the end of the sojourn on the Holy Mount, when Moses is already firmly at the head of the Jewish people and is in the process of giving them an administrative structure. This chronology is important because of the clear coincidence with an episode that takes place a few days later. As soon as his father-in-law Jethro has been sent away, Moses, with the whole Jewish people, "on the twentieth day of the second month, in the second year" (Numbers 10:11), leaves the area of the Holy Mount forever, heading north toward Palestine. The first stop is Kibroth Hattaavah, and after that, Hazeroth. It is here, in Hazeroth, that the incident occurred that is reported in Numbers 12: "And Miriam and Aaron spake against Moses because of the Cushite woman whom he had married: for he had married a Cushite woman."

Most texts, including the Jerusalem Bible and the King James Bible, translate Cushite as Ethiopian, assuming that it derives from Kush, the name then given to Nubia, a region in the south of Egypt, which paid tribute to the pharaohs and was inhabited by a negroid people. On the basis of this translation, some commentators suggest that Moses also had a black wife. This does not make any sense because, considering the chronology in the account, Moses had been joined just a few days earlier by his legitimate wife, Zipporah, a Midianite. There is nothing strange about the fact that the Cushite woman who has suddenly turned up in the Jewish community provokes the jealousy of other "prima donnas," such as Miriam and Aaron, who up to this point have experienced an exclusive and privileged relationship with Moses.

There is no doubt that the Cushite wife against whom Miriam and

Aaron mutter jealously is Zipporah herself. There is ample proof in the Bible that the term Cushite is used to define the Midianites belonging to the tribe of Jethro, and many exegetes agree with this interpretation. In Habakkuk 3:7, for example, Cushan is cited as the name of a tribe in Midian. In 2 Chronicles 14:7–13, there is a description of a war between Judah and the Cushites, clearly a people of the Sinai, and a little later, in 2 Chronicles 21:16, there is mention of the "Arabians, that were near the Cushites," from which we can deduce with certainty that the Cushites were Midianites. Definitive confirmation that Cushites refers to the same tribe to which Jethro and Zipporah belonged, however, can be found in an apocryphal text in the Hebrew Scriptures, datable to the second century BC, in which both people are explicitly referred to as Cushites.[4] The term Cushite, therefore, does not mean Ethiopian (or at least not only that), but refers instead to that particular tribe in Midian to which Jethro and his daughter Zipporah belong.*

The conclusion that must be drawn is that Zipporah, Moses's Cushite wife, remains at his side, as do his sons. But the account in Numbers 12 is also significant in other respects. It clearly shows that Moses has decided to set up his Cushite wife as the "first lady" in Israel. He severely punishes Miriam, Aaron's sister, who up to that point had played the role of first lady, banishing her from the encampment for seven days. Aaron too is severely admonished and has to bow his head and beg forgiveness.

But it is from this moment, when Zipporah is set up as the first lady of Israel, that her removal comes into play. She is no longer mentioned by name, nor is there any further reference to her sons. In the whole Pentateuch not another word is spent on them or on the fact that Moses has a family at all. It seems incredible. Chapter 12 of Numbers provides the clearest proof, if any is needed, that Moses was no different from

---

*In the book *The Apocalypse of Moses,* chapter 34:6, we read: "Moses . . . fled to Midian, to the Cushite Reuel, priest of Midian. He took as his wife the daughter of the priest, the Cushite Zipporah; two sons were born of her: Gershom and Eliezer."

the Jews of his time and of all time in his consideration of and feelings and aspirations for his family. We can be certain that he provided for his sons' future—but how? There is not a word about it in the Bible.

EVIDENCE OF CENSORSHIP IN THE BIBLE

This silence can be attributed only to two factors: either censorship removed or disguised all information regarding Moses's family or his family disappeared, for whatever reason, before the invasion of Palestine. If the latter had been the case, however, it would have been reported in the account: a chronicle so detailed that it records Miriam's banal quarrel over Moses's wife surely would have reported a fact as important as the annihilation of Moses's family.

In any case, we must admit that there was some form of censorship, either by the author of the Pentateuch or subsequently, because nothing is reported regarding a subject that would have been of primary importance in the logic and mentality of the reporter himself. Yet if the reasons for keeping silent or censoring all information regarding Moses's tomb seem clear—probably to avoid its violation and plunder—the same cannot be said about the reasons for keeping silent or censoring information regarding the prophet's family. The idea that someone wanted to eliminate it from history seems incomprehensible. Yet it is an undeniable fact.

The original account must certainly have contained information on his sons, for it contains information on figures of less importance, such as the four sons of Aaron. The account reports how the two eldest, Nadab and Abihu, are burned to death and buried at night outside the encampment. It is reported, with copious detail, how Eleazar takes the place of the firstborn son and succeeds his father. The account also provides information about the youngest son, Ithamar, listing the tasks he must perform in the management of the Tabernacle.

The censorship, therefore, is aimed specifically at Moses's family, which is carefully removed from any mention. It seems unlikely, however, given the importance of the family and of the role it must have played at the heart of Israelite society, that this operation could have been carried out without leaving a trace. Surely there must have survived in the text clues, inconsistencies, events, and names that expose the practice of censorship. Surely from these we can reconstruct the true story of this family and understand when it really disappeared from the chronicles of Israel—or if it continued to exist.

We can note such significant inconsistencies and omissions in the last book of the Pentateuch: Deuteronomy. This book narrates the events of Moses's last day on earth, when he convenes the assembly of the Jewish people and makes a great leave-taking speech, publicly handing over power to his successors. There are details that surely must have been reported in the chronicle of that day because of their importance and because they may have contributed to the main reason that the assembly was convened. It is unimaginable that this information was not reported in the original draft of the book, because it is essential to the understanding of the events of that day, which establish the future structure of the people of Israel.

The lack of this information in extant versions of the Hebrew scriptures clearly exposes the presence of censorship.

CENSORSHIP IN DEUTERONOMY

The role of Moses's family had probably been irrelevant in the first books of the Pentateuch, and therefore any censorship may not have left evident traces. Perhaps it was sufficient to suppress the occasional name—as in the case of the "Cushite wife" and a few verses here and there—to cancel any trace of the family without compromising the intelligibility of events.

The same cannot be said of Deuteronomy. At the moment of Moses's departure from this world, his family necessarily leaps into the foreground, because it is in this moment that his sons take on their inheritance or otherwise are traumatically excluded from it in favor of someone else. Normally, it is upon the death of a great leader that the events relevant to the history of a people occur, and his family is always at the center of these events. Moses's family, therefore, must have been at the center of the events that occurred on his last day on earth. By examining the events as they are reported in Deuteronomy, we realize that this is actually how it must have been in the original draft.

Deuteronomy is the book that describes Moses's leave-taking from his people and the actions by which he lays the basis of Israel's social and religious organization through handing over power to the new chiefs and laying down the rules for the future. In his great speech Moses remembers the merits of Yahweh with regard to Israel and calls for absolute faithfulness to him and to his commandments on pain of severe punishment.

He insists on two points in particular. The first is the uniqueness of the place of worship: however large becomes the territory conquered by Israel, there must be only one Temple where sacrifices to Yahweh are to be carried out and the offerings of the people are to be conveyed. He does not name the location of this Temple because he makes his speech when Palestine is yet to be conquered. He says only that it must be unique and that no sacrifice will be allowed outside of it.

The second point calls for obedience to the priestly class, which becomes not only the fulcrum of religious life, but also that of the civil life of Israel. He thus outlines a theocratic society governed by a priestly caste that regulates every aspect of the civil life of the people, with the exception of their defense. On this point—that is, regarding political power—Moses does not talk at great length. Secondary in his vision of Israelite society is who exercises political authority. Because Israel is entering a country, Palestine, which is actually still an Egyptian province,* it seems implicit that the Israelites must recognize Egyptian

---

*This is a fact that is systematically ignored by all the commentators and historians of the Bible. If the Exodus occurred in the thirteenth century BC, at the time of the nineteenth Egyptian dynasty, there is not the slightest doubt that Palestine was an Egyptian province ruled by Egyptian governors. It remained so until almost the end of the eleventh century BC, for the whole historical period covered by the book of Judges.

authority. As far as actual political authority is concerned, Moses limits himself to urging that if ever the people should feel the need to have a king, he must be chosen and consecrated by the high priest and taken from one of the tribes of Israel, not from among foreigners (Deuteronomy 17:14–20).

For the moment, he establishes a military chief, Joshua, who is charged with the task of guiding Israel in the conquest of its own space in Palestine. The whole of chapter 31 is dedicated to the nomination of Joshua as military chief of the people and to the specification of his duties.

We would expect that equal space, or even more space, would be given to the presentation of the figure who would take Moses's place as the religious leader of the people: the new high priest. Yet there is not a single word about him. We could justify this silence by saying that it was not necessary to present the high priest because he may have been installed beforehand—but this is not tenable.

There is no doubt that, for as long as he was alive, the high priest was Moses himself. It was he who consecrated the Tabernacle; he who always, to the very end, served as the interlocutor with the Lord; he who officiated at ceremonies and sacrifices, and he who ordained Aaron. The fact that Aaron is a priest is mentioned many times in the Pentateuch, but it is never mentioned that he is the high priest. It is also said that Eleazar, Aaron's son, becomes a priest on his father's death—but he is certainly not the high priest. In any case, Eleazar's son, Phinehas, considered by the exegetes as high priest on the death of his father, was never even nominated as priest. The Bible never presents him as such (apart from a note in Judges—a verse that all the commentators consider spurious). Phinehas appears for the first time in Numbers 25:7, in Bet Peor, when he kills Zimri and Coshbi with his own hands. Immediately afterward, Moses entrusts him with command of the troops that return to destroy the Midianites, and Moses personally orders him to kill Midianite women and children brought back from the raid. Further, it is to Phinehas that Joshua gives the task of bringing back to reason the tribes of Reuben, Gad, and half Manasseh, who have erected an altar on the banks of the Jordan River on the return to Transjordan. It is certainly not the image of a priest that the Bible provides for Phinehas, but rather that of the chief of Moses's Praetorian Guard. Curiously, four centuries later, the son of the chief of Aaron's family, Ahaziah, is named as the chief of David's Praetorian Guard (2 Samuel 8:18). Coincidence? In the Bible, this happens very rarely.

According to the Bible, then, Phinehas was never a priest, while Aaron and Eleazar, though named as priests, were never high priests. Who was appointed as high priest by Moses on his leave-taking from the Jewish people? Assuming that the high priest at that moment was Eleazar, we would have to expect that he was at Moses's side in his last moments, as was his military heir, Joshua—or at least that Eleazar's name would appear here and there in a book that is almost entirely dedicated to religious and priestly matters. But his name never appears in the book of Deuteronomy, except incidentally in Deuteronomy 10:6, in relation to the death of Aaron ("there Aaron died, and there he was buried; and Eleazar his son ministered in the priest's office in his stead").

In no part of the book is it ever specified who the high priest is or who has a right to the priesthood. In a book such as Deuteronomy, which is supposed to constitute the foundations of the legitimacy of political and religious appointments in Israel, this is incredible. It is all too clear that censorship was practiced in this regard.

Custom and the law enforce in all peoples, but in particular the Israelite people, that Moses had set his family above that of Aaron (as shown by Numbers 12). Logic and the natural order of things, and the nonexistence of anything to the contrary in the text, come together to lead us to conclude that Moses must have appointed his firstborn son, Gershom, as his successor as high priest—just as these factors must lead us to conclude that the descendants of the first great priest of Israel, Moses, must have inherited the position of priest.

For whatever reason, somebody wanted to cancel Moses's family from the chronicles of Israel and therefore censored all the parts of

Deuteronomy in which they appeared. In this way, a vacuum of information was created on a subject that is absolutely crucial to the history of the Jewish people—a vacuum that was arbitrarily filled by attributing to Eleazar an appointment that he never actually held and to which he had no right.

If this is true, as seems inevitable to conclude, other solid evidence must emerge from subsequent books where the role of Moses's family must have been too important to be censored without leaving a trace.

2

THE DISAPPEARANCE OF MOSES'S SONS IN THE BOOKS OF JOSHUA AND JUDGES

THE INHERITANCE OF MOSES'S FAMILY

The book that immediately follows Deuteronomy is Joshua, which narrates the conquest and dividing of Palestine among the tribes of Israel. On completion of the conquest, "the whole congregation of the children of Israel assembled together at Shiloh. . . . And the land was subdued before them (Joshua 18:1) . . . and there Joshua divided the land unto the children of Israel" (Joshua 18:10).

Of the twenty-four chapters of the book, the first twelve describe the various phases of the conquest. The next ten are entirely dedicated to the division of the conquered territory. In these chapters all the family lines of Israel are listed one by one, with the territories assigned to them. The family of Moses, absolutely the most important figure in Israel, could not be ignored in this context. Yet, incredibly, not a single mention can be found to shed light on what happened to Moses's sons.

All the Jews—even the least significant figures—receive a piece of territory. Even some of Moses's Midianite relatives receive their part of the inheritance in Palestine. In fact, Hobab the Kenite and his descendants have a territory in the middle of Israel, in the Jordan valley, near Jericho. Hobab is Zipporah's brother and therefore Moses's brother-in-law. We meet him for the first time in Numbers 10, when Moses is about to leave Mount Horeb. Moses invites Hobab to join him by saying: "We are setting out to the place of which the Lord said, 'I will give it to you'; come with us and we will do you good, for the Lord has promised good concerning Israel." Yet Hobab replies, "I will not come, but rather will go to my own land and relatives." Moses responds, "Please do not leave us, inasmuch as you know where we should camp in the wilderness, and you will be as eyes for us. So it will be, if you go with us, that whatever good the Lord does for us, we will do for you" (Numbers 10:29–32).

In Exodus, Hobab's final answer is not reported, but there can be no doubt that it is affirmative, because otherwise he would not have a territory among the Israelites. This is a clear sign that he had accepted Moses's offer and joined him, and that Moses had kept his promises. The fact that the Midianite Hobab, as Moses's brother-in-law, has a part of the inheritance in Israel is important.

This is all the more reason, then, that Moses's own sons must have received a part that suited their father's merits and position. Yet Moses's sons are never mentioned, not even fleetingly. This family seems to have vanished into thin air. It is beyond belief, however, that this omission represents simply a lapse of memory. Instead, it seems all too clear that there must have been censorship of the book in this regard.

SHILOH

This, however, is not the only instance of a lapse in the story. Because we are searching in the book of Joshua for information that should be there but is not, we must also consider another sensational omission.

After the division, the city of Shiloh, situated in the mountainous area of Ephraim, more or less in the center of the conquered territory, was set up as the most important place in Palestine. On completion of military operations, "the whole congregation of the children of Israel assembled together at Shiloh, and set up the Tabernacle of the congregation there. And the land was subdued before them" (Joshua 18:1). "These are the territories that Eleazar the priest, Joshua son of Nun, and the tribal leaders allocated as grants of land to the tribes of Israel by casting sacred lots in the presence of the Lord at the entrance of the Tabernacle at Shiloh. So the division of the land was completed" (Joshua 19:51). The tribes had left Shiloh to take possession of their territories; they were splitting up after forty years of life and war together.

That Shiloh had a central role in the vicissitudes of the Israel of Judges, before David and Solomon consecrated Jerusalem as the religious and political center of the nation, can be deduced from the penultimate chapter of Genesis, in which Jacob gathers all his sons to bless them and inform them of "that which shall befall you in the last days." On that occasion, Jacob removes Reuben's birthright, for having raped Jacob's wife Bilhah, and he also disinherits Simeon and Levi for having destroyed the city of Schechem. In the case of the fourth son, Judah, he confers on him the right to primogeniture with the words: "Judah, thou art he whom thy brethren shall praise: thy hand shall be in the neck of thine enemies; thy father's children shall bow down before thee. . . . The sceptre shall not depart from Judah, nor a lawgiver [baton of command] from between his feet, until Shiloh come; and unto him shall the obedience [gathering] of the people be."

Generations of exegetes have seen in this passage a prophecy relating to the coming of the Messiah, Jesus Christ. The Jerusalem Bible, for example, translates the word Shiloh with a pronoun: "he," to whom it (the baton of command) belongs, conjecturing a prophecy relating to the Messiah.* This, however, is clearly a strained interpretation of the text.

---

*The prophetic interpretation was favored from ancient times onward by all the translators and commentators of the Bible, who saw Jerusalem as the only center of worship and avoided highlighting the role of Shiloh before Jerusalem's advent. This verse is also testimony to the fact that the Pentateuch and the books of Joshua and Judges were written before the time of David.

These words, a clear testimony to the fact that the leadership passed at a certain moment from Judah to Shiloh, actually mean it passed to the person in charge of the Temple of Shiloh, to whom all the tribes owed obedience.

A quick investigation of the biblical text is sufficient to establish that Shiloh had risen to become the leading city of Israel from the time of the conquest of Palestine and had remained so until its destruction at the hands of the Philistines, in Samuel's time. We also find confirmation that in that interval of time, Shiloh played the same role in Israel that was later played by Jerusalem. In Jeremiah 7:12–16, the prophet, warning of the coming destruction of Jerusalem and its Temple, puts the following words into Yahweh's mouth: ". . . [U]nto my place, which was in Shiloh, where I caused my name to dwell at the first . . . therefore will I do unto the house [in Jerusalem], which is called by my name, wherein ye trust, and unto the place, which I gave to you and to your fathers, as I did to Shiloh . . ."

Shiloh had been destroyed immediately after the defeat suffered by the Jews at the hands of the Philistines, when the Ark of the Covenant was captured. Samuel's account does not talk about the destruction, but makes an explicit reference to it when it says that after the defeat there occurred such grim events "that will cause the ears of everyone who hears [them] to ring" (1 Samuel 3:11).

Judges 18:31 clearly states that at that time "the house of God was in Shiloh." It was in Shiloh, in fact, in the mountainous region of Ephraim, which was in a barycentric position with regard to the conquered territories, where a Temple dedicated to Yahweh had been erected, and in this Temple, the Ark of the Covenant was kept (1 Samuel 4:3). The great priest Eli resided at Shiloh. It was to Shiloh that the whole of Israel brought their offerings to Yahweh (1 Samuel 2:13). In Shiloh, every year, Israelites from every part of Palestine gathered, "to worship and to sacrifice to Yahweh of Armies" (Judges 21:19; 1 Samuel 1:3).

On the basis of these indications, so clear and precise, there can be no doubt that the leadership of Israel had passed to the man in charge of the Temple of Shiloh immediately after the conquest of Palestine. From then on to its destruction at the time of Samuel, Shiloh was for Israel what Jerusalem would later become.

So at the time of the division of the territory among the tribes of Israel, Shiloh was absolutely the most important city in the whole of Palestine, and the man in charge of the sanctuary, as high priest, was the highest authority in Israel. The author of the book of Joshua could not ignore what was in effect the most significant information in the whole book—that is, to whom the city and its sanctuary had been assigned. Therefore, there are only two possibilities for leaving out this information: either the author omitted it for some reason of his own or it was deleted subsequently.

Is it possible to establish, on the basis of the text, to whom the city of Shiloh had been assigned in the course of the division of Palestine? The current opinion is that at the time of the conquest, the high priest of Israel was Eleazar, who was appointed to the post just before the death of his father, Aaron. If this were true, it is logical to expect that the city had been assigned to Eleazar. Yet the book of Joshua does not say so. In fact, careful checking of the text allows us to establish with certainty that the city is not assigned to Aaron's descendants or, indeed, to any of the Levites.

The forty-eight cities that had been assigned to the Levites are named one by one. In particular, "The Levites who were descendants of Aaron the priest were allotted thirteen towns from the tribes of Judah, Simeon, and Benjamin (Joshua 21:4). . . ." The text continues:

> The children of Aaron, being of the families of the Kohathites, who were of the children of Levi, had: . . . the city of Arba the father of Anak, which city is Hebron, in the hill country of Judah, with the suburbs thereof round about it. But the fields of the city, and the villages thereof, gave they to Caleb the son of Jephunneh for his possession. Thus they gave to the children of Aaron the priest Hebron with her suburbs, to be a city of refuge for the slayer; and Libnah

with her suburbs, and Jattir with her suburbs, and Eshtemoa with her suburbs, and Holon with her suburbs, and Debir with her suburbs, and Ain with her suburbs, and Juttah with her suburbs, and Bethshemesh with her suburbs; nine cities out of those two tribes. And out of the tribe of Benjamin, Gibeon with her suburbs, Geba with her suburbs, Anathoth with her suburbs, and Almon with her suburbs; four cities.[1]

The text goes on to complete the list of names of the forty-eight cities given to the Levites, including the four in the region of Ephraim: Schechem, Gezer, Kibzaim, and Bethhoron. There is not the slightest mention of Shiloh! Therefore, it had not even been allocated to a Levite, much less to a descendant of Aaron, Eleazar, or his son Phinehas. Nevertheless, it was the seat of the Temple dedicated to Yahweh, and the highest authority in Israel resided there. The fact that in the book of Joshua there is not a single word from which it can be understood to whom the city had been allocated is an omission that is as sensational as that regarding Moses's family. Doubtless, the narrator did not ignore the most important information about the division: to whom Shiloh had been allocated and which part went to Moses's sons.

The conjecture of censorship thus becomes a certainty. By the same token, beginning to gain stature is the conjecture that a precise connection exists between Moses's family and Shiloh.

JONATHAN THE PRIEST

In the book of Joshua there is only indirect evidence in favor of the hypothesis that Moses's family went to Palestine: the absence of important information that doubtless was known by everybody at the time—and certainly the author of the book, whoever he was. In the following book, Judges, however, we begin to find the first real, direct proof.

Two whole chapters of Judges, the seventeenth and eighteenth, are dedicated to a story that is apparently strange and out of the narrative context of the book. It pertains to a certain Levite, the younger son of an unknown figure, who leaves Bethlehem in search of his fortune and is received into the house of a man identified only as Micah. This man lives on the "mountain of Ephraim" and takes on the young man as his personal "priest." After various adventures, the priest turns up in Dan, where he founds a sanctuary, becoming priest in the service of that tribe.

In the end (Judges 18:30), we discover that this unnamed Levite actually has a name, Jonathan, and is the son of a certain Gershom. Who is this Gershom? The Masoretic Text specifies that he is "Gershom son of Manasseh." The only Manasseh to have appeared in the chronicles up to this point is the firstborn son of Joseph, he who had died in Egypt at least a century earlier. It cannot, therefore, have been him. Perhaps it is an error or, worse still, an intentional interpolation? After all, in Hebrew script it is sufficient to insert an *n* between the *m* and the *s* to change the name of Moses into Manasseh. This suspicion is confirmed in the version of the Bible known as *Of the Seventy*, a text considered by many to adhere more closely to the original Text. Here, it is clearly stated that Gershom is indeed the son of Moses. It then appears that in the Masoretic Text the name of Moses was changed to Manasseh: the work of a distant descendant of our censor.

This passage, therefore, provides confirmation that Gershom, first-born son of Moses, had gone to Palestine. And that is not all: A very important piece of information provided by this excerpt from Judges is that Gershom's sons were priests by right of birth. Yet there is another detail that is extremely interesting: "Jonathan, the son of Gershom, the son of Moses, he and his sons were priests to the tribe of Dan until the day of the captivity of the land. And they set them up Micah's graven image, which he made, all the time that the house of God was in Shiloh" (Judges 18:31).

What has Shiloh to do with Jonathan? And why does he appear in reference to Gershom? It is evident from this brief mention that there must have been some kind of direct link between Jonathan and the sanctuary of Shiloh. The first explanation to come to mind is that the man in charge of the sanctuary of Shiloh was someone from his family, and therefore in all likelihood his father, Gershom, or his father's heir, Jonathan's elder brother—someone in Moses's family.

THE SLAUGHTER OF THE BENJAMITES

The following episode, which completely takes up the last three chapters of Judges, is also striking for its unjustifiable omissions. The protagonist of the events in this episode too is a certain "Levite sojourning on the side of Mount Ephraim" (Judges 19:1)—exactly where Shiloh was located. During a trip to his home in Bethlehem,* this figure, accompanied by one of his wives, makes a stopover in the city of Gibeah, where he is the object of advances by the inhabitants, who are Benjamites. To get out of a fix, he hands over to them his wife, who dies from the resulting violence she experiences (Judges 19:22–28). When he gets home, the Levite cuts his wife's corpse into many pieces and sends them, by way of messengers, to all the tribes of Israel, who assemble "as one man . . . unto the Lord in Mizpah" (Judges 20:1) and decide to avenge the anonymous Levite. As a result, Benjamin's whole tribe, thousands of people, including women and children, are slaughtered. Only a small group of young males is spared, in order not to eradicate completely one of the twelve tribes of Israel.

There are various details that are not convincing in this episode. First of all, questionable is the nature of a sin that is so serious as to deserve the slaughter of a whole tribe, women and children included. The attempts at explanation to be read in the exegetic notes to the text, which identify the sin as a violation of the rules of hospitality, are anything but convincing. It seems clear that the severity of the punishment

---

*It is the same place mentioned in connection with Jonathan, confirming the close bond between the two figures.

is justified not so much by the seriousness of the sin, as by the importance of the man it was committed against: surely not an anonymous Levite, but a personality of the highest profile in Israel, one who had the power to convene all the tribes "unto the Lord" to demand revenge. There can be no doubt that his name was well known to the writer of this episode, who must therefore have omitted it deliberately. Or, as with Moses's family, the name was the object of subsequent censorship.

Even the place where the tribes gather to decide on the form of retaliation, the sanctuary of Mizpah, seems strange. Moses had insisted at length in his last speech in the Valley of Moab, reported in Deuteronomy, that there should be a single place of worship to which all offerings should be brought. The exception to this rule, the place of worship instituted by Jonathan in Dan, is mentioned, but in connection with Shiloh, the location of the legitimate Temple—the only Temple designated for the carrying out of the "sacrifice." There were no other sanctuaries in Israel at that time, much less in the immediate vicinity of Shiloh.

Mizpah means "viewpoint" or "high place" and is normally associated with the name of a locality, as in, for example, Mizpah Ramon, the Viewpoint of Ramon. The name on its own can indicate a high place in any locality. It seems clear from the context that this Mizpah was in Shiloh. Indeed, the delegates of Israel assembled "unto the Lord" (Judges 20:1), and we know that at that time the "house of Yahweh" was in Shiloh. In the same way, just two verses later, it is said that the Israelites assembled unto God at Bethel* (Judges 20:26–21:2) to ask, "Who is there among all the tribes of Israel that came not up with the congregation unto the Lord? For they had made a great oath concerning him that came not up to the Lord to Mizpah." Immediately afterward (Judges 21:19), the author reminds us "there is a feast of the Lord in Shiloh."

Bethel means "house of the Lord"; it clearly refers to the locality of the house of God—that is, the Temple, therefore Shiloh.

The whole business of the meetings and the oaths taken "unto God," therefore, occurs in the same area and certainly in the same place, because it is inconceivable that three different sanctuaries existed in neighboring localities. The sanctuary where the elders of the tribes had gathered must have been the only one in the area: that of Shiloh, which, like that of Jerusalem later and like all places of worship at that time, was in all likelihood built in an elevated position, on a mizpah. The names Mizpah, Bethel, and Shiloh, therefore, at least in this excerpt from Judges, all refer to the same locality.

The obvious and inescapable conclusion is that the anonymous Levite, protagonist of this gruesome episode, must have been a man of great importance at the Temple of Shiloh, almost certainly the man in charge—the high priest—who at that time, as we have just seen, was Jonathan's father, Gershom. In any case, it was a person whom Israel must have considered holy and untouchable, to the point that any offense to him and any failure to comply with one of his orders resulted in annihilation. It should be noted that the inhabitants of Jabesh-Gilead were slaughtered simply because they did not attend the assembly he convened in Shiloh (Judges 21:8–12); they had to be punished by extermination.

CUSHAN THE TERRIBLE

It is evident that someone made some small alterations to the text of the book of Judges to hide the true identity of the protagonist of this episode. It is an episode of revolting barbarity, thus it would be understandable if, in the various transcriptions of the book, someone had tried to hide any connection between its protagonist and Moses in order not to stain the memory and the work of the high prophet with the wrongdoings of his descendants.

There are reasons other than cowardliness and cruelty that may justify censorship that was intended to cancel out any connection between Moses and his descendants. The first of them is the fact that Moses's descendants could not be considered true Israelites. A clue to this is provided in a brief passage in Judges 3 whose meaning has eluded explanations by the exegetes.

After Moses's death, Joshua did no more than carry out his orders point by point: he conquered a large slice of Palestine; he divided it among the twelve tribes, dispersing the Levites among them; and he allocated to the priests—to the sons of Moses, Gershom and Eliezer—the city of Shiloh.

Gershom, as high priest, was the highest religious authority in Israel, and on Joshua's death, he would again gather in his own hands—like his father Moses—both spiritual and temporal power. Why, before dying, did Moses transmit supreme command of the people to Joshua and not to his son Gershom? Was this a debt of acknowledgment to his most faithful companion? No. Blood rights came before bonds of friendship. It was probably a move by Moses to make possible, or at least facilitate, the taking of power by his sons.

We can assume that Gershom was not exactly popular among the Israelites. He had a Midianite mother and he was born and raised among the Midianites—he was therefore decidedly Midianite in culture. We saw in chapter 12 of Numbers that even Miriam and Aaron revolted against Moses's "Cushite" wife. Could the Jews, on the eve of the conquest, suddenly accept a Cushite as their supreme leader in place of Moses? Could a young man born and raised in the desert have the experience and ability to lead a military campaign of that size? Did he have the necessary stature and charisma to hold together that mass of armed men always ready for rebellion? As a Cushite, he had no chance.

It was probably the unpopularity and serious personality defects of his firstborn son, Gershom, that led Moses to entrust the fate of that military campaign, and that of his own family, to the infinitely more capable and tried and trusted hands of his faithful Joshua, who served the interests of the family to the utmost.

Before he died, Joshua gathered all the Jewish people in Schechem and beseeched them to remain forever faithful to Yahweh. Gershom was the high priest of Yahweh, in charge of the Temple of Shiloh. Joshua's words, therefore, were an explicit invitation to be loyal to Gershom and to the priestly family. Further, the insistence and the threats with which Joshua reasserted this concept are a clear indication that the man to whom he was about to pass on his powers was anything but popular in Israel. A clue to this is provided in the passage in Judges 3 in which it is said that immediately after Joshua's death, Yahweh

> . . . sold them into the hand of Cushan-Rishathaim king of Mesopotamia. And the people of Israel served Cushan-Rishathaim eight years. But when the people of Israel cried out to the Lord, the Lord raised up a deliverer for the people of Israel, who saved them, Othniel the son of Kenaz, Caleb's younger brother. The Spirit of the Lord was upon him, and he judged Israel. He went out to war, and the Lord gave Cushan-Rishathaim king of Mesopotamia into his hand. And his hand prevailed over Cushan-Rishathaim. So the land had rest forty years . . .[2]

The exegetes have always wondered who this figure might have been, for he was certainly not an Aramaic king, nor does he appear to have had an army or a seat of power or to have invaded Palestine or carried out military actions of any kind. Even his name is strange: Cushan, in fact, was the name of the territory of the Midianite tribe to which Jethro and Zipporah—respectively, Moses's father-in-law and wife—belonged. Moreover, the savior (not judge) Othniel frees the Israelites from their oppression, which lasted, according to the text, for eight years—but it does not say how he did it. The text says only that "Othniel was raised up to deliver and his hand prevailed over Cushan-Rishathaim." This is the briefest description of a military event in the whole book of Judges, which is usually rich in detail. Nothing is said about whether there was a battle with forces on the field or where this battle occurred or what happened to Cushan immediately afterward.

Such paucity of information is suspicious. It seems rather mysterious and in stark contrast to the wealth of detail with which the deeds of the subsequent Judges are reported. In fact, all the exegetes think that the text was manipulated or corrupted.

The key is probably in that name Cushan-Rishathaim. In all likelihood, it was a nickname. It is not unusual in the Bible for characters to be identified by nicknames. Esau, son of Jacob, went by the name of Edom, "the Red"; Seir, too—"the Hairy"—is very probably a nickname. This suggests that the Cushite Gershom was scornfully labeled with the nickname of Cushan, from the name of his mother's tribe, the tribe in which he was born and raised. *Rishathaim* means "from double malice" and is therefore a derogatory addition to the nickname and refers to his malign character.

Confirmation of this hypothesis is involuntarily provided by the same apocryphal writer[3] who defines Jethro and Zipporah as Cushites. A few verses later, in fact, he provides a list of Judges who dominated Israel that is significantly different from the one provided in the book of Judges. He says: "After the death of Joshua, Cushan the Terrible put himself at the head of the children of Israel for eighty years. Then Othniel, son of Kenaz and brother of Caleb, son of Jephunneh, led Israel for twenty years."

Cushan—not an invading king—is therefore the Israelite leader who immediately takes over command from Joshua, and he dominates Israel for eighty years, not for eight. Most important, Othniel succeeds him in a natural way, without wars or battles, as it says in Judges. Are these "errors" made by the anonymous chronicler of *The Apocalypse of Moses* (who, however, seems precise and accurate in all the other information he provides), or is it the text of Judges that hides the truth under an interpolated text? The latter would make sense. The name is the right one: Gershom is a Cushite, and the nickname Cushan suits him perfectly. Even the time, immediately after Joshua's death, seems correct, because it is exactly then that Gershom succeeds him to power.

Further, the appellation Terrible is consistent. In fact, it is extremely probable that Gershom is the anonymous Levite who cuts up his dead wife, after the violence to which he himself had abandoned her, and who demands terrible and unprecedented revenge: the slaughter of Benjamin's whole tribe. And it is he who orders the slaughter of the inhabitants of Jabesh Gilead, who are guilty of not having responded to his call for revenge.* Actions so disproportionate to the events preceding them show a bloodthirsty and ferocious character, which surely did nothing to increase his popularity. We must deduce that Moses's family was profoundly despised in Israel and this is probably one of the reasons why the connection between Moses and his progeny was rent asunder.

Moses had imposed and maintained his dominion over the Jewish people—and he had done so with terror. He had killed all his external opponents, having induced them to give themselves away with the business of the golden calf. He had killed all his internal opponents—including his cousins Cora, Datan, and Abiram, with their two hundred fifty supporters. In Kibroot Attahava he had killed others who were plotting against him; every time the people protested, he resolved the matter with death threats. His laws were extremely severe and provided for the death penalty for a never-ending series of offenses.

The echo of this terror is reported in his "obituary" at the end of Deuteronomy: "And there arose not a prophet since in Israel like unto Moses. . . . And in all that mighty hand, and in all the great terror, which Moses shewed in the sight of all Israel." With all those deaths behind him, he could not exactly have been loved by the people of Israel; but he was feared and respected. He was fair: he punished rebels

---

*The episode appears at the end of the book of Judges, but there is nothing that supports its placement at the end of the historical period covered by the book. Various indicators favor a much earlier placement. The historical period of Judges ends at the time of Eli and Samuel, when Israel is involved in the war against the Philistines: there is no space in this historical context for an episode such as the one narrated. In fact, Samuel chooses his own king from the tribe of Benjamin, and from the account it is clear that he has regained population and territory. Eli could not have been the author of the slaughter of the Benjamites. Without doubt, it is therefore one of his predecessors. Josephus Flavius, in his *Antiquities of the Jews,* places it shortly after the division of Palestine.

ferociously, but he rewarded the faithful and kept his promises. Most important, his violence was never gratuitous, but was always justified by the supreme interests of the new religion and was never disproportionate to its purpose.

Between him and his sons there was an abyss. The appellation Terrible leaves us to presume that Gershom governed with terror, as his father had done—but he did not have Moses's charisma and he gave nothing in return. Most important, he was not a Jew, but a Midianite, because he was the son of a Midianite mother. He was hated and despised. The nickname Cushan is an indication of profound disdain.

It was without doubt the most unpopular and disliked family of the time. This disdain is highly visible in the book of Samuel. The high priest of Shiloh, Eli, and his two sons are unpopular and disliked by everyone. They are described as greedy and dissolute swindlers who are interested only in plundering the people:

> Now the sons of Eli were sons of Belial; they knew not the Lord. And the priest's custom with the people was that, when any man offered sacrifice, the priest's servant came, while the flesh was boiling, with a fleshhook of three teeth in his hand. And he struck it into the pan, or kettle, or caldron, or pot; all that the fleshhook brought up the priest took for himself. So they did in Shiloh unto all the Israelites that came thither. . . . Wherefore the sin of the young men was very great before the Lord: for they mistreated the offering of the Lord.[4]

If we consider that these words were aimed at the sons of the high priest, heirs to the high priesthood, we can understand what kind of profound unpopularity the priestly line suffered. We can also understand why the various propagandists and copyists of the biblical text would want to omit any mention that might establish a bond between Moses and his unworthy descendants. Aaron was undoubtedly a more suitable person to take on the paternity of such progeny.

3

THE MOSAIC PRIESTLY FAMILY

WHO WAS ELI?

In the books of Joshua and Judges there is direct confirmation that Moses's family survived the death of the prophet and went to Palestine. The book of Judges also provides ample evidence that this family was in charge of the sanctuary of Shiloh. In the subsequent books there is explicit and incontrovertible proof to support this.

There is a way, in fact, to know with certainty who inherited Shiloh. Positions in Israel, like goods and cities, were always inherited, so it should be enough to confirm who the ancestors of the man in charge of the sanctuary of Shiloh were at the time of Samuel to discover who received it on the division of the territory.

In the books of Samuel, all figures are identified by their lineage, which, for the most important ones, goes back to Jacob. The first book opens with Samuel's complete lineage up to Ephraim, son of Joseph. This is all the more reason to expect that the ancestors of the great priest Eli, the man in charge of the Temple of Shiloh, the most important figure in Israel at that time, should be mentioned.

Surprisingly, however, Eli's ancestors—including the name of his father—are mentioned nowhere. Is this a sign of the usual censor at work? Perhaps, but there is a passage in which the author lets slip some information about a great ancestor of Eli's—without explicitly mentioning his name:

> And there came a man of God unto Eli, and said unto him, "Thus saith the Lord, Did I plainly appear unto the house of thy father, when they were in Egypt in Pharaoh's house? And did I choose him out of all the tribes of Israel to be my priest, to offer upon mine altar, to burn incense, to wear an ephod before me? And did I give unto the house of thy father all the offerings made by fire of the children of Israel?"[1]

On the basis of the first few words, it would seem impossible to doubt that Eli's "great ancestor" was none other than Moses himself: it was to him and him only that God appeared in Egypt; he was always the only direct interlocutor with God. Further, it was Moses who consecrated the Tabernacle and offered the first sacrifices, and it was he who anointed Aaron and his sons (Exodus 29). The fact that he was chosen from among all the tribes of Israel and wore the *ephod,* however, seems to refer to Aaron. There is no doubt, anyway, on the basis of this passage, that Eli descended from one or the other of the two absolute protagonists of the Exodus: Moses or Aaron.

All the exegetic commentaries agree that it is Aaron, just as our censor desired. This, however, makes little sense and is not confirmed by the text. The book of Joshua gives a precise list of all the cities allocated to Aaron's family, and Shiloh is not among them, whereas Gershom, Moses's son, and Gershom's son Jonathan, are associated with Shiloh. If we must choose between the two, Moses or Aaron, it seems practically obligatory to think that Eli's great ancestor, to whom the author of the book of Samuel refers, was Moses himself. If Moses's family really survived, then there can be no reasonable doubt that it must have possessed the sanctuary of Shiloh and obviously the position of high priest connected to it.

It is necessary, however, to find other certain proof that the family went to Palestine and had descendants. The mention in Judges 18:30 is insufficient, on its own, to confirm this, while the mention of Eli's great ancestor in 1 Samuel 2:7 is ambiguous and lends itself to two different interpretations. As clues they are quite solid, but to dissipate any doubt it is necessary to find a true list of Moses's descendants and precise indications as to what roles were assigned to them.

GENEALOGICAL LISTS IN CHRONICLES

In the books of Samuel, we can follow the vicissitudes of Eli's family, the one and only priestly family in Israel,* from the destruction of the Temple of Shiloh to the end of David's reign, when Jerusalem became the capital of the joint kingdoms of Israel and Judah. We are not told explicitly, however, the name of that family's "great ancestor."

The following two books, 1 Kings and 2 Kings, allow us to reconstruct the vicissitudes of the priestly family throughout the subsequent four centuries, without interruption. From them we learn with certainty that the last high priest of the kingdom of Judah, Jehozadak, deported by Nebuchadnezzar to Babylon when still a child, descends in a direct line from Zadok, Eli's grand-nephew. These books, moreover, show with virtual certainty that the priestly family and Aaron's family descended from two different progenitors, because they are always unequivocally distinguished from one another. Aaron is explicitly indicated as progenitor of the family that bears his name, however it is never said from whom the family of the priests descended—that is, who Eli's great ancestor was.

To find information relating to the ancestors of Eli and to Moses's family, we must go to the two books of Chronicles, which contain a potpourri of information assembled by the deportees from Babylon on their return to Jerusalem. Here, at last, we begin to find the evidence we have

---

*If we exclude that of Jonathan in Dan, which the books of Samuel never mention.

been looking for. In 1 Chronicles 23:14 the text says: "Now concerning Moses, the man of God, his sons were named of the tribe of Levi. The sons of Moses were Gershom and Eliezer. Of the sons of Gershom, Shebuel was the chief. And the son of Eliezer was Rehabiah the chief. And Eliezer had none other sons; but the sons of Rehabiah were very many." Regarding Gershom, only his firstborn son, Shebuel, is mentioned, but we know from Judges 18:31 that he had at least one other son, Jonathan. Regarding Eliezer, his first and only son, Rehabiah, is mentioned, but it is specified that Rehabiah had a great many sons.

It is not much, but this passage provides certainty on several points that up to now have been only conjectures, albeit well-supported conjectures. First of all, this text suggests Moses's family survived him and had descendants. Second, this fact was well known in Israel and could not fail to have been reported in the Chronicles of Joshua and Judges. Consequently, the hypothesis of censorship carried out in the text, either by the writer himself or by someone else later, becomes certainty.

Yet we still do not have precise and direct confirmation that the family went to Palestine and had played a high-profile role in the religious and political life of Israel. (We can exclude Judges 10:31, which first put us on the trail of Moses's family.) Proof is soon found, however, by continuing to read Chronicles. Two chapters on, we read:

> Shebuel the son of Gershom, the son of Moses, was ruler of the treasures. And his brethren by Eliezer; Rehabiah his son, and Jeshaiah his son, and Joram his son, and Zichri his son, and Shelomith his son. Which Shelomith and his brethren were over all the treasures of the dedicated things, which David the king, and the chief fathers, the captains over thousands and hundreds, and the captains of the host, had dedicated. Out of the spoils won in battles did they dedicate to maintain the house of the Lord. And all that Samuel the seer, and Saul the son of Kish, and Abner the son of Ner, and Joab the son of Zeruiah, had dedicated; and whosoever had dedicated any thing, it was under the hand of Shelomith, and of his brethren.[2]

According to this passage, there are six generations between Eliezer, son of Moses, and Shelomith, who lived at the time of David. This makes sense. It also makes sense that Moses's descendants were in Jerusalem at the time of David. In any case, these verses, which, for some reason, evidently escaped the censor's scissors, give us the certainty that Moses's family did not vanish in the Sinai desert, but instead followed (or perhaps led?) the Jews to Palestine and continued to play a high-profile role in the history of Israel. But what role exactly?

This passage lists in their entirety only the descendants of the younger branch, with Moses's secondborn son, Eliezer, as their chief. The main line of progeny, however, stops as usual at Shebuel, Gershom's firstborn son. Shebuel, Moses's grandson, is indicated as "ruler of the treasures," a vague and probably incorrect position, because it is stated immediately afterward that it was held by the younger line of Moses's descendants. In any case, however, it is a concrete position, which presupposes his presence in Israel. Did he have any descendants? If, in David's time, the younger branch occupied with Selomit that of superintendent of the holy treasure, the main branch must have occupied an even higher position. Yet the only higher position was that of the high priesthood.

In David's time, after the kingdom of Israel had been incorporated into that of Judah, two high priests were appointed, apparently on an equal footing: Abiathar and Zadok. Abiathar was the son of Ahimelech, the high priest, who, along with his whole family, was killed by Saul in Nob. Abiathar had managed to escape the massacre by taking refuge with David, who was at the time a bandit on the run. Ahimelech was the son of Ahitub, who was son of Eli's secondborn son, Phinehas. Zadok, as another of Ahitub's sons, was Abiathar's uncle (2 Samuel 8:17). After the massacre in Nob, Zadok had replaced his brother Ahimelech in the position of high priest of Israel, remaining loyal to Saul (1 Chronicles 12:29) and after him to his successor to the throne of Israel, Ishbosheth. When Ishbosheth died, Zadok, together with Abner, the head of the army, passed into the service of David (2 Samuel 5:1–5; 1 Chronicles 12:24), who then ruled over only the tribes of Judah and Simeon, bringing as a gift the entire kingdom of Israel with its remaining ten tribes.

Both Zadok and Abiathar, therefore, were direct descendants of Eli and, as high priests according to 1 Chronicles 23:24, had in their direct employment the descendants of Moses's younger branch. It is not likely that Moses's descendants were in a subordinate position to those of Aaron. Thus it is clear that Eli was not Aaron's descendant, but was descended from Gershom, Moses's firstborn son.

The same books of Kings systematically confirm that Eli's family—that of the priests—had nothing to do with Aaron's descendants. We have already seen, for example, that on the death of Saul's son Ishbosheth, his highest-ranking functionaries negotiated with David and gave him the kingdom of Israel. The list of the people who on that occasion went into his service is reported in 1 Chronicles 12:23–40. When it refers to the Levites, there is an explicit mention of "Jehoiada . . . the leader of the Aaronites, and with him were three thousand and seven hundred; And Zadok, a young man mighty of valour, and of his father's house twenty and two captains."

This verse portrays the situation of the Levites and the priests at the moment of the reunification of the kingdoms of Judah and Israel. On one hand, there were the priests descended from Eli: Zadok with twenty-two "chiefs," which means adult males, among whom were evidently all the descendants of Eliezer (to whom Abiathar and his family, in David's service from the very beginning, should be added). On the other hand, there were the Levites, who were not priests, and in particular Aaron's family, led by Jehoiada. It is true that the author of the text avoids leaking the name of Zadok's ancestor, but in practice he declares explicitly that it was not Aaron. This clear distinction between the priestly family and Aaron's family can already be found in the books of Samuel, where, for example, in 2 Samuel 8:15–18, it is specified that "Zadok the son of Ahitub, and Ahimelech the son of Abiathar, were the priests," while "Benaiah the son of Jehoiada was over both the Cherethites and the Pelethites" (David's personal bodyguard).

There is sufficient proof, therefore, to state with certainty that Eli's "great ancestor" was Moses, not Aaron. A quick count of the years that had passed since the Exodus, taking into account the lineages of Samuel, Saul, and David, shows that Eli was in all likelihood the son of Shebuel. We can therefore completely reconstruct the lineage of the main branch of Moses's family: Moses, Gershom, Shebuel, Eli, Phinehas, Ahitub, the brothers Ahimelech and Zadok, and Abiathar. Between Gershom and Zadok there are six generations; there are seven between him and Abiathar. The sum of the generations, therefore, fits the time available.*

Now, at last, the mystery of the "disappearance" of Moses's family seems to have been solved. The family lines of the priests of Israel were composed of the descendants of Moses, and, according to birthright, by them alone. This is a sensational conclusion, which goes against tradition, but which appears well founded on the basis of the data provided by the Bible.

WHEN THE PRIESTLY LINEAGES CHANGED

It is important now to understand when and why the Mosaic line of the priestly family was exchanged for an Aaronite one.

The Aaronite line of the family of the priests is mentioned for the first time in the Bible in a passage in 1 Chronicles, a book written after the exile in Babylon:

> The sons of Aaron; Nadab, and Abihu, Eleazar, and Ithamar. But Nadab and Abihu died before their father, and had no children: therefore Eleazar and Ithamar executed the priest's office. And David distributed them, both Zadok of the sons of Eleazar, and Ahimelech of

---

*According to most exegetic sources, Moses was born during the reign of Ramses II—that is, at the end of the thirteenth century BC. Zadok and Abiathar lived at the time of David, toward the end of the eleventh century. Between Moses and Abiathar, therefore, approximately two hundred years elapsed, perfectly compatible with seven consecutive generations.

the sons of Ithamar, according to their offices in their service. And there were more chief-men found of the sons of Eleazar than of the sons of Ithamar, and thus were they divided. Among the sons of Eleazar there were sixteen chief-men of the house of their fathers, and eight among the sons of Ithamar according to the house of their fathers.[3]

It is immediately obvious that these lineages are patently and deliberately false. Ithamar, the last of Aaron's sons, had been ordained as a priest by Moses in Exodus 29, but from then on, he completely disappears from the biblical accounts, apart from a mention in Numbers 3, where he is cited among Aaron's sons, and in Numbers 7:8, when he is entrusted with the responsibility of taking care of and transporting the Tabernacle. No descendant of his is ever mentioned in the Bible. Eleazar's descendants, instead, are listed in 1 Chronicles 5:30 and 6:35; the lists include a figure with the name of Zadok—but clearly he has nothing to do with the Zadok who was high priest at the time of Saul, David, and Solomon, because the names of the other people on the respective genealogical lists do not coincide.

In particular, among Eleazar's descendants the key figure in the priestly lineages, Eli, is nowhere to be found. This is a sure sign that Eleazar had nothing to do with Shiloh and its priestly family. In fact, none of the figures in the genealogical list is ever mentioned in the first books of the Bible, apart from Eleazar's son Phinehas (namesake of Eli's son), who appears in connection to events that occurred during the Exodus and then appears no more. There is therefore absolutely no basis for linking Eleazar and Ithamar to Zadok and Ahimelech.

Most exegetic chroniclers share the opinion that these verses reflect the covenant entered into by the two concurrent priestly branches—that of Zadok's descendants and that of the descendants of Abiathar, son of Ahimelech—after the return from Babylonian exile. In effect, they can be the fruit only of a covenant between these two priestly branches, because they definitively ratify a hierarchical order for them that is contrary to purely genealogical rights.

Ahimelech was Zadok's elder brother, so on his death the high priesthood should have passed by rights to his only surviving son, Abiathar, who, however, had gone into hiding with David. Zadok replaced his brother in the kingdom of Israel, while Abiathar became high priest in Jerusalem upon David's creation of the kingdom of Judah. When the two kingdoms were united under David, Zadok was evidently allowed to keep his position. The biblical account tells us that Zadok and Abiathar jointly held the high priesthood for the whole of David's reign, but a situation like this could not last.

On David's death, Abiathar backed Adonias's candidacy for the succession, anointing him king, while Zadok allied himself with Solomon, who turned out to be the winner. Abiathar fell into disgrace; his life was spared in consideration of merit he had acquired with David, but he was banished from Jerusalem: "Get thee to Anathoth, unto thine own fields; for thou art worthy of death: but I will not at this time put thee to death, because thou barest the ark of the Lord God before David my father. . . . So Solomon thrust out Abiathar from being priest unto the Lord" (1 Kings 2:26–27).

From then on, the high priesthood in Jerusalem was held by Zadok's direct descendants. Abiathar, however, was exiled to Anathoth and excluded from service to the Temple. Yet despite Solomon's provisions, his family did not renounce its right to the priesthood. We shall see later, in fact, that on Solomon's death, it asserted this right in the reconstituted kingdom of Israel and produced some great figures, including Elijah, Isaiah, and Jeremiah.

In any case, the two priestly branches remained estranged and rivals for more than four centuries, until they returned together to Jerusalem (from Mesopotamia, where they had been deported separately on the destruction of first Israel and then Judah), and they established a covenant for the rebuilding and the joint running of the Temple. It was then that Aaron's two sons, Eleazar and Ithamar, officially became ancestors of the two priestly branches.

Twenty-four family branches had entered into the covenant: sixteen family lines descended from Zadok were linked to Eleazar, their primacy within the priesthood thus being reasserted; eight family lines descended from Ahimelech, father of Abiathar, and were linked to Ithamar. In this way, all the priests in Jerusalem became "sons of Aaron," but nobody took the trouble to render that lineage credible, with genealogies being invented ad hoc. Apart from the verses in question, in fact, no lineage exists that directly and consistently links Aaron to any of the priests we encounter in the books of Samuel and Kings.

It is incredible not so much that the priestly family in Jerusalem wanted to substitute Aaron for its progenitor, Moses (it evidently had its good reasons for doing so), but that none of the latter-day scholars has decided to point out such an evident and blatant falsehood that has nothing at all in the Bible to support it.

EZRA'S REFORMATION

That this is a deliberate falsehood is proved by the fact that the man who stipulated the covenant between the twenty-four priestly family lines and, by writing those verses that consecrated it to history, imposed their change of lineage, was Ezra, a priest who knew the history of his people and of his family better than anyone.

It was around 458 BC when he arrived in Jerusalem, at the head of a group of thousands of ex-deportees, including hundreds of priests. A first group had already returned to the place a century before, led by Zerubbabel and Nehemiah, who had started the rebuilding of the Temple that had been destroyed by Nebuchadnezzar; but work had been suspended almost immediately, due to the opposition of the Samaritans. Since then things had dragged on in a state of deplorable degradation— so much so, in fact, as to induce Ezra to go to see the Persian king Darius and ask his permission to be sent to Jerusalem, with the task of improving Judaea's fortunes and restoring the religion of Yahweh. The first thing Ezra did was to dedicate himself to the reorganization of the priestly caste, in order to raise its status. He conducted a census of the priestly family branches present in Judaea and ascertained their origins. Whoever was unable to demonstrate their priestly origins with certainty was excluded, as were all those who did not have sons born of Jewish mothers and those priests who refused to repudiate the non-Jewish women they had married during the Babylonian exile and the sons born of them.

In the end, there were twenty-four family branches of certain priestly origin. They had grown from the branches of both Zadok and Ahimelech, on which Ezra imposed a covenant for the sharing of positions at the Temple. It was also necessary for him to establish a sort of hierarchy among the various family branches, which, in accordance with the customs of the Jewish people, should have been based on each one's genealogical rights. Unfortunately, these rights were in contrast with each one's historical rights, so it must be presumed that he found himself in some way forced to alter the lineages described in the Bible, to align them all and remove any reason for disputes in the future.

There is no doubt that he had the authority and the means to do so. He had total control over the Holy Scriptures, the books that contained the history of the people of Israel and the priestly lineages. Ezra had gained great fame and authority in Babylon for his profound knowledge of the Bible, the text he had transcribed and translated into Aramaic. Some modern scholars go so far as to say that he was the compiler—that it was he who actually wrote the first books of the Bible by putting together various oral traditions gathered from among the deportees. This conjecture is contradicted by the Bible itself, which demonstrates the existence of the Book of the Laws as far back as the time of David, and which mentions it countless times in the following centuries. This theory emphasizes an important fact, however: the version of the Bible that we read today—with very few variations—came from Ezra's pen.

Indications for this can be found in sources other than the Bible, for example in the apocryphal texts of the Hebrew Scriptures. In one of these, entitled "The Fourth Book of Ezra," in the fourteenth and last chapter, Yahweh decides to dictate the new edition of the Holy Scriptures to Ezra in a dream. He orders Ezra:

> Prepare thee many box trees, and take with thee Sarea, Dabria, Selemia, Ecanus, and Asiel, these five, which are ready to write swiftly; And come hither, and I shall light a candle of understanding in thine heart, which shall not be put out, till the things be performed, which thou shalt begin to write. And when thou hast done, some things shalt thou publish, and some things shalt thou shew secretly to the wise.[4]

So Ezra wrote at least two books: one was intended for public consumption and was the Bible recognized by the Jews as canonical.* He limited himself to transcribing this, with very little alteration, from earlier texts. The second book was intended for the "wise men of the Jewish people"—for the high priests. The contents of this book could not be divulged and probably contained secrets and provisions regarding the family. There must have been also the terms and conditions of the covenant among the twenty-four family branches, and the reasons for altering the priestly lineage must have been explained.

An operation of historical falsification of this kind could have been carried out only with the consensus and the active participation of the priestly family itself, the members of which surely knew who their progenitor had really been. Further, it could have had success with the public only in an extremely low period for the Jewish people, like the one immediately following the return from the Babylonian exile, when knowledge of the religion and history of Israel had been completely lost by the local peoples.

It remains to be understood why Ezra wanted to get rid of the evidence that the priestly family descended from Moses and why he

---

*The Jewish canon stops at the time of Ezra. It does not recognize as canonical the books of the Maccabees and the whole of the Christian Scriptures, considered canonical by Christians.

invented almost out of thin air a lineage from Aaron. We can imagine various reasons for this provision. First of all, he might have had the desire to free the figure of Moses, the high prophet, from the not-always-edifying image of his descendants. This safeguarded the figure of Moses without diminishing that of the priests, who were presented as descending from his elder brother, Aaron,[5] the man who had been ordained as a priest by Moses.

We have to presume that Ezra had something like this in mind when he introduced his reformation and that this was one of the reasons that led him to make it. Nevertheless, there must have been another reason, which we can see clearly in the book of Ezra (chapter 10). One of the cornerstones of his reformation was the imposition on the priestly family of an extremely rigid matrimonial policy: nobody could marry a non-Jewish woman, on pain of exclusion from the priesthood and from "Jewishness." He considered such marriage a grave sin, which offended God and invited his retribution onto the community. He forced all those who had married non-Jewish women to repudiate them, together with the children born of them. "Ye have transgressed, and have taken strange wives, to increase the trespass of Israel. Now therefore make confession unto the Lord God of your fathers, and do his pleasure: and separate yourselves from the people of the land, and from the strange wives" (Ezra 10:10).

At the same time that he was imposing this rule on the priestly family, could Ezra ignore what was an extremely grave original sin by the family itself—that is, the "sin" of descending from the union of Moses and a non-Jewish woman? The contradiction was too blatant and definitely unacceptable to the public. Unable to transform the Midianite Zipporah into a Jewish woman (to do so would have meant rewriting the book of Exodus from scratch), he transformed the Mosaic lineage into the Aaronite one, an operation that he was able to effect with a virtually insignificant alteration of the text (the lion's share of the censorship had already been carried out before him, as we will see).

A collateral—but no less important—advantage of this operation was the opportunity to satisfy easily the demand to provide a solid legal basis for the primacy of Zadok's priestly branch as compared to that of Ahimelech. From a genealogical point of view, the high priesthood should have passed to Ahimelech's priestly branch, but from the time of Solomon it had always been held in Jerusalem by the Zadokite branch. Evidently, in the covenant between the priestly family lines, historical rights were judged to prevail over genealogical rights, and on that occasion it was considered opportune officially to modify the lineages themselves in order to avoid second thoughts and temptations in the future. With a simple stroke of the pen, the Zadokite branch was linked to Eleazar, successor to Aaron, while Ahimelech's descendants were linked to his younger brother, Ithamar, thus legitimizing the priestly hierarchies of the time from the genealogical point of view, which was fundamental for the Jewish mentality.

So it was thanks to Ezra that the Judaic priestly family became Aaronite and invented the fairytale of the Levites elected to the priesthood, thus burying Moses and his line once and for all in the world of legend.

THE ITINERARY OF BENJAMIN OF TUDELA

If what we have said so far is true, then we must conclude that, before Ezra, the Jewish priestly family had proclaimed openly its lineage from Moses and that it continued to do so in the areas not affected by the covenant among the family branches that had returned to Jerusalem. The Bible is a text that was written and edited by these lines, so it is unlikely to find in it explicit proof of this fact. There is, however, at least one source, completely extraneous to the Bible that confirms this assertion unequivocally. This source is the *Itinerary of Benjamin of Tudela,* composed by a learned rabbi who, in the second half of the twelfth century AD, went on a long journey that took him through Jewish communities all over the world.

This is not a typical travel book, with adventures and wonderful enterprises. It is largely a list of names of cities in which there were Jewish communities, and these are presented in geographical order, from the south of France to the Far East. For every city, the text includes the number of Jewish inhabitants, a list of illustrious figures (mainly rabbis and Bible scholars), the presence of schools and biblical study centers, and all other matters of interest from the Jewish religious point of view.

Many scholars emphasize the inaccuracies and obvious exaggerations in the account and maintain that it is pure invention, but others maintain the good faith and reliability of the author and demonstrate this with hundreds of pages of patient explanation. Probably, as with all accounts of this kind, there is some reliable information and some that is a little less so. Yet there is no reason to doubt the reliability of the information provided by Benjamin of Tudela with regard to individuals—in particular rabbis and scholars of the Torah—to whom he always refers by name, attributions, and merit. Especially interesting is his report on the Babylonian Jewish community.

Not all the Jews deported to Babylon by Nebuchadnezzar had returned to Jerusalem: most had remained in the country, and among these there were certainly some members of the priestly family. If the Aaronite line of the priestly family had been officially inaugurated by Ezra only after the return to Jerusalem, as it would seem from the Bible, the priests who had remained in Babylon must have continued to proclaim themselves descendants of Moses.

In his report on the journey, Benjamin of Tudela lingers over the description of the Jewish community in Baghdad, the ancient Babylon, one of the largest of the time. Among the various items of information he provides, there is one that interests us:

In Bagdad [sic] there are about forty thousand Jews, and they dwell in security, prosperity, and honor under the great Caliph, and amongst them are great sages, the heads of Academies engaged in the study of the law. In this city there are ten Academies. At the head of the great Academy is the chief rabbi R. Samuel, the son of Eli. He is the head of the Academy Gaon Jacob. He is a Levite, and traces his lineage back to Moses, our teacher.[6]

Could this be a simple and fortuitous coincidence? This is difficult to believe. It represents further and persuasive proof that the priestly family in Jerusalem had openly declared its descent from Moses before the Babylonian exile, and that the line from Aaron was invented by Ezra only after the return from exile.

Surprisingly, a mention of a direct descendant of Moses who lived in David's time is also made by Josephus Flavius in his work *The Antiquities of the Jews*. In Book VII, section 378, he states that "the chiefs and the priests and the tribes of Levi showed great consideration in giving splendid and magnificent gifts" for the building of the Temple of Jerusalem, "and those who had precious stones brought them and gave them to the treasures, of which the keeper was Jalo, a descendant of Moses."

WHO PRACTICED CENSORSHIP OF THE MOSAIC FAMILY?

The Bible provides sufficient elements to be able to establish with certainty that Moses had a line of descendants. These elements demonstrate also that the biblical text has been the object of deliberate censorship, whose precise aim was eliminating the evidence that the priestly family in Israel descended from Moses.

It is also possible for us to assess the magnitude of the censorship carried out on the various books of the Bible. The text most affected is without doubt that of Joshua, which contains detailed and complete information on the conquest and division of Palestine among the various tribes of Israel, and which goes into great detail about which cities were allocated to which family branches. What is missing, however, is the most important information about this division—that is, what

Moses's family received and to whom the city of Shiloh, which became the religious center of Israel, was allocated. A substantial part of the book—perhaps a whole chapter—must have been dedicated to this information, and it was suppressed. Censorship of the other books must have been lighter; for these it was sufficient to correct or suppress a few names or a few verses here and there in order to get rid of any direct link between Moses and the priestly family. In any case, it was rather clumsy censorship, because it left many clues that allow us reliably to reconstruct what it intended to eliminate.

What remains is for us to discover who carried out this censorship, when, and why. The most obvious suspect is of course Ezra, who, as we have seen, was the author of the verses that establish the descent from Aaron of the twenty-four priestly family branches that had returned to Jerusalem from the Babylonian exile. Because it was he who physically wrote the copy of the Holy Book, which was then used at the Temple of Jerusalem, it would have been easy for him to omit those parts that he did not wish to make public. This, however, does not seem likely. It does not seem convincing that he, a priest, would have censored such a large part of the Holy Book and, furthermore, in such a rough and clumsy way. So most of the censorship must have been carried out before him.

Having reconstructed the lineage of Moses's descendants, we can now also reliably reconstruct the genesis of the Holy Book. Tradition attributes the writing of the Pentateuch to Moses, but this is rejected by modern exegetes, who note that Deuteronomy recounts the events of the last day in the life of the prophet. Yet if by "Moses" we mean his family, as was the custom of the Jewish people, and not the prophet personally, then it seems not just possible, but even highly likely. The Pentateuch mentions various times that Moses, or someone representing him, wrote the texts of the laws and the sermons, recorded entry into the Tabernacle, noted events, and put everything in the Ark.

It is more than obvious that his descendants, the people in charge of the Temple of Shiloh, jealously conserved this documentation, and it is likely that they added it to the deeds related to the dividing up of Palestine and to later historical events in the period of the Judges. For example, by careful analysis of the content, we can establish that Deuteronomy was written by Moses's grandson, Shebuel, who must have witnessed as a child the events narrated in the book. The book of Joshua seems to be the work of the same author.

It is legitimate to think that it was the author of Deuteronomy who deliberately omitted any information that could in any way compromise the secret of Moses's tomb. It does not seem likely, however, that it was he who censored—or else deliberately omitted—the information relating to the origins of Moses's family and to the attribution of the city of Shiloh in the book of Joshua. This information was the legitimate basis of his power and he therefore had no reason to hide it. So the guilty party must be searched for elsewhere.

KING JOSEPHAT CENSORS THE BOOK OF THE LAWS

In order to discover who it was, we must follow the destiny of those documents, step by step, in the Bible. They must have been reordered and organized into an actual book at the time of Samuel, perhaps even by Samuel himself. The book then ended up in the Ark taken by David to Jerusalem (2 Chronicles 5:10), and from then on it was kept in the Temple. The books of Samuel, Kings, and Chronicles offer sufficient information to reconstruct the events surrounding this book, known as the Book of the Laws,[7] and allow us to identify the probable author of the heavy censorship of the book of Joshua.

The perpetrator was almost certainly Josephat, the king who mounted the throne of Judah around 870 BC. Josephat wanted to divulge the contents of the Book of the Laws directly to the people, something that had never been done before, and thus "they taught in Judah, and had the book of the law of the Lord with them, and went about throughout all the cities of Judah, and taught the people"

(2 Chronicles 17:7). We are talking here about copies of the Book of Laws, and not the original, which remained jealously guarded in the Temple of Jerusalem. Yet there was something that Josephat could not allow himself to transcribe in these copies produced for instructional use.

At that time, Judah was at war with Israel. As the first act of his reign, in fact, Josephat "strengthened himself against Israel. And he placed forces in all the fenced cities of Judah, and set garrisons in the land of Judah, and in the cities of Ephraim, which Asa his father had taken" (2 Chronicles 17:1–2). In these conditions he could not in any way have publicized writings that could delegitimize the position of Judah in favor of Israel. The original Book of the Laws stated, as we have seen in previous chapters, that the city of Shiloh had been allocated to Moses's family and that obedience was given by the Jewish people to this family. Shiloh, unfortunately, was in the territory of Israel. In the copies for instructional use produced by Josephat, the whole part relating to Shiloh had to be amended—and with it any closely connected information, such as the information relating to the people in charge of Shiloh (that is, Moses's family).

It was in any case rough censorship, because the intention was not to produce a fake, but only to avoid publicizing politically inopportune information. Some time later, however, Palestine was invaded by the Assyrians. The kingdom of Israel was destroyed and disappeared from history once and for all. The kingdom of Judah survived in conditions of subjection. Manasseh, the most cruel of the kings of Judah, abolished the cult of Yahweh and dedicated the Temple of Jerusalem to the worship of the Assyrian gods. The Book of the Law disappeared. It was found only several decades later by the great priest Hilkiah (2 Kings 22:8; 23:2), when King Josiah decided to restore the Temple and the cult of Yahweh.

Doubtless, it was not the original book, which was a unique example, that was found, but one of the instructional copies produced and roughly censored by King Josephat. And it was this copy that Ezra found himself working on, in Babylon, only a little more than a century later. There cannot have been much left to do to complete the work of suppression of Moses's family and officially to transform the priests of Jerusalem into descendants of Aaron. Ezra probably limited himself to a few alterations, such as the substitution or suppression of names here and there and to suggesting, where possible, that the priests were sons of Aaron.

4

THE DESCENDANTS OF MOSES TAKE OVER AS THE HEADS OF ISRAEL

THE ORIGINS OF THE FAMILY

At this point, now that it is clear that the Judaic priestly family descended from Moses, and that only his descendants had the right to the title of priest, it is worth summarizing briefly the vicissitudes of this family, without the burden of having to look for proof of its Mosaic lineage.

It is the story of a great family, which is interwoven with the story of another great family, that of Jacob, the grandson of Abraham. According to the indications and genealogical information provided by the Bible, Jacob was of an ancient noble stock whose family tree boasted progenitors and chiefs of all the peoples in the Middle East.[1] The history of the Israelites as a separate people began when Jacob left Mesopotamia, where he had found refuge for twenty years with his family of origin, and returned to Palestine at the head of a small tribe. Here, a new name was conferred on him, that of Israel (Genesis 32:24–28): "Thy name shall be called no more Jacob, but Israel." This, from then on, would designate his whole lineage.

Israel/Jacob remained in Palestine, then under Egyptian dominion, for slightly less than thirty years, during which time it grew in wealth and numbers, incorporating among others the population of Schechem, which had been destroyed by his son Levi. The structure and social organization of the tribe were simple and linear. At the top were Jacob and his sons, who made up the noble class, the *elef* or the "chiefs" of the tribe, collectively owners of all its possessions. Below them were servants who were the property of the elef at the same level as cattle or other possessions.

When Jacob migrated to Egypt, the elef, made up of all his sons, grandsons, and great-grandsons, numbered seventy-two.* They still constituted a single tribe (apart from Joseph, who by then had set up house in Egypt), which must have numbered at least two thousand people, including servants. Four generations later,† at the time of the Exodus, there were thirteen tribes,‡ and the elef—the direct descendants of Jacob—numbered about six hundred at the head of a population that in total could not have exceeded thirty-five thousand. This number is given in Exodus 12:37, which states that six hundred elef (erroneously translated as six hundred thousand—the word *elef* also meaning "thousand") left Egypt. The figure is confirmed by two censuses carried out by Moses in the Sinai Desert, when the population of adult males fit to bear arms was found to be respectively 598 elef and 5,550 servants in the first, and 596 elef and 5,730 servants in the second.[2]

The elef made up the noble class of the people of Israel in Egypt and also subsequently, when they settled in Palestine. Slightly more than a

---

*They are listed one by one in Genesis 46:8. This number also includes Joseph's children and grandchildren, who, from a strictly technical point of view, were not part of the tribe of Jacob. They were added to reach the figure of seventy-two, highly significant because of its magical character.

†Genesis 15:13 says that the Jews remained in Egypt "for four hundred years," but two verses later we are told that this period covered "four generations." The two statements clearly contradict each other. The correct one is definitely the second, because it can be seen from all the genealogical lists in the Pentateuch that there were only four generations between Israel's entry into Egypt and the Exodus, and therefore no more than a hundred years had passed.

‡Each of Jacob's sons had founded his own separate tribe, with the exception of Joseph, who, with his greater availability of resources, had founded two tribes, one for each of his sons, Manasseh and Ephraim.

thousand years later, even the memory of them had been lost. Josephus Flavius notes with pride that in his time the noble class of the people of Israel was made up of priests,[3] who, as we saw in previous chapters, were all descendants of Moses. Yet it cannot be said of their progenitor that he was born noble, that he belonged to the class of the elef.

On the origins of Moses, many things have been said and various circumstances for his birth have been suggested, including his being an Egyptian prince, a brother of Ramses II. These hypotheses are the fruit of conjecture and pure fantasy. We cannot presume that they contain any reliable information handed down orally, because they are legends that emerged at least a thousand years later. The only source of information on the origins of Moses is the Bible, and the only certainty the Bible gives us is that he was a Jew, belonging to the tribe of Levi. Regarding the circumstances of his birth, it provides two different versions, and these contradict each other on one fundamental point: his mother. Exodus 2:1–2 says "And there went a man of the house of Levi, and took to wife a daughter of Levi. And the woman conceived, and bare a son." Given that we are talking here about the founder of the Jewish nation, it seems quite incredible that his parents are dealt with in this way, without even being named. It can mean only that there was something that could not be said or that anyway was unclear about Moses's birth: either that he was of servile status, the son of parents whose names had not been handed down, or that he was illegitimate, the son of an elef of the tribe of Levi and an unknown woman of servile status. The fact that he was brought up in an Egyptian environment, probably in the service of some temple,* bears out the second hypothesis.

---

*The Bible states that he was received by the "daughter of the pharaoh" (Exodus 2:5). That this was the sovereign of Egypt is to be excluded, because in Exodus the latter is not referred to as the *pharaoh*, but as the "king of Egypt" (Exodus 2:23). The Bible attributes the term *pharaoh* to any high-ranking Egyptian functionary. Moses's knowledge in the religious and legislative fields leads us to presume that he had been educated at a temple (as Samuel would later be). Joseph had married the daughter of the great priest of the Temple of Heliopolis, Potiphar (Genesis 42:50). We can therefore presume that the Jews had a normal relationship with this temple, and that Jewish boys were taken into its service.

A little later, in Exodus 6:20, we read: "And Amram took him Jochebed his father's sister to wife; and she bare him Aaron and Moses." (This information is repeated in Numbers 26:59 and then appears no more in the Bible.) It is likely that Moses's name was added to this verse subsequently, precisely to give him legitimate and presentable parents.* Jochebed could not have been the unnamed woman in Exodus 2:1. She was noble, the daughter of Levi, the secondborn son of Jacob, and was married to his grandson Amram, who, as an elef, must have had a very good livelihood. There is no reason why she would have had to get rid of her second son to be brought up in an Egyptian house—unless the son was a votive offering for favors received, which would have obliged her to dedicate her son to some temple, as would later happen to Samuel.

But in any case, it is gratuitous conjecture, no more well-founded than any other, and made unlikely by the fact that, according to the first piece of information, Moses's mother offered herself as wet nurse to her own son, which would have been inconceivable for a woman of Jochebed's rank. The information provided by the Bible, therefore, inclines toward an illegitimate origin for Moses. This does not exclude that his father was Amram.

How, with this status, he managed to seize power over the Jewish people is written in the Bible and described in a previous book of mine.[4] With the help of Aaron, he managed to drag Israel out of Egypt and into the Sinai Desert, where he put into action a plan to transform it from a hodgepodge of tribes into a united people by imposing on it an exclusively Jewish God and a law laid down by this God in person.

Moses did not suppress the autonomy of the tribes of Israel (which would have been detrimental to the noble class of the elef, who was at their head); he made them all subject to a superior religious authority

---

*The main suspect of these "corrections" remains Ezra. In this way he established Aaron as Moses's elder brother, therefore keeping the office of the priesthood within the same family and saving the Jewish principle that the highest position went to the firstborn son.

consisting of a priestly class, which administered the worship of this God in a temple dedicated to him.

THE PRIESTLY DYNASTY

Once he had consolidated his power as high priest, Moses's biggest concern was that of assuring the future of his descendants by making them heirs to his office. Here, too, there was an obstacle to overcome that was very serious in the eyes of that society: Moses had married a Midianite, and his children therefore had to be considered Midianites. Aaron and his sister Miriam had been the first to contest the legitimacy of his "Cushite" wife as soon as she had joined him in the Sinai Desert (Exodus 12). Moses's reaction was immediate and strong: he banished Miriam from the encampment for a whole week and publicly reproached Aaron, humiliating him in front of the whole of Israel. In this way he made it quite clear that he would not tolerate the slightest dissent on the question of his family's right to have its part in the fortunes of Israel.

Everything he did subsequently was aimed at ensuring that this right would be unassailable forever: His family had to have primacy over all others in Israel until the end of time. He also had to insure a future of abundance for his descendants, which would have been impossible to achieve if Israel were forced forever to scrape a living in the desert. First of all, he had to insure the possession of a fertile territory, where milk and honey flowed and the people could multiply and prosper, a territory over which Israel had rights, having sojourned there for a long time before migrating to Egypt: Palestine. By Moses's time, it had been occupied by other peoples, so armed conquest was necessary. Moses entrusted the task of the military training of the tribes and the conduct of the conquest to Joshua, who had proved his military skill in the campaign against the Amalekites.

And to Joshua, that man of absolute loyalty, Moses also entrusted the task of insuring the effective transition of power to his own family, once the conquest of Palestine had been carried out. To that end, Moses gave a series of very rigid provisions in his last great speech, reported in Deuteronomy. As the first and most important provision, he established that all—and only—his descendants were priests of Yahweh, and he urged Israel's absolute fidelity to this God, threatening terrible punishments for whoever turned to other gods. He then established the duties of the priests to Yahweh and those of the people to the priests, who had to be put in a position to perform their tasks through the payment of levies and offerings. To this end, he urged that, as soon as the conquest of a territory had been completed, an appropriate place was to be chosen to build a masonry Temple, where the priests could practice the worship of Yahweh, sacrificing to him animals offered by the people.

Finally, he established a fundamental rule to avoid the rapid breaking up of the people of Israel and the dispersion of his own family: the Temple would be and would remain forever "unique," and in no other place could sacrifices be performed. In Moses's intention, the Temple was to be the instrument that would insure power and prosperity for his descendants for all the generations to come—just as the Tabernacle, a genuine mobile Temple, had been the instrument that had allowed Moses to maintain his power over the Jewish people during the sojourn in the desert.

Joshua faithfully carried out Moses's instructions. In a brilliant military campaign that lasted several months, he conquered a vast territory in Palestine, and then subdivided it among the various Israelite lines. When these operations had been completed, he withdrew into private life, but not before obtaining guarantees that Moses's provisions regarding fidelity to Yahweh and a single place of worship would be respected. With his withdrawal into private life, civil power returned, as was logical, to the Egyptian authorities that controlled Palestine,* while

---

*Palestine was an Egyptian province at the time. Joshua would never have been able to conquer a part of it (thirty-one cities in all) and maintain control over them without the consent of the Egyptian authorities, to whom he must have pledged loyalty. On his death, civil power over the Jewish people must have been exercised by another authority imposed by the Egyptians, because the tribe remained within the Egyptian system of government of the Palestinian province.

religious power, with the offerings and the profits that this involved, remained in the hands of Moses's family. In the meantime, this family had built the first Temple in Israel in Shiloh, on a mizpah—that is, on a dominating hill—more or less in the center of the conquered area, which from then on was also known by the name of Bethel (House of the Lord). It was the typical Egyptian organizational system: political power was held by the pharaoh, who governed through his functionaries, called *viziers,* while religious power was held by the various temples, each one run by a priestly caste devoted to the numerous Egyptian gods, every one of which received taxes from a part of the population.

The builder as well as the first man in charge of the Temple of Shiloh was Gershom, firstborn son of Moses, who had succeeded his father in the post of high priest of Israel immediately after Moses's death. As we have learned, he was nicknamed Cushan, for his country of origin in the region of Midian. He was hated and despised not only for his Midianite origins but also for the bloodcurdling events of which he had been protagonist. It does not appear, however, that his right to the priesthood and religious primacy was ever in question. During his pontificate, one of his sons, Jonathan, in apparent violation of the provisions imparted by Moses, instituted a sanctuary in Dan. It is not clear what type of sanctuary it was. It is very likely that it was a place of worship analogous to today's synagogues, where sacrifices were not performed, given that this role was exclusively assigned to Shiloh.

According to the scanty information that survives in the Bible, Gershom should have been succeeded by his firstborn son, Shebuel, who was almost certainly born during the last few years of Israel's sojourn in the Sinai Desert. He had spent the first few years of his life in the company of his illustrious grandfather and, as a child, had witnessed Moses's last day, described in Deuteronomy. Of him and of his high priesthood in Shiloh we know nothing. To him, perhaps, we owe the books of Deuteronomy and Joshua—written, as we have seen, by the same hand—and the collection of writings and documents from which the book of Judges originated. He was succeeded by his son Eli, who appears on the scene in the first book of Samuel as high priest of Shiloh, but without his ancestors being named.

THE JUDGES

On the religious plane, the period of the pontificates of Gershom and Shebuel, which corresponds to the whole period covered by the book of Judges, appears to have been calm and without serious opposition, although the priestly family was anything but popular. Shiloh prospered, thanks to the offerings that flowed to it from all over Israel, and with it so did the priestly family. On the civil and political planes, however, the situation was more complex, although not as chaotic as a hasty reading of the book of Judges would lead us to believe.

During this period, Israel seems to have been dominated by the so-called judges, a generic name that covers a miscellaneous group of individuals that otherwise had little to do with each other. The events of which they were protagonists were banal for their time and of marginal importance for the people of Israel; they normally involved single tribes or even single individuals. They did not, therefore, disturb the sleep of the high priests who, from Shiloh, exerted their influence over the country. The only episode described in the book that directly involves the priestly family is contained in the last chapters. It tells of the near-annihilation of the tribe of Benjamin, fostered by the family itself, and provides the clearest demonstration that the true authority over the people of Israel as such was exercised from Shiloh, and that the judges were local chiefs or civil authorities at the provincial level who were subordinate to Egypt.

The first judge to appear on the scene was Othniel, son of Kenaz and brother of Caleb, who, through opportune alterations to the biblical text, was transformed into the liberator of Israel from the yoke of Cushan-Rishathaim. Actually, as we have seen, Cushan the Terrible was in fact Gershom, and Othniel never fought against the high priest of Shiloh. His name appears among the judges probably due to the fact that, after the division of Palestine, he continued military operations, conquering the Canaanite city of Kiryat Sefer (Judges 1:13).

Some of the other so-called judges were also only small leaders at the tribal level, protagonists of occasional local skirmishes. In that era, every time a pharaoh died, the viziers of the various districts and the governors of outside provinces, such as Palestine, were summoned to Thebes to attend the funeral of the deceased. Their posts remained vacant until the new pharaoh filled them with men he trusted. In this way, the provinces were left to their own devices for several months, and it was during these periods that disorder broke out and there were raids by marauders, especially in the border provinces (the conquest of Joshua most probably was made during one of these periods).

Palestine in particular, on every death of a pharaoh, was subject to raids by peoples from Transjordan and the Sinai Peninsula: Moabites, Ammonites, Midianites, and Edomites, who counted on the absence of a central authority that could muster substantial numbers of troops. Defense was made by local people who organized a few military forces at the command of local notables. The first to try their luck in an attack were the Moabites, who, perhaps on the death of Ramses III in 1156, carried out a raid in the Jordan valley. It was rebuffed by a contingent of Ephraimites on the orders, apparently, of a certain Ehud, a Benjamite who is presented as the second of the judges.

A few years later it was the turn of the Midianites to try a raid in the Jordan valley. It was rebuffed by Gideon, of the tribe of Manasseh, who was helped by the tribes of Asher, Zebulun, Naphftali, and Ephraim. After this victory, the title of king of Israel was offered to Gideon, but he refused it, saying that it lay with Yahweh, clearly in the priestly house of Shiloh.

Gideon is presented as the fifth of the judges. Before him, a certain Samgar is mentioned, who earned the title for having carried out a massacre of Philistines with an ox spur, and Deborah, who together with a certain Barak, led an army of Naphtali and Zebulun against Sisera, king of the Canaanite city of Hazor.

The last raid against the Israelites by outside peoples was carried out by the Ammonites, who invaded Gilead and were rebuffed by the Gileadite Jephthah, last of the judges to earn this title on the battlefield. But the entire episode took place on the other side of the Jordan River and only marginally interested Israel.

The remaining so-called judges carried out no military actions. The only other figure of that period who carried out actions of a military nature was Ahimelech, son of Gideon, who overreached as a result by having himself named king of Schechem and died fighting against a neighboring city. He, however, was not defined as a judge, whereas this title was conferred on a certain Tola (the sixth) of the tribe of Issachar, and on Abdon (the eleventh), of whom nothing is said. The seventh judge (Jair of Gilead), the ninth (Ibzan of Bethlehem), and the tenth (Elon of Zebulun) seem to have been mentioned in the accounts only because they were fathers of an inordinate number of sons and daughters.

A special mention is deserved by the last on the list, Samson, a violent and quarrelsome character, who on the basis of his deeds must be classified more as a bandit than as a soldier, and who repeatedly found himself in trouble as a result of his marked predilection for Philistine women.

After capture by the Philistines, Samson died toward the end of the eleventh century BC, when Egypt, in the grip of serious dynastic problems, found itself once again having to neglect its Palestinian provinces and leave them to their own devices. Here, there emerged two dominant political entities, which contended for primacy over the country: the Philistines, masters of the fertile southwestern plains, and the Israelites, who lived in the mountainous hinterland. The whole saga of Samson is about the friction that existed between these two communities and the eventual eruption into open war.

During the whole period of the judges, the priestly family, in the safety of Shiloh, had enjoyed, virtually undisturbed, the fruits of the tithes paid to it by all the tribes of Israel. With the disappearance of the Egyptian authorities, however, the family had to start assuming ever more onerous political and military responsibility. In the most critical moment, when the Philistines opened hostilities (we are already at the time of Samuel, about 1100 BC), the high priest was Eli. His sons Hophni and Phinehas led Israel's army against the Philistines, bringing onto the battlefield that powerful symbol that was the Ark of the Covenant. It did not have the desired effect. The Israelite army was scattered, Ofni and Phinehas killed, the Ark captured. A messenger raced to Shiloh to announce the rout. As soon as Eli heard the news, he fainted, fell backward, hit his head, and died on the spot (1 Samuel 4:18). In the presence of so much sudden misfortune, Eli's daughter-in-law, Phinehas's wife, who was pregnant, went into labor prematurely and died while giving birth to a son, Ichabod (Ahitub), who was rescued by Samuel. The Philistines arrived immediately afterward, razed the city and the Temple to the ground, and put all the inhabitants to the sword.

It was a terrible reversal for the Mosaic priestly family, which found itself decimated and without its essential source of power and sustenance, the Temple. It was the first of a long series of reversals that would characterize its future. At that moment, the family's fortunes were in the hands of Samuel, who had managed to escape, taking with him the newborn heir, who had become high priest even before coming into the world.

THE BIRTH OF THE JEWISH SECULAR MONARCHY

Samuel appears as one of the great figures in the history of Israel and is sometimes referred to as a judge (the last in the series) and sometimes as a prophet (the first). Actually, he was—at least initially—what in modern terms we could call a *sacristan*. He belonged to the tribe of Ephraim, in whose territory lay the Temple of Shiloh. His mother had placed him in the service of the Temple when he was still a child, in fulfillment of a votive offering. Here, little Samuel had been brought up among candles and parchment, watched over by Eli, who had apparently taken a liking to him. He was virtually considered to be one of the family, participating in its life and knowing all its secrets. Very probably he had become a sort of personal scribe to Eli. He was certainly his trusted man.

With the slaughter of the priestly family and the destruction of Shiloh, Samuel, as guardian to the newborn high priest, suddenly became the most important figure in Israel—or rather, in what remained of it. According to the Bible, Samuel took refuge in the land of his birth, Rama, in the mountainous region of Ephraim, not very far from Shiloh. Not a single word, however, is said on the subject of the priestly family, though it was closely linked to Samuel. The priestly family reappears two generations later in Nob (1 Samuel 21:2). Of this city we know only that it was a possession of Ahimelech, son of Ahitub, high priest at the time of King Saul.

According to the Bible, in the period from the destruction of Shiloh to the advent of Saul, power over Israel was exercised effectively by Samuel, who is also presented as a judge (1 Samuel 7). He personally led Israel in the counterattack against the Philistines to reconquer lost territories; he inaugurated the monarchy, choosing and anointing the first king of Israel, Saul; and he chose and consecrated King David, the founder of the monarchy of Judah. All of this apparently was done without the slightest intervention by the priestly family, to whom Samuel was in service. Yet this is unlikely. It is clearly a case of boasting on the part of Samuel or whoever wrote the books that bear his name—very probably a member of his family.

He certainly must have operated in the name of and on behalf of the high priest, and, it would seem, he looked after the interests of his pupil with skill and loyalty, in order not to diminish the prestige and prerogatives of the post. He did not succeed, however, in avoiding what was a natural and urgent evolution in the political organization of Israel in those circumstances. The defeat by the Philistines had highlighted the inadequacy of the priestly institution to the task of taking on the military defense of the country, so the people demanded and obtained the establishment of a monarchy.[5]

The negotiations were conducted by Samuel, who had previously been decidedly against this concession (1 Samuel 8:6). In the end, though, he let himself be persuaded. From his subsequent actions we can clearly deduce that he hoped to create a monarchical institution that was completely subjugated to the interests of the high priest. First, he put into writing the duties of the king, the most important of which was observing the law of Yahweh and putting his orders into practice (Deuteronomy 17:19).

Next, he made sure that it was absolutely clear that the king's authority emanated from God through the high priest, who consecrated him with the anointment ceremony.[6] Finally, he chose a king who, at least in his wishes, would be politically too weak and isolated to pose a serious threat to the primacy of the priestly family. Moses had imposed his descendants—Midianites—as the first family in Israel, and after them the Levites, descendants of Aaron. Outside the religious field, however, the ancient hierarchy among the tribes established by Jacob in his will (Genesis 50) was still valid. Judah had been nominated heir, and if a king were imposed on Israel, it was from this tribe that he was to be chosen (as actually happened subsequently).

Yet Samuel deliberately looked for this king in the bosom of the tribe that had the least right to that position and which was among the least of his family branches. The chronicler can do no less than record Saul's surprise when Samuel informs him that he has been chosen as the first king of Israel: "Am not I a Benjamite, of the smallest of the tribes of Israel? And my family the least of all the families of the tribe of Benjamin? Wherefore then speakest thou so to me?" (1 Samuel 9:21). Actually his was the smallest of the tribes both in hierarchical terms, because Benjamin was the last of Jacob's sons, and in number, due to the extermination campaign (carried out by Gershom) that had brought it to the brink of extinction. Evidently, Samuel was counting on this fact to be able to keep the newly elected monarch under his guardianship: he would never have had sufficient authority to govern the country without the backing of the high priest.

Unfortunately, Samuel had miscalculated. This calamitous choice would spell infinite trouble for the people of Israel, and in particular for the priestly family. Saul revealed himself to be anything but a docile tool in the hands of the high priest, as Samuel had intended, and when he tried to remedy the situation by naming another king, it almost caused the total annihilation of the Mosaic family.

The Bible tells us that it was Samuel who chose Saul and that he himself "anointed" Saul king (1 Samuel 10:1). While the first piece of information is undoubtedly likely, because as guardian and factotum to the high priest this task was one of his duties, the second piece is not credible. Samuel was not a priest and could not carry out actions such as that of consecrating the king, either in the name of or on behalf of the high priest. Samuel would certainly have been present at Saul's anointment ceremony, and we must assume that he was also its promoter and director, but it was Ahitub who consecrated Saul king of Israel. We cannot imagine how Ahitub must have felt: one of his ancestors had almost exterminated the tribe of the man whom he was rising above the whole of Israel. Perhaps it was intended to be a reparatory gesture through which it would be possible to achieve closure with the past.

Yet this was evidently not Saul's intention,[7] and as soon as an occasion presented itself, he took his revenge on the priestly family. He was without doubt an able and skillful king who knew how to unite the whole of Israel behind him and improve its fortunes with regard to the Philistine enemy. From the little that we are told about him, we can see that he was a great sovereign, the true creator of the structure of the state of Israel. Unfortunately, accounts of him were all written during the reign of the rival dynasty, that of David, so they are very short on information, especially regarding details of embarrassing matters. For example, it is not even known where the capital of the new kingdom was located. The Bible says that Saul lived in "Gibeah," a rather common and generic name from which it is only possible to infer that it was a raised place, on the top of a hill.

As the first capital of the kingdom of Israel, it could not have been

some insignificant little village. It could have been Shiloh, rebuilt by
Saul on its original hill. The Bible does not say where the priestly family
resided or whether Ahitub had built a place of worship to replace the
Temple destroyed by the Philistines. It does, however, provide information here and there from which we can gather that Shiloh had effectively
been rebuilt and that it had remained the religious center of Israel. For
King Saul's anointment ceremony, for example, Samuel called the people "unto Yahweh, in Mizpah," a locality that the exegetes think was a
little north of Jerusalem, but which, as we saw in chapter 2, could have
been Shiloh, or more precisely the place where the Temple was situated,
almost certainly on a raised hillock.

The accounts do not even mention the relationship between
Samuel—and through him the priestly family—and the newly elected
monarch, which, to judge from events, must have been anything but
idyllic. Some time later, in fact, we find Samuel in Bethlehem, searching
for another king to propose as an alternative to Saul, this time respect-
ing the criteria of priority among the tribes. His choice was David, son
of Jesse, direct descendant of Judah. According to the biblical account,
David was anointed king on that same occasion and by Samuel. This
is the usual boasting, but it is not at all credible because it contrasts
with the story, recounted a little later, of David in flight from the court
and hunted by King Saul, but respectful to the end of Saul's right to
the crown of Israel. It is revealing, however, of the relationship between
Saul and the priestly family at the time and of the role of Samuel as the
inspiration behind the family's policies.

Actually, the idea of replacing Saul with David must have come
about after David had risen to the rank of national hero by killing the
Philistine giant Goliath and had thus been admitted to the court of Saul.
It was a full-scale plot, hatched by Ahitub's firstborn son, Ahimelech.
By that time, Samuel had been dead for a long time, and so had Ahitub,
who had died young. Ahitub had left two sons: Ahimelech, the firstborn, and Zadok. According to hereditary rights, Ahitub should have
been succeeded in the position of high priest by his firstborn son, but

the Bible does not confirm that this occurred. The only high priest who appears in the service of Saul, in fact, is Zadok, who presumably lived in the same city as the king: Gibeah. Ahimelech, however, lived in a village that appears in the biblical account for the first and last time only on this occasion and of which we know nothing else: Nob.

One hypothesis that could explain events consistently in the absence of explicit information is that Ahimelech, for some unknown reason, was removed from power by Saul in favor of his brother, Zadok, and banished to Nob (as would later happen to his son Abiathar, exiled by Solomon to Anathoth). Fortified by his right of primogeniture, Ahimelech had plotted to depose Saul and establish a king who would restore Ahimelech's rights. David, apart from being very popular for his exploits against Goliath, also had the great merit of belonging to the tribe of Judah. As a matter of fact, he descended in a direct line from Judah himself,* he who Jacob had designated as his heir by saying, "The sceptre shall not depart from Judah, nor a lawgiver from between his feet" (Genesis 49:8–12). David, therefore, unlike Saul, had the right cards in his hand to aspire to the title of king of the twelve Israelite tribes. It is easy to imagine that the disinherited Ahimelech would have been counting on him to restore the legitimacy of the religious and political posts in Israel.

Saul suspected—or discovered—the plot, and reacted rapidly and ruthlessly. He gave the order to capture David, who managed, however, to escape in time, thanks mainly to the help of Saul's son, Jonathan, who loved him like a brother. So Saul turned on Ahimelech and killed him along with his whole family and all the inhabitants of Nob.[8] It was the second great massacre suffered by the Mosaic priestly family. One of Ahimelech's sons, however, Abiathar, managed to escape with his life and team up with the fugitive David, sharing his fortunes from then

---

*David was the son of Jesse, son of Obed, son of Boaz, son of Salmon, son of Nahshon, son of Amminadab, son of Ram, son of Hezron, son of Pharez, firstborn son of Judah: a well-documented lineage that clearly demonstrates David's right to the throne of Israel.

on. Both of them were the legitimate heirs to the two highest positions in Israel, one to the high priesthood, the other to the crown. Yet they would have to spend many years in hiding before they could restore their rights.

With David in hiding, intent on creating his own personal kingdom at the expense of the Philistines, Saul continued to prosper, apparently unaffected by the horrible crimes visited on the priestly family. On the contrary, it almost seems that from then on his power was bolstered, because no one challenged it any longer, not even David, who recognized him as "the Lord's anointed one," the legitimate sovereign of Israel.[9] Not even Abiathar seems to have challenged the right to the high priesthood of his uncle Zadok. Saul and Zadok governed Israel unchallenged until Saul's death, which occurred on the battlefield against the Philistines.

DAVID'S REIGN

After various adventures, David managed to create his own kingdom in the territory of his tribe, Judah, apparently by tearing it from the hands of the Philistines. We must infer that Judah had been subjugated to the Philistines before Saul was named king and therefore had never been a part of his kingdom.* David conquered the citadel of Jerusalem, which up to then had been independent and in the hands of the Jebusites, and he made it the capital of his kingdom. Abiathar, his high priest, anointed him king of Judah. Along with the tribe of Judah, his kingdom incorporated the remains of that of Simeon, who never appears again in the story.

Now there were two kings in Israel, both of them legitimate, one of them reigning over the ten tribes in the north, and the other reigning over the two tribes of Judah and Simeon in the south. The tribe of Levi

---

*Very probably the territory of Judah, which bordered that of the Philistines, had been subjugated by them since the time of Eli.

was dispersed between the two kingdoms. The priestly family was also divided into two branches: one loyal to Zadok, Saul's high priest; the other to Abiathar, David's high priest. On his death, Saul was succeeded to the throne of Israel by his son Ishbosheth, who certainly did not have the political stature of his father or of his adversary David. Zadok and the head of Saul's army, Abner (who was actually Ishbosheth's uncle), secretly negotiated with David for the unification of the two kingdoms. Ishbosheth was killed and his kingdom passed en masse into the service of David, who, for the first time, united the whole population of Israel under one fully legitimate king, with a high priest who was also completely legitimate. Actually, there were two high priests because, according to the Bible, Zadok and Abiathar exercised the high priesthood jointly for the whole period that David remained alive. This was clearly a situation that could not last; sooner or later one of them would eliminate the other, as happened regularly on the death of the king.

David made another mistake that would subsequently prove fatal for the unity of the kingdom. As soon as unification had taken place, the priestly family took their revenge on Saul's family for the massacre in Nob. They asked for and obtained the handing over of seven males from Saul's line to be hanged from a pole on the mount sacred to Yahweh. David did this willingly, but he refused to hand over the sons of Jonathan, Saul's firstborn son, in recognition of the fact that he had been helped by Jonathan.* So he spared the lives of Saul's legitimate heirs,[10] a sure recipe for future trouble, because sooner or later they would stake a claim to the kingdom of Israel, and in fact that is exactly what they did.

At that moment, however, this threat seemed remote. What did happen on David's death, in fact even before his death, was the showdown between the two high priests. Strictly speaking, the title should have gone to Abiathar, the son of Ahitub's firstborn son. Abiathar made

---

*Jonathan helped David to evade capture by his father Saul, but in return asked him to swear that he would never turn against him or his descendants.

an alliance with Adonijah, David's firstborn son, because he felt he had the right to succeed his father, who was by then old and decrepit. They also induced Joab, head of Judah's army, to be on their side. It was a fatal error because David bore a strong grudge against Joab, whom he could not forgive for having killed Abner, the chief of Israel's army. Like Zadok, Abner had passed into David's service in return for precise guarantees that his life would be saved (2 Samuel 3:12)—but he was killed by Joab (2 Samuel 3:24), who was evidently afraid for his own position, before he even got to Jerusalem.

The trio tried to speed things up and, before David died, held a great banquet to announce Adonijah's coronation. But Zadok knew how to play his cards. He allied himself with the prophet Nathan—who was very probably one of Samuel's grandsons and who had great influence over David—and to Jehoiada, head of Aaron's family and who had also been in David's service at one time. Nathan managed to persuade the old, dying king to nominate Solomon as his successor and to have him crowned on the spot, which Zadok arranged. Adonijah's supporters melted away like snow in the sun and Solomon became king, without a shot being fired in anger. Adonijah's life was spared at first, but he was killed subsequently, on his first false move, as was Joab.

Abiathar, however, was spared by virtue of the services he had rendered to David, but he was excluded from the priesthood and banished to Anathoth. Though this was generous and humane on Solomon's part, from a political point of view it was an error, because the priestly family of Anathoth did not cease to consider themselves the legitimate heirs to Moses, and thereby heirs to the high priesthood. They obviously made sure they would get the office back at the first favorable opportunity, and they allied themselves in this instance with the other great disinherited family, Saul's descendants, who continued to consider themselves rightful sovereigns of the ten northern tribes.

At that moment, however, nothing seemed to tarnish the triumph of David's dynasty and that of Zadok, who was now the only high priest of Israel. To seal the everlasting alliance between the royal family and the priestly one, Solomon and Zadok embarked on the construction of the first Temple in Jerusalem, which became the new political and religious capital of the united kingdoms of Israel and Judah. The city held this position only for about forty years—for as long as Solomon's reign lasted. This would never happen again in its history, but that brief period was enough to consecrate it forever as the Holy City par excellence, although for the next two centuries it again had to give way to the rival city of Shiloh.

THE GREAT SCHISM BETWEEN ISRAEL AND JUDAH

The break-up of the united kingdom of Israel and Judah was already looming on the horizon during Solomon's reign. 1 Kings 11:29 tells us that a certain "prophet Ahijah the Shilomite" had predicted that one of Solomon's functionaries, Jeroboam, would reign over the ten tribes of Israel, while Solomon's successor, Rehoboam, would reign over only two. As a result of this prophecy, Jeroboam was forced to flee to Egypt, but he returned directly after Solomon's death, when the united Jewish kingdom split in two again, returning to the situation that existed at the end of Saul's reign: In the north was re-created the kingdom of Israel, encompassing ten tribes and headed by Jeroboam. In the south the kingdom of Judah, with only the two tribes of Judah and Simeon, went to Rehoboam.

Of the two kingdoms, Israel was by far the most prosperous and important because, apart from the fact that it was home to ten tribes as opposed to two, its territory was vaster and more fertile than that of Judah, which was mainly desert. In addition, it boasted historical precedence because it had been the first Jewish kingdom on Palestinian soil. Judah had the Temple of Jerusalem, but even in this its rights of precedence were nonexistent because Israel possessed Shiloh, which had been the first center of worship of the Jewish people and the site of the first Temple. It is beyond question, therefore, that Israel enjoyed absolute primacy with respect to Judah from both the political and religious points of view. This fact, however, is not specified in the Bible, because Israel's vicissitudes are known to us only from accounts written by its historical adversary, Judah, who had a vital interest in affirming its own primacy in regard to its "big brother."

The kingdom of Judah survived its rival Israel by more than a century, and the history of this period—or at least the history that has reached us through the books of Samuel, Kings, and Chronicles—was written by priests* from Judah who were careful to delete from the accounts any detail that might in some way cast a shadow over the legitimacy and precedence of David's dynasty and the Jerusalem priestly branch, as compared to Saul's dynasty and the Shiloh priestly branch. Objectivity and integrity of information did not lie within their cultural horizons, so it would be naive to accept what they wrote as the undisputed truth. A minimal amount of critical reasoning allows us a much more reliable vision of how things stood, at least on matters concerning the rights of the four family branches, and enables us to search for clues that corroborate that vision.

Of Saul's dynasty, for example, which was the first in Israel and was definitely legitimate because it was officially consecrated (David, too, as long as Saul was alive, always recognized him as the one legitimate sovereign of Israel), nothing more is said in the biblical accounts. Yet it is historically certain that it survived its founder because this is confirmed by chroniclers from Judah itself. The Jerusalem priestly family limited itself to executing only seven of Saul's male descendants in retaliation for the massacre of Nob, but all the others—including the sons of Jonathan, the king's firstborn son—were spared on David's specific orders. We lose track of them simply because the chroniclers from Judah avoided highlighting the fact that they belonged to Saul's

---

*The chronicler of the books of Kings certainly belonged to the Jerusalem priestly class, a fact we can infer from the slant of his report, which is completely centered on the religious aspects of the story and is constantly determined by divine wrath about the idolatry deviations of the sovereigns.

dynasty, not because they disappeared from the history of Israel.

We would not understand, in the Jewish context, why Jeroboam, right after Solomon's death, was named king of the ten tribes that at one time had belonged to Saul if he had not been someone who had indisputable rights to that position. The chronicler of 1 Kings 11:26–40 says virtually nothing about Jeroboam's origins, limiting himself to mentioning his father's name (and, surprisingly for the accounts of the time, also that of his mother), for which he suggests, without much conviction, an Ephraimite origin. Given that we are talking here about the figure who founded the dynasty that would from then on reign over Israel, it is impossible that the chronicler did not know his true origins; his reticence on this matter clearly means that Jeroboam was Saul's most direct descendant. It is the only possible explanation.

In some way, however, the chronicler had to justify the fact that the ten northern tribes had elected Jeroboam as their king without hesitation or resistance. He attributed it to the prophecy pronounced on Jeroboam by "the prophet of Shiloh," Ahijah (1 Kings 11:29). It is an illuminating detail. In this way, he not only confirmed Jeroboam's royal line, but also revealed who his main allies were in his regaining the throne. Ahijah, as we shall see shortly, was a priest of the Anathoth branch and certainly could not have promised the kingdom of Israel to someone who did not have a right to it. Excluded from service at the Temple of Jerusalem by Solomon and banished to Anathoth, Abiathar's descendants had tried to get their revenge by allying themselves with the descendants of the man who had exterminated their family, and by providing them with invaluable help in winning back the throne. Thus the words of Ahijah sound as a covenant between Saul's royal family and Abiathar's priestly one to gain back the positions they occupied before David.

The support of the Anathoth priestly family, however, was not enough on its own to allow Jeroboam to ascend the throne. The support of Egypt was crucial. After the covenant with Ahijah, Jeroboam was forced to flee, to avoid being killed by Solomon, and he took refuge in

Egypt, at the court of the pharaoh Shosenq I (the Shishaq of the Bible).[11] On Solomon's death, Shosenq invaded Palestine, apparently with the precise aim of reinstating Jeroboam on the ancestral throne. Significantly, in the accounts of his military campaign that are written up on the portal of the Temple of Bubastis in Karnak, there is a list of all the conquered cities in Palestine, which practically includes the whole kingdom of Israel,[12] a sure sign that Jeroboam was instated as vassal of the pharaoh. None of the cities of Judah appears in this list, but from the accounts in 1 Kings,[13] we know that Shosenq (Shishaq) carried out a military campaign against Jerusalem, stripping the Temple and the Royal Palace of all their treasures. Clearly, it was a campaign to dissuade Rehoboam once and for all from trying to gain revenge on Israel. (Rehoboam had in fact assembled an army to make war against Jeroboam.)[14]

THE NORTHERN PRIESTLY FAMILY: THE GREAT PROPHETS OF ISRAEL

The political secession of Israel led to religious secession, and this caused the splitting of the priestly family into two branches, which formed the priestly class in both rival kingdoms. Curiously, while the two ruling dynasties got back their ancestral kingdoms, the two branches of priests connected to them exchanged roles: the descendants of Zadok, who had begun his career as high priest with Saul in the kingdom of Israel, remained in Jerusalem, and the descendants of Abiathar, who with David had been the creator of the kingdom of Judah, settled as priests in the new kingdom of Israel.

The religious capital of the northern kingdom was once again Shiloh, and from a copious amount of mentions and clues disseminated in the Bible, it seems clear that the city again occupied the position that was its due, both for its historical precedence over Jerusalem and for Abiathar's precedence with regard to the high priesthood. It emerges from the accounts that the kingdom of Israel had undoubted religious primacy, as well as political primacy, over Judah.

The chronicler of Kings always tries to hide this fact, but he usually obtains the opposite result, highlighting the strident contradictions in his account. For example, he states with insistence that the priestly caste that had settled in the kingdom of Israel was illegitimate, because, according to him, it had been chosen directly by the people and had not risen from the priestly family of proven Mosaic lineage (1 Kings 12:13–33). Yet he is not at all convincing because he often contradicts himself. First, he tries to pass off the creed practiced in Dan and Bethel (Shiloh) as idolatry because it is addressed to two statues of bullocks. Further, the priests who administer it are grouped together with the "priests of the high places" of the Canaanite religions. He is forced to say, time and time again, however, when speaking of the great religious figures of Israel, that they were "men of Yahweh."

His preoccupation with not legitimizing the priestly class in the kingdom of Israel in any way is simply too clear and betrays the fact that this was an extremely embarrassing matter for him as a member of the Judaic priestly branch. He cannot proclaim the historical precedence of the rival family. His lies, though, are ineffective, because he cannot ignore, for example, that the sanctuary of Dan had been created by Jonathan, son of Moses's eldest son, Gershom, and that his clergy, as a result, was anything but illegitimate, boasting as it did an unarguable Mosaic lineage. In the same way, he cannot ignore the fact that Shiloh had historical precedence over Jerusalem, but he takes great care not to name it in connection with the religious capital of Israel. He usually refers to it by the name of Bethel or Mizpah. Yet the name Shiloh, in connection with the "prophets of Yahweh," those in charge of the Temple of Bethel, escapes him more than once—as, for example, with the prophet of Shiloh, Ahijah, maker of the covenant with Jeroboam.

The Shiloh priestly family clearly belonged to the Anathoth branch, exiled by Solomon on the day after his coronation. Anathoth, as the writer of the book of Jeremiah takes pains to point out (Jeremiah 1:1), was in Benjamin's territory, which had previously become part of Jeroboam's kingdom (1 Kings 12:20), and it is only natural that

Abiathar's descendants had gone back to what had been the first religious center in Israel.

For Jeroboam, they were manna from heaven because they placed the final seal on the legitimacy of his kingdom, something he certainly did not let the rival kingdom forget. It seems clear that the priestly family of Bethel (Shiloh) did not fail to assert its primacy over that of Jerusalem and actually had religious primacy for the whole period of Israel's existence. It is the chronicler of Kings himself who repeatedly provides elements that demonstrate this fact.

Particularly significant in this regard is an episode of which the protagonist was the king of Judah, Hezekiah. In a clumsy attempt to reestablish Jerusalem's prestige as a religious center, he invited all the tribes of Israel to a Passover celebration, with the result that he covered himself in ridicule (2 Chronicles 30:10–11). Among other things, he was even off by one month regarding the date of Passover—a clear sign of the cultural degradation into which David's and Solomon's capital had plummeted. After the secession, the Temple of Jerusalem immediately lost its central role in the life of Israel. In fact, it was plundered and stripped of all its vestments by the pharaoh Shishak just five years after Solomon's death.

For the whole historical period in which the northern kingdom was in existence, Jerusalem and its priestly class remained in the shadows. There are no priests from the kingdom of Judah who emerged into the historical spotlight. The great religious figures of that period all belong to the kingdom of Israel. The chronicler, however, not wishing to present them as priests and having denied the existence of a legitimate priestly class in Israel, presents them instead as prophets. Historians have always wondered why the phenomenon of the prophets arose in Israel and was limited to that period and the one immediately following it, and then disappeared completely. There is a simple explanation: the term *prophet* is a little expedient devised by the writer of the books of Kings to avoid having to use the term *priest* for the members of the rival family. Yet we can see through this on several occasions. According to the first verse of the book that bears his name, for example, the prophet Jeremiah was "the son of Hilkiah, of the priests that were in Anathoth": an authentic priest, therefore, because he was a descendant of Abiathar.

That the "prophets of Yahweh" of the kingdom of Israel were, for all intents and purposes, priests is also proved by the fact that they had the power to anoint kings (1 Kings 19:15–16; 9:1–10), a right reserved for the high priest. We can find a posthumous acknowledgement in 2 Kings 17:28–33, where the chronicler admits that the priests of Israel had been deported by the Assyrians and then sent back to Samaria to reintroduce the cult of Yahweh. Because the chronicler of Kings could not delete the great priests of Israel from history, he limited himself to deleting them from the priestly family tree by presenting them as prophets.

From their deeds we can deduce that the Mosaic priestly family was prosperous and powerful in the kingdom of Israel and that it held this primacy for centuries, driving into shadow the Jerusalem family descended from Zadok. From Zadok's family they were divided by an irremediable rivalry. Of course, this priestly family had its highs and lows and reversals of fortune. For example, it was nearly wiped out in the time of one of Israel's greatest kings, Achab, whose wife, Jezebel, tried to impose the cult of Baal, and ordered the killing of all the prophets of Yahweh (1 Kings 18:3; 18:13). Only because of the intervention of Abdias (1 Kings 18:4) did about a hundred of them escape with their lives.

There are clear indications that the primacy of Israel's priestly caste was recognized even by Jerusalem itself. The prophet Elijah, for example, one of the greatest men of Yahweh of all time, crossed the kingdom of Judah to go to Mount Horeb (1 Kings 19:1), and he did not have any scruples about writing to Jehoram, king of Judah, to reproach him for his lukewarm Yahwist faith and to threaten him with divine retribution (2 Chronicles 21:12). Elijah is one of the greatest priestly figures in the history of the Jewish people—so much so that he was even taken up into heaven (2 Kings 2:1–11). He was succeeded by another great prophet, Elisha, who moved the northern sanctuary to Samaria, to Mount Carmel (2 Kings 4:25), probably because Bethel was threatened or had been destroyed by the king of Judah, Asa (2 Chr 15:8), or by his son Josephat (2 Chronicles 17:2).

THE DESTRUCTION OF THE KINGDOM OF ISRAEL

The story of the northern priestly branch, therefore, remains to be told. History, alas, had a sad destiny in store for it. Shortly after Elisha's death, the Assyrians attacked Palestine. In 753 BC, during the reign of Menahem, the Assyrian King Pul marched against Israel and made it pay taxes to him (2 Kings 15:19). Thirteen years later, the Assyrian king Tiglathpileser was not content with just a tax, but devastated huge tracts of the territory of Israel, and deported its inhabitants to Assyria (2 Kings 15:29–30). Just a few years after that, the Assyrians were again in action against Israel, this time providing assistance to the king of Judah, Ahaz, who obtained their aid at the price of the treasure of the Temple of Jerusalem (2 Kings 16:17). Once again, in 730, the king of Israel, Hoshea, submitted to the Assyrians, and paid them a heavy tax.

Very soon, however, Hoshea tried to get out of paying the tax by allying himself with Egypt. Faced with yet another betrayal, the Assyrian king Shalmaneser decided to put an end to the kingdom of Israel. He invaded it with a powerful army, imprisoned Hoshea, and attacked the city of Samaria, capital of the kingdom, which fell in 722 BC after a three-year siege. The surviving inhabitants were deported to Mesopotamia "in Halah and in Habor by the river of Gozan, and in the cities of the Medes" (2 Kings 17:6). Immediately afterward, Shalmaneser sent for the populations "from Babylon, and from Cuthah, and from Ava, and from Hamath, and from Sepharvaim, and placed them in the cities of Samaria instead of the children of Israel" (2 Kings 17:24).

The surviving priests were deported to Mesopotamia along with the rest of the population and they shared its destiny (the same destiny that the deportees from Judah would also share, little more than a hundred years later). Some time later, however, it is not known when exactly, some priests were sent back to Samaria (2 Kings 17:27–28) to reestablish the ancient Yahwist faith, giving origin to that community of Jews known as Samaritans, either Cuthians or Gutians, who continue to this day to claim their primacy over the Judaic faith.

Assyrian domination was carried out with a heavy hand over Judah, too—so much so, in fact, as to bring the Jerusalem priestly branch almost to extermination. In 714, the Assyrian King Sennacherib imposed a heavy tax on the king of Judah, Hezekiah, who was forced to strip the Temple completely to pay it. Sennacherib, however, not content with simply attacking Jerusalem, decided to plunder it as well. The breakout of a mysterious pestilence in his army forced him to withdraw (2 Kings 19:35), and shortly afterward, he was murdered. Judah escaped destruction, but not vassalage. Manasseh, Hezekiah's successor, was taken as a prisoner to Mesopotamia (2 Chronicles 33:11) and was returned to the throne of Judah as a faithful subject of the Assyrian king. In the fifty-two years of his reign he tried in every possible way to eliminate the Yahwist faith. The Temple was dedicated to the worship of an Assyrian god and the Zadokite priestly branch was subjected to severe persecution. "Manasseh shed innocent blood* very much, till he had filled Jerusalem from one end to another" (2 Kings 21:16).

It was certainly one of the blackest periods for the Jerusalem priestly family, which almost risked extinction. Its fortunes began to rise again with the collapse of the Assyrian empire at the hands of the Babylonians. King Josiah (641–609 BC), Manasseh's successor, restored the Yahwist faith and the Temple. After more than fifty years, Jerusalem once again had a high priest, Hilkiah, from the Zadokite branch, who reconsecrated the Temple to Yahweh. He even found the Book of the Laws of Moses, the Pentateuch (2 Kings 22:8), on which Ezra would subsequently work. It had been lost in Manasseh's reign, and with its return, Hilkiah restored Mosaic Law. With him, Zadok's

---

*Priestly blood, obviously.

family regained primacy among the Jewish people and Jerusalem was once again and forever more the Holy City, home of the only Temple dedicated to Yahweh.

The rival branch—without a sovereign state, dispersed among the communities of deportees in Media and, without autonomy, in Samaria, where it had been reinstated by the Assyrians—would never again play a central role in the history of the Jewish people.

JEREMIAH

Yet not all the members of the northern priestly family shared the destiny of their political homeland. A certain number of them threw in their lot with Judah, and after the further tragedy, which very soon would hit the priestly family, they reunited with the Zadokites.

After the destruction of the kingdom of Israel, we can find some prophets of Yahweh operating in the kingdom of Judah. Among these were Amos, his son Isaiah, and Jeremiah. Amos began his career as a prophet in the kingdom of Israel, before its destruction. We meet him for the first time in Bethel, where he is busy arguing with the local priests and thus giving the lie to the chronicler of Kings, who always calls them prophets. Moreover, it says clearly in the book of Amos that in Bethel there was "the Temple of the nation of Israel" (Amos 7:10–14), thus confirming that Bethel and Shiloh were the same place. Amos's prophetic activity mainly consisted of prophesying misfortunes for the kingdom of Israel. After the destruction of Israel, it seems he took refuge in the kingdom of Judah, probably in Tekoa, a village nine kilometers south of Bethlehem,* which in the book of Amos is noted as his place of origin (Amos 1:1).

The prophet Isaiah appears for the first time in the biblical accounts

---

*It is better, however, not to put too much trust into the identification of these places, because we do not know what the actual geography was at that time—nor do we know on what elements the identification was based.

in Jerusalem, at the time of King Hezekiah, a few years after the fall of Israel. Regarding his origins, it is only said that he was Amos's son, implying that he was a native of Tekoa. Given the title attributed to him—prophet—Isaiah must have been a priest from Bethel who had escaped together with his father when the city had fallen into the hands of the Assyrians. He must have been of very high rank, perhaps even high priest, because he enjoyed enormous prestige and authority with Hezekiah, far superior to that of the priests of Judah. It was to him, in fact, that the king turned for advice when Sennacherib ordered the unconditional surrender of the city. Isaiah incited him to resist with every means possible, and fortune smiled on him because the Assyrian army, decimated by the mysterious pestilence on the eve of the attack while positioned by the walls of Jerusalem, had to withdraw.

The prophet Jeremiah, who lived several decades later, at the time of King Josiah (641–609 BC), is presented in two passages in 2 Kings (23:31; 24:18) as a native of Libnah, identified by the exegetes as the city of the same name that had belonged in ancient times to the kingdom of Judah. This is perplexing, because this city had rebelled against King Jehoram (848–841 BC) two centuries before (2 Kings 8:22) and, since then, had passed into the hands of the Philistines. Much more significant for establishing who Jeremiah was and where he came from is the first verse of the book that bears his name, in which we learn that the prophet was "the son of Hilkiah, of the priests that were in Anathoth." This is very important, because it immediately qualifies him as a priest belonging to the main branch of the Mosaic family, the one that had Abiathar at its head.

Jeremiah is best known for his Jeremiads. Few know that he was also a political figure of great importance and in a social position that was among the highest of his time. The exegetes usually neglect this aspect of his history, probably because it does not fit in very well with the stereotypical image of this figure, who is depicted as a voice crying in the desert, almost a beggar, avoided by everybody and persecuted by both the political and religious authorities. The reality that emerges from the books of Kings and Chronicles is quite different. We meet him for the first time in the Bible at the court of the king of Judah, intent on composing a funeral chant for the death of King Josiah (2 Chronicles 35:25), in 609 BC.

His presence in Jerusalem on that occasion was not fortuitous. His daughter, Hamutal, had married King Josiah, and two of her sons (Jeremiah's grandsons) succeeded to the throne of Judah. When Josiah died (609)* he was succeeded by Jehoahaz, son of Hamutal, a sign that Hamutal was Josiah's main wife. Jehoahaz reigned for only three months, after which he was captured by the pharaoh Nechoh and deported to Egypt. He was succeeded by Jehoiakim (609–598 BC), son of Josiah and his second wife Zebudah, then by his son Jehoiachin (598–597 BC), and finally by Zedekiah (597–596 BC), second son of Hamutal and the last king of Judah.

Jeremiah therefore held a position of the highest importance in the political life of Judah, a fact that is also emphasized in the book that bears his name, which states that he had been entrusted while still a boy with a special mission "over the kingdom of Judah" (Jeremiah 1:10). It remains to be understood why a priest of the Anathoth branch, which throughout the history of the kingdom of Israel had exercised the priesthood in open rivalry against Jerusalem, should find himself on a mission in the kingdom of Judah and was strictly related to the royal family. Jeremiah was born in about the middle of Manasseh's reign (687–642 BC) around 665 BC. The kingdom of Israel had been destroyed half a century before, in 722.

Where had Jeremiah been born and brought up before coming to Jerusalem? When the kingdom of Israel was destroyed by the Assyrians,

---

*Josiah died at the age of thirty-nine when Jehoahaz was twenty-three. The latter, therefore, was born in the sixteenth year of Josiah. The marriage to Hamutal must have taken place at the end of his sixteenth year and the first son arrived in the same year. A couple of years earlier, Josiah—only just an adolescent—had a son, Jehoiakim, probably by an unofficial wife. In fact, Jehoiakim became king after Jehoahaz, despite being older than him.

its priests, who belonged to the Anathoth branch, were deported to Mesopotamia. It is possible that a certain number of them managed to escape, taking refuge elsewhere, as we have seen in the cases of Amos and Isaiah, who ended up at Hezekiah's court. But after Hezekiah, the kingdom of Judah had ended up in the grip of Manasseh, who had been subjugated by the Assyrians and, apparently, was not prepared to give asylum to defecting priests from Israel.

The mention of belonging to the priestly family of Anathoth and of coming from Libnah are the only information given about the origin of Jeremiah, but both details are very significant. The Canaanite city of Libnah had fallen under the dominion of the Philistines in about 840.[15] It is not unlikely that the priestly family, including Jeremiah's parents, had found safety from Manasseh's persecutions in Philistine territory and had then returned to Judah with the advent of Josiah. There is, however, a much more likely possibility. All Jeremiah's intercessions at the court of Judah were desperate exhortations not to betray the king of Babylon, and then, after the war broke out, to surrender to him without conditions (Jeremiah 27:12–17).

There is not the slightest doubt, therefore, that Jeremiah was unfailingly loyal to Nebuchadnezzar, and tried by all means to prevent Jerusalem from siding with Egypt. And there is no doubt that Nebuchadnezzar knew him personally and numbered him among his faithful followers. He gave precise instructions to his general Nebuzaraddan to free Jeremiah and place himself under his command as soon as Jerusalem was captured (Jeremiah 39:12). Jeremiah, therefore, given the position he held at court, appears to have been an agent for the king of Babylon in the kingdom of Judah, with the task of insuring fidelity to him—an equivalent figure to Nehemiah and Ezra subsequently, who were sent to Jerusalem as trusted men of the king of Persia.

This presupposes that Jeremiah had entered into the Babylonian sovereign's favor before being sent to Jerusalem and that he had therefore been born and brought up in Mesopotamia. From a historical point of view this coincides perfectly with—and is consistent with—the indications provided by the Bible. In 722, the Assyrians had deported Israel to Mesopotamia. The areas in which the deportees were settled were to the east of Assyria, along the Habor River, a tributary of the Euphrates, and to the south, in the area known as Gutea* along the Tigris, between Assyria and Babylon. The main city of this region was Assur (modern Calaat, or Seergat), which subsequently took the name of Libanah.[16] Because Hebrew vowels are not written, Libnah and Libanah are spelled in the same way. The mention in 2 Kings, therefore, must refer to this city rather than the Philistine village of the same name.

Proof that Jeremiah had lived in Mesopotamia is provided by the anecdote he tells in chapter 13 of his book: he hides a linen belt on the banks of the Euphrates—clearly impossible if he had lived in Palestine. Another thing that links Jeremiah to Mesopotamia is the fact that his personal scribe, ever present in his adventures, the prophet Baruch, lived in Babylon. This is where we find Baruch at the beginning of the book that bears his name, intent on collecting offerings to send to the Temple of Jerusalem from among the Israelite deportees, and commanding them to be loyal to Nebuchadnezzar (Baruch 1).

THE SAMARITANS

The Bible does not provide explicit information on the community of deportees from the kingdom of Israel. We must presume, however, that under the Assyrians its conditions and organization, from the socio-political point of view, were analogous to those of the deportees from Judah under the Babylonians. The priests were the elite class of the community and guarantors of its loyalty to the sovereign. As priests they enjoyed his respect and eventually they also gained his trust. This is proved by the fact, reported in 2 Kings 17:27–41, that the Assyrians had sent some priests back to Samaria to reestablish the cult of Yahweh.

---

*The Samaritans, according to Josephus Flavius, originated from the priests sent back by the Assyrians to Israel from Mesopotamia. This is very probably the reason that they were also known as Cuthians.

This obviously must have involved the rebuilding of a Temple at Mizpah and the conferring of political power on the priests who administered it. The former kingdom of Israel, therefore, had been transformed into a province governed on behalf of the Babylonian sovereign by the high priest of the Temple of Mizpah.* Mizpah must have been, as usual, a hill where the House of God was rebuilt (most probably not Shiloh, but Mount Gerizim). Jeremiah 41:4–5 testify that here stood the House of Yahweh (Bethel), where people from all over the territory that had belonged to Israel (Schechem, Shiloh, and Samaria) gathered to bring their offerings. (We cannot forget that it was under pressure from Israel that Manasseh, also a vassal of Assyria, eliminated the cult of Yahweh at the Temple of Jerusalem, which was seen as a rival to Shiloh.)

In the course of the seventh century BC, the Babylonians replaced the Assyrians in the dominion of Mesopotamia, and among the first cities to fall into their hands were those of the Gutians. The Israelite community had to accept the change of regime and offer their loyalty to the new sovereign. The community must have been represented by its priests, who must therefore have had access to the court and to the sovereign. They were priests of the former kingdom of Israel, belonging therefore to the Anathoth branch, the same branch to which Jeremiah belonged. It is not unlikely that they had won the full trust of the Babylonian sovereign. When the kingdom of Judah fell under the dominion of Babylon, the king had to send someone there as his trusted envoy and representative—someone whose loyalty was certain and at the same time who had lineage and religion in common with the new subjects.

Hilkiah, Jeremiah's father, was probably the head of the priestly branch in Babylon, or at least was one of its leading members, and as such he must have had a relationship with the king. It is explicable that the choice of fiduciary to the king would fall on one of his sons.

---

*The same happened later in the province of Judah, after the return from the Babylonian exile, when the high priest of the newly built Temple of Jerusalem was established as the leader of the country.

According to Jeremiah 1:6–10,* Jeremiah was sent to Jerusalem (exactly as Ezra and Nehemiah would later be sent as the trusted men of the Persian king) when he was still a boy.[17] At his side was placed a person of great experience and proven trustworthiness, Baruch, who also belonged to the Babylonian Israelite community, and who, from then on, always appears as Jeremiah's personal scribe and maintained ties with Babylon.

We know how things went then. Josiah died from his wounds while trying to impede the passage of the pharaoh Nechoh, who was at war with Nebuchadnezzar. His son Jehoahaz reigned for only three months, after which he was captured and deported to Egypt by Nechoh, who instated Joaquim, a man loyal to him, on the throne of Judah. Jeremiah very probably went back to Babylon, to return to Jerusalem only several years later when Nebuchadnezzar reconquered it and instated Hamutal's son Zedekiah on the throne. When Zedekiah was forced by circumstances to side with Egypt, Jeremiah, who had opposed the betrayal with all his might, was imprisoned, to be freed eventually by Nebuchadnezzar when he recaptured and destroyed the city.

Nebuchadnezzar definitively suppressed the kingdom of Judah and entrusted the administration of its territories to a certain Gedaliah (Jeremiah 40:5; 2 Kings 25:22–26), who lived in Mizpah (Jeremiah 40:6; 40:10; 2 Kings 25:23), capital of the province of Samaria. No indications in the text allow us to infer who Gedaliah actually was, which is not in the least surprising if we suppose that he was the high priest in Mizpah and as such governor of Samaria for the Babylonian sovereign.

---

*Jeremiah 1:6–10 almost certainly refers to the investiture of the king of Babylon: "[T]hou shalt go to all that I shall send thee, and whatsoever I command thee thou shalt speak." This is a strange concept in reference to Yahweh, but comprehensible if the order comes from a sovereign in flesh and blood. The words "Before I formed thee in the belly I knew thee; and before thou camest forth out of the womb I sanctified thee" mean that the respect enjoyed by Jeremiah was not so much due to his personal merits as to the fact that he belonged to a family held in great esteem by the king. In all likelihood, then, that family was the priestly branch of Israel that held sway in the community of the deportees in Mesopotamia.

Because he was from the Anathoth branch, the chroniclers of Judah likely censored his role as priest, as they did for all of his predecessors.

The survivors of the kingdom of Judah were taken to Mizpah, which was under the control of the governor (Jeremiah 40:5–7; 41:1–3). Jeremiah, who had been given the choice of going back to Babylon or remaining where he was (Jeremiah 40:4), also decided to stay, and he went to Gedaliah, together with Baruch (Jeremiah 40:6). It is not clear from the biblical text what he did afterward or where he died. Some time later, Gedaliah was murdered by a rebel, a certain Ishmael.* The refugees from Judah who were in Mizpah found themselves in difficulties because they were suspected of connivance with the killers (Jeremiah 41; 2 Kings 25:25) and planned to take refuge in Egypt, fearing retaliation by the Babylonians. They turned again for advice to Jeremiah, who, as usual, urged them to remain loyal to the Babylonian sovereign, threatening them with extermination if they abandoned the country (Jeremiah 42). They, however, did not trust him, and openly accused Jeremiah and Baruch of wanting to hand them over to the king of Babylon. They took refuge in Egypt, taking the two prophets with them (Jeremiah 43:6), probably as hostages. The historical information provided by the Bible ends here, in Tahpenes, with Jeremiah prophesying the arrival of Nebuchadnezzar, who would put Egypt to the sword.

Whether he actually died in Egypt, as the Jewish tradition has it, or whether instead he went back to Israel to die, as a Christian tradition has it,† is not known. With him, in any case, the history of the people of Israel and its priestly family in the land of Palestine comes to an end. Not that the priests of Israel transplanted to Samaria disappear into thin air: when, seventy years later, the Jews return to Jerusalem from

---

*The fact that he was killed by Ishmael, whom the author of Jeremiah 41:1 presents as being of "the seed royal," is an indication that Gedaliah governed as priest. Ishmael was evidently from the ruling house of Israel, a descendant of Saul, and as such, laid claim to power in place of Gedaliah.

†According to the apocryphal book Paralipomena of Jeremiah, the prophet was stoned in Jerusalem by an enraged crowd for having announced the coming of the Messiah.

Babylonian exile, we find them there, and they continue to be there—as Samaritans—for centuries to come.

From then on, however, the biblical chronicler only and always considers them enemies extraneous to the cult of Yahweh, and never gives any of them the title of priest, let alone that of prophet. In fact, Judaic historians continue to deny, even to this day, that they had ever originated from the Jewish people. Josephus Flavius derisively calls them "Gutians" or "Cuthians," and states that they descended from pagan peoples who had originated in Mesopotamia and who had been transplanted to Samaria by the Assyrians after the destruction of the kingdom of Israel.

Initially numerous and powerful, from Ezra onward the Samaritans lost their predominance over Palestine and were subject to persecutions and mass exterminations, including those by the Judaeans, who brought them to the brink of extinction. Today, the Samaritans have been reduced to a few hundred individuals who live in Israel in the area of Mount Gerizim, which they consider sacred. At the head of the community there is a high priest who claims primacy over Jewish priests, not just from a doctrinal point of view, as possessor of the most ancient and authentic version of the Pentateuch, but also and especially from a genetic point of view, given that he declares himself to be the most direct descendant of the founder of the priestly line. In theory, he is the most direct descendant of Moses alive today.

5

RECONSTITUTION OF THE KINGDOM OF JUDAH

THE COVENANT AMONG THE TWENTY-FOUR PRIESTLY LINES

The Jewish community during the so-called Babylonian exile was made up of two distinct components: one that came from the kingdom of Israel, which had been deported to Mesopotamia by the Assyrians in 722 BC; and the other from the kingdom of Judah, which had been deported by Nebuchadnezzar in two successive waves, in 598 BC, when he had defeated and taken prisoner the eighteen-year-old King Jehoiakim, an ally of Egypt, and eleven years later, when he destroyed Jerusalem once and for all.

Various elements lead us to think that the two components then fused together, after the reorganization of the community carried out by the Babylonian sovereigns. We have already seen that Nebuchadnezzar had sent Jeremiah and Baruch, both members of the northern priestly branch, to the kingdom of Judah as his agents, and that after the destruction of Jerusalem, he had placed Judaea under the jurisdiction of the Samaritan Gedaliah. We might not understand, therefore, why he would have had to keep separate the two Jewish communities in Babylon. His successor, Amel-Marduk, who came to the throne in 561 BC, freed Jehoiakim and put him at the head of the Jewish community, creating the institution of the exarch, which would last for nearly two thousand years under the descendants of David, until Genghis Khan's Mongols annihilated the entire Babylonian population.

The exarch reestablished the unity of the people of Israel, and obviously this must have involved the reconciliation of the two priestly branches, the Anathoth branch and the Zadokite branch, which were forced to settle their disputes because they had to live together in the same community. This is proved by the fact that among the priests who returned to Jerusalem after Ezra, there were members of both family branches. In Samaria the descendants of the priests originally reintroduced by the Assyrians continued to survive; but no one in Babylon had to feel subjection toward them or cultivate ties of any kind with them. At most, there persisted a revanchist desire in members of Judaic origin, who must have seen as historical anomaly the fact that Jerusalem was subjugated to Shiloh and who did not renounce the idea of being able to reestablish themselves one day in their own ancient dominions.

The opportunity presented itself with the fall of the Babylonian kingdom and the advent of the Persian sovereign Cyrus, who favored the restoration of Jerusalem as the religious center of Judaea. A first wave of Jews returned to their home country in 538 BC, led by Zerubbabel and the priest Joshua, son of Josedec, who had been deported to Babylon when still a child after Josedec's father, Seraiah, the last high priest of Jerusalem, had been killed in Riblah by Nebuchadnezzar. They were accompanied by other priests, probably all from the Zadokite branch, who intended to rebuild the Temple and the city walls and thus throw in their lot with the Persian monarchy.

Yet they found themselves immediately having to deal with the Samaritans, who obviously did not look favorably on the resurgence in Jerusalem of an independent and competing religious and political center. As soon as Zerubbabel and Joshua started rebuilding the Temple and restoring the walls, the Samaritans went to the Persian king and managed to get him to suspend the work, thus impeding the demographic and economic revival of the city.[1] The pipedream of independence and the restoration of the Zadokite family's primacy, which had been promised by Joshua, remained just that. Those who had been repatriated got by as best they could, in a half-empty city with no defenses and almost certainly in a subordinate position to the Samaritans. The state of the Judaic community of Jerusalem and its priestly family was so pitiful that a few decades later one of King Artaxerxes' favorites at the Persian court, the priest Ezra, successfully asked to be sent to Palestine to improve its fortunes.

Ezra returned to Jerusalem, bringing with him thousands of ex-deportees, including hundreds of priests. The rebuilding of the Temple was resumed immediately and completed. From this moment on, Jerusalem started to rise again and its ascent became unstoppable. Essential to the recovery of its ancient prestige and well-being was the rebuilding of the city walls, carried out, according to the Bible, by Nehemiah, who had also been sent by King Artaxerxes. There has always been a lively debate among biblical exegetes as to which of the two, Ezra or Nehemiah, came first to Palestine, and in what role. Both were favorites of King Artaxerxes and were sent by him. During the period in question there were two Persian kings with this name: the first, Artaxerxes Longimanus (Long Hands), reigned from 465 to 424 BC, and the second, Artaxerxes Memor, from 405 to 358 BC.

The majority of exegetes think that Nehemiah was sent by the first and Ezra by the second, but there are some who invert the order. The most probable thing is that they were sent together by Artaxerxes Longimanus around 458 BC, and they worked together, albeit with different responsibilities. It is not likely that there were two separate rebirths of Jerusalem, one essentially civil, the second only religious. The two components must have gone ahead, side by side. Nehemiah, who was not a priest, held political responsibility, and it was given to him to reestablish Jerusalem's administrative autonomy with respect to the Samaritan authorities and to restore its defenses.

The priest Ezra, on the other hand, held power over the Temple and the religious life of the country. The first thing he did was to dedicate himself to the reorganization of the priestly family. His main objective was to surmount once and for all the ancient division between the rival branches. The priests who returned to Jerusalem after him belonged, in fact, to both family branches: the family led by Zadok, first high priest of Jerusalem, and the one led by his brother Ahimelech and Ahimelech's son Abiathar, who had been exiled by Solomon to Anathoth. Ezra imposed a covenant on them, which is described in 1 Chronicles 24:1–6.

Twenty-four family lines entered into this covenant, and the branches from then on shared among themselves the positions at the Temple and its income and, most important, claimed the exclusive right to the priesthood. All the other family branches of Mosaic origin, who at that moment were out of Jerusalem, in Babylon or Samaria or Egypt, were excluded. It was then, as we can see in the verses in question, that the twenty-four branches officially took Aaron's two sons as their ancestors: sixteen lines descending from Zadok linked themselves to Eleazar, to reassert their primacy in the priesthood; eight lines descending from Ahimelech linked themselves to Aaron's younger son, Ithamar. In this way all the priests became "sons of Aaron," but nobody took care to make that lineage credible; they just invented it ad hoc.

It is not very clear to which of the two houses Ezra belonged. It is possible that he belonged to one on his father's side and one on his mother's. The figure of the mother thus assumed an extraordinary importance in Ezra's reformation and would from then on be fundamental in Jewish society, in which only the son of a Jewish mother can be considered Jewish. This is almost certainly the reason why the priestly family changed its founder from Moses to Aaron.

It is unlikely, however, that the priestly family disowned its origins in private. In the secret books to be handed to the "wise men" of which Ezra's apocryphal texts speak, the true origin of the family must have been indicated. The wise men, we can imagine, must have been the leading figures in the twenty-four family branches, and they must have been part of an organism created by Ezra with the task of applying the covenant and safeguarding the prerogatives and the unity of the priestly class. It was probably a secret organization, because no information is provided about it by historical sources and it did its work in absolute secrecy, as testified to by Ezra's apocryphal texts. Yet there can be no doubt about its existence, because there must have been a mechanism for handing out posts and resources among the various family lines; settling disputes; making decisions on the great religious, political, and administrative questions that involved the priestly class; keeping a register of who was entitled to be part of it; and so on.

The organization created by Ezra for this purpose was without doubt efficient and durable, because otherwise it would be impossible to explain how such a covenant, among such a great number of family branches, could have held up for centuries, weathering all historical vicissitudes and the inevitable bitter rivalries that arose among the branches. Later, we will look at the nature and structure of this organization. For the moment, we must note that only the family lines that had a part in it had a right to the administration of the Temple of Jerusalem.

All the other priests scattered around the world who had not entered into the covenant were excluded from the organization that administered it. Almost certainly, however, the twenty-four family branches that constituted the organization had neither the intention nor the power to "excommunicate" the other priestly family branches in the Jewish communities, thus depriving them of their right to the priesthood. They simply intended to restore the Temple of Jerusalem as the place of worship delegated to carry out sacrifices to Yahweh and to make sure that they had an exclusive right to its income. By excluding the interference of the outside branches, the pact among them aimed at sharing both the tasks involved in the running of the Temple and the resources that became available. Thanks to this, Jerusalem soon became prosperous and powerful again and expanded its influence in Palestine and in the Jewish world in general—but this inevitably led to an escalation in the conflict with the Samaritans, which eventually resulted in the disavowal of their priestly status and of their being part of the Jewish people.

The apple of discord was the Temple as the delegated place of sacrifices, which, according to Moses's instructions, should have been "unique." It was not only a religious question, but also—and especially— an economic one, for to this Temple flowed the offerings and tithes that all the faithful had to pay.

Until Solomon's death, in fact, there had always been only one Temple in Israel delegated for sacrifices: at first in Shiloh, and then in Jerusalem. With the division of Israel into two separate and rival kingdoms, there were also two Temples dedicated to sacrifice: the Temple of Shiloh (or Bethel or Mizpah) was rebuilt, and from then on it placed itself in opposition to and in competition with that of Jerusalem. After the destruction of the kingdom of Israel, the Temple of Jerusalem was again, for some time, the only place entitled to hold sacrifices, until the priests sent back to Samaria by the Assyrian King Esar-haddon rebuilt the Temple and resumed the celebration of sacrifices to Yahweh (Ezra 4:2).

After the destruction of the kingdom of Judah by Nebuchadnezzar, his territory passed under the direct administration of the Samaritans, whose Temple once again became the only place delegated to sacrifices. This situation lasted until the return to Jerusalem of the first wave of exiles from Judah, in the wake of Zerubbabel and Joshua, who began the rebuilding of the Temple and resumed the offering of sacrifices (Ezra 3:6), provoking, as we have seen, the reaction of the Samaritans, who managed to interrupt the building work (Ezra 4) and almost certainly, though the Bible does not say so, to bring to an end the practice of sacrifice in Jerusalem.

It was only with Ezra that Jerusalem finally had its Temple again, along with its right to sacrifice—tied to which was the right to collect tithes and offerings. The Temple of the Samaritans, however, continued to survive for a few years, until the vicissitudes of history turned the wind decidedly in the favor of the house of Judah. In 423 BC, King Darius II (423–404 BC) came to the throne of Persia, and, reversing the policies of his predecessors, he placed Samaria under the direct administration of Jerusalem. It was on that occasion that the northern Temple was destroyed, and the Samaritans were forbidden to offer sacrifices.

The Samaritans got their revenge less than a century later, when the Persian empire was conquered by Alexander the Great. Bolstered by their position as victims of the persecution of the past regime, they demanded and obtained from the Macedonian sovereign independence from Jerusalem and permission to rebuild a Temple on Mount Gerizim with the right to sacrifice. The Temple of Gerizim was completely destroyed two centuries later, in 128 BC, by the Hasmonean Hyrcanus I, high priest of Jerusalem. Since then, as has already been mentioned, the history of the Samaritans has been a continuous succession of persecutions and massacres, which has brought them to the brink of extinction.

FROM PRIESTS TO KINGS

Let us go back to Jerusalem, to the day after the return of the exiles from Babylon, led by Ezra. He is a fundamental figure in the history of the Jewish people and particularly that of the priestly family. Ezra was the instigator of a profound religious reformation, which came about essentially through the reorganization of the Jerusalem priestly family, on which a perfectly regulated structure and strict rules regarding marriage and behavior were imposed. This was aimed at preventing any future degeneration of the priesthood and of the religion for which they were the only ministers. To guarantee the family's means of survival and the successful running of the Temple, he had established, or rather restored and regulated, the system of tithes, which provided an abundant and regular income. The family's fortunes were more than ever based on the possession and administration of the Temple and of the religion connected with it.

With the rebuilding of the Temple and the walls, Jerusalem rose once more, growing rapidly in population and prosperity, and Judaea again became totally Jewish. Concurrently, the influence and wealth of the priestly family—or rather the twenty-four priestly lines, which together controlled the whole country—grew. At the head of Judah there was no longer a king from David's dynasty, but instead the high priest, who governed in the name of and on behalf of the Persian sovereign. For this whole period the post of high priest continued to be attributed on a hereditary basis to the direct descendants of Zadok.

In 333 BC, Alexander the Great, having defeated the Persian king Darius at Issus in Cilicia, conquered Syria and carried out the Siege of Tyre. The Samaritans flocked to the Macedonian king, hailing him as a liberator and bringing him supplies and soldiers. In exchange, Alexander recognized their autonomy from Jerusalem and granted them permission to rebuild their own Temple on Mount Gerizim with the right to sacrifice. The Jerusalem priestly family, however, which owed its good fortune entirely to the Persian kings, refused to take his side, declaring themselves loyal to the defeated Persian sovereign—an act that ran the risk of dire consequences. When the Siege of Tyre had been completed, Alexander headed toward Jerusalem with the apparent intention of destroying it and instating a Macedonian governor in Judaea. The high priest, Jahdo, however, sought an audience with him. Somehow he managed to calm down Alexander, and he obtained honorable conditions for the city and for himself: Judaea was allowed to continue to govern itself according to its own laws and Jahdo was reconfirmed in his post.

Little or nothing is known about what happened in Jerusalem in the following ten years of Alexander's reign or during the war that broke out among his generals to divide up the spoils of the empire. In the end, we find Judaea again under the dominion of Egypt, ruled by the Tolomeans, who put into practice a policy of Hellenization of the country without encroaching on the privileges and prerogatives of the Jerusalem priestly family. The sovereign, however, gave himself the right personally to nominate—or in any case to confirm the nomination—of the high priest, usually on payment of substantial sums. In this way, the hereditary principle was often ignored and the post began to pass from one priestly family group to the other, creating rivalry among them and often bitter disputes over the attainment of the position of high priest.

In 199 BC, Judaea was occupied by Syria, which was ruled by the Macedonian dynasty of the Seleucids. For the priestly family branches, this was the start of very difficult times, because the Seleucids greatly escalated the policy of the Hellenization of the country, an attempt to transform Jerusalem into a Greek city. This policy culminated in 168 with the sacking of the Temple by Antiochus IV and the massacre of a great number of priests. The Jewish religion was outlawed, the Temple was dedicated to the cult of Zeus, and—the supreme outrage—a pig was sacrificed there.

It did not take long for a revolt to occur, led by a certain Mattathias from the Hasmonean priestly family, who, together with his five sons, massacred the Syrian emissaries who had been appointed to force the people to sacrifice to Zeus. Two years later, in 165 BC, his son Judah succeeded in liberating Jerusalem, and he rededicated the Temple to Yahweh, after having first purified it. The ceremony of the rededication of the Temple would forever more be remembered by the Jewish people in the holiday of Hanukkah, celebrated in memory of this event. Judah is known by the nickname of Maccabee, meaning "hammer," which was probably given to him in recognition of his successes in beating the Syrians (though some people maintain that it was because of the shape of his skull). Although Syria remained nominally master of Judaea, in fact Judah Maccabee acted as an independent sovereign, to the extent that in 161 BC he drew up a mutual-aid treaty with Rome.

It did not last long: Judah was killed in battle and the Syrians returned to the country in great numbers, forcing his brother Jonathan, who had succeeded him in command, to retreat into the desert with just a handful of loyal supporters. A few years later, in 153 BC, things improved for Jonathan, who had in the meantime succeeded in assembling a substantial army. To guarantee his support, the new sovereign of

Antiokya, Alexander Balas, named him first as high priest and then as governor of Judaea.*

Jonathan died in battle between 144 and 143 BC and was succeeded in the post of high priest by his brother Simon, Mattathias's only surviving son. A little later, in 143 BC, the Syrian king Demetrius II relieved Judaea of the payment of all taxes, and the following year Simon drove out the Syrians once and for all. For the next eighty years Judaea was an independent state under the guidance of the Hasmoneans, who each governed as high priest, a position to which the title of king was very soon added. In 141 BC, a great assembly was convened in Jerusalem, which confirmed Simon as high priest, despite the fact that he did not belong to the Zadokite branch, and also conferred on him the title of Sar am El, prince of the people of God, never before conferred on anyone who did not belong to David's line.

Simon was murdered, five years after his nomination, by a relative who was jealous of his power. He was succeeded by his son Johanan, also known as Hyrcanus I, who considerably extended the borders of the kingdom of Judah, conquering, to the north, Samaria, whose Temple, erected two centuries earlier on Mount Gerizim, he destroyed, and, to the south, Idumea, which he converted to Judaism. He was succeeded by his son Judah, known also by the Greek name of Aristobulus, who finally succeeded in having himself proclaimed king, despite some opposition due to the fact that he was not of David's lineage. After more than three centuries, the Jewish people again had a king. He founded the third royal dynasty, drawn from the line of the priests. For the first time in the history of the Jewish people the positions of high priest and king were joined in the same person, something that would later provoke bitter opposition.

Aristobulus continued the expansion of the kingdom, completing

---

*The Hasmoneans did not belong to the Zadokite branch of the priestly family. With their power, the high priesthood returned to the branch of Abiathar, despite the protests of those who demanded respect for the traditions.

the conquest of Galilee and annexing territories in Lebanon, which had never been part of either of the Jewish kingdoms. He died in 104 BC and was succeeded by his brother Jannaeus—Alexander, in Greek—who reigned for the following twenty-seven years, the most turbulent years in the history of the Hasmonean monarchy as a result of his despotic and bloodthirsty character and his dissolute lifestyle, unworthy of a high priest.

In 78 BC, Jannaeus was succeeded to the throne by his wife, Salome, known also by the Greek name of Alexandra, who ruled for nine years and would be remembered as a great queen, the first and only in Israel. On her death, the kingdom of Judah was ravaged by a civil war for the crown between her sons Hyrcanus II and Aristobulus II. The two pretenders ended up asking for the arbitration of Pompey the Great, who, in 63, had annexed Syria to Rome by conquering Damascus. Pompey settled the dispute between the brothers by occupying Jerusalem and confirming Hyrcanus II as high priest. Nevertheless, he abolished his title of king and named him simply governor on Rome's behalf, thereby considerably curtailing his jurisdiction, because wide territories in the north were annexed to Syria's Roman province. Thus Judah's independence ended forever.

After Pompey's departure, Judaea enjoyed a period of relative peace. Hyrcanus II continued to hold the post of high priest, but the Romans transferred civil power to the family of an able and ambitious figure of Idumaean origin, Antipater. Julius Caesar conferred Roman citizenship on Antipater and named him prosecutor of Judaea, which meant effectively Rome's representative in the country. Antipater's son, Phasael, was named governor of Jerusalem and a second son, Herod, governor of Galilee.

The priestly family reacted by allying itself to the Parthians, who at that time were at war with Rome. With their help, in 40 BC the son of Aristobulus II, Antigonus, succeeded in recapturing Jerusalem and instating himself for a brief period, by having himself named high priest in place of his uncle Hyrcanus, who was deported to Parthia, and by taking back the title of king. It was the last swish of the tail of the Hasmonean dynasty.

Herod escaped to Rome and so effectively convinced the senate of his capabilities and loyalty that he was unanimously named king of Judaea. It was in this way that he returned to Palestine, accompanied by the Roman legions, which, in 37 BC, again captured Jerusalem and, after executing Antigonus, instated as sovereign the newly elected Idumaean. In order to legitimize his position in the eyes of the Judaeans, Herod hurriedly married a Hasmonean princess, Mariamme, granddaughter of Hyrcanus II, to whom he had been betrothed some years earlier. He named Mariamme's brother, Aristobulus III, as high priest, keeping the post firmly within the grasp of the Hasmonean family.

With Herod, the priestly family lost the throne once and for all but acquired a new Temple, incomparably grander than the previous one, thus increasing their prestige and income. With the huge increase in the population of Judaean faithful, the Temple built by Ezra on the top of Mount Moriah had become inadequate to the task of receiving the countless pilgrims who were coming to Jerusalem. In 22 BC, Herod started the work of enlarging it. He ringed the top of Mount Moriah with impressive walls and filled in the surrounding areas in order to create level ground with a surface that was more than double that of the previous one.

Later, we will look at an interesting detail with regard to possible relationships: the fact that, for the building of the new Temple, Herod created a corps of mason-priests who were the only people authorized to enter and work in the inner sanctum. This corps remained in service in order to carry out routine maintenance, and continued to embellish the Temple right up to the eve of its destruction.

With the death of Herod the Great in 4 BC, the kingdom of Judah was divided up among his three sons—Archelaus, Herod Antipas, and Phillip—to whom, however, the Romans denied the title of king. The first was named ethnarch and the other two tetrarchs. After their deaths, Judaea became a Roman province and, for the next sixty years, was governed by a prosecutor sent by Rome—save for one interval of seven years, between AD 37 and 44, during which it again had a king of partly Hasmonean origin, Agrippa I, son of Aristobulus, eldest son of Mariamme and Herod, who had been brought up in Rome together with Caligula. When Caligula became emperor, he named him king of Judaea, a title confirmed by Caligula's successor, Claudius.

On his death, Judaea was once again ruled by Roman prosecutors, who set themselves up in Cesarea, a largely pagan city situated on the coast. At that time, Judaea was no more a state with a unique established religion for a while, because in many big cities, especially those on the coast, the Hellenized pagan population was in the majority, and the prosecutors, while having the right to name the high priests, did not treat the Jewish religion with any more regard than the other religions. At the entrance to the Temple was affixed a golden effigy of the imperial eagle, and anyone attempting to remove it was crucified.

Jerusalem remained the point of reference for all the Jews in the Roman Empire who had created numerous and prosperous communities outside Judaea and continued to pay tithes to the Temple. The Jerusalem priestly family remained the only element of unity for the Jewish people and reached the peak of its power and wealth. It was then that it let itself be dragged into anti-Roman sentiment and eventually into a full-scale revolt, which caused its ruinous downfall. Judgment Day was coming.

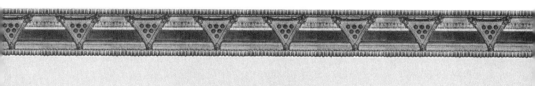

PART TWO

Sol Invictus Mithras

6

JOSEPHUS FLAVIUS

MASTER OF SURVIVAL

The fateful year of AD 70 saw the Mosaic family at the height of its power. The twenty-four priestly lines who had shared power in the days of Ezra, based on the exclusive ownership of the Temple and the exclusive administration of the priesthood, were all still there, more numerous and richer than ever and firmly entrenched in the running of the Temple and the country. Their descendants numbered in the thousands, and many of them had royal blood in their veins because they descended from or were related by marriage to the Hasmoneans. The Roman domination had brought peace and prosperity, but it had been marked by passionate tensions on the religious level, which had provoked a series of revolts, the last of which, in AD 66, was fatal for the Jewish nation and for the priestly family. With the destruction of Jerusalem by Titus Flavius Vespasianus in AD 70, the family was practically wiped out.

The Temple, the instrument of family power, was razed to the ground, never to be rebuilt. From that moment on, the priestly family disappeared from the stage of history, never again to play a visible role. Was this the end of a great line, which went back a thousand years?

The historical facts would appear to confirm this, but reality looks different. It is certain, in fact, that the family did not materially disappear. There were several survivors, members of the top social class who were extremely wealthy and enjoyed the protection of the Romans. We are informed of them by the Jewish historian Josephus Flavius, who lists them one by one, starting with himself.

Josephus, the son of Matthias, was a priest who belonged to the first of the twenty-four priestly family lines; he had royal blood in his veins because, through his mother, he was related to the Hasmoneans. At the time of the revolt against Rome, he had played a leading role in the events that tormented Palestine. Sent by the Jerusalem Sanhedrin to be governor of Galilee, he had been the first to fight against the legions of the Roman general Titus Flavius Vespasianus, who had been ordered by Nero to quell the revolt.

Barricaded inside the fortress of Jotapata, he bravely withstood the Roman troops' siege. When the city finally capitulated, he withdrew into a cistern, and after lengthy negotiations, he surrendered, asking to be granted a personal audience with Vespasian (*The Jewish War*, III, 8, 9), who, incredibly, gave his consent.* Their meeting led to an upturn in the fortunes of Vespasian, as well as in those of Josephus: the former was shortly to become emperor in Rome, while the latter not only had his life spared, but not long afterward, he was "adopted" into the emperor's family and assumed the name Flavius. He received Roman citizenship, a patrician villa in Rome, a life income annuity paid by the state treasury, and an enormous estate.

Josephus Flavius justified these extraordinary favors by claiming that during their meeting after the fall of Jotapata, he had predicted that

---

*After the city of Jotapata was captured by the Romans, Josephus took refuge in an underground cistern with forty of his men. In his account, he tells that the forty had decided to kill one another rather than be taken prisoners, and they consequently drew lots to establish the order. By chance, the last place fell to Josephus Flavius, and when all the others had killed one another, except for him and one other, he thought that he would better serve the will of God by staying alive, in order to announce to Vespasian the good news that Vespasian would become emperor, as had been revealed to him in a dream.

Vespasian would become emperor.* Yet the Roman historian Suetonius testifies that this prophecy made by Josephus was only the last in a series of similar predictions, which started on the day that Vespasian was born. Everybody knew of the existence of these prophecies—it was thus totally absurd to imagine that Vespasian covered a vanquished rebel with unprecedented favors simply because he had repeated an omen that was generally known. There must have been something else. The Roman general was under a terrible handicap in his race for the imperial purple robe: he was broke (it is Suetonius again who confirms this†), but in order to become emperor, he needed ample financial means. Josephus provided them.

During his governorship in Galilee, Joephus had put aside a considerable sum of money, both from the collection of the tithes due to the Temple and, above all, from the requisitioning of the gold, silver, and precious objects that had been plundered by the inhabitants of Tiberias from the palace of Herod the Tetrarch (*The Jewish War,* II, 21, 3; *Life,* 66). He immediately handed over his personal savings to Vespasian, thus earning the sparing of his own life, and he promised a far greater patrimony in exchange for the benefit that he subsequently received: the treasure of the Temple in Jerusalem. His own works contain sufficient indications to accuse him.

In the triumph celebrated in Rome some time later by Titus and his father, Vespasian, the showpiece was represented by the treasure from the Temple in Jerusalem. This is testified by Josephus Flavius,‡ and his

---

*The fact that there were prophecies about the imperial destiny of Vespasian was not novel. In his *Lives of the Caesars,* Suetonius dedicates a whole chapter[1] to the omens, which, from his birth, forecast that Vespasian was predestined to wear the emperor's purple robe. Last in the list comes the prophecy of Josephus. It is historically certain, therefore, that this subject was mentioned in the conversation between Josephus and Vespasian.

†Suetonius puts great emphasis on Vespasian's greed and his need for money. He says of Vespasian: "The only defect of which he can justly be accused was his greed for money." Further on, he defines him as "extremely greedy by nature."

‡"[A]mong all the objects, those taken from the Temple of Jerusalem stood out, a gold table weighing many talents and a candlestick also made of gold . . . this was followed by the last of the spoils, a copy of the Jews' law" (Josephus Flavius, *The Jewish War,* VII, 5, 5, 148–50).

words are confirmed by the representation of the triumph engraved on the arch of Titus,[2] clearly showing the menorah, the large candelabra with seven arms, in the procession together with other precious furnishings from the Temple.

There is no doubt, then, that Vespasian took possession of the treasure of the Temple, but how and when did this happen? Reading of the circumstances in which the siege of Jerusalem and the final attack on the Temple took place, we should expect that when the Romans succeeded in capturing it, little remained of the original treasure: the Temple had been occupied for months by the Zealots, who had not hesitated to strip it completely. When they finally realized that any kind of defense was out of the question, they set fire to it and destroyed everything of any value that remained in order to prevent it from falling into Roman hands. The Romans found themselves the owners of a building gutted by fire and sacked by its own defenders.

The certainty that emerges from the story of Josephus Flavius is that the Temple treasure was not captured by Titus, the son of Vespasian, but was handed over to him by members of the priestly family in exchange for safe conduct and economic benefits. The treasure was undoubtedly hidden in various secret hiding places, even if Josephus does not reveal where these were and he is somewhat confused and contradictory about the times and methods of consignment. Above all, he is careful not to reveal the role that he himself played in the handover.

THE COPPER SCROLL

We can reconstruct the facts with the help of an extraordinary document that came to light only two thousand years later: the Copper Scroll. It was discovered in 1952 in cave 3Q, at Qumran. The scroll is composed of three attached sheets of copper rolled up like a sheet of paper. On the inside of this document was engraved a text in Hebrew. In view of its antiquity, it was not possible to unroll the scroll without ruining the text. It was therefore transferred to Manchester, where it was cut into vertical strips corresponding to the columns of the text. As the strips were cut and cleaned, they were translated by the famous Qumranist J. M. Allegro.

The text is largely a list of locations where treasures had been hidden. Initially, it was thought to refer to the treasure of the Essene community of Qumran, and the text was considered with profound skepticism because it seemed to be impossible for that small community to possess such enormous riches. Among other things, most of the locations mentioned in the text are situated in the neighborhood of Jerusalem. Nowadays, scholars are practically unanimous in their belief that the Copper Scroll refers to the treasure from the Temple in Jerusalem (partly because a large portion of it is made up of the tithes), which was hidden in preparation for the siege.[3]

The scroll begins directly with the list of hiding places:

At Horebbeh, in the valley of Achor, underneath the steps that go eastwards, forty cubits deep: a silver coffer, the total weight of which is 17 talents.

In the funeral monument of Ben-Rabbah from Shalisha: one hundred gold ingots.

In the large cistern in the enclosure of the small peristyle, stopped up by a stone with a hole in it, in one of the bottom corners, opposite the upper opening: nine hundred talents.

On the hill of Kohlit: vases of offerings collected, half-measurements and ransoms, all the offerings collected for the treasury in the seventh year and the tithes . . .

It goes on in the same way for the rest of the document, listing as many as seventy-four different hiding places and the contents of each of them. Needless to say, none of these treasures is found in the place indicated. (J. Allegro has carried out searches—without success—in all the locations that he had succeeded in identifying on the basis of the description.) This was only to be expected: the last sentence on the Copper Scroll states, "In the cave of Kohlit, . . . there is a copy of this document, with the explanation, the measurements and a complete inventory, object by object."

The Copper Scroll found at Qumran, then, is only a reserve copy of an original, which had been hidden in the cave of Kohlit, in the neighborhood of Jerusalem. Whoever had hidden the treasure must have taken every possible precaution to be able to take possession of it again once the storm had passed. He had written out the list of hiding places on a nonperishable substance—copper—and obviously, given the importance of the document, he had made two copies and had them hidden in two different places. Both copies must have been written and hidden by the people who had organized the hiding of the treasure. There can be no doubt about their identity: the owners of the treasure—that is to say, the heads of the priestly family lines of the Temple, undoubtedly including the treasurer.

At this point, what remains is only to put together two and two. The scroll must have represented for some of them safe conduct in order to escape the destruction of the Temple and the following slaughter and to insure a future for themselves and their families. Josephus Flavius was the first of the Jewish priests to fall into the hands of the Romans, and he was the one who obtained the greatest favors. Seeing that he not only belonged to the first of the priestly families, but also occupied a very high position of responsibility in Israel, as governor of Galilee, and that he had a profound knowledge of the desert of Judah, where he had spent three years of his youth, it is legitimate to believe that he knew about the operations to hide the treasure and was perfectly capable of finding the hiding places.

During his private audience with Vespasian immediately after his capture, Josephus must have negotiated his own safety and future prosperity in exchange for the Temple treasure. The proposal would have been irresistible for the penniless Roman general, who thus saw the possibility of securing the necessary means for his ascent to imperial power. On that occasion, the two of them probably made a pact, which was to change the destinies of the world.

Initially, Vespasian "did not free Josephus, but gave him a robe and other objects of value, treating him with favor and respect" (*The Jewish War*, III, 8, 9). He also gave him "a young prisoner, one of those captured at Caesarea" (*Life*, 414) to be his wife. This was just the beginning of an incredible series of favors and gifts that Vespasian and his son, Titus, reserved for their former enemy. Some time later, as soon as the legions stationed in Egypt proclaimed him emperor (though he was far from having purchased the throne) and the Roman governor Tiberius Alexander put himself at his disposal, Vespasian freed Josephus and took him with him to Alexandria in Egypt. Subsequently, Josephus remained at the side of Titus, the son of Vespasian, for the rest of the war in Jerusalem. After the fall of the city, "Titus several times attempted to convince him to take whatever he wanted from the ruins of his homeland" (*Life*, 418). In the same period, he made him a gift of a vast land estate around Jerusalem. Eventually, he took Josephus with him to Rome on board his own ship (*Life*, 422).

When he arrived in Rome, Josephus received even greater gifts and honors. Vespasian gave him the house that had been his private home before he became emperor, and he granted Josephus Roman citizenship, a life income annuity, and the ownership of enormous estates in Judaea, and he even went so far as to "adopt" him into his own family. These incredible donations are a clear charge against Josephus, with the result that the Jews of his period and the following centuries considered him to be a traitor. The benefits he received must have been proportional to those that his treachery secured for Vespasian. We can be reasonably certain that during the siege of Jerusalem or immediately after its destruction, a group of soldiers loyal to Titus, accompanied by Josephus and perhaps a few other priests, went out in great secret into the desert of Judah and unearthed the treasures, one after another, listed in the original copy of the Copper Scroll found at Kohlit. The reserve copy, now useless, was left where it was, at Qumran.

This secret treasure hunt gave Vespasian a great advantage: he did not have to present an account to anybody for the treasure that he recovered, and he could dispose of it as he willed. The discovery of the reserve copy of the list allows us to appreciate precisely how great the sum was that Vespasian suddenly found at his personal disposal. From this point of view, the favors granted to Josephus and his companions appear to be amply justified.

The most conspicuous objects used in religious worship, such as the menorah and the sacred vessels, were put aside for the triumph celebrated in Rome and the public treasury. After the triumph, they were deposited in the Temple of Peace, built by Vespasian.[4] In 455, they were seized by the Vandals under Jensericus during the sack of Rome, and were taken to Tunis. Here, they were captured during the following century by the Byzantine general Belisarius, who took them to Constantinople, where all trace of them is lost.[5]

On the contrary, the money from the tithes, the jewels, and the loose gold and silver were all confiscated by Vespasian, who thus managed to pay for his rise to power, and, once on the throne in Rome, to build a luxurious palace, compared to which his old family villa became so insignificant that he gave it to Josephus. The latter settled in Rome, where he created a family for the third time, and after a few years, Josephus started to write down the events of which he had been a protagonist and the history of the Jewish people, for which his name has gone down in history.

THE SURVIVORS OF THE PRIESTLY FAMILY

The siege of Jerusalem and the city's subsequent destruction witnessed the death of a striking number of people, estimated by some scholars at about one million. It is certain that thousands of members of the priestly family line were massacred. It was such a sweeping, methodical slaughter that no further mention was made of the Jewish priestly family. We know with certainty, however, that several members escaped, because in his book *The Jewish War*, Josephus Flavius lists them one by one. From the early stages of the siege of Jerusalem, many Jews deserted, passing over to the Romans. Josephus Flavius tells us (VI, 2, 114):

> Among them, there were two heads of the priestly family, Joseph and Jesus, and some sons of heads of this family, like the three sons of Ishmael, who had been decapitated at Cyrene, the four sons of Matthias and the son of another Matthias, who had fled after the death of his father, who had been put to death by Simon, the son of Joras, together with three of his sons, as has been said above. Caesar received them with benevolence and . . . pledged to give back their possessions to each of them, as soon as he had the possibility at the end of the war.

This case involved ten members of the priestly family, including two of a high rank, and we can imagine that they subsequently received their returned possessions.

After the capture of the Temple—or rather, what remained of it—a group of priests who had defended it to the end surrendered to the Romans, asking them to spare their lives. Titus's behavior toward them was completely different: "He answered that the time of forgiveness had passed for them; the only reason that he might have had for sparing their lives was the Temple, and that was completely burnt down; it was only right, therefore, for the priests to be exterminated together with their sanctuary. And he had them led away to be executed" (VI, 6, 1, 321).

This did not stop him from guaranteeing, only a few days later, a safe conduct for two high-ranking members of the priestly family:

> During the same period, a priest named Jesus, the son of Thebuthi, having obtained from Caesar a guarantee, under oath, that his life would be spared, on condition that he delivered certain precious objects of worship, went out and handed over . . . two candlesticks similar to those that were deposited in the Temple, some tables,

some drinking chalices and cups, all of solid gold. He also handed over the curtains, the robes of the high priest, with the precious stones and many other objects used for sacrifices. And the guardian of the Temple treasure, a certain Phineas, who had also been taken prisoner, handed over the priests' tunics and belts, a large quantity of purple and scarlet cloth . . . and also a considerable amount of cinnamon and other aromas, which they mixed and burnt every day as incense for God. He likewise handed over to the Romans many other treasures from the Temple, and also a large quantity of the sacred ornaments, thanks to which, even if he was a prisoner of war, he obtained the amnesty reserved for deserters.[6]

Josephus Flavius tries to lay all the blame for handing over the Temple treasure to the Romans on the two priests, Jesus and Phineas (evidently of such a high rank as to be depositaries of the treasure), who betray in exchange for safe conduct and economic benefits. Yet it is beyond doubt that he himself must have played a leading role in this scenario. This is demonstrated first of all by the vagueness of his narration. There are some inaccuracies in this passage, and several details are omitted. First of all, the capture of the two priests takes place when the Temple had already been gutted by fire and what remained of it was in Roman hands. Consequently, it is impossible that, as Josephus tells us, the objects were lowered down by Jesus "from the top of the sanctuary wall." Further, it is unlikely that this happened before the fall of the Temple, because the walls were teeming with defenders who would never have allowed such an operation. Next, he presents the two priests as low-ranking figures, though they must have been at the top of the priestly organization in order to be the custodians of the Temple treasure. Last, he covers up the fact that the objects handed over had obviously been hidden in some secret hiding place. Phineas could not have had them with him at the time of his capture.

The fact remains—which emerges with certainty when we look closely at Josephus's writing—that the Temple treasure was handed over to Titus by members of the priestly family in exchange for safe conduct, and everything tends to indicate that in this operation Josephus Flavius played a leading role. Otherwise, it would not be possible to explain the incredible favors he received. As well as those we've already learned of, he obtained the right, immediately after the fall of Jerusalem, to free whomever he wanted. In his autobiography (*Life*, 417–19), he says:

> I advanced a request to Titus to free some prisoners, and I obtained . . . the release of my brother and fifty friends. On being authorized by Titus to visit the Temple, where many prisoners were confined, with women and children, I freed all my friends and acquaintances that I recognized, for a total of about 190 people, and I obtained their release without the payment of any ransom, restoring them to their previous conditions.

In all, therefore, Josephus lists twelve high priests, to whom we should add his brother and himself, who had their lives spared thanks to their betrayal and had their possessions returned. Besides these, he mentions two hundred forty other people, all friends and acquaintances of his, who were freed thanks to his agency and "restored to their previous conditions." These were probably about fifty adults and their families. We can be reasonably sure that the majority of these, if not all of them, belonged to the priestly class.

The group of priests who survived the massacre in Jerusalem was undoubtedly large, much more numerous than on various occasions in the past, when the priestly family had been reduced to dire straits—for example, after the defeat and the destruction of the Temple at Shiloh by the Philistines at the time of Samuel; or after the massacre of Nob perpetrated by King Saul, who tried to exterminate the priestly family; or after the massacre of Manasseh, who inundated Jerusalem with the blood of the priests; or, last, after the massacre of Nebuchadnezzar, who had all the "great men of the Temple" put to death. After all these circumstances, the family had risen from its own ashes, stronger and more influential than ever.

This time, however, it seems to disappear definitively from the scene. It is never mentioned again, at least in official historical documents. It seems to vanish into thin air, as if by magic. What came of it?

7

THE DESTINIES OF THE PRIESTLY FAMILY

THE SPIRITUAL TEMPLE

From the narration of Josephus Flavius, we know for sure that there were hundreds of survivors. At least fifteen of these formed a homogeneous group, which we may consider compact, because they were linked by circumstances that united them in the same destiny. All of them belonged to the leading priestly lines; all of them had been spared because they were more or less involved in handing over the Temple treasure to Vespasian; all of them were considered by the rest of the Jews to be traitors of their homeland and of the most precious things that existed for a Jew; all of them, therefore, were interested in remaining in the background, maintaining their anonymity, at least in the Jewish world.

It is not realistic, however, to imagine that they committed a sort of genealogical suicide, denying their origins, their past, and their traditions and bringing to an end the most significant and glorious chapter of Jewish history. They were linked by family ties, by one thousand years of history, and by powerful traditions. They all possessed considerable financial means, because, as Josephus Flavius tells us, they received their returned possessions from Vespasian, together with generous donations. Individually, each of them was perhaps richer than the single members of the family had ever been, even at the height of their power and prosperity. Furthermore, they enjoyed the favor and the protection of political power, because their most prominent exponent, Josephus, had been "adopted" into the imperial family. Last, they were part of a compact, proven family organization, created by Ezra, which had not been destroyed together with the Temple, but must have continued and maintained its tradition, its structure, its contents, and all its potential.

It is not possible for a family of this kind to disappear into thin air. It simply couldn't. That we do not have any news of it may be due to the fact that the family had decided to disappear from the world stage, withdrawing into clandestinity. It must have been a change of strategy, with the aim not of a collective suicide, but of the perpetuation of its fortunes. We do not know what happened to any of the priests who survived after the destruction of Jerusalem, except for the one who, from that moment on, we are forced to consider as their representative: Josephus Flavius. With regard to him, however, we have only the information that he himself decided to leave us in his works. These speak at some length of his wartime feats but say little or nothing about his private life or his affairs or relationships in Rome. We do not know how or when he died or what happened to his family, whose traces are lost.

With regard to the other high-ranking priests who survived, we may take it for granted that they left Palestine for more hospitable lands. Neither they nor any of their descendants ever appear again in the history of that country or of any Jewish community inside or outside the Roman Empire. This was perfectly understandable: they were considered to be traitors, and their presence must have been wholly unwelcome among the Jews. On the other hand, they were too conspicuous for their presence to pass unobserved in any provincial town. We are led to believe, therefore, that at least initially they followed Josephus to Rome, a megalopolis with inhabitants from all over the Empire, people of all religions, where they could easily disappear into anonymity.

What did they do in the capital? We have no idea. We only know about the activity of Josephus Flavius as a writer because his monumental work is extant today. On the basis of this work, however, we can make a complete evaluation of his personality—his incredible ability to turn the most desperate situations to his advantage and the enormous ambition that prompted him. A character such as Josephus, who had arrived at the top of his physical and mental strength and his personal power, could not have limited his activities simply to writing his memories.

Once just a governor of a province of Palestine, he eventually found himself at the center of the Roman Empire as an honorary member of the imperial family. His horizons had expanded from Judaea and the Jewish people to the whole world. Given this, he must have felt responsible for the destiny of the priestly family, the most noble of the families that existed on the face of the earth because they descended from Moses himself. The other survivors must have gathered around the one who, during the whole course of his life, had shown extraordinary leadership capacities.

The first great effort to which he dedicated all his energies, as his works show clearly, was to find a justification for the betrayal that had been committed and to create a new basis for the reconstruction of the role and fortunes of his family. As usual in cases such as this, the justification is provided by the Divinity himself. Josephus had passed over to the Romans after the fall of the town of Jotapata. On that occasion, he had taken refuge in a cistern, together with forty companions, and all of them had decided to kill each other rather than hand themselves over to the hated enemy, in accordance with an established tradition among the Jews of that period. Yet when he and one other were left, Josephus handed himself over to the Romans with the excuse that God had forced him to save himself in order that he might give Vespasian the news that Vespasian would become emperor and in order that he might carry out an important mission for which he had been chosen.

At that time, it seemed God had abandoned Israel and had irreversibly granted his favor to the Romans. Josephus could not oppose his will, but was forced to become an instrument of his will in spite of himself.

This is his justification for his betrayal, and this was the justification that the other priests were also forced to adopt. In this way, the Mosaic family linked its destiny to the destiny of the Roman Empire. From that moment on, its stage was no longer Judaea, but the whole world.

There is no historical information about how Josephus Flavius accomplished his mission, how he reorganized the priestly family and what new role he assigned to it. There is, however, a nonhistorical source—whose nature and reliability we will investigate later—that provides us with information about the activities of the group. We learn from this source that immediately after the destruction of the Temple, a group of priests who had survived met among the smoking ruins to decide the destiny of the family. The subjects discussed are the same as those that make up the leitmotif of the works of Josephus Flavius: God has abandoned Israel and has taken sides definitively with Rome; it is not wise to oppose his will. The power of the Roman Empire was at its height. It was absurd to hope for a change in fortune that would allow the reconstruction of the Temple in Jerusalem in the foreseeable future.

The priests therefore decided to continue the traditions of the family, but in Rome and in clandestinity, and not to entrust their destiny, as in the past, to a material Temple, which was too subject to profanation and destruction. They decided instead to dedicate themselves to the construction of a "spiritual" Temple.

According to this source of information, therefore, the Mosaic priestly family maintained its identity and its organization in the aftermath of the catastrophe, but changed its strategy, passing into clandestinity and entrusting its survival and its fortunes to an immaterial institution. The Temple in Jerusalem had allowed the family of Moses to survive and prosper for several centuries. The spiritual Temple was to serve the same purpose for the future—a future in which the very existence of the family was never to be revealed publicly, so that its members would not be vulnerable, as in the past, when they had been the objects of campaigns of extermination.

This, too, was a part of the family tradition. On their return from exile in Babylon, the priests had chosen not to proclaim publicly their descent from Moses, but instead had established as their forefathers the children of Aaron. The members of the family who escaped from the definitive destruction of the Temple must have judged that their survival was better protected if their very existence remained secret. The family organization from then on remained secret, invisible, and thus no longer vulnerable.

If this reconstruction of the facts is correct, then we must conclude that their descendants subsequently reemerged in the forefront of history with other names and invented genealogies. Yet it should be possible to discover the traces that they must necessarily have left behind them, and these ought to be sufficient to identify at least some of the historical characters belonging to the priestly family.

JOSEPHUS FLAVIUS AND ST. PAUL

Traces and members of the priestly family can be sought in the Christian world, and not in the world of the Jews. There are various elements that link to Christianity Josephus Flavius and the group of priests that were with him.

The arguments used by Josephus Flavius to justify his own betrayal and that of his brethren seem to echo the words of St. Paul, who is considered by universal consent as the one who created the ideological basis for the construction of the Roman church. The two seem to be perfectly in agreement with regard to their attitude toward the Roman world. Paul, for example, considered it his task to free the church of Jesus from the narrowness of Judaism and from the land of Judaea and to make it universal, linking it to Rome. They are also in agreement on other significant points: for example, both of them declare their belief in the doctrines of the Pharisees, which were those that were wholly received by the Roman church. (The Pharisees, unlike the Sadducees, believed in the resurrection of the dead, the existence of the soul, angels, and so on.)

There are sufficient historical indications to lead us to consider it possible, if not certain, that the two knew each other and were very close friends. In the Acts of the Apostles, we read that after preaching in Jerusalem, Paul was brought before the high priests and the Sanhedrin to be judged (Acts 22:30). He defended himself:

"Brethren, I am a Pharisee, the son of a Pharisee: of the hope and resurrection of the dead I am called in question." And when he had so said, there arose a dissension between the Pharisees and the Sadducees: and the multitude was divided. For the Sadducees say that there is no resurrection, neither angel, nor spirit: but the Pharisees confess both. And there arose a great cry: and the scribes that were of the Pharisees' part arose, and strove, saying, "We find no evil in this man: but if a spirit or an angel hath spoken to him, let us not fight against God." And when there arose a great dissension, the chief captain, fearing lest Paul should have been pulled in pieces by them, commanded the soldiers to go down, and to take him by force from among them.[1]

Josephus was a high-ranking priest and he was in Jerusalem at that time, and so we must conclude that he was present at that assembly. He had joined the sect of the Pharisees at the age of nineteen (*Life*, 2.12), and so he must have been among those priests who stood up to defend Paul. The apostle was then handed over to the Roman governor, Felix, who kept him under arrest for some time, until he was sent to Rome, together with some other prisoners (Acts 27:1), to be judged by the emperor, to whom, as a Roman citizen, Paul had appealed. In Rome, he spent two years in prison (Acts 28:39) before being set free in AD 63 or 64.

In his autobiography, Josephus says,

Between the age of twenty-six and twenty-seven [thus in 63–64] I embarked on a journey to Rome, for the following reason. During the period when he was governor of Judaea, Felix had sent some priests to Rome to justify themselves before the emperor; I knew them to be excellent people, who had been arrested on insignificant charges. As I desired to devise a plan to save them, . . . I journeyed to Rome.[2]

This was an adventurous journey—with even a shipwreck, which recalls very closely that of Paul narrated in the Acts of the Apostles. Somehow, Josephus succeeded in reaching Puteoli, near Naples, where he made friends with Aliturus, a Jewish mime who was appreciated by Nero. Thanks to Aliturus, he was introduced to Poppaea, the wife of the emperor, and through her agency, he succeeded in freeing the priests (*Life,* 3.16).

The correspondence of dates, facts, and people involved is so perfect that it is consequently difficult to avoid the conclusion that Josephus went to Rome to free Paul and his companions and that it was due to his intervention that the apostle was released. This presupposes that the relationship between the two was much closer than that of a simple occasional acquaintance. At any event, even if we do not accept that Josephus made the journey to Rome at his own personal risk specifically to free Paul, we cannot avoid recognizing that he must necessarily have had contact with the apostle on that occasion. Paul's case had been discussed by the main leaders of the Jewish community in Rome (Acts 28:17–23), and it is unthinkable that it was not brought to the attention of Josephus, who was in that region precisely to solve cases of the kind.

According to the Acts of the Apostles, Paul never lost the opportunity to "preach the kingdom of God and teach those things, which concern the Lord Jesus Christ" to anybody that he met. Thus Josephus must have known much more about Christianity than he admits in his works, and his knowledge came directly from the teaching of Paul, of whom, in all likelihood, he was a disciple. Obviously, he never mentions this and he gives no names or facts connected to his first stay in Rome, apart from those mentioned previously, which is highly significant.

Those were the years of the fire in the capital and the first anti-Christian persecution, which followed the fire. Josephus Flavius never says a word about these events in his various works, even if he was an eyewitness to them, nor does he speak about his relationships in this period with the Jewish community in Rome or with the family of the emperor. Nor does he say anything about the names of the priests that he helped to release—the men who must have been important to him, given that he had gone to such lengths to free them—or what happened to them afterward. For a loquacious historian, Josephus's silence is more deafening than a confession because it seems deliberate. For some reason, he did not want it known publicly that he had played a role in these events. It is anything but a simple coincidence, then, that this silence reaches to his relationship with the person who is universally recognized as the true founder of the Roman church, and thus with the newly formed Christian community in the capital.

In the same way, a veil of silence was cast over all the facts regarding the Roman church during the period when Josephus Flavius was in the capital. In the thirty years from AD 70 to 100—the time following the arrival of Josephus Flavius in Rome—we know next to nothing about what happened in the Roman church. It is almost a complete blackout—which is puzzling, because it is a crucial period in the history of the formation of the church, a time when it was completely transformed, both in its doctrine and, above all, in its hierarchical structure. Further, it was in this period that the Christian community in Rome assumed the leadership of all the Christian communities in the Empire. From the information in our possession, it is legitimate to suspect that Josephus Flavius and the other priests with him played a decisive role in the events that determined the transformation of Christianity in that period.

During the apostolic period, there was no single Christian church, but instead a group of independent churches, each led by a council of elders and all situated, without exception, in the eastern, Hellenizing part of the Empire. From the end of the first century on, however, the direction of the churches assumed a monarchic structure in which each of them was led by a bishop with absolute power, and all of the bishops were subject to the authority of the bishop of Rome, who was a figure equivalent to the high priest in Jerusalem. This was the beginning of a prodigious expansion, which led Christianity to become the state religion of the whole Empire within two centuries.

THE PRIMACY OF THE CHURCH OF ROME

The very first testimony of the primacy of Rome over other churches is provided by Pope Clement* in his famous "Letter to the Corinthians,"[3] probably written toward the end of the reign of Domitian (95–96). In it, he calls to order the Christian community of Corinth because it appears that they had rebelled against the authority of the elders (XLIV, 4 and 6), which had evidently been imposed from elsewhere. He invites them to submit, under penalty of exclusion from the "flock of Christ" (LVII, 1 and 2). We also learn from the letter (LXIII) that he had sent his representatives to Corinth with the task of reestablishing order.

Never before this moment had one Christian community interfered in the affairs of another. The early Christian communities were completely independent from one another, and they recognized the authority of only the apostles on doctrinal questions. Further, in any case, they looked to Jerusalem, and not to Rome. Clement's letter is the clear demonstration that in the years following AD 70, the community of Rome, which previously did not have the slightest significance in the Christian world, had suddenly become most important in the Empire and had

---

*According to the list of Irenaeus, bishop of Lyon (AD 180), Clement was bishop of Rome from 92 to 101, after Peter, Linus, and Anacletus. According to Tertullian, however, Clement was ordained by Peter himself and succeeded him immediately. Likewise, in the sequence illustrated by the portraits painted in the Basilica of San Paolo fuori le mura (fifth century) Clement follows Peter immediately, and the same order is given in the fourth-century *Liber Pontificalis*. Because it is not at all certain that Peter was ever bishop of Rome, Clement was in reality the first pope.

imposed its authority on all the other Christian communities of the period. Eusebius of Caesarea testifies that Clement's letter was regularly read in many churches (H.E. III, 16), which was a sign that the bishop of Rome had established his authority. How could such a radical, sudden change have taken place?

The Christian community in Rome is never mentioned before the age of Nero, and we do not even know if any Christians existed in the capital. It is certain that none of the apostles had ever gone there to preach. The first one was St. Paul, who, in AD 61 or 62, was taken to Rome, together with some of his disciples, as a "prisoner awaiting judgment." It is possible, therefore—or indeed, quite probable—that the Christian community in Rome was formed on that occasion by Paul and his companions. He was free to receive visitors to his house, and during the two years of his imprisonment, he dedicated himself to an active apostolic ministry.

The justification for the primacy of the church of Rome over other Christian churches has always been that Peter, the prince of the apostles, designated by Jesus Christ as his earthly successor, chose, at a certain moment in his life, to become the first bishop of Rome, where he died the death of a martyr during the persecution under Nero, and where he was subsequently buried. This, however, is mentioned only in a tradition that developed at least a century after the facts in question. Naturally, on such an important question, all the historians of the church rallied around to demonstrate the truth of that tradition, but their efforts only achieved the result of revealing the total absence of any direct testimonies on the subject.[4]

The Acts of the Apostles narrates the story of Peter in detail up to AD 42, when the apostle miraculously escaped from the prison of Herod Agrippa (the same who saw to the decapitation of John the Baptist). From this moment on, we are not given any more direct information about him. Peter disappears from history. According to a tradition that developed in the fourth century (from the catalog of the popes compiled by St. Jerome in 354), Peter went to Rome immediately after his escape and stayed there until his death in 67.

On the contrary, a more ancient tradition (mentioned by Origen and Eusebius) says that after his escape from Jerusalem, he went to Syria, where he founded the episcopate of Antioch, which does not negate the fact that he may have gone subsequently to Rome. As proof of this, historians indicate a passage by Clement himself saying that Peter and Paul were martyred—even if Clement does not say when or where, or if they faced this destiny together. Only in AD 170 does Bishop Dionysius of Corinth state explicitly that Peter and Paul were martyred in Rome. The first statement that attributes the foundation of the church of Rome to Peter comes even later: it was issued by the bishop of Lyon, Irenaeus,* between 180 and 190, when he compiled the first list of the bishops of Rome.[5]

The only contemporary direct testimony for the sojourn of the apostle in a precise place is contained in a passage of the First Epistle of Peter (5:13), which says: "The church that is at Babylon, elected together with you, saluteth you." From this we may deduce that at the time when Peter wrote the letter, he was in Babylon. The church historians, on the contrary, immediately stated unanimously that by "Babylon" he meant Rome, the corrupt capital of the world, and they quote this passage as proof of his stay in Rome. This interpretation is debatable, however. Revelation had not yet been written, therefore there was no notion of associating the Great Babylon of St. John with Nero's Rome. It is extremely doubtful that any Jew (and even less, a Gentile) at the time of Peter would be able to understand a reference to Rome as a Babylon. Among other things, even if this were true, it would seem to be inappropriate for the apostle, in an official letter, to use offensive terms to label the city where he was a guest.

Moreover, at that time, Babylon actually existed and was the center of the largest and most ancient Jewish community outside Judaea. This

---

*Irenaeus writes: "But as it would be too long . . . to list the successions of all the churches, we shall take the great, ancient church known to everyone, the Church founded and established in Rome by the two glorious apostles Peter and Paul. . . . With this Church, in view of its most excellent origin, every Church must necessarily agree."

community was bound to attract the apostles' attention sooner or later. The fact that the letter was really written from Babylon would seem to be confirmed also by the list of the addresses: the Christians of Pontus, Galatia, Cappadocia, Asia, and Bithynia—all localities in Asia.

This obviously does not exclude the possibility that, in the end, Peter came to be martyred in Rome, but it is a fact that there is no contemporary testimony to this effect or any kind of indication of the circumstances or the date of this hypothetical journey. Given the importance attributed to the person of Peter and the facts regarding him, it appears to be surprising and definitely suspicious that none of the sources of the period gives the slightest information about the destiny of Peter after his escape from prison, especially considering the extent and the detail of the narration about other questions regarding him. An accidental loss of historical information about such a subject would be unlikely. It is more likely, instead, that the oversight was manipulated in order to confuse the situation: in a vacuum of information, it is easy to construct more or less credible legends. Further, the manipulators would have been the same as those who omitted the information about Paul and the story of the Roman church under the Flavian emperors.

Among other things, these manipulators are also the inventors of the myth of the primacy of Peter, which does not appear in the gospels apart from the famous sentence attributed to Jesus—"Thou art Peter, and upon this rock I will build my church"—which is mentioned only in the Gospel of St. Matthew (16:18). The lack of any direct information about Peter's stay in Rome is a significant element in favor of the hypothesis that he did not play any significant role in the foundation of the church in Rome. If the activity of Peter had created the basis of the legitimacy of Rome's primacy among the Christian churches, that same community would presumably have registered and handed down the most significant episodes of that activity—and yet nothing of what was written in that period (and undoubtedly, a great deal was written) was kept or transcribed for posterity. This significant indication, if not certain proof, is not exactly in harmony with the tradition, which some subsequently wished to credit.

Only one fact is certain on the basis of the historical evidence: the Roman church developed and imposed its authority on all the other churches of the Empire during the period of the Flavians. Somebody must have performed this miracle. If it was not Peter or Paul (the former because he was never seen in Rome, the latter because he was killed before the advent of the Flavians), it must undoubtedly have been someone who had assumed control of the church of Rome at the time of the Flavians and who used Peter and Paul's names and authority to extend this control to all the churches of the Empire. All the clues point to Josephus Flavius and the group of priests associated with him.

JOSEPHUS FLAVIUS AND POPE CLEMENT

The first bishop of Rome for whom we have certain historical information (and probably the very first according to various ancient testimonies) was Clement, and as we have seen, it was during his pontificate that Rome imposed its primacy over all the other Christian churches. Who was Clement? What we can conclude with certainty from his extremely long letter is that he was a Roman citizen.[6] He loves Rome, and in talking about its leaders and institutions, expresses himself exactly as a citizen of Rome would. It appears certain, however, that Clement was a Jew. In substance and in form, the letter appears to be the work of a Jew: there are many references to the Hebrew Scriptures, and the writer reveals a detailed knowledge of the Bible. This, among other things, clearly reveals his priestly status. Furthermore, his culture is that of Hellenizing Judaism, because he quotes the Bible in the version of the Septuagint and frequently refers to Greek authors, such as Euripides and Sophocles.

This is the perfect identification for Josephus Flavius: a priest with a Hellenizing culture who possessed a detailed knowledge of the Bible, and a Roman citizen (even if acquired citizenship) who lived in

Rome. The idea that the two characters are one and the same person is unlikely, however, because it could not have passed unobserved, given the importance of both figures. We know, however, that together with Josephus, other priests had come to Rome who corresponded to this description and were part of his entourage, and they enjoyed the protection of the family of the Flavian emperors. We cannot eliminate the fact that the bishop of Rome could have been chosen from among these priests and that he assumed the name Clement in honor of his august protector, the consul Titus Flavius Clemens. This consul belonged to the house of the Flavians and was a cousin of the emperor, and it is certain, therefore, that he must have enjoyed a good relationship with his acquired relation, Josephus Flavius, or at least with some of the priests in his following. The clearest proof of these relationships is the charge brought against him by Domitian as a pretext for his execution: "deviation toward Judaic customs."

Also, Flavius Clemens has been proposed by some as the identity of the pope of that name, and there are valid reasons to support this hypothesis, including the fact that both of them figure as martyrs. If this was the case, it would mean that the Roman consul had profoundly assimilated Jewish priestly culture from Josephus Flavius or from some other priest in his same conditions. Yet this does not appear to be likely, because the palaeo-Christian sources would not have failed to underline the fact that a pope belonged to the imperial family. Furthermore, the identikit of Pope Clement corresponds to that of a Romanized Jew, and not vice versa.

There is one last character that fits perfectly into this description, which was proposed since the third century by Origen, Eusebius of Caesarea, and others: Clement, "whose name is written in the book of life," is mentioned in the letter to the Philippians as a close collaborator of St. Paul (Philippians 4:3). Given that he was a disciple of Paul, we may conclude that he was among the prisoners sent to Rome together with Paul and freed two years later as a result of the intervention of Josephus Flavius.

Whichever hypothesis of his true identity is correct, Pope Clement must be in some way connected to Josephus Flavius and the group of priests with him.

THE JEWISH PRIESTLY FAMILY AND THE CHURCH IN ROME

Another indication that a close relationship existed between the Jewish priestly family and the church of Rome comes, once again, from the nonhistorical source of information mentioned above. In it, we find the surviving priests meeting in Rome as followers of Jesus and subject to persecution by Domitian, who succeeded to the throne on the death of the great protector of Josephus, Titus. Yet they pass practically unscathed through this persecution.

This information is extremely interesting and consistent with our historical data. One of the most significant points of this source is that the surviving priests reconstructed—or better, continued—the priestly organization created by Ezra. They maintained the structure, the contents, and the rituals, but in secret, thus making it invisible to the secular world. Second, they were converted to Christianity.

That Josephus Flavius was converted to Christianity appears to be at least probable on the basis of his writings and the historical circumstances that we know. This conversion, from an ideological and doctrinal point of view, was not a great step for Josephus Flavius and his brethren. Nor was it for Paul, whose conversion did not entail the denial of any of his past convictions, but only the acceptance that Jesus was the long-awaited Messiah. Accordingly, when Paul was placed on trial by the priests in Jerusalem, he stated with full conviction that he was a Pharisee.

Jesus was a Jew, and had never rejected the Mosaic Law; on the contrary, he taught it, even to the priests in the Temple. He was not condemned for his religious ideas, but for political reasons, because he declared that he was the Messiah. His preaching was that of a Jew for other Jews, and the contents of his preaching was in line with the way of living and thinking of the sect known as the Essenes, who are normally considered to be very close to, if not precursors of, the Christians. Yet the doctrinal contents of Christianity as it emerged from this period of Roman blackout are extraordinarily close to those of the sect of the Pharisees. This is no surprise, given that it is universally recognized that it was Paul who provided Christianity with its doctrinal and liturgical framework.

The Christianity imposed by Paul in Rome had little to do with the religious vision preached by Jesus in Palestine and put into practice by James the Just, who was subsequently the leader of the Christian community of Jerusalem. The Roman church fully accepted the doctrines of the Pharisees and the theories of Paul, which were somewhat different from those of James. The Jerusalem church, instead, had sprung up within the Essenes and fully accepted their philosophy and way of living. For Paul, Jesus was only a pretext to set up a new religious movement, freed of orthodox Judaism's interpretation of Mosaic Law.

In his works, Josephus Flavius dedicates a great deal of space to the Essenes and does not hide his sympathy for them. As a young man, he had spent three years in the desert of Judah, together with a holy man called Bannus,[7] living as a hermit. At the end of this Essene experience, however, when he came back to Jerusalem, he resumed his life "following the precepts of the Pharisaic school," the same as that of Paul.

We cannot, therefore, speak of conversion as if he accepted the ideas of Jesus—or better, of Paul—while denying the beliefs he had professed up to that moment. In fact, he had to deny no aspect. The real change, what distinguished a Jew from a Jewish Christian, was the acceptance of Jesus as the awaited Messiah.

The great majority of the Jews thought of the Messiah as a sovereign (for this reason, he had to be a member of the family of David), who would materially reestablish the kingdom and the power of Israel. Instead, Jesus, in proposing himself as the Messiah, clearly specified "my kingdom is not of this world." What he was proposing, therefore, was a spiritual kingdom—a concept that we nowadays accept as normal, almost banal. At that time, however, it was an extraordinary novelty, and it had been totally espoused by Paul and also by Josephus Flavius and the priests who were with him, who had decided never again to build a material Temple, but instead to dedicate themselves to the construction of a spiritual Temple.

A spiritual Temple would be constructed for a spiritual kingdom. Was this a simple coincidence? It appears extremely likely that there was a relationship between the two concepts, presupposing that the builders of the spiritual Temple had recognized Jesus as the Messiah and had become the supporters and promoters of his kingdom. We have precise confirmation of this. In a famous passage in *Jewish Antiquities* (the so-called *Testimonium Flavianum*),* Josephus Flavius writes:

> In the same period lived Jesus, a wise man, if he may be called a man; because he performed surprising deeds, and was the master of people who gladly accepted the truth. He was the Christ. When Pilate heard that he was charged by our leaders, he condemned him to be crucified. Those who had loved him from the beginning did not stop following him. On the third day, he appeared to them again, alive: because God's prophets had prophesied these facts, together with countless other wonderful things about him.[8]

Words of this kind can come only from a Christian *in pectore,* because they demonstrate his acceptance of two essential points: the resurrection of Jesus, and Jesus's identification with the Messiah of prophecy. The Christian sympathies of Josephus Flavius also emanate clearly

---

*Origen explicitly affirms that Josephus Flavius did not convert to Christianity. This is the main reason why many scholars reject the authenticity of the *Testimonium Flavianum* (which, however, Origen knew perfectly well), because it was considered to be in contrast to the religious faith of a high-ranking Jewish priest. Also, the opposite reasoning is valid: the *Testimonium Flavianum* shows the interest of Josephus Flavius in the figure of Jesus, even if he never publicly declared himself a Christian.

from other passages of the same work. In XVIII, V, 2, he speaks with great admiration about John the Baptist and his behavior and preaching, underlining the validity of baptism and condemning Herod for the Baptist's murder. In XX, IX, 1, he expresses the same sympathy for James, the brother of Jesus.

A further indication is offered by the fact that the anti-Christian persecution under Domitian mentioned by Christian sources never actually took place. The only Roman martyrs of the period listed as Christians are figures close to the imperial family, the most famous of whom is the senator and former consul Titus Flavius Clemens, who was executed not because he was a Christian, but on the alleged charge of "atheism" and "deviation toward Judaic customs." In reality, religion had little to do with this execution: the emperor was extremely moody and ruthless and had members of his entourage executed for totally banal reasons—including, sometimes, for his simple personal dislikes.

Titus Flavius Clemens, however, is claimed by tradition to be a Christian, which means that someone must have converted him. What Christian in those years could be in a position to have contact with, and convert, such a high-ranking figure? Moreover, we know for certain that he must have had contact with Josephus Flavius and the group of priests associated with him. Further, who else except a church linked to the group of Josephus Flavius could claim Flavius Clemens as one of their martyrs? The Christian martyr Flavius Clemens thus offers a precise link to the priestly organization of Josephus Flavius and a substantial indication that this organization played an important role in the church of the period.

The inclusion in the Christian community of the period, initially composed mainly of Jews, of such a conspicuous and numerous group of surviving priests could not fail to have profound consequences on the organization of the community. Hated by the other Jews because they were considered traitors, the priests must have been welcome among only the Christians—and above all those converted from paganism, who accepted without reserve the priests' justification that they had been chosen by God for the construction of the spiritual kingdom.

We should observe, however, that the priestly family, which had guided the destinies of the Jewish people for over a thousand years, and its members who had royal blood in their veins, could not accept inferior roles in the community of which they had become a part. Josephus was even less able to accept such a role. If he ever took part in the birth of the Roman church, he undoubtedly must have had the reins firmly in his own hands, which was quite possible in those circumstances: the Roman community was just emerging from the first bloody period of persecution at the hands of Nero and had suffered the death of its leader and founder, Paul. The leadership—or at least, the protection—of an adopted member of the imperial family must have been welcomed as a gift from heaven. Further cause for welcome: this person was a high-ranking priest and had been instrumental in obtaining Paul's release from prison. He could therefore claim, without any risk of denial, that he had been Paul's disciple and had been invested as his successor.

Yet Josephus Flavius was too much in the public eye to assume any direct responsibility in the management of the Roman church. We are forced to hypothesize that he limited his role to controlling the secret priestly organization, imposing on the Christian community a hierarchy drawn from the circle of priests who were members of it, such as Paul's old disciple, Clement. With regard to the doctrinal contents, he drew on the preaching of St. Paul, but with regard to the liturgy and the hierarchical structure, he referred to the long-experimented model of his family in Jerusalem.

Not surprisingly, the irresistible rise of Christianity started from that moment, and within the incredibly short period of two centuries, it became the state religion of the Roman Empire. This unbelievable rise, which amazed the subsequent Christian historians, is not so surprising if we accept the hypothesis that the protagonists were the survivors of the Mosaic priestly family who had taken refuge in Rome. We know for certain what their specialization was, what know-how they possessed, as the fruit of more than a thousand years' experience: they knew better than anyone else how to organize and run a religion independently of its doctrinal content.

They must have put their experience and themselves at the service of the newborn Christian religion, designing it in accordance with patterns that were well tested, but with one essential novelty: its opening up to the pagan world. Peter himself had started to welcome pagans into the Christian community, amid protests from the other Jews, who demanded that the new converts should fully respect the Mosaic Law.[9] Paul made the entry of non-Jews systematic, creating the necessary doctrinal justifications. Seeing their problems with the Jews, the proselytizing of Josephus Flavius and his priestly colleagues in Rome had to be addressed preferably to the pagans. This was the trump card, which decreed the success of the new religion.

The origin of the church in Rome is a delicate subject, which arouses deep feelings, and many will undoubtedly reject the idea that Josephus Flavius played a leading role in it, protesting that there is no proof of this. This is true, at least up to now, given that there are no known writings or direct testimonies that provide documentary evidence of it. Yet the coincidences are numerous and are such as to make it likely that in the aftermath of the destruction of the Temple in Jerusalem, the Mosaic priestly family took firm control of the newborn Christian religion and from then on guided its destinies.

8

BUILDING THE
SPIRITUAL TEMPLE

RECONSTRUCTION OF THE EVENTS
OF THE PRIESTLY FAMILY

After the destruction of the Temple in Jerusalem, the Judaic priestly family had to inaugurate a new strategy of survival: disappearing into clandestinity but continuing to maintain the secret organization created by Ezra in his times and substituting for the material Temple, as its means of sustenance and power, a spiritual Temple that was the Christian church. The secret organization controlled the visible institution, the church, which in turn controlled the ranks of the faithful. This was a perfect system, concealing the family from its enemies as a clearly identifiable target and sheltering it from campaigns of destruction. Any persecution—as actually happened—would be against the visible target, the church, leaving practically unscathed the organization from which it arose.

Among the indications that confirm this scenario, I have quoted the information provided by what I have called a nonhistorical source—a source composed of material that cannot be taken into consideration by historians. These are not contemporary documents or testimonies but Masonic rituals and traditions, as we know them today. Their content

138

always regards exclusively the Jewish priestly family—to the point that it seems legitimate to suspect the existence of a connection between this family and Freemasonry. We will see further on in this text what kind of relationship this is, when we look into the nature and the origin of Freemasonry.

For the moment, it is interesting to examine its traditions and rituals. On analyzing them, we realize that they all refer to biblical themes, facts, and characters that cannot have been inspired by the Bible. Instead, they date back to an independent, equally ancient parallel source. What is quite clear from an analysis of the rituals of Freemasonry is that they reproduce in a present-day form not facts narrated by the Bible, but events from the lives of the priestly family of Jerusalem. The characters are those of the Bible—Solomon, Hiram, Jeremiah, Nathan, and so on—but they are surrounded by the constant presence of the priests of the Jerusalem Temple, who are always identified as Freemason brothers.

INFORMATIVE CONTENT OF THE MASONIC RITUALS

The Masonic rituals are always based exclusively on these themes: the Judaic priestly family, its Temple, its vicissitudes, and its secrets. We may wonder what the origin of these rituals was, whether they possess any informative content, and what value we should give to the information they transmit.

At this point, we must reflect on the nature and informative content in general of rituals. There is no human organization, whether religious or political, military, or of any other type, that ignores the importance of rituals to drum into the minds of individuals of different social and cultural backgrounds the so-called team spirit and a common set of moral principles, convictions, and ideals—all in the name of making individuals fit to carry out particular tasks. Participation in rituals is unifying and gives a greater sense of belonging to a group, category, caste, or society. Rituals have the magical power to mold human minds, to transmit messages and values and to root them deeply in the conscience of the participants. It is no surprise that all religions transmit their essential values to the faithful by means of rituals.

Yet how do they originate and what do they really represent? It is common opinion that they are ceremonies of an essentially symbolic character, with symbols specially created to transmit the desired messages. This, however, is not true—or, at least, not always. When we discover the origin of a rite, we realize that it is almost always inspired by a fact—one that actually took place or is presumed to have taken place—reenacted by the participants. Catholic rituals, for example, cover the history of Jesus Christ at a distance of two thousand years, making the most significant episodes come to life again. The same may be said for the rituals of Jewish feasts, which recall the most important episodes of the history of that people, from the Exodus from Egypt and the crossing of the Red Sea to their exile in Babylon and so on. It is an extremely effective system to transmit indefinitely the remembrance of events that are at the origin of a given organization.

Obviously, the ritual always presents an isolated episode not included in the historical and environmental context in which it took place and charges it with the problems and expectations of those who are taking part at that moment. Consequently, the original meaning is inevitably lost and is substituted by a symbolic meaning. The context and the environment continually change, giving the fact continually new interpretations—and as a result, it would be an illusion to expect to reconstruct a reliable history starting only from the rituals that represent it. For example, we would certainly not be able to reconstruct the history of the Jewish people or that of Jesus Christ starting only from the rituals that are performed during the various feasts of the Jewish or Christian liturgical year. We are, however, able to recognize with certainty which events the rituals refer to, thanks to their informative content of a historical character, which can be transmitted unchanged for very long periods of time.

This characteristic of rites, of reenacting the most important moments of a history—that is to say, those in which the participants recognize their roots, whether cultural, religious, or otherwise—is of particular interest in the case of an organization such as Freemasonry, which is characterized by an important, well-structured set of rituals. If we suppose that these recall, in the same way as Jewish and Christian rituals, the salient facts of a real history, we have an instrument that will allow us to verify and to complete the relevant information that comes to us from the actual historical sources.

As has been said, then, the Masonic rituals and legends always refer exclusively to fundamental episodes in the history of the Judaic priestly family. Some are known to us from the Bible because they are narrated as part of the general history of Israel; others are new because they do not appear explicitly in any official historical chronicle.

For example, let us briefly examine the story narrated in the rituals of the so-called Scottish Rite,* composed of thirty-three degrees. The rituals from the first to the twelfth degree all take place in Jerusalem at the time of King Solomon and relate to events that revolve around the building of the first Temple—not from a historical perspective, as told in the Bible, but from point of view of the priestly family. The protagonists are characters that we find in the biblical chronicles: Solomon, Hiram, Adoniram, Nathan, Zabud, and all the priests of the Temple, with their various hierarchies, functions, and tasks. The episodes of which they are protagonists are not always confirmed directly in the Bible, because they are important only for the priestly family, but they fit into the biblical narration without any contradiction, completing it in a consistent manner.

The ritual of the thirteenth degree, the Royal Arch, takes place in the audience hall of King Solomon, and is centered on the existence of

---

*Today, there are various Masonic rites, among which the most important are the Scottish Rite and that of York. All those that are officially recognized are more or less similar in content.

a secret crypt where there are hidden the treasures of the priestly family, including the Ark of the Covenant. The ritual of the following degree (the fourteenth) recalls episodes that took place four centuries later, with the destruction of the Temple by Nebuchadnezzar, the deportation of the priests to Babylon, and the definitive loss of the crypt.

The ritual of the fifteenth degree takes us about seventy years further in time. Its performance is divided into three distinct phases: It begins in the palace of King Cyrus in Babylon, with the scene of the Persian monarch granting Zerubbabel permission to return to Jerusalem and giving him back the treasures of the Temple sacked by Nebuchadnezzar. This is followed by the scene of the crossing of the Jordan, where the priests coming back from exile are attacked and have to fight strenuously in order to get across. The third scene takes place among the ruins of the Temple in Jerusalem, when the priests decide to rebuild it. The story continues in the ritual of the sixteenth degree, Prince of Jerusalem, which regards the construction of the second Temple.

The rituals of the seventeenth and eighteenth degrees return to the theme of the loss of the secret of the crypt. The ritual of the nineteenth degree again involves a step forward of more than four hundred years: it is connected with the destruction by the Romans of the Temple in Jerusalem, the one built by Herod the Great. The ritual of the twentieth degree is the one, mentioned in the previous chapter, that narrates the decision of the surviving priests never again to build a material Temple, but instead to construct a Temple that is completely spiritual.

The rituals of the twenty-first and twenty-second degrees develop themes taken from the book of Genesis: the tower of Babel and Noah and the construction of the ark. Those that number from twenty-three to twenty-five, on the contrary, reenact three important episodes from the life of Moses. They are all clearly taken from the Pentateuch. After the Mosaic interlude, the twenty-sixth degree again takes up the story of the priestly family, moving to the times of Domitian: the story takes place in an underground room and shows how the priestly family succeeds in surviving during the persecution unleashed by the emperor. In this ritual, the participants are Christians and are responsible for the destiny of the church of Rome.

The rituals of the following degrees take us, with a step forward of one thousand years, to the history of the Templars, who are thus fitted into the environment of the history of the priestly family. Whether this is the same story or another one, we will see later. For the moment, it is of interest to underline the fact that the rituals of the twentieth and twenty-sixth degrees deal with the specific subject of our investigation, confirming and integrating in a consistent manner the hypotheses advanced here with regard to Josephus Flavius and his colleague-priests. These Masonic traditions, therefore, not only show that they are directly connected to the priestly family of Jerusalem; they also show that this connection passes through the group of surviving priests who gathered around Josephus Flavius in Rome.

How and by what channels modern Freemasonry may have acquired the historical information contained in its rituals is a question that we will deal with later. What we can reasonably hypothesize is that Masonry somehow derived from or at least received some of its essential elements from the organization that the surviving priests of Jerusalem must have created once they settled in Rome.

This organization must have been re-created by Josephus Flavius and the other surviving priests without any significant variations compared to the priestly organization created by Ezra in his times, except for two essential points, which completely distorted its character. First, the subject of the agreement was no longer the management of the Temple in Jerusalem and a well-consolidated religion, but a spiritual Temple and the creation and management of a new religion, which had to open up space for itself amid a hostile world. Second, the number of priestly branches that were party to the new agreement must have been smaller than the original number of twenty-four, because not all of them may have been represented among the survivors, and also not all the surviving priests must necessarily have been included in the new organization.

We have no explicit, direct historical information about the existence of a Judaic priestly organization created in Rome after the destruction of Jerusalem. We know only that it must have existed because various Jewish priests arriving in Rome must necessarily have maintained among them their traditional connections and maintained its secrecy or at least disguised it so that its true nature would not be revealed. Further, this organization was essentially composed of members of the priestly family—that is, direct descendants of Moses. We also know that this organization must have been perpetuated for a long time.

And yet an organization of the kind that operated successfully for centuries, causing Christianity to triumph over the pagan world, is bound to have left clear traces, at both the archaeological and the historical level, of its existence and its work. If it truly existed, in one way or another we should be able to identify it and recognize its links to the Judaic priestly family.

THE STRATEGY OF JOSEPHUS FLAVIUS TO CONQUER THE ROMAN WORLD

Let us go back to this family in the aftermath of the destruction of the Temple of Jerusalem. From the book *The Jewish War,* it is clear that Josephus Flavius and the other priests who had passed over to the Romans during or at the end of the siege had close relationships among them. One pseudohistorical trace of these relationships and their nature can be found in the Masonic ritual of the twentieth degree, which regards a meeting of the surviving priests held amid the ruins of the city, during which they decided to construct the spiritual Temple.

This meeting, which we may conclude actually took place and was presided over by Josephus Flavius, unquestionably the strongest and most important character in that group of people, marks a fundamental milestone in the history of humanity. During the course of it, the priests must have examined the situation of the priestly family and decided on a strategy to improve its fortunes. We may wonder whether this strategy was devised only with the aim of ensuring safety and prosperity for the descendants of the family, or whether, on the contrary, they had consciously set themselves the objective of conquering the Empire that had humiliated them and destroyed their homeland. The second hypothesis appears far more likely, because this strategy was conceived by the man who, on the bottom of the cistern at Jotapata, faced only with the alternative of an honorable death at the hands of his men or an ignominious one at his enemy's hands, adopted a plan that was to lead him to become a member of his enemy's own imperial family.

His works clearly reveal the brilliance, together with an unrepeatable experience of life, of this man. He possessed a wide-ranging culture, which included a detailed knowledge of three different worlds—the Jewish world, the Hellenistic one, and that of the Romans—and an experience of life that saw him involved in the front line in every field: civil, religious, political, military, economic, and literary. Years of life as a hermit in the desert, the exercise of the priesthood in Jerusalem, a shipwreck, the intrigues of the imperial court of Nero, the governorship of Galilee in times of extreme turbulence, the exercise of military command, political plots, military victories and defeats, imprisonment, the humiliation of betrayal, literary glory: there is nothing that this man did not experience with unrivalled intensity. Furthermore, he passed unscathed through every defeat and personal catastrophe and succeeding invariably in transforming them into springboards to pick himself up again and rise even higher than before.

A man of this kind was capable of conceiving, consciously and lucidly, a plan that, in those circumstances, would have appeared to anybody else to be the utmost folly. This man, sitting amid the smoking ruins of what had been his fatherland, surrounded by a few humiliated, disconsolate survivors rejected by their fellow countrymen, aspired to no less than conquering that enormous, powerful Empire that had defeated him, and establishing his descendants and those of the men around him as the ruling class of that Empire. He knew in his heart that at the end he would win.

We have already seen the first step in that strategy: taking possession of the newborn Christian religion and transforming it into a solid power basis for the priestly family. Having come to Rome in the entourage of Titus, and thus strong in the emperor's protection and well supplied from an economic point of view, the priests of the new secret organization could not have encountered undue problems in taking over the leadership of a tiny group of Christians who had survived Nero's persecution, legitimated as they were by the relationship of Josephus Flavius, in the past, with Paul. Only six years had passed since he sought Paul's freedom from Roman imprisonment. The apostle of the nations must have died at least three years before. But Josephus must have appropriated Paul's doctrine, sensing its potential for propagation in the Roman world, and he dedicated himself and his organization of priests to its practical implementation. Once he had created a strong Christian community in the capital, it could not have been difficult for the priestly organization also to impose its authority on the other Christian communities scattered around the Empire—above all, on those that had been created or catechized by Paul himself.

The construction and consolidation of the church in Rome began with the creation of a centralized ecclesiastical hierarchy that was the exact replica of the Jewish one. There was one important, substantial difference, however, aiming to preserve the power and the safety of the secret priestly organization: In the Jewish religion, the class of priests was public and the right to exercise the priesthood was hereditary, transmitted from father to son. In the new religion, the hereditary principle of the priesthood had to be safeguarded, but at the same time, the existence of the priestly line had to remain a secret. These two conditions appeared to be irreconcilable. The hereditary nature of ecclesiastical appointments in the Jewish world necessarily meant that all the members of the priestly family that occupied them, and their position in the order of succession, must be publicly known and recognized. This is exactly what the new religion sought to avoid.

Josephus Flavius and the priests of his group found a solution, which nowadays may appear obvious but, for that period, was revolutionary:[1] the eligibility of the prelates who made up the public ecclesiastic hierarchies, and their celibacy.* At all costs, they had to belong to the priestly line, united in the secret organization, but this membership did not need to be publicly known. It was necessary, therefore, to find a different form of legitimation of ecclesiastic appointments. From then on, in order to occupy a priestly position in the church, it was necessary to be consecrated by a bishop, and the bishops were considered to be the successors of the apostles whose appointment had to be necessarily approved, if not made, by the successor of the prince of the apostles, the bishop of Rome. In this way, the secret priestly organization could completely control the attribution of ecclesiastic positions while continuing to remain in the background. The celibacy of ecclesiastic figures became indispensable at this point in order to avoid the creation of priestly dynasties that would quickly deprive the secret organization of its power or that would make it inevitable for its members to come out of clandestinity.

It is easy, therefore, to understand the need to set alongside Paul—the true founder of the Roman church who, however, had never met Jesus—a true apostle invested by the Messiah himself with the mission

---

*Jesus never preached celibacy and neither did any of his apostles—not even St. Paul, who limits himself to recommending that bishops should be married only once and should lead a moral life. Until then, no priest in the ancient world had been subject to any obligation of the kind, even in the primitive apostolic church. Among the priests in Jerusalem, celibacy was even a sin that contradicted God's commandments. Starting from the first century, however, it became compulsory for the pope and Catholic bishops (but not for the lower clergy). The reason for this apparently inexplicable fact lies in the secret priestly organization that controlled the church. In order to maintain control over ecclesiastic positions, it was necessary to avoid their becoming hereditary, and the only way to do so was to prevent people who occupied these positions from having legitimate heirs, thus inaugurating dynasties, which could escape from the control of the secret priestly organization. With the imposition of celibacy, every time a pope or a bishop died, the successor was chosen by the secret organization from among the most capable and most deserving members of the organization itself, without any claims on the part of heirs. Starting from 306, with the Synod of Elvira in Spain, the obligation of celibacy was extended to all ecclesiastics.

of creating his church and perpetuating it. Peter, therefore, was to provide the public legitimation of the priesthood, and above all, the legitimation of the primacy of the church of Rome over the other churches.

The letter of Pope Clement informs us that both of these preliminary operations had been concluded at the time of Domitian, with Josephus still alive. This was the beginning of the phase of expansion of the Christian religion in every corner of the Empire. Less than one century later, we find Christian communities and bishops obedient to Rome in almost all the main cities of the Empire, even in faraway Britannia. From the documents and the accounts of Christian historians, however, it is impossible to understand how this happened.

It is impossible to understand the causes and the manner of this prodigious expansion without taking into consideration an essential part of the strategy adopted by Josephus Flavius. He knew all too well that no religion has a future unless it is an integral part of a system of political power. It was a concept innate in the DNA, so to speak, of the priests of Judah that religion and political power should live together in symbiosis, mutually sustaining each other. It is unimaginable that he could think that the new religion would spread throughout the Empire independently, or even in contrast to political power. His first aim was, therefore, seizing power.

Thanks not only to the millennial experience of his family, but also to his own experience of life, Josephus knew all too well that political power, especially in an elephantine organism such as the Roman Empire, was based on military power, and military power was based on economic power, and economic power on the ability to influence and control the financial leverage of the country, including its bureaucracy and trade. His plan must have taken into account that the priestly family would sooner or later take control of these leverages. Then the Empire would be in his hands, and the new religion would be the main instrument to maintain control of it.

What did Josephus do to bring about this incredible success? What instruments did he use for this purpose? What was his strategy? Such an enormous plan could not have come to pass by chance. If it is true that Josephus had a prearranged plan, it must be possible to discover the lines of its development. Through the historical events that led, within two hundred years, to the triumph of Christianity all over the Empire, which placed the priestly family at the top of Roman society, we can reconstruct and follow the essential lines of this plan in all its simplicity and brilliance.

9

SOL INVICTUS
MITHRAS

CHRISTIANS AND THE PUBLIC CAREER

It is unrealistic to hope to find documentary proof that explicitly confirms the hypothesis presented in chapter 8. (We will shortly see why it is extremely unlikely that any direct testimony in this sense may have survived.) Yet if this reconstruction of the facts corresponds to the truth, at least in its general outline, it must be supported by a mass of convergent factors, as numerous as they are circumstantial. In order to accomplish his plan, Josephus must have adopted a strategy that, even if not noticed by contemporaries, could not escape the attention of an a posteriori historical analysis.

If the secret priestly organization actually existed, we should be able to identify it and follow its developments and the effects of its strategy by tracing the steps of the historical protagonists in the success of Christianity in the Roman world. Among these characters, there are some who, in view of the role they played in the history of Christianity, had to belong to the group of Judaic priestly branches and the secret organization formed by them—or at least had close relationships with them.

This is the point, however, where we find ourselves faced with serious contradictions that would seem to demolish the entire theory of the existence of a secret priestly organization. For example, the author of the decisive turning point in the history of Christianity (and consequently of the priestly family), Constantine the Great, is presented by historians as a pagan son of pagans. In addition, some of the most prominent characters in the history of the church in this period—such as Tertullian, St. Augustine of Hippo, St. Ambrose of Milan, and so on—are presented in their biographies as sons of pagans and initially pagans themselves. This does not fit in very well with the theory of the secret priestly organization, because we should be able to recognize such characters as Christians and sons of Christian parents.

In order to overcome this difficulty, we might hypothesize that men of an exceptional level were sometimes accepted as members of the ecclesiastic elite, even if they did not come from priestly family branches. Given that celibacy was instituted for high-ranking ecclesiastic figures, there was no danger that the positions occupied by them might fall into the hands of a nonpriestly dynasty. Yet this appears to be difficult to accept for characters such as Ambrose of Milan, who enjoyed an enormous prestige and also a political authority out of all proportion to his position. We cannot imagine that he would have enjoyed such a great authority with the clergy and political authorities belonging to priestly family branches, if he had not been a member of these branches himself.

With regard to Constantine, historical reconstruction based on the supposition of the existence of a secret priestly organization requires that he should have been a member of it. In this case, he could not have been a pagan, nor could his father, Constans Chlorus—at least, not in the classic sense of the term. The question of the alleged paganism of Constantine and his so-called conversion has long been debated—and still is—by historians of Christianity, and quite rightly so. *Pagan* usually means a polytheist, one who believes in, for instance, an Olympus populated by a plethora of gods, even if there is one among these who emerges over all the others. On the contrary, it is beyond doubt that

Constantine and his father, Constans Chlorus, professed a sort of syncretistic monotheism centered on the worship of Sol Invictus. More than a real religion, it was an esoteric association that had spread during the second and third centuries among the officers of the army and the upper imperial bureaucracy, which appear to be linked by profound subterranean connections to Christianity.*

Before dealing with the question of the relationship between Sol Invictus and Christianity, however, let us consider an extremely significant aspect of Christianity in the third and fourth centuries. We know for certain that in that period, the high-ranking functionaries and bureaucrats of Christian families were not baptized except when they were about to die, and they avoided appearing in public as Christians. The historians of the church, for example, describe as pagan the father of St. Ambrose, who belonged to the Roman senatorial nobility, and they use the same term for Ambrose himself, who had been launched on a bureaucratic career as a young man. Judging, however, by what he himself says in his autobiography, there is no doubt that his family was Christian and lived in a profoundly Christian environment. From his childhood, Ambrose loved to play the part of bishop, and in the year 353, in St. Peter's, his sister Marcellina, still a young girl, received the veil of the consecrated virgins from Pope Liberius himself.[1] Formally, however, he remained a pagan until he was designated bishop of Milan. He was actually baptized only fifteen days before being consecrated bishop, on December 7, 374, at the age of 35. Further, this was a period in which Christianity had obtained freedom of worship and had been the official religion of the Empire for more than fifty years!

The father of St. Augustine was also described as a pagan because he was not baptized. His mother, however, was a Christian, and Augustine was brought up in the Christian faith, even if in his youth

---

*The great misunderstanding is to consider Mithraism a religion. The word *cult* so often used to define it is misleading. It was not a cult, but an esoteric secret association—so esoteric and secret, in fact, that it has been defined as the Freemasonry of antiquity.

he was attracted by the beliefs of heretical sects. It was only at the age of thirty-three, however, in the year 387, that he was baptized in Milan by St. Ambrose, and a few years later, he was in turn consecrated bishop of Hippo. The fact is that in that period, Christians destined for a public career were baptized only at the point of death, or else when, for one reason or another, they decided to embrace the ecclesiastic career. This was normal practice. The senator Nectarius, who was designated bishop of Antioch by the council of Constantinople in 381 (on the advice of Emperor Theodosius, who considered him to have a highly suitable physical aspect for that position), was forced to postpone the consecration ceremony because first he had to arrange his own baptism.

Constantine was also baptized only at the point of death. While for him historians have invoked a sort of psychological resistance of the inveterate pagan to accept baptism, the same cannot be said for his children, who were born Christians from a Christian mother and were brought up in a rigorously Christian environment, but they too were baptized only at the point of death.[2]

The same practice was adopted by the emperors of the succeeding dynasty, yet the most Christian Valentinianus II (375–392) was never even baptized: feeling that he was threatened by the rhetor Arbogastus, a Gallic general, he sent for St. Ambrose, with the notion of being baptized, but Ambrose did not arrive in time. The fine funeral speech that he pronounced for the emperor's death is extant, and in it he introduces the concept of baptism of desire: "I understand that you wail because he did not receive the sacrament of baptism. . . . Well, then, is it not true that whoever desires grace receives it? Is it not true that whoever asks for it receives it? This is the reason why he received it."[3]

This prudence among the important Christian families was the norm in the second, third, and fourth centuries, especially among high-ranking bureaucrats and military men—and not only for a kind of expediency in the area of religion, which made it advisable for individuals not to publicize membership of a minority creed. It also probably helped to avoid being judged sinful or even apostate. Public positions necessarily entailed participation in ceremonies and manifestations linked to pagan religion. (For example, the emperors, even if Christian, occupied the position of *pontifex maximus,* and officiated the pagan rites connected to this position.) Until they received baptism, even if functionaries were intimately Christian, they could officiate in pagan ceremonies without denying their own faith. It was a deeply rooted conviction in that period that baptism washed away all past sins, not only Original Sin. For this reason, Christian emperors and public figures of that period waited until their last day to be baptized and in this way washed away from their souls every wickedness they had committed during their entire lives. (The classic example is Constantine, who had gone so far as to execute his own son and wife.)

The fact that they were not baptized, therefore—as in the case of the father of St. Ambrose; Ambrose himself; Constantine; and his father, Constans Chlorus—does not mean they were pagan, as historians and biographers tend to say. Yet if they were not baptized and did not publicly profess Christianity, which they could not do, what was the religion that they professed in public?

ORIGIN AND SPREAD OF THE WORSHIP OF MITHRAS

All these supposed pagans were followers of Sol Invictus. The worship of the Invincible Sun was elevated to the level of an official religion of the Roman Empire by Aurelianus. A native of Pannonia, he had been elected emperor in 270 by the army, where this so-called religion was particularly widespread. After the victorious conclusion of the campaign against the Persians with the brilliant victory of Emesa, he elevated Sol Invictus to the level of the highest divinity in the Empire and in his honor built a splendid Temple, which was solemnly inaugurated on December 25, 274.[4] This was the day of Natalis Invicti, which from then on was the main religious festivity in Rome. Of course, he declared the day of the sun to be a public holiday, which the Christians already dedicated to the worship of the Lord, according to the testimony of Tertullian.

In spite of its clear historical importance, the vast majority of people are unaware of the doctrinal contents and characteristics of Sol Invictus, perhaps because scholars normally avoid speaking about it or explaining how it succeeded in reaching such an elevated position. Above all, they avoid referring to it by another name, which is well known to the general public: Mithras. The reason for this reticence may lie in the widespread conviction that the worship of Mithras was for people of humble origins, slaves and freedmen, whereas Sol Invictus numbered among its followers emperors, senators, high-ranking bureaucrats, and military leaders. Yet there is no doubt that Sol Invictus and Mithras were one and the same. This is absolutely certain from countless inscriptions found in mithraea* and on monuments dedicated to this divinity, where the name Mithras is always preceded by the appellation Sol Invictus or Deus Invictus.

Mithras and Sol Invictus are the same and inseparably linked to the same esoteric institution. The social differences found between its followers at the beginning of the second century and those in the early fourth century simply reflect the incredible rise of this institution in Roman society during the course of these two centuries. We should note, interestingly, that this rise is exactly parallel to the rise of Christianity, which, from its origins, was a religion of slaves and freedmen and, in the same two centuries, succeeded in counting among its followers emperors, senators, high-ranking bureaucrats, and military leaders. Further, in many cases that are historically proven (for example, in the case of Constantine), the followers of Sol Invictus were exactly the same as the followers of Christianity. It does not appear to be inappropriate, therefore, to try to understand the progress of Christianity by following that of the so-called cult of Mithras. We must, however, keep to the facts as

---

*[Places of "worship" of Mithras; singular mithraeum. —*Editor*]

they have been gathered from historical and archaeological testimonies and must not be influenced by the interpretations and deliberate misinformation provided by ancient and modern historians.

Most historians hypothesize—or better, postulate—that the cult of Mithras was imported into the Roman Empire from Persia, perhaps by soldiers who had served in the East. Yet this is only a hypothesis, somewhat vague and not backed up by any evidence. Among other aspects, it does not take into consideration the substantial difference in form and content that existed between the Oriental cult (actually of Mesopotamian, not Persian, origins) and the religion practiced in the Roman Empire.

Given the scarcity of written documents on the subject, the origin and the spread of the cult of Mithras are known to us almost exclusively from archaeological evidence (remains of mithraea, dedicatory inscriptions, iconography and statues of the god, reliefs, paintings, and mosaics) that has survived in large quantities and in a conserved state, due to the fact that mithraea were usually underground and thus escaped the destruction and deterioration often suffered by buildings at ground level and due to the fact that mithraea are very often situated under Christian churches. These archaeological testimonies prove conclusively that apart from their common name, there was no relationship at all between the cults of Mithras as it was practiced in the Roman world and that practiced in the Orient. In the whole of the Eastern world, in fact, there is nothing that can be compared to a Roman mithraeum.

Almost all the archaeological evidence comes from the Western Empire, particularly from the city of Rome itself and from the port of Ostia. Several mithraea, statues, and dedicatory inscriptions have also been found in the military fortresses scattered along the Danube, in Pannonia; along the Rhine border; in Britannia, especially along Hadrian's Wall; in Spain; and in North Africa. They have been found along with military garrisons. Almost all these monuments can be dated with relative precision and bear dedicatory inscriptions. As a result, the times and the circumstances of the spread of the cult of Mithras in the Roman Empire are known to us with reasonable certainty. Also known are the names, professions, and responsibilities of a large number of figures connected to it.

The first mithraeum discovered was set up in Rome at the time of Domitian, and there are precise indications that it was attended by people close to the imperial family,[5] in particular freedmen—that is, foreigners who had acquired Roman citizenship. Our thought goes immediately to the great freedman Josephus Flavius, who at that time and in that environment was reconstructing the secret organization of the Judaic priestly family. The elements that identify Josephus Flavius and the Jewish priests of his entourage as the founders of the cult of Mithras are anything but irrelevant. They add up to more than merely a coincidence of time and place and the historically confirmed fact that in that period the Jews met in underground environments. This specific mithraeum was dedicated by a certain Titus Flavius Hyginus Ephebianus, who was undoubtedly a Jew because his name indicated that he was a freedman of the emperor Titus Flavius.

It is important to underline that Sol Invictus Mithras was not a true religion, as the majority of historians continue to affirm, any more than modern Freemasonry is a religion dedicated to the worship of the Great Architect of the Universe. What is defined as the cult of Mithras was in reality an esoteric organization divided into seven degrees and wholly analogous to modern Freemasonry. The mithraea were similar to Masonic lodges: followers met there not to render homage to the solar divinity, but to celebrate rituals of initiation whose purpose was to consolidate unity and solidarity among members of the group. Certainly members of the group deliberated on questions of common interest.

Another fundamental difference between Mithraism and a classic religion—a difference that distinguishes it as an esoteric organization—is the fact that the cult of Mithras was reserved exclusively for men (as in traditional Freemasonry) and did not possess a priestly caste. All the participants, at least from the fourth level on, were priests, and among them there were differences only of hierarchy and knowledge of the secrets of the institution (the so-called mysteries) established by each level of initiation. Furthermore, it was definitely not a mass religion, because the mithraea were always hidden and were normally small in size. At most, forty people could be seated in each of them.

Mithras was not even considered an independent divinity, but rather, more than anything else, as a messenger or even the personification on earth of the one who was considered to be the Supreme Being: the Invincible Sun. This detail is interesting and significant because it suggests Mithraism was a cover-up to conceal, under the name of a divinity widely accepted in the pagan world, an institution whose followers believed in a syncretistic Superior Being, which derived from the Jewish world. The Greek name of the sun god Helios is clearly similar to the names El, El Elyon, and Elohim, which are attributed to the Divinity in the Bible. Also, the place of origin of the name of Mithras, as the sun god, creates a direct link to the Jewish priestly family. It is mentioned for the first time in a document of 1375 BC, a peace treaty stipulated between the Hittites and the Mitanni. Both of them invoked the sun god as the guarantor of the treaty. The Mitanni called him by the name of Mithras. According to the Bible, Abraham was born at Nahor and from there he moved to Haran, both cities of the Mitanni.[6] Thus the roots of the Jewish religion can be be found in the empire of the Mitanni.

Last, we cannot ignore the connection provided by Freemasonry, the source that we have defined as nonhistorical but which possesses information whose contents are probably historical. The ritual of the twenty-sixth degree of the Scottish Rite speaks of secret meetings of surviving priests in a place defined as a catacomb to defend themselves from the persecution of Domitian. Given that the Christian catacombs did not yet exist at that time, the underground place in question can be identified as a mithraeum.

SPREAD OF THE CULT OF MITHRAS
IN THE EMPIRE

Regardless of what its faraway origins were, the fact remains that the first appearance of the so-called cult of Mithras took place in Rome at the time of Domitian, and its followers were freedmen of the imperial family of the Flavians—and consequently, in all likelihood, Romanized Jews. They were doubtless the same who, as indicated in chapter 8, took possession of the Roman church and adopted a strategy for the spread of Christianity.

It is not surprising, therefore, that most of the information about the cult of Mithras comes to us from Christian authors. We may start with Tertullian, one of the church fathers. He was born in Carthage in 155 to a Roman centurion who was a follower of the cult of Mithras. He is the one who gives us the first information about the "religion," informing us that it consisted of seven initiatory degrees,* the highest of which was called Father. (St. Jerome also lists the seven Mithraic degrees.[7]) The supreme head of the Mithraic organization was called the *pater patrum,* or pope, and he resided in Rome in the Vatican grotto.[8] Tertullian also tells us that full membership in the order was obtained only by third-level initiation, the level of Soldier, during which the candidate was offered a crown on the tip of a sword. He was to refuse it, declaring that Mithras was his crown. Also, Porphyrius speaks of initiatory levels, but he states that the assumption of the first three levels did not authorize the candidate to participate in the real mysteries of the Mithraic organization. The followers of the first three levels were the "servants" of the cult. Starting only from the fourth level—the Lion—did they enter into the operational level of the organization and have access to its mysteries.[9]

The existence of a connection between Christianity and the sun

---

*Mithraism consisted of seven stages or degrees, ranging from the lowest, the Raven, to the highest, the Father or Pater. Between these two grades were the degrees known as Occult, Soldier, Lion, Persian, and Courier of the Sun.

cult from the earliest times is recognized by the church fathers, too. Tertullian writes that the pagans ". . . believe that the Christian God is the Sun, because it is a well-known fact that we pray turning towards the rising Sun, and that on the Sun's day we give ourselves to jubilation" (Tertullian, *Ad Nationes* 1, 13).

Both the written sources and the archaeological testimonies demonstrate that from Domitian on, Rome always remained the most important center of this organization, which had become deeply rooted at the very heart of the imperial administration both in the palace and among the Praetorian Guard. In fact, the second oldest testimony referring to Mithras is that of a certain Alcimus, the administrator of the estate of Claudius Livianus, the prefect of the praetorium under Trajan, who commissioned a statue of the god.[10] The archaeological evidence shows that the organization spread almost immediately to the nearby port of Ostia, where, in the course of the second and third centuries, almost forty mithraea were built. Eighteen have been found, limited to the part of the town that has so far been excavated.[11] Subsequently, it spread to the rest of the Empire, except for the Hellenized East (apart from a few exceptions, linked to the presence of Roman troops).

The first mithraea to arise outside the Roman circle were built along the Danubian border shortly before AD 110—in the military garrison of Carnuntum, in Pannonia, and at Poetovium, also in Pannonia, the main customs center of the region, and then in all the Danubian provinces (Rhaetia, Noricum, Pannonia, Mesia, and Dacia). The followers of the cult of Mithras included the customs officers, who collected a tax on every kind of transport dispatched from Italy (via the Brenner Pass or Aquileia) toward central Europe and vice versa;[12] the imperial functionaries who controlled transport; the post; the administration of finance and mines; and last, the military troops of the garrisons scattered along the border. Almost in the same period as in the Danubian region, the cult of Mithras started to appear in the basin of the Rhine, at Bonn and Treves. This was followed by

Britannia, Spain, and North Africa, where mithraea appeared in the early decades of the second century, always associated with military garrisons and administrative centers.

SIMILARITIES BETWEEN THE CULT OF MITHRAS AND CHRISTIANITY

The fact that the cult, apart from Rome itself, is connected to military sites and administrative centers is extremely significant, as is its geographic distribution. The regions where it was most deeply rooted provided almost all the functionaries and military officers, followers of the cult of Mithras, who in a second movement proved to be Christians.

The coincidence is all the more significant because the cult of Mithras (or Sol Invictus) prospered almost in symbiosis with Christianity—to the point that Christian churches very often rise above or next to places of Mithraic worship. This is the case, for example, with the basilicas of St. Clement, St. Stephen Rotundus, St. Prisca, and so on, which sprang up over grottos dedicated to the worship of Sol Invictus.[13] An exceptional testimony confirming the connection between the cult of Mithras and Christianity comes from Pope (and St.) Leo the Great, who wrote in AD 460: "This religion of the Sun is so highly respected that some Christians, before entering the basilica of St. Peter the apostle, dedicated to the one true living God, after climbing the steps that lead to the upper entrance hall, turn toward the Sun and bow their heads in honor of the bright star" (St. Leo the Great, seventh sermon held on Christmas, AD 460, XXVII–4).

Almost one hundred fifty years had passed since Constantine's Edict of Tolerance, and more than eighty years had passed since the official abolition of the worship of Sol Invictus; Christianity had completely taken the place of paganism. Yet the conviction that Sol Invictus Mithras and Jesus were one and the same was still deeply rooted in the conscience of many Christians,* as testified by the words of Leo the Great.[14]

It is true that both he and Tertullian and other fathers of the church officially deny this connection, and that St. Ambrose goes so far as to affirm that he had never heard of Mithras.† But it is equally true that a long series of analogies exist between Mithras and Jesus: On December 25 Mithras was born in a stable to a virgin, surrounded by shepherds who brought gifts. He was venerated on the day of the sun (Sunday). He bore a halo around his head. He celebrated a last supper with his faithful followers before returning to his father. He was said not to have died, but to have ascended to heaven from where he would return in the last days to raise the dead and judge them, sending the good to Paradise and the evil to hell. He guaranteed his followers immortality after baptism.

Furthermore, the followers of Mithras believed in the immortality of the soul, the last judgment, and the resurrection of the dead at the

---

*Constantine believed that Jesus Christ and Sol Invictus were both aspects of the same Superior Divinity. He was certainly not the only one to have this conviction. Neoplatonism contended that the religion of the sun represented a "bridge" between paganism and Christianity. Jesus was often called by the name Sol Justitiae and was represented by statues that were similar to the young Apollo or sun. Clement of Alexandria describes Jesus driving the chariot of the sun across the sky, and a mosaic of the fourth century shows him on the chariot while he ascends to heaven, represented by the sun. On some coins of the fourth century, the Christian banner at the top reads "Sol Invictus." A large part of the Roman population believed that Christianity and the worship of the sun were closely connected, if not the same. One significant case is that of the bishop of Troy, who openly continued to profess his worship of the sun even during his episcopate (see Michael Grant, The Emperor Constantine [London: Phoenix Press, 1998], 135). Another important example in this sense is that of Synesius of Cyrene, a disciple of the famous Neoplatonic philosopher Apathias, who was killed by the mob in Alexandria in 415. Synesius, not yet baptized, was elected bishop of Ptolemais and metropolitan bishop of Cyrenaica, but he accepted the position only on condition that he did not have to retract his Neoplatonic ideas or renounce his worship of the sun.

†This was clearly a lie. As a member of a senatorial family and as a senator himself, it is unthinkable that he was unaware that the most eminent members of the senate were at the head of the organization of Sol Invictus Mithras. This is all the more unimaginable because his father, one of the closest collaborators of Constantine, undoubtedly belonged to the institution.

end of the world. They celebrated the atoning death of a savior who had risen on a Sunday. They celebrated a ceremony corresponding to the Catholic Mass during which they consumed consecrated bread and wine in memory of the last supper of Mithras—and during the ceremony they used hymns, bells, candles, and holy water. Indeed, they shared with Christians a long series of other beliefs and ritual practices, to the point that they were practically indistinguishable from each other in the eyes of the pagans and also to many Christians. Tertullian narrates this fact, and together with other fathers of the church, he attempts to justify this substantial commonality to the eyes of the Christian faithful, attributing it to Satan's plagiarism of the most sacred rites and beliefs of the Christian religion.[15]

Last, the Mithraic organization was presided over by a supreme head known as the pater patrum, or pope, who governed from a grotto on the Vatican hill in Rome, where Constantine had the basilica of St. Peter built in 322. This cave of the Vatican (the so-called Phrygianum, which is still situated at the foot of the present basilica) remained the central seat of the cult of Mithras until the death of the last pater patrum, the senator Vectius Agorius Praetextatus, in AD 384. Immediately afterward, the cult of Mithras was officially abolished and the cave was occupied by Syricius (the successor of the bishop of Rome, Damasus), who adopted the name of the head of the Mithraic sect, pater patrum, or pope, for the first time in the history of the church.[16] He also adopted the same clothing and sat on the same chair, which became the throne of St. Peter in Rome. Mithraic designs were—and still are—engraved on this throne. Sol Invictus Mithras, who, according to historians, had the belief of the majority in the Roman senate, in the army, and in the public administration, vanished almost immediately, without any killing, persecution, exile, or forced abjuration. Overnight, the Roman senate, stronghold of the cult of Mithras, discovered that it was totally Christian.

In this light, we are forced to conclude that Sol Invictus Mithras and Christianity were not two religions in competition, as we often read, but were two institutions of a different nature that were closely connected. Rather than being a simple hypothesis, this is practically a certainty. It is unthinkable that the Roman church continued to extend hospitality to the head of a rival pagan religion for more than half a century and at the heart of its most exclusive property, the basilica dedicated to the prince of apostles. The Mithraic pater patrum and the bishop of Rome must necessarily have been closely linked.

After the death of Praetextatus, his prerogative and functions were assumed by the bishop of Rome, and the church seized all the property of the Mithraic organization. The seat, the robes, the title, and the prerogatives of the pater patrum were not the only things that passed from the cult of Mithras to the church. Besides the similarities in doctrines and rituals, we find in Christian churches the stone table in front of the apse—the altar where the disc of the sun was exhibited in the mithraea. We also find the stole, the bishop's headpiece (still called a mitre), the robes, the colors, the use of incense, the aspergillum, the candles lit in front of the altar, the genuflexions, and not least of all, the most representative object that dominates the Christian rite: the exhibition of the Host, which is contained in a disc from which the sun radiates, the monstrance.

Further, the rays of the sun surround God's head, or his triangular symbol, in myriad Christian representations. The symbol of the sun is omnipresent in Christian churches and in a large number of Christian depictions. It can be found in the rose window at the center of cathedral facades, and when there is no rose window, the sun itself is represented in myriad churches, either by itself or on the back of the cross. We need only look around to discover it everywhere in Christian symbolism. Obviously, all the feasts and anniversaries of the cult of Mithras have been incorporated into the Christian religion. Historians justify this fact by insisting that the church incorporated pagan feasts and symbolism, but this is not true. It is only the feasts and symbols of Sol Invictus, not those of the other pagan cults, which have entered Christianity en masse.

So were the cult of Mithras and Christianity the same thing? Not exactly—there were substantial differences between them. First of all, as has been said, the so-called cult of Sol Invictus Mithras was not a religion, but an esoteric association reserved exclusively for men. All the participants were priests, at least from the fourth level up, and among them, there were differences only of hierarchy determined by the level of initiation.

If we add to this the fact that the followers of the solar organization who are known to us from history usually had mothers and wives who followed the Christian faith, and that bishops and Christian emperors came from their families, we must conclude that the so-called cult of Mithras was none other than the organizational expression of the secret brotherhood of branches of the priestly family, which controlled the Christian religion. Further, the mithraea were places where they met secretly to celebrate their traditional rites, to establish the hierarchies within the family, and to agree on action to be taken. They were the places of government of the priestly family, and naturally the mithraeum of Rome, with its seat in the grotto of the Vatican, was the most important one, with jurisdiction over all the others. It was presided over by the supreme head of the family, the pater patrum, a figure equivalent to the high priest of Jewish memory. The Christian church was the public religion open to women and to the pagan world and created and controlled by the priestly family. Sol Invictus Mithras and Christianity were therefore two faces of the same coin,* one directed to the world and exposed to its attacks, and the other secret and well entrenched in all the power centers of the Roman empire.[17]

THE JUDAIC PRIESTLY FAMILY IN THE CULT OF MITHRAS

There are various indications that confirm that the followers of the cult of Mithras belonged to branches of the priestly family and considered themselves to be priests, even if they were not part of the hierarchic

---

*This is perhaps expressed best by certain coins minted by Constantine toward the end of his reign. These present the symbol of Sol Invictus on one side and the Christian Chi Rho symbol on the other.

structure of the church. The classic example is St. Ambrose, who passes directly from being a pagan to being bishop of one of the most important sees of the period. Yet the most illuminating and best-attested example is that of the emperor Constantine. Even if he was not baptized until he was at the point of death and was consequently considered by historians to be a pagan to the end, he was in the habit of defining himself as "God's servant," and he himself declared that he was "the bishop established by God for humanity outside the Church" (*Life of Constantine,* IV, 24). His biographer Eusebius goes so far as to define him as "the new Moses"* and "a sort of universal bishop."

Even if he was still formally a pagan, he promoted and presided over the Council of Nicaea, a milestone in the history of the church, sitting at the center of the assembly on a throne of gold and guiding the choices. The Greek church subsequently venerated him as a saint, together with his mother, Elena. Indeed, he was even considered equal to the apostles or the thirteenth apostle—and as a result, he was buried in the Church of the Holy Apostles, built specifically for this purpose, where the relics of the twelve apostles had been gathered.† The bishops who were invited to dine with him declared that they felt honored as if they had taken part in a banquet with the apostles, even comparing Constantine to Jesus.

Not bad for someone who had not even been baptized! These attributions can be explained only by his priestly status, regardless of whether he had been baptized or not. He was a high priest by birth and by right. The mastery that he displayed in all the questions of the Christian religion from the beginning of his alleged conversion, the passion that he put into the defense of its unity and its doctrinal content,

---

*Together with Eusebius, various panegyrists refer to him in a similar fashion. This connection between Constantine and Moses is significant, especially if we consider that as a priest, the former descended from the latter.

†Significantly, Constantine erected over the basilica not a cross, as would be logical to expect, but a five-pointed star, exactly like the one that stood over the entrance to the Temple in Jerusalem.

interfering energetically in the work of the Council of Nicaea, and all his religious policies show that his roots were Christian and not pagan. It is no surprise that Eusebius also considers as Christian and even a saint Constantine's father, Constans Chlorus, implying that Sol Invictus of which he was officially a devotee was the same Supreme Being as that of Christianity.

Membership in the priestly family must have been a necessary and sufficient condition to become part of the ecclesiastic hierarchy of the church. Of this we have no proof, but we do have substantial indications. For example, St. Jerome, one of the great church fathers, was born (between 340 and 347) in Pannonia, a stronghold, as we have seen, of the cult of Mithras. His parents were Christians or at least he states that they were—but this does not exclude that his father was a follower of Sol Invictus, and he must have been of priestly origins. Otherwise, it would not be possible to understand the declaration made by Jerome himself a few years later, in Rome, when he was a candidate for the position of pope. Speaking of the excessive luxury of Roman prelates of his period, he writes:

> Sometimes people of my own condition are ordained deacons or elders in order to consort more freely with ladies. They curl their hair and go around with rings on their fingers. Seeing them dressed in such an unusual guise, you would take them more for dandies in love than for priests. Some of them spend all their efforts and their scholarship in learning the names, addresses, and habits of rich Roman ladies.[18]

Apart from the glimpse of Roman ecclesiastic life of the period, which is already significant, his words give us some essential information about those who had a right to the priesthood; he affirms that in order to be appointed deacons or elders, it was sufficient to be "people of his same condition." It couldn't be clearer! Those men were priests by right of birth, and not on the basis of moral worthiness or anything else. The ecclesiastic career was an option that "people of that condition" could exercise (or could be obliged to exercise, as in the case of Augustine, Ambrose, and various others) at any moment of their lives.

CULT OF MITHRAS AND FREEMASONRY

It is not by chance that modern Freemasonry seems to a large extent to be a tributary of the cult of Mithras. The points of similarity are numerous and substantial, not only in initiatory structure, but also in ritualistic content: continuous references to the sun; the most significant anniversaries; the constant link to the solar cycle; the architecture and decoration of the Masonic Temple itself, which has maintained the shapes and dispositions of the mithraeum. If we enter a Masonic Temple today, we will see on the wall opposite the entrance the sun on the left and the waxing moon on the right. On the right-hand and left-hand walls are the signs of the zodiac, six on each side, which begin with Aries on the left, and finish with Pisces on the right. Alternating with the signs of the zodiac are the statues of Minerva, Hercules, Venus, and Saturn. On the ceiling there is a starry sky. Along the sides are benches where the followers take their seats. On the back wall is the throne where the venerable master sits, and at his side are the chairs of the important people of the lodge. All is exactly as was in a mithraeum. The substantial difference is that behind the throne there is no image of Mithras with the bull, but instead there is a triangle with an eye at the center (and normally the sun in the background). Along with this image is the inscription T.G.O.G.A.O.T.U., which means: To the Glory of the Great Architect of the Universe. We should note that G.A.O.T.U. is the term that the Pythagoreans used to indicate the sun (and Pythagoras is indicated by the Masonic tradition as one of its founders). Indeed, the sun is one of the most important elements in Freemasonry: it stands in the center of the grand master's apron and in Masonry coats of arms and is omnipresent in the rituals. The main Masonic anniversaries (solstices and equinoxes) are linked to the sun.

The points of similarity with Sol Invictus Mithras do not stop here. Another typical characteristic inherited from the cult of Mithras is the handshake,* which today is used universally, but which maintains an almost sacred meaning allowing Masonic brothers to recognize each other. Mithraic initiates were defined by the term *syndexii,* which means "united by shaking the right hand." The handshake was, in fact, a characteristic of the cult. The follower became almost a vassal of the pater, the highest level in the Mithraic lodge.[19] In addition, the initiation ceremony represented in various mithraea is very closely related to the one celebrated in Masonic initiations: The new initiate is presented kneeling down, naked, with his eyes blindfolded and his hands tied. Beside him on one side is a character wearing a white tunic who acts as a guide, and on the other is the pater, who hands him a cup from which to drink. Further, the four constituent elements of reality—earth, air, water, and fire—also appear to be linked to the ritual of initiation, as in modern Freemasonry.

Another ceremony represented in numerous mithraea and almost identical to the modern one is that of the ritual dinner, during which the followers were served by the neophytes. Also, the fact that an individual became a member of the real Mithraic organization only from the third level up exactly corresponds to modern Freemasonry, in which only after reaching the third level—that of master—can an individual aspire to the higher levels of the various rites.

It is indisputable: modern Freemasonry presents such a close affinity to the organization of Sol Invictus Mithras that a link must exist between them. Of course, a great deal of time has passed and many evolutions of every kind have taken place since the time of the Mithras cult and the time of modern Freemasonry's birth. The latter cannot be

---

*On the graffiti of Dura-Europos we read: "An homage to all those who are united by a handshake" or "an homage to Geminiano, a good syndexios," and so on. The term is also used in Latin. When a pater named Ebutius Restitutianus built a new mithraeum in Rome, he declared in the inscription that he had built it "so that everybody who was linked by the handshake could joyfully celebrate their solemnity forever." We should note this last sentence for its similarity to the modern Masonic formula: "Everything in this Temple must be serenity, joy, and jubilation."

considered automatically to be a continuation of the former. Yet what appears legitimate is the hypothesis that Freemasonry reproduces the organization of Josephus Flavius exactly as a fossil reproduces the forms of a living being that has been extinct for countless ages. This allows us to obtain information about the original organization, just as a fossil allows us to obtain essential information about the creature from which it derives, even if the living matter has been entirely substituted by stone and many parts and characteristics have vanished.

KEEPING THE SECRET IN THE UNDERGROUND PRIESTLY ORGANIZATION

The elements that connect the esoteric organization of Sol Invictus Mithras to Josephus Flavius and the other surviving members of the Judaic priestly family and to Christianity are numerous, important, and consistent, as we will see in chapter 10. Nevertheless, they remain only indicative. There are no written documents that prove this connection with certainty, just as there is no document or written testimony that refers to any meeting of Sol Invictus, who took part in it, or what decisions were made.

It is absolutely certain, however, that meetings were regularly held in the mithraea, and we are necessarily forced to conclude that during the course of these meetings, problems connected with economic and political life were discussed and decisions of great importance for the Roman Empire were made, given that the participants in the meetings all belonged to the upper echelons of the state bureaucracy. History tells us, for example, that from a certain point on, the Roman emperors were proclaimed, almost always, by the army or by the Praetorian Guard. It is unthinkable that an organization such as Sol Invictus, which included among its members the majority of high-ranking officials in the army and the praetorium, should not have any say in those elections. We must necessarily conclude that the decisions about who was to be elected were made in the secret of the mithraea, even if no written document exists to confirm this and, consequently, no historian dares to affirm it, however hypothetically.

Yet what the lack of any written documentation removes is not the certainty that given decisions were made, but only the information about when and in what circumstances they were made and who made them. We are therefore forced to hypothesize on the basis of indications and historical findings—what in modern terms may be defined as searching for hidden motives. Starting from the premise of the existence of the secret Judaic priestly organization, we obtain a completely new, infinitely more realistic and understandable interpretation of history. Nevertheless, it is an essentially circumstantial process, because the secret nature of the organization leads us to exclude a priori the existence of written documents to prove explicitly its existence, activities, membership, and decisions.

The recognition of Freemasonry as the descendant of the primitive priestly organization allows us to establish with certainty that the maintenance of the secret about the participants and the activities carried out in the mithraea was an absolute priority. The fact that it was an absolute obligation to keep the secrets in the Masonic organization, ever since its faraway origins, is proved by the content of the rituals as they have been handed down to us. Nowadays, the neophyte smiles, albeit with a shiver down his spine, when the venerable master asks him to pronounce the solemn oath that accompanies every initiation:[20]

Initiation at the sixth degree, Intimate Secretary

I promise and swear that I will never reveal to anybody, directly or indirectly, what is revealed to me, especially to brothers of a lower degree. . . . If I should fail to respect my oath, may my body be opened up, my guts torn out, my heart cut to pieces, and all be thrown to wild beasts to be devoured.

Initiation at the seventh degree, Irish Master

I promise to maintain, as a sacred secret, all the mysteries that are revealed to me, and to observe all the rules that are imposed on me by the Grand Council of the Princes of Jerusalem: if I should fail to respect my promise, as well as the preceding punishments, may my body be cut in two and may my intestines be torn out . . .

Initiation at the ninth degree, Elect Master of Nine

When you were initiated a Mason, you saw all the brothers armed; you know that it was to defend you if you were exposed to any danger—but you also know that those arms will be used for your destruction, to be sunk into your heart, if you are so wicked as to betray your oaths. . . . Are you also ready to avenge Freemasonry, killing every possible traitor? Even if it were your best friend, you must put aside all sentiment and leave place only for vengeance . . . you will take this dagger, and will stab him, first in the head and then in the heart and then you will cut his head off . . .

Initiation at the tenth degree, Illustrious Elect of Fifteen

I promise and swear on the Holy Bible . . . to keep all the secrets that are revealed to me closed in my heart; if I should not maintain my oath, may my body be cut perpendicularly and exposed for eight hours in the open air, so that poisonous flies may eat their fill of my entrails, may my head be cut off and placed on the uppermost pinnacle . . . and I will always be ready to inflict the same punishment on those who reveal the secrets of this level and betray their oath . . .

Initiation at the twelfth degree, Great Master Architect

I promise to maintain the secret . . . to be faithful to my king, and to be charitable to my neighbors and brothers; if I should fail to respect this promise, may my body be cut in two, may my memory be damned and may I be considered a perjured villain.

These oaths are a clear demonstration that the rituals to which they refer developed in a period of barbarism (and undoubtedly before firearms began to be used). Nowadays, as in the eighteenth century, nobody would think of invoking such truculent punishments for failure to maintain a promise, and even less of applying them. The oaths pronounced by initiates at the various levels of Freemasonry are pure folklore to which nobody would dream of assigning a real meaning. In the ancient period when the very survival of the organization and its ability to maintain the levers of power depended on the secret being maintained, whoever pronounced those words really meant what he said. The secret, therefore, was always kept, and if anyone ever failed to do so, he was undoubtedly eliminated, together with his testimony.

CONCLUSIONS

We can never hope to find direct written testimonies about the acts carried out and the decisions made in the mithraea in order to obtain explicit confirmation of the theory that the priestly family held there. This, however, does not mean that it is impossible to obtain confirmation of its validity. We can reconstruct the historical events of the Western Empire, by setting the events in the framework created and verifying their consistency. The Judaic priestly family, Christianity, the organization of Mithras, and Freemasonry appear to be closely connected as the protagonists of a history that begins to make sense—a history based on factual elements linked coherently and supported by myriad convergent factors.

These factors lead us to believe that Sol Invictus Mithras was the cover behind which hid the secret esoteric organization re-created in Rome by the Mosaic priestly family that had escaped the massacre in Jerusalem. The proof that we were searching for—proof of the survival of the Judaic priestly family and proof of its relationship to the Christian religion—exists as circumstantial evidence, it is true. Yet it provides a solid basis for the hypothesis formulated at the beginning of this section, and allows us to develop it in an increasingly confirmed and credible frame and on the basis of facts.

Starting from these premises, we can form a precise idea of the methods used by the priestly family to seize possession of the Roman Empire and impose the Christian religion, and we can also succeed in identifying, with a high degree of reliability, the leading characters. Last, we can try to give sense to a story that up to now appeared to be a chaotic series of coincidences determined by characters who had no connection among them—people who miraculously succeeded in achieving an aim that seemed to be preordained from the beginning. Christian historians attribute it to the unfathomable designs of Divine Providence. Our theory, on the contrary, allows us to understand the background of this story and the motivations that prompted its protagonists—and to understand the vast and extremely solid network of relationships that linked them.

They were all linked by blood ties, members of an organization, which operated secretly, even when its existence was publicly known, and which had succeeded in penetrating into all the vital institutions of the Roman Empire and controlling them. One striking aspect of this organization that relates to its geographical distribution is that it appears to be confined to the Roman Western part of the Empire, but seems to be absent in the Hellenized part—that is, Greece, the Middle East, and Egypt. It is possible—or better, probable—that the Oriental members of the priestly family were gathered around the Neoplatonic school whose ideological positions were extraordinarily close to those of Sol Invictus and whose exponents were so fully accepted and appreciated in Christian environments that they exercised a great influence at the court of the Christian emperors and occupied high positions in the administration of the state. In any case, the head of the Mithraic organization and its most important "lodges," where the decisions fundamental for the priestly family were made, were in the West, which was soon to split away from the East and to follow its own autonomous evolution. For our purposes, therefore, we may limit ourselves to following in detail only this part of the story, which happens to be the most linear and the easiest to document and the part that interests us most directly.

THE STRATEGY OF THE PRIESTLY FAMILY TO CONQUER THE ROMAN EMPIRE

THE CULT OF MITHRAS IN THE PUBLIC ADMINISTRATION

The very first testimony referring to followers of the cult of Mithras goes back, as we have learned, to the time of Domitian, and has to do with a person who is close to the imperial house. It is a dedicatory inscription to Mithras left by a certain Titus Flavius Hyginus Ephebianus, almost certainly a freedman of the emperor whose name he assumed: Titus Flavius. He was likely a Jew who came to Rome after the destruction of Jerusalem, and it is more than likely that he was one of the priests of the circle of Josephus Flavius. The Mithraic organization was simply an apparently pagan cover-up created by the Judaic priestly organization to conceal its true nature from the outside world.

In these secret meetings in this first Roman mithraeum, the survivors of the Judaic priestly family, led by Josephus Flavius, had to devise a strategy that would one day allow their descendants to take possession of that omnipotent Empire, which had destroyed their Temple and their homeland. We can reconstruct precisely the guidelines of this strategy and the manner of its application by following not so much the events of Christianity, but rather the expansion of the cult of Mithras and its seizure of the fundamental mainstays of the Empire: bureaucracy, finance, its army, and finally even its religion, as we will see.

The second archaeological testimony (in chronological order) is represented by a statue dedicated to Mithras by a certain Alcimus, a farmer in the service of Tiberius Claudius Livianus, the prefect of the praetorium under Trajan (the successor of Domitian). Alcimus was one of the two commanders of the emperor's personal guard and in many respects was practically the emperor's representative.[1] From that moment on, Sol Invictus was a constant presence in the Praetorian Guard. The greatest concentration of mithraea in Rome, in fact, is in the vicinity of the Praetorian barracks.

Another statue dating back to the same period, around AD 100, is that dedicated to Mithras by a certain Melichrysius, a functionary at Novae, in the province of Mesia (Bulgaria). He was in the service of the general contractor of the customs in the area of the lower Danube. This was the bridgehead of a whole host of functionaries who adhered to the cult of Mithras. In the following decades, they took control of the customs services of all the Danubian provinces, the Publicum Portorium Illyrici, which extended from the sources of the Danube to the Black Sea. The head office was at Poetovium, in Pannonia, and the contractors were a certain Julius Capito and his brothers Julius Januarius and Julius Epaphroditus, who are celebrated in the mithraea scattered all over their district, which were erected by functionaries in their service. This long list of names testifies that the followers of the cult of Mithras had, within a few years, assumed total control of this enormous, extremely important tax district, which was even larger than the subsequent Austro-Hungarian Empire.

Penetration of the cult of Mithras in this area was not limited to the customs offices; it also extended to the imperial functionaries who controlled transport and the important postal service (the *cursus publi-cus*), and those running administration of finances and mines. Its pen-etration into the state administrative machinery was not limited to the provinces. In Rome, a long list of freedmen (a condition that betrayed their non-Roman origins) who were followers of the cult of Mithras occupied positions of great importance at the court and in the impe-rial administration.[2] Already, at the end of the second century, practi-cally all public money—or at least a large slice of it—passed through the hands of followers of the cult of Mithras (that is, according to our starting hypothesis, members of the priestly family).[3]

No less attention, judging by archaeological findings, was dedicated by the priestly family to other vital sectors of the economy, such as, for example, trading. Josephus Flavius and his fellow priests possessed extensive financial means and connections all over the Mediterranean. It would seem, then, that the world of business and trade offered a natural outlet for their resources. It is not by chance that mithraea are particularly numerous in Ostia, the port with the greatest volume of trading in the world in that period. There, goods and foodstuffs from every part of the Empire arrived to delight the insatiable appetite of the capital.

If this identification of the followers of the cult of Mithras as the members of the Judaic priestly family is correct, we have definitive proof that by the end of the second century they controlled the main levers of economic and financial power, together with the public administration of the Roman Empire. We may well imagine what an enormous finan-cial fortune the family had amassed and what influence it was able to exert in society.

Besides bureaucracy, trading, and finance, the attention of the fam-ily had been turned, from the very beginning, to the army, the other great power structure of the Roman Empire. The usual iconography has led us to consider Christians as opposed to violence and always ready to turn the other cheek; we cannot see them in the role of warriors. Perhaps this is true for the masses of the faithful, but it is definitely not true in the case of the followers of Sol Invictus. In actual fact, the Judaic priestly family had glorious military traditions, starting from the Maccabees and ending with Josephus Flavius. It is logical and natural that they saw the army as an indispensable instrument for their affirmation in the Roman world. Josephus Flavius knew, from direct experience, that the army could become the arbiter of the imperial throne. His great protector, Vespasian, was the first emperor who was proclaimed by the army. He undoubtedly obtained assent for his office by bribing the officials who commanded the legions stationed in Egypt with the gold provided by Josephus Flavius. From then on, the Roman emperors owed their position not so much to political or social forces (which, however, were indispensable to maintain the position), but to the army. Whoever controlled the army controlled the Empire.

The main aim fixed by Josephus Flavius for the Mithraic organization, therefore, must have been infiltrating the army and taking control of it. This was his winning move, which accelerated the triumph of the priestly family—and together with it, Christianity, which was its emanation. It was favorable for the priestly family that most of the troops were deployed along the borders of the Empire, and that the leading citizens, especially the noble and rich, were loath to live far away from Rome. In these borderlands, a Romanized Jew possessing extensive financial resources could easily emerge and re-create a Roman "virginity." Soon, mithraea sprang up in all the places where Roman garrisons were stationed. The first that we know of was built at the garrison of Carnuntum, in Pannonia, practically at the same time as the mithraeum of the nearby customs center of Poetovium: between AD 100 and 110.[4] Subsequently, mithraea multiplied all over the region—besides Carnuntum, they can be found in Vindobona (Vienna), Brigetium and Aquincum (Budapest), in Dacia, and in the area of the lower Danube: all places where military garrisons were situated. At the same time, mithraea were erected along the border with Germany, in particular at Wiesbaden, Heddernheim, Mainz, Treviri, Gros-Krotzenburg, Lorsch, and numerous other places in the Palatinate and in Alsace. In Britannia, at least fifteen mithraea have been discovered; eight are scattered along Hadrian's Wall and the others can be found in the territory around the main military garrisons (London, York, St. Albans, Segontium, etc.). In Spain, at least twenty-five sites dedicated to Mithras have been found. They have also been found in Africa, mainly at Lambesis, and in Tunisia, at the post of the only legion stationed on that continent.

The archaeological testimonies are clear and incontrovertible: within a century, the priestly family, by means of the cult of Mithras, had succeeded in controlling all the Roman legions stationed in the provinces and along the borders. In fact, the worship of Sol Invictus Mithras is often considered by historians to be the "religion" typical of Roman soldiers.

Even before the army, however, the attention of Sol Invictus was concentrated on the Praetorian Guard, the emperor's personal guard. It is not by chance that the second known dedicatory inscription of a Mithraic character regards a commander of the praetorium and that the concentration of mithraea was particularly high in the area surrounding the Praetorian barracks. The infiltration of this body must have started under the Flavians. They could count on the unconditional loyalty of many Jewish freedmen who owed them everything—their lives, their safety, and their well-being. The Roman emperors were somewhat reluctant to entrust their personal safety to officers who came from the ranks of the Roman senate, their main political adversary, and so the ranks of their personal guard were mainly filled by freedmen and members of the equestrian class, rather than men of Roman origin. This must have favored Sol Invictus, in particular, which made the praetorium its unchallenged fief from the beginning of the second century on.

CHRISTIANS IN THE ROMAN ARMY

The existence of profound links between Christianity and Sol Invictus helps us to understand a fact that seems impossible given the professions of pacifism and disengagement from public life made by the church in the early centuries: surprisingly, at the end of the third century, Christians were massively represented in the army and occupied many of the highest positions. Christian sources testify to this.[5] They describe the purges carried out by Diocletian in the army. According to the declaration of Bishop Eucherius of Lyon in 450, he went so far as to massacre an entire legion of Christians, the so-called Theban legion. Historians unanimously judge that this story is exaggerated, but at the same time, it confirms the importance of the presence of Christians in the army. Large numbers of Christians served in the army of Constantine some time before he revealed his sympathies for Christianity, and just as many—or more—served on the other side, in the army of Maxentius in Rome.

Yet how did a minority religion in the Empire that professed pacifism become such an important presence in the army? Once again, the explanation lies in the fact that Christianity and the cult of Mithras were two sides of the same coin. Wherever Mithras arrived, the Christians arrived, too. The primary aim of the priestly family's strategy was seizing power in the army. This was achieved in two ways: First, the upper ranks were occupied by members of the family who were part of the Mithraic organization and who supported one another. Second, the army became Christianized. It is legitimate to imagine that the institution favored the spread of Christianity among the soldiers in every possible way, and they favored Christian soldiers in the advancement of their careers. A Christian soldier was easily controlled by the Mithraic organization through its connections with the ecclesiastic authority.

The fact that the secret priestly organization was behind the penetration of Christians into the army is proved by the legend of the Quattuor Coronati Saints, which connects Freemasonry and four high officers of the army who were executed by Diocletian. The Quattuor Coronati Saints have always been considered the patron saints of masons, and thus of Freemasonry. In fact, they occupy a very important place in the Royal Manuscript (a document of the fifteenth century, which traces the history of Freemasonry), and a large number of Masonic lodges all over the world are dedicated to them. The legend is mentioned for the first time by a hagiographic work of the sixth century, the *Passio Quattuor Coronatorum,* probably written by a cleric from Pannonia who was employed in the basilica on Mount Celio in Rome, and it was composed on the occasion of the new feast of the Celio.

The Quattuor Coronati Saints were high officers in the army who originally came from Pannonia. According to the Christian story, they refused to offer incense during the inauguration of a temple to the god Aesculapius that was built in Rome by Diocletian. For this, they were executed by the emperor. Their bodies were recovered by Pope Melchiades, who had them laid to rest in the catacombs of Via Labricana, in Rome. Since then, they have been known as the Catacombs of the Quattuor Coronati Saints. Subsequently, in the sixth century, the basilica on Mount Celio, called at first Titulus Aemilianae (Glory of Emiliana), became Titulus SS. Quattuor Coronatorum (Glory of the Four Crowned Saints), probably because some relics of the martyrs were placed there. The four are indicated explicitly in the tradition as master masons, despite the fact that they were soldiers ranked as *cornicularii,* from which derived the name Coronati (crowned): they wore the crown of the centurion, which was the highest rank of noncommissioned officer in the Roman army.

This legend offers some significant insights for our study. First, the four were natives of Pannonia, a stronghold of the cult of Mithras. Furthermore, the appellation of master masons identifies them as belonging to the branches of the priestly family. The fact that, two centuries later, they are defined as *artifices mirificos in arte quadrataria—* "artisans expert in the art of squaring stones" (the same definition that is attributed to modern Freemasons)—means that the secret priestly organization assumed the present-day masonic characterization immediately after the official abolition of the cult of Mithras.

Last, the Four Crowned Saints offer a clear demonstration of the policy adopted by the priestly organization to occupy the highest ranks of the army. This was not at all difficult for Roman families of elevated social conditions who possessed extensive financial resources. Interestingly, the strong influence of Christian officers was not impaired in the slightest by Diocletian's purges. On the contrary, it grew in the following decades until it assumed total control of the army. Starting with Constantine, the Roman legions always proclaimed emperors exclusively from Christian generals, and for almost one hundred years they all came from Pannonia. We can conclude that they were in some way linked to the four officers killed by Diocletian. During the persecution under Diocletian, the Christian martyrs in the Empire numbered in the hundreds or even thousands. The fact that, among so many, the Four Crowned Saints were honored with catacombs—and even a Roman basilica—dedicated to them as if they were apostles is a sure sign of their importance to the priestly family.

PART THREE

The Conquest of the
Roman Empire

11

THE TAKEOVER OF THE IMPERIAL OFFICE

THE SEVERANS, THE FIRST SOL INVICTUS EMPERORS

Despite the absence of official documents, the identification of Sol Invictus Mithras as the secret organization of the Judaic priestly family allows us to follow step-by-step its strategy for conquest of the Roman Empire—its primary objective. As far as we can judge with hindsight, the goal of the strategy was the complete substitution of the ruling class of the Roman Empire with the descendants of the priestly family that had survived the destruction of Jerusalem and the Temple. This result was achieved in less than three centuries, by which time all the ancient religions had been eliminated and substituted with Christianity, and the primitive Roman nobility had been virtually annihilated and replaced by members of the family of priestly origin that had accumulated all the power and wealth of the Empire.

The seizure of power in the Empire occurred in distinct phases, which we can perceive clearly from an historical perspective. We have already looked at the first phase: consolidation of the Christian religion and seizure of the levers of power. Throughout the second century AD, the initiates of Sol Invictus Mithras occupied all the main positions in the public administration and the army, becoming the dominant class in the outlying provinces of the Empire—especially in central and northern Europe.

In Rome the Mithraic organization instated itself solidly within the imperial administration and the emperor's personal guards, the Praetorian Guard. At the same time, it seized control of trade and other key economic activities, as we can see, for example, in the abundance of mithraea in Ostia, the port of Rome. Yet most important of all was that the spread of Christianity proceeded at the same pace. Wherever the representatives of Mithras arrived, a Christian community immediately sprang up. By the end of the second century, there were already at least four bishop's sees in Britannia, sixteen in Gaul,[1] sixteen in Spain, and one in practically every big city in North Africa and the Middle East. They all had buildings for worship and revenue-producing land, and they were all operating in relative freedom, despite the creeping persecution of Christianity.

Christianity remained a *religio illicita* until the end of the second century—therefore it was subject to recurrent, often bloody persecutions, especially in the eastern provinces. It must be said, however, that throughout this period the Roman emperors, with the possible exception of Marcus Aurelius, never fomented the persecutions. If anything, they tried to limit the excesses of their more zealous governors by prohibiting the pursuit of Christians unless they had perpetrated crimes or had been reported by other citizens. (This is demonstrated by a well-known letter from Trajan to Pliny.)

In any case, Christianity remained largely a minority religion, involving less than 5 percent of the population of the Empire (except in some privileged areas, such as Nabatea, where the percentage was much higher). Its proportion was too small to carry any weight in society. Even the vast majority of the senate consisted of the ancient patrician families who had held power in Rome for more than seven centuries and who had been responsible for creating its greatness.

In opposition to the senatorial aristocracy an "equestrian" class was formed. This was the backbone of the imperial administration, and it consisted mostly of new families that had emerged in the course of the second century. Almost all of these families were initiates of Sol Invictus, which, as we have seen, had seized possession of the administrative bureaucracy and the army. It was an occupation so complete that by the end of the second century, Sol Invictus was even able to get its hands on the imperial office. Born within the palace at the time of the Flavians, the organization of Mithras never strayed far from there throughout its existence. From the time of Trajan onward, as we have seen, it was a presence in his personal bodyguard, the Praetorians. Yet it was also present in the more intimate circle of palace functionaries, until it succeeded in gaining among its ranks the emperor himself.

Fundamental to understanding the priestly family's strategy is Porphyry's assertion that an adept could be initiated to the mysteries of Mithras only from the fourth grade upward: people from outside the priestly family could be affiliated with the first three grades. These outsiders could then be influenced and maneuvered by the members of the priestly family, who were the only ones to have access to the higher levels, the very existence of which had to be unknown at the first level of the Mithraic organization.*

On the death of Marcus Aurelius, probably the most zealous and efficient persecutor of Christianity of the emperors who succeeded Nero, the Empire passed to his son Commodus, who was initiated into the Mithraic organization. For more efficient influence over Commodus, he was given a Christian concubine, Marcia, who, for the entire duration of his reign (AD 180–192), had the prerogatives and powers of an empress. Commodus has gone down in history as one of the most ferocious and extravagant of the Roman emperors; he sent thousands of people to their deaths for the sheer pleasure of it. Among these people, however, there was not a single Christian, because he put an end to the persecutions of his father and showed favor to Christianity in every way.

---

*This type of structure is practically universal in esoteric organizations that feature initiation, including modern Freemasonry.

Commodus was certainly not of priestly lineage, and his unpredictability made him difficult to maneuver for the Mithraic organization, which eventually decided to eliminate him. (It seems the emperor had profaned the rites of Mithras by killing people while they were in progress.[2]) Marcia was the instrument of his elimination, and was helped by Quintus Aemilius Laetus, prefect of the Praetorian Guard, which, by then, was completely under the control of Sol Invictus. The substitute was ready: Publius Helvius Pertinax, a sixty-six-year-old illustrious unknown from Liguria, was named emperor the following day, January 1, 183. He was killed by the Praetorians less than three months later. In all likelihood he was also an initiate of Sol Invictus, because his successor, Septimius Severus (193–211), avenged his death ferociously, to the point of disbanding the corps of the Praetorians.

Septimius Severus, born in Leptis Magna, in North Africa, to an equestrian family of high-ranking bureaucrats, was certainly an affiliate of the Mithraic organization—he married Julia Domna, sister of Bassianus, a self-professed priest of Sol Invictus. This status must have been the key to his political success. On the death of Pertinax, he was governor of Gaul and resided in Lyon. He was proclaimed emperor by the legions of Pannonia, who were already by that time completely under the control of the Mithraic organization.

Septimius Severus showed favor in every way to Christianity and to the emerging equestrian class to which the branches of the priestly family belonged. They were by then well established in the provinces, but were finding it hard to penetrate Italy, which was still under the solid dominion of the senatorial nobility of Roman and Italic origin. His policy was aimed entirely at diminishing the authority of the senate, greatly strengthening imperial power, and raising the status of the equestrian order to which the imperial bureaucracy and the army belonged.

Under Septimius, the senate lost almost all its authority and played only a very small part in the administration of the state. Authority was instead concentrated in a group of friends and companions of the emperor who were chosen from among the equestrian order, the militaries and the most famous jurists (all of them, it must be presumed, belonging to Sol Invictus). To these functionaries was entrusted the status reserved previously for the senators, and they were always assigned positions that by right and by tradition were previously held by members of the senatorial order. In other words, Septimius's entire policy was aimed at favoring Christianity and eliminating the old Roman senatorial class by replacing it with men from his entourage belonging to the equestrian order.

Septimius Severus died in Britannia in 211 of natural causes. He was succeeded by his son Antoninus Bassianus (named after his maternal uncle, the priest of the sun), better known to history by the name of Caracalla, born in Lyon in 188. Caracalla, like Commodus, was accused of the worst possible crimes against humanity, but he never raised a finger against the Christians, to whom he did indeed show extraordinary favor. He was, however, much harder than his father on the Roman senatorial nobility, to whom he soon dealt a fatal blow. In AD 212, he granted Roman citizenship to all the free subjects of the Empire. Suddenly, the great families that had emerged in the boundless provinces under the aegis of Sol Invictus found themselves competing in terms of wealth and power with the Roman senatorial families, which were eventually swept away.

Caracalla was killed in 217 by his prefect of the Praetorian Guard, Marcus Opellius Macrinus, who succeeded in having himself elected emperor after three days. He did not last long. Following a series of ignominious defeats in the war against the Parthians, which had made him unpopular with the military, the Mithraic organization decided to replace him. In 218, an established member of the priestly family was elected emperor. Varius Avitus was a boy of just fourteen, son of the Roman senator Sextus Varius Marcellus and Semides, daughter of the priest of the sun Bassianus, brother-in-law of Septimius Severus. He was, by birthright, priest of the sun himself, and for this reason he was given the name Elagabalus (from the Syro-Phoenician sun-god).

Historians of the time attributed his election to a vague resemblance to Caracalla, insinuating that he was Caracella's son, born as the result of his rape of his cousin Semides. It is obvious, still, that a boy of fourteen could not have become the master of the world without the will and support of a powerful organization that possessed the principal levers of power—and this organization could have been none other than Sol Invictus Mithras.

More than emperor, the boy continued to be priest to his god. *Sacerdos amplissimus Dei Invicti Solis Elagabali* was what he liked to be called, and he wanted the sun to be raised above all other gods. His total disdain for the traditional pagan religion, culminating in the unheard-of sacrilege of his marrying a Vestal Virgin, earned him the undying hatred of the Romans, who attributed to him all sorts of iniquities. Worse still, he was notoriously infatuated with the Jewish, Samaritan, and Christian religions, which he dreamed of uniting in a single religion under his priesthood (a clear indication of his belonging to the Judaic priestly family). His ties to Christianity were strong and well known, so much so that he dragged Pope Callixtus into his own ruination. After less than three years of his reign, the boy was killed in a revolt by the Praetorians, and his body was thrown into the Tiber river. Immediately, the mob attacked the pope, slaughtering him along with the priests Calepodius and Aslepiades and throwing their bodies in the river to join their protector.

The young sovereign had disappointed the expectations of those who had raised him to the imperial purple by proving he was depraved and incapable. His killing was no doubt arranged by Sol Invictus, which, as we have seen, had complete control over the Praetorian Guard. In his place, another self-professed Sol Invictus priest was immediately created emperor: his cousin Marcus Aurelius Alexander, known to history as Severus Alexander (222–235), who was not yet fourteen years old and was the son of Mammea, sister of Semides. Alexander realized expectations and governed with wisdom and moderation, guided by the organization of which he was a priest. He too, of course, was a fervent supporter of Christianity—so much so that he raised an altar to Jesus of Nazareth in his own palace.

THE REACTION OF THE SENATE AND
THE PAGAN WORLD

Alexander Severus was killed at just twenty-seven years old, in a revolt by the army. Soldiers were irritated by his shameful conduct of a military campaign in Gaul and by his subjugation to his mother, Mammea. In his place, a former Praetorian from Thrace was elected, Gaius Iulius Verus Maximinus. He was an unfortunate choice, and for some time the situation seemed to slip from the hands of Sol Invictus. In 238, a popular revolt in North Africa was set up in opposition to the coarse and brutal neoemperor. Pro-Consul Marcus Antonius Gordianus, an eighty-year-old candidate from the ancient Roman senatorial nobility and a descendant of the Gracchi and of Trajan, was immediately acclaimed by the senate. He had put to death the prefect of the Praetorian Guard, Vitalyn, and all the supporters of Maximinus present in Rome. Gordian joined forces with his son Gordian II and barricaded himself in Carthage with irregular troops, but the Third Legion Augusta, stationed in Africa and entirely under the control of Sol Invictus, moved against the two Gordians, defeated them, and killed them.

On hearing the news, the Roman senate panicked, but in a last, desperate jolt of pride they named two emperors, Maximus and Balbinus, from their own ranks. They added as caesar the thirteen-year-old Gordian III, grandson of Gordian II on his mother's side, and they recruited soldiers from all over Italy to face up to Maximinus, who was preparing to invade the peninsula from Pannonia. Maximinus would have had no difficulty in routing the senate's irregular troops if he had not been killed in Aquileia by his own soldiers. The senate triumphed; the ancient republic appeared to have been revived and the two emperors seemed like the consuls of old. Yet it was a momentary illusion. That same year, on August 9, 238, the two emperors were slaughtered by the Praetorian Guard, which continued as ever to be under the control of Sol Invictus.

The young Gordian III was proclaimed emperor, but not before marrying the daughter of the prefect of the Praetorian Guard, Furius Sabinus Aquila Timesitheus, who actually held power. Three years later,

Gordian III and Timesitheus left Rome to fight, first against the Goths and immediately afterward against the Persians. In the course of this military campaign, in 243, Timesitheus died. The historians insinuated that he had been poisoned by the man who succeeded him as head of the Praetorian Guard, Julius Philipus, known as the Arab because he was a native of Bosra, the capital of Arabia Nabatea.* The following year, in 244, the seventeen-year-old Gordian III was killed by his troops and Philip the Arab was elected emperor. The usual gossipmongers insinuated that he was behind the killing of his predecessor.

Sol Invictus was again in command. Philip the Arab was the first emperor that the tradition of the church (according to the testimony of Eusebius)[3] openly declared as Christian. Both he and his wife, Otacilia Severa (of the family of the Severans and therefore of priestly origin), had a regular correspondence with one of the great fathers of the church, Origenes. Further, before admitting him to the church, the bishop of Antioch, Babylas, imposed a public penitence on him in expiation of a massacre carried out in Thessalonica.[4] To him went the honor of celebrating the millennium of the foundation of Rome in AD 247. This was an extraordinary irony if it is true that he was a direct descendant of Josephus Flavius, as we will see later.

Philip's public declaration of adherence to Christianity, however, cost the Christians dearly, for they were finally identified as being responsible for the misfortunes that had befallen paganism and the senate in the previous decades. Sol Invictus had complete control over the army, the Praetorian Guard, and the imperial administration—but given the absolute secrecy of its meetings and of the decisions it made, nobody at the time was able to perceive or understand the role it had in the management of public matters.

---

*Place of birth, however, was not very significant for the initiates of Sol Invictus, who, as imperial functionaries, always were extremely mobile. Indeed, seventy years later, the Pannonian Licinius, co-drafter with Constantine of the Edict of Tolerance issued in Milan in 313, declared himself to be a descendant of Philip the Arab. He was probably the son of an imperial functionary sent to Bosra.

The tough measures that were adopted against the senate and the outrages inflicted on the traditional pagan religion were attributed by contemporary historians to the depravity of individual emperors, whose elevation to the imperial throne, according to these historians' reports, was due to the caprice of the Praetorians or of the soldiers of one legion or another. These are ridiculous explanations if we consider that those emperors governed a population of more than fifty million people in a territory today divided among more than twenty-five nations. The Empire was held together as a result of the iron discipline of its soldiers. It is inconceivable that those soldiers (or the Praetorians) could have acted against the will of their officers. We know for certain that the majority of the officers, both in the army and the Praetorian Guard, were at that time members of Sol Invictus Mithras and undoubtedly carried out its orders.

It would appear, however, that the senate and the pagan world in general never identified Sol Invictus as being responsible for their misfortunes. The public profession of Christianity flaunted by Philip the Arab offered them, finally, a well-identified target against which they could work out their frustrations. It was then that the senate found the strength to react and attempt a restoration. In 249, Philip was assassinated by Quintus Traianus Decius, a general from Pannonia who bore the name of an ancient Roman senatorial family. It was Philip himself who had put him in charge of the Syrian troops who had then made him emperor. Once in Rome, Decius unleashed a violent persecution of the Christians, whom he may have perceived as being responsible for the assault on the Empire. He did not cause any serious harm, because the Christians were the wrong target, and also because he immediately had to go to the Danube to deal with a barbarian invasion. He died after just two years of his reign, in 251, killed in battle with the Goths.*

---

*Other emperors disliked by the Christians died in battle (or were captured by the enemy). The battlefield was the ideal place for getting rid of inconvenient leaders without being accused of assassination.

A violent and dramatic period followed during which there were simultaneously as many as four emperors, fighting among themselves and against the barbarians who were pressing all over the Empire. Eventually, in 253, Licinius Valerianus, who belonged to the senatorial nobility, prevailed, and he ruled for all of seven years, until 260. It is difficult to establish Valerian's position with regard to Sol Invictus—whether he was initially one of its initiates and at which level. Contemporary Christian sources, from Dyonysius of Alexandria to Commodianus, concur that in the first years of his reign, Valerian showed favor toward the Christians and "that his whole house was full of Christians and was a Church of God."[5] Then, however, in 257, he promulgated a persecutory edict that led to the deaths of Pope Martin and numerous Christian members of the clergy, the senate (which had already been "infiltrated" by numerous family lines of priestly origin, adherents of Sol Invictus), and the equestrian class. It also led to the confiscation of cemeteries and other ecclesiastical property. It was a persecution aimed at Christians of the highest classes only in the city of Rome,[6] and it was unleashed for reasons that remain unknown, though it is possible that it was due not so much to doctrinal motivation as to reasons of a political nature—or even to personal reasons.

As a result of the distinct separation between the church and the secret organization that controlled it, the latter came out unscathed from the anti-Christian persecutions of Decius and Valerian and continued to operate undisturbed. It created and eliminated emperors as it saw fit, although for reasons of prudence several of these emperors were presumably affiliated with the first ranks, and did not belong to branches of the Judaic priestly family.

Poor Valerian came to a sticky end unique among Roman emperors. During a military campaign in the East in 260, as a result of incredible and inexplicable imprudence on his part, he was captured by the Persian king Shapur and lived out the rest of his days in prison. After a few years of harsh detention, he was killed and his body was displayed in a temple. His son Egnatius Gallienus,[7] who had been associated with the throne, abandoned him to his fate and succeeded him in the imperial office. Gallienus was very clearly affiliated with Sol Invictus, because on the occasion of his investiture, he raised a huge statue to the sun in Rome, and he lost no time in taking measures that were obviously dictated by Sol Invictus.

The first of these was to revoke his father's persecutory edicts against the Christians by issuing an Edict of Tolerance (in 261) that gave back all confiscated property and, for the first time, recognized Christianity as a legitimate religion. From then on there would no longer be legal reasons for persecuting it. The second measure concerned the senate and was clearly intended to remove, once and for all, the last political force that was in opposition to the undisputed dominion of Sol Invictus and to subjugate it completely. The senate was stripped of the privileges that it had regained under his predecessors, and it was oppressed in every possible way, as it had been in the time of the Severans.

More important, Gallienus issued a decree that resumed a policy that had at one time been inaugurated by Septimius Severus and which was intended to lead quickly to the overwhelming of the ancient senatorial families through the accelerated introduction of families from the equestrian class (lines of priestly origin). He established that all those who had held the position of provincial governor or prefect of the Praetorian Guard—both positions reserved for the equestrian order—had the right to enter the senate. Despite these measures of great importance for Sol Invictus, Gallienus's throne was ensnared by a throng of claimants such as had never before been seen. He managed to prevail over all of them, but he died in 268, struck by a "stray" javelin during a siege in Milan.

He was succeeded by one of the most brilliant generals in the army, M. Aurelius Claudius, who earned undying fame by defeating the Goths, and for this reason he was deservedly given the title of Gothic. Unfortunately, he died that same year, in 270, of plague, which had been brought by the Goths. In spite of the brevity of his reign, Claudius was important for two reasons: First, he inaugurated the series of emperors native to Pannonia.* From then on, all the emperors and aspiring emperors for more than a century would be natives of this region, which had been a fiefdom of Sol Invictus since the beginning of the second century. Second, he figured among the ancestors of Constantine the Great, thus qualifying as a figure of certain priestly lineage.

On his death, the army named as emperor Domizius Aurelian, another officer from Pannonia. It is not known whether he was of Judaic priestly lineage, but he was certainly affiliated with Sol Invictus. It was he who, on his return from a series of victorious military campaigns in the East and in the Balkans, dedicated a magnificent temple to the sun in Rome in 274, and he proclaimed as holidays throughout the Empire the days dedicated to the sun: Sunday and Christmas Day. He was killed in a plot by the military organized by one of his scribes, apparently for personal reasons.

After his death, something incredible happened, something that had never occurred before: for seven months it was impossible to find anyone who was prepared to be emperor. The army and the senate bounced the choice back and forth among themselves. In the end, the old ex-consul Claudius Tacitus was forced against his will to accept the position, and he performed it with moderate success for nearly seven months, at the end of which he was killed, in 276, by the same plotters who had killed his predecessor.

The division within Sol Invictus was evident on this occasion, too, because the Praetorians elected the prefect of the Praetorian Guard, M. Annius Florianus, as emperor, while the army proclaimed M. Aurelius Probus, a valiant general from Pannonia, who had been Aurelian's right-hand man. Probus easily prevailed over his adversary and devoted the next five years to fighting the barbarians, who, from every direction, were attacking the Empire, as well as the new claimants to his office. He was killed in 282 by his soldiers, because they were annoyed at having been

---

*Actually, Decius too came from Pannonia, but the series had been interrupted by emperors of other provenance.

forced to plant a vineyard. This, at least, is what the chronicles tell us—but it is more likely that his death was decided by an opposing faction of Sol Invictus (of which Probus was an affiliate). The organization had already set up two different claimants against him, elected by the legions in Gaul and Germany and immediately eliminated by him. The true reason, perhaps, lies in Probus's policy regarding the barbarians, whom he settled in great numbers within the Empire: a hundred thousand Bastamae were settled in Thrace and Moesia and as many Vandals and Franks were settled respectively in Britannia and Pontus. Demonstrating this is the fact that M. Aurelius Carus was elected before Probus had even been killed.

Carus, as usual, was an officer from Pannonia, as well as prefect of the Praetorian Guard. He died the following year, in 283, apparently struck by lightning (but there are those who believe he was killed by his soldiers). He was succeeded by his son Numerian, who, however, did not long survive him. He was found dead in his litter, in an advanced state of decomposition, during a trip to the Middle East. The commander of his bodyguard, Gaius Aurelius Valerius—who, from his homeland, Dioclea, would later take the name Diocletian—took advantage of the situation to accuse Numerian's father-in-law, Arrius Aper, prefect of the Praetorian Guard, of having murdered his son-in-law. He tried him on the spot and immediately carried out the execution, strangling him with his own hands. After that, he had himself proclaimed emperor by the soldiers of his guard. It was a masterpiece of cunning, unscrupulousness, and ferocity if it is true, as was later insinuated by some historians, that it was he who actually killed Numerian. It was November 17, 284.

DIOCLETIAN

Diocletian deserves a section of his own, because, according to historians, it was through him that the senate and the pagan world made one last desperate attempt to react to the enemy that was in the process of wiping them out: Christianity. This analysis might even appear correct in hindsight, because, only a few years later, Christianity became the state religion. Yet in light of that period and of the protagonists of those events, it appears to be open to question. Christians at that time made up much less than 20 percent of the population of the Empire and held no positions of importance. All the levers of power were in the hands of the initiates of Sol Invictus Mithras. To speak of a last epic effort by the Empire to suffocate a religion that was legally legitimate is tempting, but surely it is a misleading exaggeration.

Diocletian himself was an affiliate of Sol Invictus Mithras,[8] as were all the high-ranking officers in the army. He was probably not of priestly lineage and was affiliated at the first level of the Mithraic organization—the one that stopped at the third rank. As we have seen, in the second half of the third century the job of emperor had become extremely dangerous and precarious. (This was demonstrated by the fact that after Aurelian, for seven months neither the senate nor the army could find anyone prepared to be emperor.) It is quite likely that the heads of the branches of the priestly family, who monopolized the higher levels of the Mithraic organization, were reluctant to take on the office themselves and preferred to govern through expendable pawns affiliated at the first levels—and were ready to eliminate them as soon as they deviated from their instructions or disappointed expectations.

It was a policy that seemed to work wonderfully well, until an exceptionally able and unscrupulous man such as Diocletian appeared on the scene. Of course, Diocletian was careful not to come into conflict with Sol Invictus, to which he remained faithful throughout his reign and with whose support he defeated and killed Carinus, the imperial candidate set against him by the senate. Initially, he even showed great favor toward Christianity to the extent of marrying a Christian woman, Prisca, and of allowing his daughter Valeria to be educated as a Christian. Further, he filled the court with Christians.[9] When he instituted the system of the tetrarchy, he chose his companions in government from among the ranks of Sol Invictus.

We should not forget, however, that Diocletian governed an

Empire in which over 80 percent of the population was pagan and that as emperor he was the head of all religions, a position he held in his capacity as pontifex maximus. None of the emperors who preceded him had renounced this office, nor would any of those who followed him for another century, even though they were self-professed Christians. Obviously, he did not renounce it either, but even on the subject of religion he displayed, at least initially, a behavior that was perfectly in line with the dictates of the Mithraic organization.

Indeed, after his victory over the usurper Carausius in 287, he had himself proclaimed son of Jupiter, assuming the appellation Jovius.[10] This was not, as it might seem, a challenge to Sol Invictus. In fact, it was exactly the opposite: Sol Invictus had developed a particularly syncretistic vision of God, as we will see in more depth later. Every Mithraic level was dedicated to a particular planet represented by a particular god. The statues of Jupiter, Mercury, Venus, and Saturn, and a rich symbology connected with them* were always present in the mithraea as expressions of the various qualities of that uniquely superior god in whom the initiates were required to believe, independent of name. With these statues were the figures of Minerva, the representative of wisdom, and Hercules, the symbol of strength. (Interestingly, in modern Freemasonry, the initiates must declare their belief in a Superior Entity, whatever that may be, and representations of Minerva, Hercules, and Venus are still present in all the lodges in the world.)

Diocletian's Jupiter was not the head of a swarm of minor gods, but rather the representation of the supreme god, perfectly in line with the philosophy of Sol Invictus and its symbology. The fact that then, in his capacity as pontifex maximus, he continued to give formal tribute to all

---

*The various levels of Mithraic initiation were linked to the planets. The fourth rank, the Lion, was dedicated to Jupiter and was often symbolized by a sheath of thunderbolts or an eagle with thunderbolts in its claws. In the Mithraic relief in Osterburken there are two scenes: in the first, Saturn (god of the seventh rank) gives the sheath of thunderbolts to Jupiter; in the second, Jupiter raises in his right hand the thunderbolts with which he is about to strike some giants.[11]

the other gods meant nothing. The Christian Philip the Arab did the same, as did all the subsequent Christian emperors, until 379, when St. Ambrose[12] forced the Christian emperor Gratian to renounce the office of pontifex maximus.

On the same day (July 21, 287) Emperor Maximian was proclaimed son of Hercules, another unequivocal Mithraic symbol, and he assumed the appellation Herculeus. The titles of Jovius and Herculeus then passed, in 305, to Galerius and Constans Chlorus respectively, despite the fact that Eusebius indicates the latter was a Christian.

The fact is that Diocletian and Maximian and their successors, Galerius and Licinius, belonged to Sol Invictus, and their loyalty to the organization is proved beyond all doubt by numerous historical testimonies and by an inscription that the four of them placed in a mithraeum in Carnuntum (a well-known stronghold of the organization) in 308. They had met in the same mithraeum, restored for the occasion, in an attempt to find a remedy to the extreme chaos that had been created in the Empire following the resignations of Diocletian and Maximian as emperors in 305. Before going their separate ways, as an undying testimony to their meeting, they had the following inscription placed in the mithraeum: "To Sol Invictus Mithras, benign protector of their Majesties, the successors to Jupiter and Hercules, devoted emperors, which restored the sanctuary."[13]

Marcus Aurelius Maximian, also from Pannonia, had been associated with Diocletian's government in the capacity of caesar in 285 and had been named emperor in 286. In 293, each of them named their own caesar, thus founding the system of government known as the tetrarchy. Maximian chose Constans Chlorus, who married his stepdaughter Flavia Maximiana Theodora, while Diocletian named Galerius Valerius, giving him his own daughter Valeria in marriage.

According to most historians, the tetrarchic system was devised by Diocletian to insure the enduring governability of the immense Empire. The system provided for its division into two parts, Eastern and Western, subject to the authority of an emperor. In turn, each emperor named a caesar who was destined one day to succeed him. To this caesar he assigned the government of half of his territory: a quarter of the Empire. If the objective was as stated by historians, it was an immediate failure—predictable even for much less able and worldly-wise people than Diocletian.

Actually, his real objective must have been that of ensuring his own position and personal safety by removing from Sol Invictus—at least, within his own lifetime—the initiative to create rival emperors.* Each of the four colleagues—all from the same geographical area, Pannonia, tied to each other by bonds of personal loyalty and committed to reciprocal support—was able to control the Mithraic organization within his own territory, thereby making it impossible to form coalitions capable of standing up to them at the same time. From this point of view, the system was very efficient, because it assured Diocletian and his colleague Maximian of undisputed government until they themselves decided to withdraw.

Yet it degenerated as soon as they withdrew into private life in 305, leaving the office to Galerius Valerius and Constans Chlorus respectively. In just two years, there were five emperors at the same time, to whom was added, in 308, a sixth: Flavius Licinius was appointed during the meeting of Sol Invictus in Carnuntum, without even having to be a caesar first. The other emperors in those years, proclaimed directly by their troops or otherwise convinced, were Flavius Severus Maxentius, Constantine (elected in Eboracum—York—on the death of his father in 305), Maximinus Daia (grandson of Galerius), and later Maximian (father of Maxentius and father-in-law of Constantine). This inunda-

---

*The historian William Seston expresses an opinion in the same tone. He maintains that the tetrarchic system was instituted to remove from soldiers and senators any possibility of influencing the choice of emperor, thus eliminating the possibility of usurpations and revolutions.[14] An analogous opinion is expressed by other historians such as Michael Grant,[15] who states: "The tetrarchic division, with its military implications, was a safeguard against internal usurpers, of whom, during the past half-century of political upheaval, there had been too many."

tion of emperors was in all likelihood provoked by the reaction of Sol Invictus to the anti-Christian persecutions imprudently unleashed by Diocletian, and it must have been aimed at finding candidates who would put an end to this madness. Indeed, this quickly came about.

As we have seen, Diocletian initially favored Christianity to the extent of filling his house—and even his bedroom—with Christians. The man who dragged him against his will into what turned out to be one of the bloodiest persecutions in history was his caesar, Galerius Valerius. Galerius, course and brutal but valiant and of proven loyalty to his lord, was Diocletian's dark alter-ego, and he eventually induced him, in 303, to issue a first edict that targeted the property of the church and places of worship, probably with the aim or the excuse of raising financial resources.

Galerius hated the Christians not so much for ideological reasons, for he ended up asking to be included in their prayers,[16] as for petty personal reasons. This hatred had been instilled in him by his mother, Romula, who had sworn revenge for a series of grave slights by some Christian noblewomen who had absented themselves from her receptions on the pretext that the receptions had been arranged during times of fasting and prayer.[17]

It may seem a banal reason as the main cause of the spilling of so much Christian blood, but matters of these kinds can easily degenerate into mortal hatred and give rise to unheard-of massacres if the person who feels that hatred happens to hold absolute and uncontrollable power. Historical examples are innumerable: to give just one, Caracalla exterminated tens of thousands of citizens in Alexandria and divided their city in two with a wall just because they had given him a derisory nickname.[18] On the other hand, Diocletian's pretext for justifying his first anti-Christian edict, inspired by Galerius, seems no less banal. According to the Christian historians Eusebius and Lactantius, it was due to the complaints of some pagan diviners who attributed the failure of one of their prophesies to the presence of Christians who had made the sign of the cross. Actually, no persecutory edict followed that episode: the enraged emperor ordered all those who had been present to make sacrifices to the gods and then extended the obligation to all the palatines and all the soldiers. If they refused, they were forced to resign.[19]

Some bloodless purges followed in the army and among the palatines, coordinated by a special office in the imperial palace in Nicomedia. When this office was burned down in 302, Diocletian interpreted it as intimidation and reacted, after long consultations with Galerius, by promulgating in February 303 an edict that ordered the destruction of the basilicas and the liturgical books of the Christians.[20] A new fire broke out immediately afterward in the imperial palace in Nicomedia.[21] The Christians were blamed (probably rightly so), and this triggered an angry reaction from the sovereign, who immediately had priests and deacons of the city arrested and executed. Following this, that same year and the next, there were issued three other edicts, all on the instigation of Galerius, which imposed the performance of sacrifices to the gods first on priests and then on all Christians.[22]

It is probable that Diocletian did not at all intend to trigger a duel to the death with the Christian religion, as is supposed by most historians, and that he was the first not to believe in the effectiveness of his own edicts. He did very little to enforce their application. At first, he limited himself to executing the perpetrators of the fire in Nicomedia, a few army officers (the famous Four Crowned Saints), and some prelates. There is no evidence in the chronicles that he personally went much further. In any case, he stopped all persecutory acts two years later, in 305, when he withdrew into private life in his splendid villa in Solona. We should not overlook the probability that this decision was in some way encouraged by his desire to get out of the crisis provoked by his edicts.

In Rome, where Augustus Maximian ruled, the application of the edicts was much blander, limited to the confiscation of some of the church's property, and the prosecution ceased completely in 306, when his son Maxentius, who was proclaimed augustus by the troops, reestablished freedom of worship and returned all confiscated property. In the prefecture of Gaul, though, the fiefdom of Constans Chlorus, father of

Constantine the Great, the persecutory edicts were not applied at all and the Christians remained undisturbed.

Only in the East did Galerius take advantage of the edicts that he had inspired to vent his deep-rooted hatred, indulging himself in an orgy of blood, which the reports of the martyrologists have made famous among Christians throughout the ages (although it is the unanimous opinion of Christian historians that they were highly exaggerated). In this he was helped and even outdone by his nephew Maximinus Daia (his sister's son and therefore also brought up with a hatred of Christians instilled by his grandmother Romula), who was created augustus in 306 and placed in charge of the government of Syria and Egypt.

Galerius, however, like his predecessors and Diocletian, did not even touch the Mithraic organization to which he continued to belong and whose decisions he had to accept. At the summit meeting in Carnuntum in 308 an old fellow soldier, Licinius, was placed at his side as augustus, with the job of bringing him back to reason.

According to analysis, Flavius Licinius, another officer from Pannonia and self-professed member of Sol Invictus, certainly belonged to a family of priestly origin. Indeed, Eusebius, before his conflict with Constantine, exalted him as a Christian of sure faith as much as Constantine was. He declared himself to be from a Christian family when he stated that he was a descendant of Philip the Arab. The prayer that he imposed on his army to recite before every battle had a clear Christian content, and he filled his court with Christians.

It was Licinius who eventually convinced Galerius to desist from his pointless persecution and inspired and cosigned with him the famous Edict of Nicomedia (or of Serdica), in April 311. This edict gave complete freedom to the cult of Christianity, and in it Galerius even asked the Christians to pray for him, hinting that the persecution had been the result of a "misunderstanding."* Five days later, he died, leaving

---

*In the edict, Galerius blames the Christians "for not having understood his intentions, and of having drawn the wrath of God to him, while at the same time begging them to pray to this God for him."[23]

Licinius free to confront the last enemy of the Christians, Maximinus Daia, who continued to govern Syria and Egypt.

With the Edict of Nicomedia, the great persecution, depicted by triumphant Christianity as pagan Rome's last desperate attempt to arrest its expansion, came to an end. If we examine the facts, however, we can see that this is absolutely not true. The persecution affected almost exclusively the Hellenized East, while Rome and the West were hardly touched. Moreover, the persecutors belonged to the same "pagan" organization, Sol Invictus, to which belonged those who put an end to the persecutions—from Maxentius to Licinius and Constantine. It is true, however, that this persecution gave them the pretext for a rapid and radical forced Christianization of the Empire.

12

THE CONSOLIDATION
OF POWER OVER
ROMAN SOCIETY

THE GENS FLAVIA

The shake-up caused by the policies of Diocletian and his right-hand man Galerius were healthy for Sol Invictus and provoked a radical shift in the priestly family's policies. From historical consequences, it seems that the priestly family decided no longer to entrust the responsibility of the Empire to people who did not belong to the priestly lineage, even if they were Sol Invictus initiates. Instead, only members of the priestly family would assume the imperial office.

The first result of this policy was the appointment of Constantine as augustus (proclaimed by the troops in Britannia on the death of his father) and Licinius (nominated at the Sol Invictus summit meeting in Carnuntum). In 312 Constantine eliminated his rival Maxentius*

---

*Maxentius was also a Sol Invictus and probably belonged to the same group of Pannonian priestly branches as Constantine. He was favorable toward the Christians to the extent that many Christian soldiers and officers served in his army and he had the full backing of the Roman clergy. Maxentius died at Milvian Bridge, but Constantine spared his father, Maximian, who was his own father-in-law. Maxentius was therefore Constantine's brother-in-law. It was a war en famille, as would become the norm and as it had always been in the bosom of the priestly family in the kingdom of Judah.

at the famous battle of Milvian Bridge, thus remaining sole master of the West. Directly afterward, at the beginning of 313, Constantine and Licinius met in Milan. There, they fraternally acknowledged each other's respective spheres of influence and sealed their agreement with the marriage of Licinius to Constantine's sister, Flavia Constans. They also agreed to eliminate jointly the last enemy of the Christians, Maximinus Daia, which they did soon afterward.*

The Milan meeting in 313 heralded a fundamental change in world history—not because on that occasion was issued the famous Edict of Tolerance, which at last gave full freedom of worship to Christianity, as is claimed by the majority of historians, who credit Constantine. Actually, the so-called Edict of Tolerance issued in 313 jointly by the two emperors was only a confirmation of the Edict of Nicomedia, signed two years earlier by Galerius and Licinius. It extended the earlier edict to the whole of the Empire and expanded some of its clauses (in particular with regard to the restoration of the church's confiscated property). Letters were sent to the provinces' respective governors with instructions for its application.† Ironically, it is from one of Licinius's letters, reported in full by Eusebius and Lactantius, that we know what actions they took.[1]

Credit for the confirmation of the Edict of Tolerance and Christianity's consequent definitive triumph was wholly attributed to Constantine, but it should have been shared equally by the two. But, as we know, the victor is always right. It was inevitable that sooner or later a

---

*The decisive battle against Maximinus was fought on April 30, 313, in the Campus Serenus, between Heraclea and Adrianople. There, it is said, Licinius made his soldiers say the following prayer to Deus Summus et Sanctus: "Almighty God, to thee we pray—Heavenly Father—to thee we pray. Each good cause we commend unto thee; our salvation we commend unto thee—our empire we commend unto thee. . . ."

†They started by exonerating the African clergy from municipal taxes and continued with the so-called Edict of Milan, "an excellent law and fully in favor of the Christians" (Eusebius IX, 9, 12), which finally allowed full freedom of cults, restored seized property to the church, gave the bishops a publicly recognized civil jurisdiction, and made Sunday (the day of the sun) a holiday.

conflict for supremacy would break out between Constantine and Licinius. After a few years of relations that oscillated between the fraternal and collision, in 324 they faced each other in a decisive confrontation. Constantine had the better of it and reunited the Empire.

The real turning point, however, was due to the two emperors' secret agreements, which settled once and for all the policy of the priestly organization—and thus decided the fate of the Empire. From that moment on, the conquest of civil society proceeded openly and extremely rapidly on two fronts: the forced Christianization of the Empire[2] and the destruction of what remained of the old ruling class and its substitution with new men. We can be reasonably certain that in the majority of cases these new men were members of branches of the priestly family.

If Licinius had won, history would probably not have changed much, at least regarding Christianity. Both Constantine and Licinius belonged to Sol Invictus; both imposed Christian prayers and symbols on their armies; both depended on Christianity and showed favor toward it in every way (Licinius perhaps even more openly than Constantine, because he could claim a direct lineage from the first Christian emperor Philip the Arab). In addition to being brothers-in-law, they both belonged to the same lineage, the Gens Flavia. In all likelihood, this was at the center of the agreements between Flavius Constantine and Flavius Licinius at their meeting in Milan in 313. We have already said that the decisions of the Mithraic organization were an inviolable secret of which we cannot expect to find any trace in any historical document. Of this particular detail, however, given its importance and resonance within the priestly family, there is perhaps an indirect mention in the historical chronicle of a contemporary writer, Aurelius Victor.[3]

In his chronicles *De Caesaribus,* he says that after the victory over Maxentius, the paters (an ambiguous term that can mean either the senate or the heads of the Mithraic lodges, who went by the name of paters) dedicated a basilica in Rome to Flavius Constantine. Directly afterward, he adds that *sacerdotium conferitum Flaviae Genti*—literally, "priesthood was conferred on the Flavian lineage."

A sentence of this kind is highly ambiguous from the pagan point of view. The only meaning that we can attribute to it is that a priestly body was instituted that was devoted to the cult of the Flavian lineage, and certainly not that the members of that family were made priests, for the office of pontifex maximus was automatically connected to that of the emperor. Further, from the Christian point of view, it makes no sense at all. It does make sense, however, from the point of view of the Judaic priestly family. To understand the meaning of this conferring, we must bear in mind who Aurelius Valerius was, who the Gens Flavia were, and what this meant exactly for the different interpretations of the word *priesthood*.

Valerius Aurelius, born in Carthage (like St. Augustine, his contemporary), was from an equestrian family and is defined as pagan by historians. He had a brilliant career in the imperial administration before 389, when he became prefect of a Rome that by that time was already completely in the hands of the Christians. It is inconceivable that in a situation of this kind the highest civil office would have been left in the hands of a true pagan. Valerius was surely a pagan as Constantine, Ambrose, and other emperors had been—that is, a member of Sol Invictus, in whose hierarchy he must have held a high-profile position.

Almost unanimously, historians state that the Roman senate at the time consisted in large part of pagans. Yet it is St. Ambrose himself who confirms that they were pagans exactly as he had been: he states repeatedly in his writings that the Christians constituted the majority in the senate.[4] This was confirmed in 383, when the Roman senate voted by a huge majority to abolish paganism in Rome and throughout the West.[5] Valerius Aurelius, elected prefect six years later, was certainly a high-level member of Sol Invictus Mithras with the rank of pater, like most of the senators at that time, and therefore he must have been well-informed of its secret matters.

Let us now see who these Gens Flavia—the lineage of the Flavians—were. Historians agree that they had nothing to do with the family of emperors of the first century, and they often restrict this definition exclusively to Constantine's family. This is certainly inexact; at the very least it must also have extended to Licinius's family. As we have seen, the cult of Mithras started to appropriate Pannonia at the beginning of the second century, and we can assume that Constantine and Licinius's ancestors arrived in the area exactly in that period. There can be no doubt that over two centuries they must have established a vast network of interrelated families that held an almost absolute prominence all over the region. (We must not forget that Constantine claimed to descend from the Pannonian emperor Claudius the Goth and Licinius from Philip the Arab. It was a genuine imperial dynasty.) Further, they were all connected through the Sol Invictus organization.

Finally, we must consider the interpretation of the word *priesthood*. As high-ranking members of Sol Invictus, those who belonged to the Gens Flavia were priests by birthright. In the Bible, however, and in Josephus Flavius, the attribution of the priesthood to a priest often means the attribution of the high priesthood, a status with which, in the Hasmonean tradition, the highest political office of the state was also connected. (The Hasmoneans combined within the same person the offices of king of Judah and high priest.) What Valerius Aurelius seems to have wanted to communicate in his writings, albeit it in a cryptic form comprehensible only to initiates (in order not to give away any secrets), is some information of extreme relevance: on that occasion, the high priesthood was conferred on the Gens Flavia.

What does this mean? From what we have seen from our examination so far, the imperial office from Commodus onward had been conferred almost exclusively on members of the Sol Invictus organization, independent of the rank they held in the organization and whether or not they belonged to whatever branch of the priestly family. This had caused an interminable series of internecine struggles, which had certainly not helped the cause of the priestly family.

At the meeting in Milan, the two Flavians, Constantine and Licinius, must have persuaded the priestly organization of Sol Invictus to decree that from then on the high priesthood—and consequently the imperial office connected to it—would go by right exclusively to their lineage. This interpretation of Valerius Aurelius's phrase may not be correct, but it is certainly plausible. A decision of this kind must have been made on that occasion, because from then on, all the Roman emperors were always and exclusively chosen from among the members of the Gens Flavia.

The presence of this name, Flavius, would become almost an obsession from then on among the members of the imperial families, starting, obviously, with Constantine. His father's full name was Marcus Flavius Valerius Constans Chlorus. His first wife (although she would go down in history as his concubine) was Flavia Helena. Constantine's mother and Constans's second wife was Flavia Maxima Theodora. Indeed, the name Flavius appears in almost all the descendants of Constans Chlorus, starting with Constantine, who, incidentally, also married a woman of the same gens, Flavia Maxima Fausta. From among them we can cite Flavius Julius Crispus, Flavius Julius Constantine, Flavius Julius Constantius, Flavius Julius Constans, Flavia Julia Constans, Flavius Dalmatius, Flavius Hannibalianus, Flavius Gratian, and Flavius Claudius Julian, known as the Apostate, the last representative of the Constantinian dynasty, but certainly not the last of the Gens Flavia, which would continue uninterrupted.

On the death of Julian, a general by the name of Flavius Jovianus was elected, and was emperor for a few months. His successor, Valentinian I, was the founder of a new dynasty of Flavians, which included Gratian and his grandson Valentinian II. Flavius was the name given to Theodosius, the Spanish general who founded the subsequent dynasty,* and it was also given to most of his descendants, both male and female.[6] Flavius was the name given to the general Constans, created augustus by Flavius Honorius, son of Valentinian. Flavius was also the name of the usurper Eugenius, created augustus by Arbogast in oppo-

---

*In Spain too, from which both Theodosius and Maximus came, the Gens Flavia has left in the toponymy clear signs of its dominion: the capital of Galicia, for example, is called Aquae Flaviae.

sition to Theodosius. Another Flavius was Magnus Maximus,[7] who, like Theodosius, came from Spain and from whom the most important province in Britannia took the name Flavia Caesarensis Maxima.[8] Flavius was the name of the Roman general who in 406 was proclaimed emperor in Britannia, with the name Constantine III. Flavius was the name of that Marcian who, in Constantinople, founded the dynasty that followed that of Theodosius—and Flavius would be the name given to Justinian, founder of the third dynasty in the East, who would be instated in Constantinople in 518, and so on.

Even Odoacer, once he had conquered Italy in 576 and had been created patrician, hurriedly assumed the name of Flavius. The fact that the name Flavius was adopted in adulthood even by figures who were probably not of priestly lineage does not in any way weaken the argument that the imperial office was reserved exclusively for the Gens Flavia. On the contrary, it strengthens it, because whoever aspired to the office—for himself or for his sons—hurried to assume the name, usually by having first married a woman from the Gens Flavia. This establishes a direct link to Josephus Flavius, who claimed descent from the Hasmoneans on his mother's side, and to the custom of the priestly class after Ezra's reforms: priestly status was inherited from the mother. This custom is still observed today by the Jews.

The Visigoth king Favritta assumed the name Flavius after marrying a Byzantine noble. He therefore felt entitled to ask Theodosius for the rank of patrician and a life annuity.[9] Similarly, Stilicho, thought to be of Vandal origin, took the name Flavius after marrying Theodosius's granddaughter, Flavia Serena. Marrying a woman from the Gens Flavia certainly did not confer on the consort any right to the imperial crown—but it did to their sons, because they inherited this right from the mother. Indeed, Stilicho planned to have his son from Serena, Flavius Eucherius, created caesar, and this was probably the reason he and his son were condemned to death. Odoacer, too, who for himself claimed only the title of patrician, dreamed of a future as emperor for his son Flavius Telane, whom he had proclaimed caesar.[10] It was a dream that must have cost him the throne and his life, because it was probably the reason that the Eastern emperor Zeno unleashed Theodoric's Ostrogoths against him.

The same fate awaited the Visigoth king Ataulf, who dreamed of an imperial future for his lineage (it was part of his hope for the restoration of the Roman Empire). In Narbonne in January 414, he married the sister of Emperor Flavius Honorius, Galla Placidia, who was captured during the sack of Rome in 410. The following year she bore him a son, whom he named Flavius Theodosius.[11] Ataulf was killed the following year by the Goths, and Galla Placidia was restored to her brother Honorius and given in marriage to the general Flavius Constans, who was of the right lineage and was immediately proclaimed augustus. From their union the future emperor Flavius Valentinian II was born.

Evidently, the "pure" members of the Gens Flavia were not prepared to tolerate competition from the "bastards" or accept them in their ranks, and they resorted to every means to eliminate them. Other barbarians in that period cultivated the same dream of the restoration of the Roman Empire through offspring. The Vandal king Geiseric, for example, gave his son Huneric in marriage to Eudocia, one of the daughters of Valentinian III who was captured in the sack of Rome in 455. He gave the other daughter in marriage to the Roman senator Flavius Anicius Olybrius, whom he managed to impose as emperor for some time in 473. His dream, apparently, was that of instating on the Western throne one of his own grandsons, who was legitimized for the imperial office by his mother.

Yet where did the Gens Flavia originate? The one certainty, as we have seen, is that they bore no relation to the imperial Flavians of the first century. It was a family that was clearly linked to Sol Invictus Mithras and had been instated in Pannonia since the beginning of the second century and immediately afterward in Spain, in the wake of the Roman legions stationed in Galicia, and in Britannia. It was a family that had spawned at least two emperors in the third century, of whom one was a self-professed Christian. We have seen, in fact, that Licinius counted among his ancestors Philip the Arab, who was certainly not an Arab, although he was born in Bosra.*

The Gens Flavia, then, was a family of priests, all members of Sol Invictus Mithras, traditionally linked to Christianity, and with an almost divine right to govern. Its members apparently drew on an ancestor named Flavius. It does not require much imagination to conclude that we must be talking about the descendants of Josephus Flavius, member of the first line of the Judaic priestly family, descendant of the Hasmonean royal family, founder of the Mithraic organization, as well as, on the basis of our initial reconstruction, promoter of the church of Rome.

In little more than two centuries, his descendants had completely and irreversibly taken control of that hugely powerful Empire that had almost annihilated his race, reducing it to exactly what the kingdom of Judah had been for the priestly family at the time of the Hasmoneans. Josephus Flavius's impossible dream had become reality: the Mosaic priestly family had become for Rome what it had been for Jerusalem at the peak of its power—mistress of economic and political power and undisputed arbiter of religion. Its direct descendants were its high priests as well as sovereigns of the Empire by birthright. The only difference was that outside the secret organization, nobody even suspected the existence of the Judaic priestly family and therefore nobody knew of the bonds of kinship and solidarity among the families who constituted the ruling class of the Empire.

CONSTANTINE'S SUCCESSORS AND THE CHRISTIANIZATION OF ROMAN SOCIETY

Let us proceed with our examination of the history of Rome, which acquires a completely new dimension and clarity in light of the priestly theory.

---

*The equestrian families that emerged from the imperial bureaucracy had great mobility, so the place of birth of a figure from this class is not necessarily helpful in establishing his origin.

First, it is understandable why Constantine spared no efforts in showing favor toward Christianity and spreading it as much as he could, to the point of proclaiming it, in 324, the state religion of the Empire. This was political opportunism, say the historians, according to whom Constantine decided to straddle Christianity because he saw it as a secure basis for his power. Yet it is difficult (indeed impossible) to accept this explanation if we consider the numbers involved. Out of a population estimated at fifty million inhabitants in the whole of the Roman Empire, there were no more than seven million, or at the very most ten million, Christians.[12] They were therefore a negligible minority that hardly made up 20 percent of the whole population and that was faced with an overwhelming majority of pagans. It was certainly not for political gain that Constantine married the Christian cause in such an open and decisive way, but rather because it was the mission of the family of which he was a member—the mission that he openly proclaimed to have been given by God, declaring himself "universal bishop."

Constantine died in 337 and was succeeded by his three sons, Flavius Julius Constantine, Flavius Julius Constantius, and Flavius Julius Constans. Despite the fact that the Council of Nicaea, promoted by Constantine in 325, had condemned Arianism as heretical, Constantine was himself baptized on his deathbed by the Arian bishop Eusebius of Nicomedia. Constantius, who succeeded Constantine, was an Arian, like his father. On his death in 361, one of Constantine's grandsons, Julian, came to the throne. He had been brought up as a Christian but was nicknamed the Apostate because he forcefully revived the syncretistic policy of Sol Invictus (of which he was an initiate), restoring the ceremonies and the pagan priestly colleges.

His policies did not last long, however. In 363, Julian the Apostate died under circumstances that were not very clear, during a military campaign against the Persian empire. The commanders of the legions of the West and East, who found themselves reunited in war, proclaimed as the new emperor an officer from Pannonia who had never before appeared in the historical chronicles: a certain Flavius Claudius Jovianus, whose chief merit seems to have been that he had the right name.

Despite being Christian (of Arian faith), one of Jovian's first acts was to confirm the primacy of Sol Invictus by excluding the concession of further privileges to the Christians. There was not enough time, however, for his intentions to become reality, because soon after, he was found dead in his tent, having almost certainly been murdered. The army commanders were fast and unanimous in their choice of a new successor, once again a Christian and once again from Pannonia. He too was unknown to the chronicles up to that point: Flavius Valentinianus (known as Valentinian I), on whom the commanders imposed the immediate appointment of a coruler. He presented his brother Flavius Valens to the army. Valens was also a Christian, but not baptized, like all the so-called Christian emperors of this period, and was proclaimed augustus.

The two brothers divided up the Empire between them: Valentinian took the West and established his court in Milan; Valens took the East and moved first to Constantinople and then later to Antioch. One of Valentinian's first acts was to appoint as leader of the troops in Britannia Flavius Theodosius, a Christian general from Galicia (another Sol Invictus stronghold). Theodosius defeated the Picts in Britannia, driving them into Scotland, then he drove the Scots, who had invaded Wales, into Ireland, and finally he liberated London from a siege by mercenary Saxon troops, thus pacifying and giving security to the island.

Some years later, in 373, Theodosius was sent to Africa to tame a revolt by the Berber tribes. For reasons that were never clarified, he was executed in 376 by Valentinian's son, Flavius Gratian, who had been proclaimed augustus in Amiens in 367 at the age of eight. Yet two years later, Gratian admitted his victim's son—who had the same name as his father, Flavius Theodosius (the future Theodosius I)—to the government of the Empire, making him augustus.

In the meantime, another Christian general from Spain, Flavius

Magnus Maximus, had been sent to command the troops in Britannia in place of General Theodosius. Despite the fact that Valentinian's family came from Pannonia and Theodosius's from Spain, it is blatantly obvious that we are talking here about the Gens Flavia. These two families were without doubt bonded by inflexible solidarity and also by ancient kinship, as testified by that shared name.

Magnus Maximus, co-religionist and fellow countryman of Theodosius, whose place he took in Britannia, was Theodosius's relative. His appointment could hardly have been a coincidence. Despite the fact that historians insist on defining him as a usurper,* it seems clear that he asserted dynastic rights that were no less valid than those of Valentinian and Theodosius and that he enjoyed no less support from the army and the country. Indeed, in 381 he had himself proclaimed augustus first by his troops and then, in 383, by the garrisons in Belgium and Germany, where he had gone to live in Trier, having abandoned Britannia. Maximus was recognized[13] and accepted by his fellow augusti, a sign that he was considered their equal, and vied with Theodosius in the struggle against the heretics. In the end, however, he allowed himself to be blinded by ambition to become the only emperor, and he clashed first with Valentinian II, forcing him to move out of Milan, and then with Theodosius, who, however, defeated and killed him in 388.†

Valentinian, Magnus Maximus, Gratian, and Theodosius dealt the fatal blow to paganism and what little still remained of the ancient Roman senatorial aristocracy. Starting in 368, Valentinian introduced a

---

*Historians refer to Magnus Maximus as a usurper who passed through Roman history like a meteor, without leaving a trace. It is definitely a false depiction, because Magnus Maximus was recognized as augustus by his colleagues Valentinian and Theodosius and left a deep mark on the history of the West, especially in Great Britain, where various reigning families declared themselves to have descended from him.

†A substantial indication that Theodosius and Magnus Maximus were related is the fact that once he had defeated and killed his rival, Theodosius saw—at his own expense—to the maintenance of Maximus's aged mother and the education of his orphaned daughters.[14]

large number of Christians into the senate, conferring the title of *clarissimus* (which went only to senators) on high-ranking functionaries of the court and also on army commanders. In 369 he seized the property of many pagan senators who had opposed him, he sent others into exile, and he put still others to death.

In 380, in Thessalonica, Theodosius I promulgated an edict that obliged all the Christians in the Empire to profess the faith of the bishop of Rome.[15] In 392, he promulgated a decree that outlawed paganism, forbidding any manifestations of pagan cults, including the Olympic games, which were held in honor of Zeus.

This measure provoked strong resentment, which was taken advantage of by the *magister militum* Abrogast, who in March 392 saw to the murder of Valentinian II (Gratian's successor to the Western throne) and the election as emperor of Flavius Eugenius. In return, Eugenius reestablished the syncretistic policy of Sol Invictus, once again allowing freedom of cult to paganism. This provoked the immediate reaction of Theodosius, who in 393 wiped out Eugenius and his whole army.

From that moment on, any manifestation of a pagan nature was completely forbidden throughout the Empire, and Christianity triumphed undisputedly. Of course, so did the many branches of the priestly family: Christianity's promoters and secret masters.

THE POWER OF THE SECRET PRIESTLY ORGANIZATION

From Commodus onward, the pagan world, despite its initial huge numerical advantage and its undoubted historical legitimacy, was impotent against both the Sol Invictus emperors and the subsequent Christian emperors. Indeed, it never managed seriously to threaten either, not even when, less than a century after Constantine had taken power, Theodosius handed down paganism's definitive death sentence.

It is clear that in the course of the second century AD, without realizing it, paganism had lost all control over Roman society, which had passed into the hands of the esoteric organization of Sol Invictus Mithras. Throughout the third century, Sol Invictus created and got rid of emperors at its pleasure. Only Diocletian managed for a while to evade its will with the system of the tetrarchy, but he never succeeded in denting its power. On the contrary, he determined a radical shift in Sol Invictus policy, with its consequent choice of the forced Christianization of the whole of Roman society.

It is equally clear that control over civil society did not pass immediately into the hands of the Christian emperors who put this policy into effect—not even after the official abolition of the pagan cults, including that of Mithras. It was an abolition that suppressed external public manifestations of a pagan nature but did not damage in any way the secret organization and power of Sol Invictus. Albeit under a different name, Sol Invictus continued to have an authority superior to that of the emperors themselves and to determine their political choices, especially in matters of religion. For a long time, it was still able to get rid of emperors whenever they deviated from its instructions.

The historical evidence in this regard is eloquent. In the course of a century, four Christian dynasties succeeded to the imperial throne. All of them issued from the same group of families, and all of them terminated in violent and often obscure ways—always for reasons connected with matters of religious orthodoxy. The first dynasty, the one established by Constantine, was jettisoned just as soon as his scion, Julian, betrayed expectations that had been placed on him and tried to save the pagan traditions by reuniting all the religions under a single syncretistic creed. The history of these vicissitudes is truly exemplary, because it clearly demonstrates that control of the secret priestly organization always remained in Rome, which never ceased to be the real capital of the Empire.

With the Council of Nicaea in 325, Constantine had decreed the condemnation of Arianism and the triumph of Catholic orthodoxy, sanctioning the primacy of the papacy in Rome over the church. He himself, however, then began to favor the Arian heresy, recalling from exile the Arian bishop Eusebius of Caesarea and having himself baptized, on his deathbed in 337, by the Arian bishop Eusebius of Nicomedia. (He was buried by his son Constantius II in the Church of the SS Apostles, which the emperor had built for this purpose.)[16]

Constantine was succeeded by his sons Constantine II and Constantius, both of Arian tendencies, who divided the Empire between them: the West to the former, the East to the latter. The third son, Constans, at the time just fourteen years old, remained landless. Unlike the first two sons, however, Constans was (or more likely came to be) of an incorruptible religious orthodoxy (although he privately led a scandalous life)—and therefore he had the full backing of the clergy and the Roman senate. Called to Rome, he was provided with a political secretariat and an army, which he used to defeat and kill his brother Constantine II at Aquileia in 343. At just twenty years old, he became the sole master of the West. In the following years there were various attempts to heal the fractures that had been created in the Christian world, but they all failed due to the intransigence of Constantius, who had bent the Eastern bishops to his will (while in the West it was the bishops who dictated Constans's policies).

The situation came to a head in 350, when Constans fell victim to a popular revolt led by a pagan officer from Gaul, Magnentius. In the face of this danger, the Christian forces regrouped. Rome accepted Constantius's envoy, his grandson Nepotianus, and the following year Magnentius was defeated (he committed suicide in Lyon in 353).

Constantius entered Rome as victor in 357 and imposed more or less Arian policies on the Christians, deposing some bishops and Pope Liberius, who refused to accept them.[17] With this he brought about his own ruin. In February 360 the army of Gaul proclaimed as augustus one of Constantine's grandsons, Flavius Claudius Julianus, who seemed to offer solid guarantees of religious orthodoxy, having been educated by a priest from Ancyra, Gregorius, who had obliged him to study the Christian theologians.[18] The church of Rome, of course, greeted his appointment with enthusiasm.

With his position in the West consolidated, Julian moved against Constantius, who, however, died in 361, before arriving at a direct confrontation. Becoming master of the Empire without striking a blow, Julian interpreted this opportune death as a gift of Providence and, in his capacity as pontifex maximus, thanked the Divinity with public sacrifices of the pagan rite. The Christian world, which had had such high hopes for him, was horrified and branded the young sovereign with the epithet Apostate,* accusing him of having carried out the worst possible infamies against Christianity and of wanting to restore paganism.

Actually, Julian (a zealous supporter of Sol Invictus) never did anything against the Christian church. He did not persecute the bishops, nor did he try to bring back paganism to its ancient splendor. His was an attempt of a very different kind, perfectly in line with his position as high priest of a cult devoted to the supreme God: from the measures he took directly after Constantius's death and the reunification of the Empire, it seems clear that he was aiming to unite the two religions—pagan (which, let us not forget, continued to be the religion of the majority) and Christian—under a single priestly caste. He even contemplated rebuilding the Temple of Jerusalem, and his plans fell through only because of an earthquake that took place as the work was beginning.[19]

It was probably a design conceived in his youth. In the solitude of the villa in Cappadocia, his tutor Maximus, in addition to assigning the Christian theologians, had started him off on Neoplatonic authors such as Porphyry and Iamblichus. From this fervor of study he had conceived the idea of fusing all the confessions in the Empire into a single super-religion with a single priestly caste and a unified, syncretistic liturgy.

He began by recalling from exile and reinstating the orthodox bishops that had been banished by his predecessor, and at the same time he published an edict restoring to paganism property and freedom of cult. He then devoted himself to the reorganization of the hierarchy of

---

*The appellation Apostate, incidentally, is not fully correct, given that the sovereign, like all his colleagues, was not baptized.

the pagan priests along the lines of the Judaic priestly organization. For every province, he created a high priest not only for the imperial cult, but also for the whole set of cults that paid tribute to the gods, including the Christian cult. With regard to these measures, we can read various letters by Julian that appear to be genuine encyclicals, or pastoral letters. In them the emperor deals with the recruitment, lifestyle, training, and payment of the priests; with divine services, which had to be held three times a day; with the foundation of convents for virgins devoted to the ascetic life; and with hospices. Moreover, Julian saw to the publishing of informational booklets for priests as well as books of instructions for religious teaching.[20]

It is clear from these measures that Julian had received priestly training at a high level, and that he felt he had been invested with a mission of epochal significance. Yet his vision turned out to be utopian. It was opposed by pagans as well as by Christians—and it was the Christians who eliminated him and decided to replace Constantine's dynasty (of which various descendants of Arian faith still survived) with one that was more reliable in terms of religious orthodoxy. After just two years of his reign, Julian was assassinated during a military campaign against the Persians. The official iconography has him mortally wounded in battle in the act of acknowledging the victory of his great antagonist, Jesus, with the famous phrase *"Vicisti, Galilee!"* Actually, Julian was struck from behind by a spear at the end of the battle—and the spear had definitely not been thrown by a Persian: the Christian historian Libanius says explicitly that it was a Christian soldier who killed him. The pagan Ammianus Marcellinus, however, who could not afford to attack the Christians, presents the event simply as a tragic accident.[21]

The army commanders immediately proclaimed a new emperor, but their choice did not fall on a member of the ruling dynasty, as it would be legitimate and logical to expect (it is practically a historical rule). Surprisingly, a new man, an officer previously unknown to the chronicles, Flavius Jovianus, was chosen. For history, one Christian dynasty had ended and another one had started. For the secret priestly organization, however, it must have been simply an alternation within the same group of families. Jovian, in fact, was a Christian, from the same region as Constans Chlorus—Pannonia—and from the same gens, as demonstrated by his name. These are coincidences that have always appeared fortuitous to historians, but cannot be considered so in the light of this new theory on the priestly family.

Neither can we consider as fortuitous coincidence the fact that Jovian was eliminated a few months later, as soon as he revealed his intention to proceed along the road of religious tolerance with regard to paganism. He was found dead in his tent.[22] The army commanders lost no time on an investigation, but immediately and unhesitatingly appointed a successor, once again ignoring the rights of the past dynasty. Again, it was a new man unknown to the chronicles, Flavius Valentinianus. He too was a Christian, he too was from Pannonia, and he too belonged to the same group of families.

It was 364. His dynasty would not endure even for thirty years. Again, the change would be brought about in a dramatic and bloody way and, what is more, with the collaboration (whether willing or forced is not known) of the family in office. The reason for the change, in any case, appears to be the usual one: religious orthodoxy. In fact, Valentinianus I, while conducting a ruthless fight against the last remnants of the ancient pagan aristocracy, was not equally intransigent in matters of Christian orthodoxy. His second wife, Justina, was an Arian, and she gave birth to Valentinianus II. He was just four years old in 375 when his father died and he was elected augustus. For the whole of his short life he was dominated by his mother, who favored the Arian heresy, dominant in the East, in contrast to the orthodoxy of the church of Rome, which was dominated at that time by the great figures of Pope Damasus and Bishop Ambrose of Milan.

The other son of Valentinianus I, Flavius Gratian, from his first wife Marina Severa, had a weak character and was subject to Arian influence—but after suffering a terrible defeat while trying to help the Arians in 379, he became completely loyal to Damasus and Ambrose and carried out their orders faithfully, to the extent of fighting with intransigence all the heretical churches. Indeed, he was the first Roman emperor to remove the mantle of pontifex maximus, eliminating the Vestal Virgins and the pagan priestly colleges.[23] It was probably on Damasus and Ambrose's insistence that Gratian, that same year, appointed as augustus Flavius Theodosius (whose father he had executed just two years earlier). Flavius Theodosius, being from Spain, was immune to the Arian influence and of safe orthodox faith.

So it was Gratian himself who prepared the substitution of his own dynasty,* and with this act he must have signed his own death warrant. The young emperor was assassinated in Lyon in 383 (at the age of twenty-four), apparently on the orders of Flavius Magnus Maximus (a Christian of sure orthodox faith and from the same region as Theodosius). His brother Valentinianus II came to the same end in 392, at just twenty years of age, killed by the barbarian Arbogast on behalf of Flavius Eugenius, a former functionary of Theodosius.[24] Theodosius became the only emperor, with the full blessing of the church of Rome.

Thus the third dynastic change of the Christian empire was complete. This was also determined by reasons of defense of religious orthodoxy (and therefore of the unity of the many branches of the priestly family that made up the secret ruling group of the Roman church). Once again, the choice of successor took place, as we have seen, within the families belonging to the same priestly branch—the Gens Flavia.

In the East the dynasty of Theodosius, who died in 395, continued with Arcadius and then with Theodosius II for another tormented half century. Then, in 450, there was a bloodless change of dynasty with Flavius Marcian, a soldier who became emperor by marrying Arcadius's daughter, Pulcheria. Marcian took up the cause of a group of Eastern

---

*Ironically, it was Gratian who saw to the execution of Theodosius's father just two years earlier. The reasons for this execution have always been a mystery, but it is probably not far from the truth to suppose that it was due to the fact that Theodosius did nothing to hide his ambitions for the imperial throne, to which his belonging to the Gens Flavia gave him right.

bishops who were trying to shake off the tutelage of the Vatican. In fact, he and his descendants progressively distanced themselves from Rome, favoring the monophysitic heresy, which imposed itself rapidly throughout the East to the extent that it caused a serious split in Christianity. It was this that eventually caused the banishment of his dynastic line.

On the death of Emperor Anastasius in 518, despite the existence of legitimate claimants to the succession, the commander of the Constantinople guard, Justin, was proclaimed emperor. He was a soldier from Illyria (a region where the noble families of Pannonia had taken refuge when Pannonia had been conceded by Theodosius to the Visigoths) and an orthodox Catholic devoted to the pope in Rome. The monophysitic heresy was outlawed and the unity of the church was reestablished.

His son Flavius Justinian tried to rebuild the territorial unity of the Empire, reconquering most of Italy and North Africa, but he got no farther than that. What is striking about this emperor (and about his father too) was his intransigent defense of the primacy of the bishop of Rome over the whole of Christendom. This is inexplicable for a sovereign whose capital was in Constantinople and who reigned over a territory of which Rome occupied a marginal and precarious corner. Logic and political expediency should have led him to transfer the religious capital to Constantinople, under his direct control, as his predecessors had unfailingly done and as would be done again half a millennium later.

This incongruence can be explained by what we have said so far with regard to the secret priestly organization that was instated in Rome and was preoccupied with maintaining the unity of Christendom. All previous dynastic changes were provoked for this reason. The succession, however, always occurred within the same group of families, all of them equally authorized to wear the imperial purple because they all belonged to the Gens Flavia.

Christian historians have seen in the events that characterized this century—so crucial for Christianity and for the whole world—the constant intervention of divine Providence. Non-Christian historians have seen a series of random events, bearing no clear relation to one another, miraculously imposing Christianity on the world. The hypothesis of the secret priestly organization, however, offers a clear and reasoned view of these events, showing how they correspond to a precise design, which develops logically. It explains why certain choices were made and it reveals the relationships linking the various protagonists.*

Direct documentary proof might not exist, but the evidence of the historical facts certainly favors this hypothesis.

---

*Even some episodes that Christian historians refer to generically as anti-Christian persecutions, when seen in light of the new hypothesis, appear more like an internal struggle in the priestly organization for control of the Christian religion than like persecutions perpetrated by pagans to suppress the new religion.

13

THE PRIESTLY FAMILY AND THE SO-CALLED FALL OF THE ROMAN EMPIRE

THE DONATION OF CONSTANTINE

Among the decisions made by the secret priestly organization directly after Constantine's victory, one in particular has always escaped the attention of historians, but had extremely important consequences. We have no direct proof of this decision, but on the basis of an examination of subsequent historical events, it is certain that it was made at that time—probably in Milan, on the occasion of the encounter between Constantine and Licinius in 313, at that Sol Invictus meeting that had given the imperial office in perpetuity to the Gens Flavia. As a collateral measure it must have been established that the seat of the Emperor and his administration would remain forever a long way from Rome.

It is incontestable that from that moment on no "Roman" emperor ever resided again in Rome, not even when the West and East had separate emperors. The last emperor to reside in the capital was Maxentius. Before having a tailor-made capital built for him on the Bosporus,

Constantine lived in Milan, Arles, Trier, Aquileia, Sirmium, and Serdica. Meanwhile, however, he continued to lavish enormous resources on embellishing Rome with monuments, basilicas, churches, and other grandiose public buildings.[1] There was a frenzy of building the likes of which few had ever seen before, and this constituted the clearest demonstration that the city continued to be the real capital of the Empire. Its position was never in question, and the flow of supplies needed to maintain its exuberant population was never cut.

So what was it that stopped Constantine from establishing himself in Rome? And why did the Western emperors decide in the end to make a little city in the middle of swamps—Ravenna—their administrative seat, while continuing to pour enormous amounts of money into the defense and maintenance of Rome? The explanations in history books are always vague, generic, and unconvincing, and are tied to the preferences of this or that person or to contingent circumstances at that moment. Apart from Diocletian, who lived there for only four weeks, all the Roman emperors before Constantine, whatever part of the Empire they came from, had always placed their capital in Rome. How do we explain that after Constantine no one ever thought of establishing their seat in what was still and would remain the *caput mundi*?

Was it a free and independent choice of all the Roman emperors from Constantine onward, or was it an imposition by the secret priestly organization? The first alternative seems unlikely; we must exclude it a priori. That leaves the second. In attributing the imperial office in perpetuity to the Gens Flavia, the secret priestly organization must also have taken measures to safeguard its independence and power. It was a decision that can be explained only by the existence of two powers: one public—constituted by the emperor, who was head of the army and the civil service—and the other secret—constituted by the priestly organization itself, and endowed with an exclusively moral power exercised by the Mithraic lodge system. Each lodge was presided over by a pater, who recognized the authority of the pater patrum, who resided in Rome, in the Vatican Grotto. Strictly related to the pater patrum was the religious power of the Catholic bishop of Rome, who from the same Vatican exercised his primacy over all the bishops in the Empire.

The two powers could not coexist in the same seat. The secret organization was the expression of the lines of the priestly family as a whole and it therefore claimed a power superior to that of the emperor, who belonged to just one of those lines. The organization did not fill directly any public office of a political, administrative, or military nature. Thus the only chance of insuring its own existence and independence was by keeping the seat of the imperial administration far away from Rome. Rome, moral capital of the Empire, was and had to remain the property of the priestly family as such, not of individual emperors. These emperors would inevitably have fought and neutralized a power that was both outside of their control and capable of influencing them. The only way to avoid this very real risk was to separate physically the civil and religious authorities, giving Rome a sort of extraterritoriality compared to the rest of the Empire—that is, making it a sort of modern Vatican *ante litteram,* with moral authority over the whole Empire, but especially in its western part, where it also had a sort of political primacy.

A precise and detailed reference to this decision is probably constituted by a famous document of the eighth century known as the Donation of Constantine. This is presented as a decree by Constantine addressed to Pope Sylvester. In it the emperor grants the pope and all his successors a higher status than his own secular throne, imperial honors, and revenues (*insignia et regalia*). He gives the pope the Lateran Palace, the city of Rome, and "all the provinces, places, and cities of Italy and of the western regions." As a result of this donation, he moved his capital to the East. He also declares the supremacy of the pope over the Eastern patriarchs.

This document was almost certainly written around 754, during the pontificate of Stephen II, and is therefore unanimously considered a fake, which is certainly true with regard to the form, but not the content. The historical evidence demonstrates that it faithfully reflects a decision made at the time of Constantine in that fateful year of 313, because from then on the de facto jurisdiction over Rome and central Italy was always exercised by the senate and the church. Moreover, the historical evidence shows that from then on, the whole Western Empire was an "area of influence" reserved for the pope in Rome, and the imperial authorities limited themselves to providing for its defense against internal and external enemies.

The decision to separate the seat of the imperial administration from Rome was always respected. Further, it certainly changed the course of history in ways that we cannot even begin to imagine. We can try for a moment to think how different the situation might have been if Constantine had placed his capital in Rome and if Rome had remained forever, as it had once been, the imperial seat. Would an Eastern Roman Empire ever have existed? Would the barbarians ever have prevailed over the West? Would the Roman Empire ever have fallen? What would have happened to the papacy and Christianity? It is pointless to hypothesize, but these questions give an idea of the historical significance of that decision, though no contemporary document gives the slightest mention of it. Nevertheless, factual evidence indicates it was indeed made.

This separation led to the division of the Empire into two parts, one subject to the religious authority of the church (or rather, initially, to the priestly organization that controlled it), the other to the political authority of the emperor of the East. Formally, the authority of both extended to the whole empire. It was a compromise that for a long time seemed as though it might work. For centuries, in fact, relations between the family's political leader, the emperor, and its religious leader were very good—albeit the two were often in conflict—and the two leaders sustained and legitimized each other, but in two worlds that were politically and territorially distinct and separate.

It was inevitable, however, that sooner or later they would split completely and go separate ways. We cannot doubt that the decision likely made in Milan in 313—the decision that forbade Roman emperors from residing in Rome—was the main cause of the so-called fall of the Western Roman Empire, which occurred just a century and a half later. Historians are almost unanimous in attributing the fall of the Western Empire to the incursions within its frontiers of an uninterrupted series of barbarian populations. An objective analysis of the facts, however, shows a completely different reality. The deposition of Romulus Augustus in 476 was the final act in the crisis of the imperial institution in the West that had begun at the moment that Constantine had built his new capital on the Bosporus. From then on, the emperor of the West, when there was one, always had limited authority that was completely subjugated—even from a purely civil point of view—to the interests of the church of Rome and the families that controlled it (the great landowners that constituted the new, omnipotent senatorial class in that part of the Empire).

This is evident since the death of Constantine. Then, Rome imposed as emperor of the West Constantine's youngest son, Constans, a Catholic, in place of his brother Constantine II, an Arian who was appointed by his father. Constans's successors Valentinian and Gratian were dominated by the church—in particular, by Pope Damasus and by Ambrose of Milan, who among other things forced Gratian to lay down the pontifical mantle and subsequently accept Flavius Theodosius, champion of Catholic orthodoxy, as augustus.

Though Spanish and elected in the West, Theodosius moved to the East as soon as he could. He was the last emperor to unite the whole Roman Empire under his dominion. On his death in 395, the Empire was divided between his two sons, Arcadius, who got the East, and Honorius, who got the West. This had been the usual way of dealing with such circumstances since the time of Diocletian—but this time, the division was definitive, although at that moment no one realized it. From then on, the destinies of the lines of the priestly family that were under the emperor, on one hand, and the pope, on the other, began to take different roads.

In the East, the priestly family came up against a progressive loss of power and autonomy in favor of the imperial office. The Eastern church became completely subjugated to the emperor, who of course tended to control any power capable of influencing his own personal power. The secret priestly organization, therefore, assuming it had a network of "lodges" in the East, was progressively deprived of significance and ended up disappearing.

In the West, however, the imperial office progressively lost importance and power until it disappeared completely, leaving power entirely in the hands of the organization of the branches of the priestly family and the pope in Rome, who was its expression. Honorius (395–423) and Valentinian III (423–455) were emperors more in name than in practice. Political power was actually in the hands of the army and those who commanded it, the three greatest military figures of the century: Flavius Stilicho, Flavius Constantius, and Flavius Aetius, who expressed the interests of the great landowners of Italy and Gaul—the greatest of which was the Catholic church. The emperors of the following twenty-one years were transient and insignificant figures who exercised no real power, but were in fact constant sources of instability and conflict.

In the end it was the Roman senate that decreed the "fall" of the Western Empire, as we will see. The imperial office died without trauma, leaving a West that was apparently subdivided among various independent barbarian entities, but which—under the guidance of the church of Rome and all Western bishops who answered to it—was actually more united and autonomous than it had ever been. This clearly testifies to the fact that the end of the Empire did not mean the end of the privileges of the priestly family branches. It merely heralded the beginning of a new phase in their history: under the protective umbrella of barbarian armies, which defended them against threats from all directions, their power, no longer influenced by the charismatic figure of an omnipotent emperor, became complete and stable in a way that it had never been in the past.

THE PRIESTLY FAMILY AT THE END
OF THE FOURTH CENTURY

To discover how the Judaic priestly family navigated through these vicissitudes, what part it played in them, and in what condition it emerged in the end, it is indispensable to establish first what position it had attained in Roman society at the end of the fourth century, at the peak of its power and expansion.

We have seen how the descendants of the Judaic priestly family that came to Rome in the wake of Titus in AD 70, through the Mithraic organization created by Josephus Flavius, immediately began to infiltrate the imperial administrative apparatus (as distinct from the senate), mercantile traffic heading for the capital, customs, the Praetorian Guard, and the army. Along with their presence in Rome and Ostia, in the beginning of the second century we find them instated in all the peripheral areas of the Roman Empire where there were important centers of imperial administration and frontier legions. They were family groups that possessed substantial capital, and their members were in positions of power in the nerve centers of the administration. They were blessed with innate entrepreneurial gifts, backed by a formidable network of interpersonal relationships, and supported by a powerful secret organization that was well established in the court and that had influence throughout the Empire. They cannot have had any difficulty in amassing large fortunes and emerging as the ruling class, especially in the regions outside Italy, where they did not have to face competition from the great noble families that made up the primitive Roman senatorial class—for these senate families were unwilling to leave the capital to settle in the distant and barely civilized periphery.

The family branches of priestly origin came to constitute the backbone of the so-called equestrian class, which emerged with the consolidation of the imperial bureaucracy, and which would eventually provide all its administrative managers. Starting in the third century, the emperors (apart from sporadic exceptions, such as Decius and the Gordians) always came from the equestrian class and always governed in clear opposition to the senate. These emperors completely relied on the equestrian families, which practically monopolized the civil service.

The extension of Roman citizenship to the whole Empire effected by Sol Invictus favored the consolidation of the positions of the equestrian families to the detriment of the senatorial nobility. Along with this came a dizzying increase in equestrian economic resources, which were invested in the formation of great landed properties. In the course of this century, the priestly family branches acquired (or rather consolidated) complete control of the army, Praetorian Guard (the prefecture of the Praetorian Guard was the last career stage of every bureaucrat of the equestrian class), and the civil service. They also collectively took over most of the economic resources of the Empire.

Conversely, their hold on civil society was a long way from being complete. Due to the favor of Sol Invictus emperors (and to the actions of the functionaries belonging to this organization), Christianity had spread discreetly but relentlessly throughout the Empire, to the extent that by the end of the third century, there were bishops' sees in all the main cities as far as its extreme frontiers in Britannia. Yet the vast majority of the population, at least 80 percent, was still pagan, and the Roman senate, though largely stripped of its powers and prerogatives, humiliated, impoverished, and already infiltrated by a majority of families of equestrian origin, still possessed a substantial nucleus of ancient Roman and Italic noble families. These were custodians of the pagan traditions, and as such, they were still able to constitute a pole of attraction for the majority of the population. It was this that made possible paganism's last swish of the tail at the time of Diocletian and Galerius. This in turn eventually made the descendants of the priestly family decide to proceed with the forced Christianization of the Empire and the complete marginalization—if not the actual physical elimination—of what remained of the original Roman ruling class.

Despite its numerical inferiority in 324, Christianity was proclaimed state religion of the Empire and paganism was subjected to a growing series of restrictions, until it was completely prohibited in 380 by an edict of Theodosius that was confirmed by the Roman senate in 383. In 393, Theodosius also prohibited all holidays and public manifestations that were linked to paganism, including the Olympics. In fact, the last Olympics were held that year. By the end of the fourth century, therefore, every single Roman citizen was Christian—at least formally—and subject to the authority of a bishop.

The elimination and substitution of the ancient Italic and Roman senatorial nobility proceeded at the same pace.* The strategy adopted for this purpose by the Christian emperors in the fourth century was, however, very different from that of Sol Invictus emperors in the third century. The Sol Invictus emperors placed themselves in open opposition to the senate, humiliating it, depriving it of its prerogatives and wealth, and striking it physically with the exile and execution of a great number of its high-profile members. Further, they completely relied on the equestrian class for the civil and military administration of the state. The Christian emperors, instead, restored to the senate—at least officially—the central role it had always had, reintegrating or even increasing its ancient privileges, but not before they had completely replaced the original senatorial families with others from the equestrian class.

The policy of introducing equestrian families into the senate had been initiated by Septimius Severus and imposed by decree by Gallienus (who, we must remember, was also the author of the first Edict of Tolerance toward Christianity in 261). As we have seen, it established that all those who had had the position of provincial governors or prefects of the Praetorian Guard, both appointments reserved for the equestrian order, would enter by right into the senatorial order. This right was then extended by the Christian emperors to other categories of functionary, starting with the so-called *comites* (the future comtes, or counts)—who were both civilian and military functionaries chosen by

---

*The senatorial nobility of ancient republican origin had already been renewed in the first century AD. Tacitus (*Annals,* III, 55) states that between the Battle of Actium and the reign of Vespasian, the senate had been gradually filled with new families from Italian cities and colonies.

the emperors from among their own companions in arms (or in lodge)—and extending to the great bureaucrats and high-ranking army officers. Within a few decades, virtually the whole equestrian class passed into the ranks of the senate, outnumbering the families of the original Italic and Roman aristocracy.

At the same time, the old guard was subjected to a campaign of persecution both on the physical level, with executions and exile, and on the economic level, with expropriations and selective taxation. These ended up by wiping them out completely. From the economic point of view, the Christian emperors did everything in their power to favor members of the lines of the priestly family. To start with, the bishops were exempted from taxes and revenues, and property was guaranteed to the churches. Then a series of laws was introduced that favored the formation of great landed properties in the "right" hands, which were in turn exempted from the payment of taxes. The final measure, which was to complete the transformation of the senatorial class (the noble class of the Empire) was the reform introduced by Valentinian I. This subdivided the senators into three levels based not on the antiquity or nobility of the family or on the positions held, but exclusively on the wealth of the family measured on the basis of landed property. The wealthiest were at the top, forming the true senatorial class, the poorest were at the bottom. Naturally, in accordance with the thesis that we have been developing up to now, at the top there must have been only descendants of the family of priestly origin, which by that time had taken over almost all the arable land.*

For these descendants, the fourth century was a golden time. There were two career paths open to any young man of this status—such as, for example, the young Jerome, who was born in Pannonia, the region from which all the Christian generals of the first imperial dynasties came: the

---

*Actually, the great landowners were Christians (for example, Basil of Caesarea; St. Melanie, who owned sixty farms, each of three hundred hectares; and so on) and were exempt from the payment of taxes. Evidently, they were all members of branches of the priestly family.

bureaucratic career or the religious one. The first offered the prospect of rapid and immense enrichment, but the second was not without its satisfactions, given the enormous expansion that Christianity enjoyed in those years and the dizzying increase in the ecclesiastical patrimony (due to the generous donations and tax exemptions of the Christian emperors).

A testimony to the "land of plenty" atmosphere that reigned among the ecclesiastical hierarchies in that golden period is provided by a pagan historian, Ammianus Marcellinus, who writes:

> Those who set themselves to reach the much-sought-after pontificate use every weapon at their disposal, because they are sure that, once elected, they will become rich with the offerings of the matrons, ride in luxuriously fitted carriages, and take part in elegant banquets that surely surpass those laid on the royal tables. The bishops could bring a positive contribution to the life of the people, if they would only disdain the riches of Rome . . .[2]

These are words that we have seen confirmed by Jerome during his Roman sojourn.

SOL INVICTUS AND THE PAGAN RELIGIONS

Most historians think that toward the end of the fourth century, the Roman senate still had a pagan majority. This opinion is motivated by the fact that in 380 a statue of Victory still dominated the hall of the senate, and most senators were ministers of pagan cults. In addition, surviving were the Vestal Virgins, who kept alight the sacred fire of Vesta.

In 382 in Milan, Emperor Gratian promulgated an edict for the suppression of the emperor's title of pontifex maximus; for the abolition of the maintenance of the Vestal Virgins and the other priestly colleges in Rome; and finally for the removal of the altar opposite the statue of Victory, where incense was burned at the beginning of every sitting of the senate.[3] Symmachus, one of the richest and most influential senators, went to Milan to persuade the emperor to revoke the measure, but he was not even received.

The following year, in 383, the senate almost unanimously approved the decree, voting for the abolition of paganism and all its symbols in Rome and throughout the Western Empire. That same year, Gratian died in Lyon, killed by an emissary of Flavius Magnus Maximus. Symmachus took advantage of this to make another attempt. Elected prefect of the city of Rome, as well as pontifex maximus representing the emperor, he wrote a letter to Valentinian II, urging him not to diverge from the tradition of tolerance toward the symbols of the ancestral religion that had been upheld by his predecessors, which had shown itself to be so useful for the security and prosperity of the Empire. The letter was refuted point by point by the bishop of Milan, Ambrose, who persuaded Valentinian to reject it. Two years later, on November 3, 386, the last public remnants of the cult of the sun were canceled by a decree that transformed the *dies solis,* instituted by Aurelian, into *dies dominicus,* or Sunday, the day of the Lord.[4]

According to historians, the open and passionate defense of the syncretistic tradition of Sol Invictus made by Symmachus in the name of the majority of the senators is clear testimony to the fact that these senators were still pagans. If this means they were not baptized, it is certainly true. That they were pagans in the true sense of the term, however, is unsustainable: they were pagans exactly as Constantine and Ambrose had been. Indeed, Ambrose, who came from a senatorial family and who must have known a great deal more about Roman matters than modern historians do, stated several times that it was the Christians who were in the majority in the Roman senate.[5]

That the more-or-less openly Christian senatorial families were in the majority is also proved by the words of Marcellinus and Jerome when they state that the Roman matrons (belonging to senatorial families) generously subsidized the Catholic clergy. It is equally true, however, on the basis of incontrovertible historical and archaeological testimonies, that the majority of the senators in the fourth century were initiates of Sol Invictus and, therefore, technically pagans according to historians. The most important testimonies come from the Vatican itself, from the basilica of St. Peter, built on the site of a Mithraic temple: the so-called Frigianum, which was in use up to the end of the century[6] (that is, for at least sixty years after the basilica had been erected by Constantine in 322). On the foundations of the basilica's facade have been found numerous devotionals written in a period of time (305 to 390) by Roman senators who included their religious titles—among which stands out the title of pater of the Mithraic cult. As many as nine of the senators who appear on the list hold the title of pater patrum— that is, supreme head of the Mithraic organization—which confirms that it resided in the Vatican.

Also in St. Peter's Square, a marble altar was found in 1949. It had been dedicated to Mithras on July 19, 374, by the pater patrum Alfenius Caeionius Julius Camenius, a senator who appears in various other Roman inscriptions and who was a cousin of Emperor Julian.

Various Roman mithraea are clearly connected to senatorial residences and bear inscriptions with the titles of their owners. In the Campus Martius, where the Sol Invictus temple erected by Aurelian stood, a series of dedications celebrate the promotion to a higher rank of members of the Mithraic organization in the years 357, 358, 359, 362, and 376. Along with those who had been promoted, there are also the names and titles of the officiants, the pater patrum Nonius Victor Olympius and his sons, Aurelius Victor Olympius and Aurelius Victor Augentius, both paters. All the figures cited are *vires clarissimi*—senators.

Among the other senators indicated in the inscriptions as paters of the Mithraic organization are Ulpius Egnatius Faventius, Junius Postumianus, Caelius Hilarianus, Rufius Caeionius Sabinus, Sextilius Agesilaus Aedesius, C. Rufius Volusianus, Publius Caeionius Caecina Albinus, and Vettius Agorius Praetextatus. This last, who held the supreme rank of pater patrum, is well known from the chronicles of the time and is considered by historians, together with Symmachus and Flavianus, as the main exponent of pagan senators' resistance to Christianity. Yet it was he in 367, as prefect of Rome, who personally defended Pope Damasus, driving the antipope Ursinus out of the city and absolving Damasus of the charge of murder.* In addition, he was prefect of the Praetorian Guard for Italy, Illyria, and Africa in 383, when the senate voted solidly for the abolition of paganism.

The senator Varius Nicomachus Flavianus, Symmachus's cousin, also figures among the paters of Mithras. This did not prevent him from interfering in the affairs of the Christians, supporting the Donatist heresy in Africa in 377 (for which he was punished by Valentinian), or from being appointed prefect of the Praetorian Guard for Italy by the devoutly Christian Theodosius in 389. In this office, in Milan in 391, he published an edict for the proscription of paganism, directed at the prefect of Rome, Clodius Albinus.[7] In it he reasserted the ban on any public or private sacrifice, including the traditional ceremonies of the state still in use in Rome, and the closing down of the temples.

The archaeological and historical evidence therefore confirms that virtually the whole of the Roman senate was made up either of paters of Sol Invictus or self-professed Christians (none of whom, however, had been baptized).

This same evidence reveals an important and interesting point that has always escaped analysis by historians and which has not been mentioned here. The inscriptions that appear in the Frigianum and on other Roman Mithraic monuments reveal a fundamental aspect of Sol Invictus: it is crystal clear—and perhaps shocking—that the organization had infiltrated not only the civil service, Praetorian Guard, and army, but also the traditional pagan religions of the Roman Empire. Which is quite natural for an organization of priests who were determined to conquer all the levers of power and who were more aware than anyone that religion constitutes the most important and enduring power in a society.

---

*On the election of Pope Damasus in 366, two opposing factions clashed, resulting in about a hundred deaths.

It is true that Christianity remained their original and favorite creation, destined in the long term to take control of the whole of Roman society. In the meantime, however, Sol Invictus could not have ignored one of the fundamental pillars of the state: the traditional religion. The Sol Invictus emperors, like their Christian counterparts, never renounced the office of pontifex maximus, supreme head of all the religions, until the eve of the complete suppression of every pagan cult. Yet the inscriptions on the Mithraic monuments prove conclusively that they also infiltrated the individual pagan cults, occupying the highest offices of their respective priestly colleges, at least with regard to Rome and the West. In fact, alongside the titles of *vir clarissimus* (senator), magister, hieroceryx, pater, or pater patrum* in the cult of Sol Invictus Mithras, all the senators who figure in the Roman Mithraic inscriptions also list a long series of other religious offices: *sacerdos; hierophanta; archibucolus* of Brontes or of Hecate, Isis, and Liberius; *maior augur; quindecimvir sacris faciundis;* and finally even pontifex of various pagan cults. Further, they were in charge of the college of the Vestal Virgins and of the sacred fire of Vesta. In the senate, there was no manifestation of cult tied to the pagan tradition that was not celebrated by a senator adhering to Sol Invictus.

That senator, almost certainly, was backed up by a Christian family, and it is likely that he himself, in private, shared its doctrine. This did not stop him from exercising in public, with dignity and conviction, the duties that his pagan priestly office required. (As we have seen, Christian emperors, too, exercised the duties of pontifex maximus, which involved invocations and sacrifices to the pagan gods.) All the members of Sol Invictus were priests by birth and believed in a single Superior Entity. In the course of the second and third centuries, however, they had formulated a singular syncretistic philosophy that allowed them to reconcile monotheism with the multiplicity of

---

*There were seven ranks in the Mithraic organization, but no senator ever held a rank lower than that of pater.

pagan divinities: these were considered expressions or aspects of the recognized unique divinity represented by the sun.* This philosophy was expressed explicitly in the writings of various Mithraic exponents, among whom was the last pater patrum, the senator Vettius Agorius Praetextatus. It is also dealt with in an in-depth way by the writer Macrobius, proconsul in Africa in 410 (a fully Christian era), in his work *Saturnalia*. This work collects conversations from among the most authoritative scholars of the time who met in Rome, at Praetextatus's house, and in the houses of Nicomachus Flavianus and Aurelius Symmachus. These three men were the great senatorial defenders of the pagan tradition of Sol Invictus.

This explains why all the main pagan divinities found hospitality in the mithraea and why devotees of Mithras declared themselves to be sons of Jupiter and Hercules and did not disdain to preside over the priestly colleges of divinities considered competitors. It also explains Julian's attempt to unify all the religions, because there was nothing else he could do but officialize a situation that already existed in practice (although he obviously met decisive opposition from the Catholic hierarchy, for this recognition meant equating Christianity and the pagan religions and putting all on the same level). Further, it explains why, in Rome and in the West in general, the pagans seldom resorted to violence against the Christians (unlike in the Hellenized East); why the Roman senators voted solidly in favor of the abolition of pagan cults; why the Roman population, notoriously ready to rise up for any trifle, accepted the decree without question; why, directly after the decree, the senate and the Romans immediately discovered themselves to be Christians; and so forth.

---

*This identification might seem to contrast with the Jewish concept of divinity. We should not forget, however, that the Jewish God was indicated by the name El or Elyon. The affinity with the Greek name of the solar divinity—Helios—could not have gone unnoticed in the profoundly Hellenized Jewish society, and in particular by Josephus Flavius.

THE PRIESTLY FAMILY AND THE ROMAN SENATE

The fervent and passionate advocacy of Symmachus in favor of the conservation of the pagan symbols in the senate should be seen more as an attempt to defend the many power centers of Sol Invictus, rather than as an impossible attempt to restore paganism, as historians have interpreted it. We cannot underestimate what has been insinuated by some historians (Gibbon, for example): it was also motivated by the desire to conserve the rich stipends that were tied to religious offices. After all, a river of money dried up with the abolition of the pagan temples. This explains why Symmachus was not punished for his action. On the contrary, he was actually raised to the consulate by Theodosius, the most fanatical, intransigent, and antipagan of the Christian emperors. It also explains why Symmachus's family immediately became one of the pillars of Christian Rome, providing, eventually, men of government, popes, and even a saint.

It is not clear when the family entered the senate or what its origins were. At the time of Septimius Severus a certain Symmachus, known as the Ebionite—who supposedly translated the Bible taken from Epiphanius and Jerome—enjoyed great renown among Christians. He is cited as a Judaean who converted to Christianity, but it is probably not just a simple coincidence that he was called Symmachus and that he lived in the time of Severus, to whom many equestrian families owed their good fortune. In 319, a certain Aurelius Julian Symmachus, grandfather of the senator in question, was proconsul in Achaea (or, according to others, vice-prefect in Macedonia). He was therefore an imperial functionary of the equestrian class. This office gave him the automatic right to pass into the senate. His son Aurelius Avianus Symmachus, who was prefect of Rome in 364, was in fact a senator. There can be no doubt that the Symmachuses at the end of the fourth century, one of the richest senatorial families in the whole of the Roman Empire, were of priestly status.

Some (not many) Roman senatorial families in the fourth century had names that were also found in the republican era. Yet this does not necessarily mean that there was a direct genealogical lineage. We have seen this with regard to the Gens Flavia, which had no genetic relationship to Vespasian's family. In ancient Rome nothing was easier than usurping the name of a great family. It was practice for freedmen, when they were liberated and took Roman citizenship, also to take the name of the family that had freed them. For example, at the time of Augustus, more than a thousand people suddenly became Julii, because they had been freed by him. In the same way, Josephus took the name of Flavius, and with him also an unknown number of Judaic priests freed by Titus, including the Titus Flavius Iginus Ephebianus whose name appears in the first Roman mithreum. Perhaps he was a relative of Josephus or one of the friends freed by him in Jerusalem. We can presume that other noble Roman families in this way yielded their name to family groups of Judaic priestly origin, who then supplanted them in the senate. (They might also have passed their name on through adoption or marriage. Indeed, we have seen that from the fourth century onward, it was enough to marry a woman from the Gens Flavia to assume her name and prerogatives.)

Among these we can include the family of Deci, which figures among the senatorial families from the republican era onward. Decius, however, was appointed prefect of the Praetorian Guard (an office, we can remember, reserved for the equestrian order, not for the senators) by Philip the Arab, and then had himself proclaimed augustus by the army, later killing his patron—yet he was not Roman, but came from a family from Pannonia, the undisputed fiefdom of Sol Invictus. The fact that he then unleashed anti-Christian persecutions means nothing: perhaps he did so to soothe his guilty conscience and to attempt to eliminate those who were in a position to make him answer for his misdeeds. In any case, it was a fruitless attempt, because less than two years later, he was eliminated in battle against the Goths. The fact, however, that the family survived the fall of the persecutor of Christians, Decius, and kept its senatorial rank, is a strong indication in favor of its priestly origin.

The most eminent and richest of the Roman senatorial families at the end of the fourth century was the Anici family. The historian Prudentius cites its members as the first to openly profess themselves to be Christian, directly after Constantine's victory over Maxentius.* Yet the family had certainly been Christian beforehand, for some of its members figure among the martyrs of Diocletian in Illyria and are venerated as saints.[8] With regard to their origins, they were apparently extremely ancient and undoubtedly Roman. The first Anicius to appear on the Roman scene was a certain M. Anicius Gallus, tribune of the people in 247 BC. He was succeeded in this office two years later by a Quintus Anicius. It was a family of modest origins, therefore; Titus Livius (XIV, 43) counted it among the petty provincial nobility. Nevertheless, it rose to the heights of the consulate in 160 BC and again in AD 65 under Nero. Then it disappeared from the chronicles for a century and a half, to return to the consulate in 214, under Caracalla, priest of the sun and sworn enemy of the senators, on whom he performed unheard-of massacres.[†] It is likely that the consul Anicius who distinguished himself for his flattery to the sovereign, so much so as to be pilloried by Tacitus,[9] belonged to a priestly family that had been raised to the ranks of the nobility by Caracalla (or by his father Severus, who introduced numerous equestrian families into the senatorial nobility). The family, then, was unrelated, from a genetic point of view, to the Anicis of republican memory.

In any case, when it reappeared on the scene, the Anici family demonstrated a sure connection (though not an actual lineage) to Emperor Probus, initiate of Sol Invictus and a native of Pannonia. The Gallic branch of the family, to which the saints mentioned belonged,

---

*Gibbon suggests that the senator Anicius Julian converted in order to be forgiven by Constantine for the fact that he had sided with Maxentius. This, however, makes no sense, for at that time Constantine was still a pagan.

†According to Cassius Dio, Caracalla, having killed his brother Geta in 212, killed at least twenty thousand suspects among his supporters in Rome, including an unknown but certainly high number of senators.

was related to Emperor Carinus (Sol Invictus, great protector of the Christians in Gaul), and had landed properties in Pannonia. The family's fortunes were improved beyond measure by the senator Probus Anicius, who shared the consulate with Emperor Gratian and was four times prefect of the Praetorian Guard. His strong ties to the church are shown by the fact that he was buried in a monumental tomb in the Vatican, where the basilica of St. Peter stood (and where the pater patrum of Sol Invictus had his seat). The Anici family became the most influential and richest in the senate, with landed properties throughout the Empire, and would maintain its primacy in the West for several centuries to come, providing emperors and popes.

The remaining senatorial families were largely of recent acquisition from the equestrian class, so their connection to Sol Invictus—and therefore their priestly origin—is more immediate and evident. Many of them, unable to demonstrate a link to the noble families of the past, were not above creating ad hoc lineages to connect them to great historical figures. An illuminating example in this regard was the senatorial family of matron Paula, the scandalously rich* benefactress of St. Jerome who manufactured a fictitious lineage that made her a woman of royal blood—a descendant of no less than the Homeric hero Agamemnon.[10]

In conclusion, on the death of Theodosius in 395, the situation regarding the ruling class of the Western Empire must have been this: the ancient nobility of pagan origin had virtually disappeared or had been deprived of all its wealth and power.[11] The great nobility that identified itself with the senatorial class of landowners consisted of descendants of Judaic priests. On the religious level, paganism had been banned and Christianity had become the religion of all the inhabitants of the Empire and was controlled by ecclesiastical hierarchies endowed with immense landed properties and quasi-royal powers within their sees.

The Mosaic priestly family had become the absolute master of that

---

*She owned sixty farms of three hundred hectares each.

same Empire that had destroyed Israel and the Temple of Jerusalem. All the high offices of the Empire, both civil and religious, and all its wealth were in its hands, and supreme power had been entrusted in perpetuity, by divine right, to the most illustrious of the priestly tribes, the Gens Flavia. Three centuries earlier, its founder, Josephus Flavius, had written with pride: "My family is not obscure, on the contrary, it is of priestly descent: as in all peoples there is a different foundation of the nobility, so with us the excellence of the line is confirmed by its belonging to the priestly order" (*Life* 1.1). By the end of the fourth century his descendants had every right to apply those same words to the Roman Empire.

Yet the mass of the population did not know that the whole ruling class of the Empire belonged to a priestly order that had been deleted from the historical chronicles three centuries earlier.

THE ROLE OF THE BARBARIANS IN THE VICISSITUDES OF THE WESTERN ROMAN EMPIRE

At the end of the fourth century the social situation in the western part of the Roman Empire was analogous to what would exist more than a millennium later in France, on the eve of the Revolution: on one hand, there was an omnipotent clergy and senatorial nobility, owners of almost all arable land; on the other, there was the great mass of the population, oppressed and impoverished. This explosive situation gave way to a series of social revolutions known to historians as Bagaudae rebellions.

The Bagaudae were armed bands formed by rebel slaves, artisans, and peasants ruined by taxation, deserting soldiers, and political refugees of every type—united by their hatred of the dominant classes. They revolted, burning churches, seizing land and killing or enslaving the owners. Bagaudae rebellions occurred on several occasions in the West, starting from the second half of the fourth century in Gaul, Spain, and Noricum, and a considerable amount of the Western Empire's military resources were required to supress them. They were the dominant class's enemy number one and were crushed without mercy by the great family champions—Stilicho, Constantius, and Aetius—who in this struggle used the barbarian populations to their own advantage in various ways.

It was in this context, in fact, that the great barbarian invasions, considered by historians to be directly responsible for the so-called fall of the Western Roman Empire, took place. A brief look at the events that characterized the period of the barbarian invasions will allow us to see from a very different perspective the role that these invasions had in the decline of the imperial institution in the West, and, much more important, in the ascent of the fortunes of the priestly family.

As we have seen, when Theodosius died in 395, the priestly family was at the peak of its power and the Roman Empire was at the peak of its expansion. For a long time, however, whole barbarian populations had been settling within the Empire's frontiers and had been to some extent assimilated. Most of these settlements had come about in a peaceful way and by the will of the Roman ruling classes.* From an objective analysis of the events of that era, in fact, we can see that the barbarians were always deliberately used by the Romans not only to defend the Empire from outside aggression, but also to fight internecine wars for the conquest of the imperial office and even to defend the privileges of the dominant class against the Roman population. (A profound analysis of the conditions of the barbarians in the Roman Empire is provided by Prof. E. A. Thompson, showing the reverence that the barbarians had for the Romans.)[12]

---

*Up to AD 406, no barbarian population had ever succeeded in entering the Empire and remaining there without the consensus of the Romans. The invading barbarian peoples had always been exterminated or driven out, from the Cimbri and Teutones wiped out by Marius to the Goths defeated by Claudius the Gothic (ancestor of Constantine) and including the Sarmatians, Alans, Swabians, Franks, Saxons, and so on, driven out by Aurelian, Probus, Constantine, and so on at the end of the third century and the turn of the fourth. In 405, Radagaisus's Ostrogoths were destroyed by Stilicho at Fiesole.

Sol Invictus had initiated the policy of acceptance and assimilation of the barbarians within the frontiers of the Empire. Indeed, as we should remember, the residents of the Roman empire were made up of myriad populations, and for this reason the barbarians were not perceived as foreigners once they had been accepted within its frontiers. In 273, Aurelian had incorporated into his army a large group of Vandals. A few years later, Probus had settled whole populations of Franks, Bastamae, and Swabians in Anatolia and Britannia. This policy was continued by almost all his successors, especially after Constantine's military reform, which divided the army into frontier troops, stationed along the borders, and *comitales* legions, stationed in the cities in the hinterland and subject to rapid redeployment from one end of the Empire to the other. Reform increased the necessity of the recruitment of soldiers, which was made ever more problematic by the concession of wide privileges and exemptions to the great landowners—that is, to the senatorial class and the clergy. (Traditionally, military conscription was carried out among free farmers.)

It became ever more necessary, then, to resort to the recruitment of barbarian warriors, in particular to fill out the frontier legions cheaply. Whole barbarian populations were installed along the borders as *foederati* and given the incentive to settle by the distribution of arable land. In return, they saw to the defense of the frontier even against their fellow countrymen. Hence, for example, the settlement of the Salian Franks and Ripuarian Franks along the frontier of the lower Rhine and subsequently of the Alamanni in what is now Switzerland.

Even the comitales legions made ever more use of barbarian auxiliaries. The need of barbarian soldiers had grown to such an extent that when, in 376, two hundred thousand Visigoths, pressed by the Huns, asked Emperor Valens for permission to enter the Empire, he gave it immediately, with the hope of solving his recruitment problems. (The previous year, Valens had issued a decree that revoked—in the East— the privileges given to the great landowners with regard to recruitment, but the effects of the decree had not yet taken hold.) The Roman frontier legions actually helped the Visigoths to cross the Danube. Valens's calculations turned out to be wrong and were thwarted by the greed and incompetence of some of his high-ranking officers, who transformed this operation into a disaster. Two years later, in 378, Valens, together with his whole army, was killed by the Visigoths in the battle of Adrianople.

Valens's successor, Theodosius, drew up a treaty with the Visigoths, which gave them the status of foederati and possession of a territory in Pannonia. (In so doing, he brought down on himself the hatred of the priestly family branches that were native to the area. Traditionally, it had been the stronghold of the Gens Flavia, but Theodosius instead belonged to the Spanish branch of this Gens.) In return, the Visigoths committed themselves to defending the Empire whenever asked to do so. Indeed, a great number of them were enlisted into the army and fought under the orders of Flavius Stilicho.[13] Stilicho himself is considered by many historians to have been of Vandal origin, but this is anything but certain. He was made a general by Theodosius, whose granddaughter, Serena, he had married,* and he had continued to serve his son-in-law Honorius in the West, to whom he had given his own daughter, Maria, in marriage. He employed an army made up largely of Gothic troops and other Germans to drive the Saxons from Britannia and the Vandals and the Alans from the Rhine frontier. Then, however, when the Visigoths, led by Alaric, incited by the regent of Constantinople, Eutropius, invaded Italy, Stilicho drove them out with an army made up from the legions that had been withdrawn from Britannia in 401. These were reinforced by contingents of Vandals and Alans, who were later installed in Italy as foederati.

In 405, a horde of Sarmatians and Ostrogoths led by Radagaisus crossed the Danube under pressure from the Huns and went down into

---

*It is possible that Stilicho took the name Flavius after marrying Theodosius's granddaughter, Serena. There are various examples of barbarians who took the name Flavius after marrying women from the Gens Flavia; subsequently they claimed for their sons the rights of the Gens Flavia. This custom would continue into the Middle Ages.

Italy. Stilicho annihilated them at Fiesole, near Florence, at the head of an army made up largely of Visigoths, Alans, and Huns. The situation appeared to get suddenly worse in the winter of 406. It was a particularly severe season, during which the Rhine froze over completely. It was on the frozen river, on December 31, that an avalanche of barbarians— Vandals, Sarmatians, Alans, Swabians, and Alamanni, in all more than two hundred thousand people—crossed the border of the Empire at Mainz, overwhelmed the Roman garrisons (made up largely of troops of Franks), and flooded into Gaul, abandoning themselves to pillage and destruction.

The Gauls called for the help of Flavius Claudius Constantine, who had been proclaimed emperor in Britannia as Constantine III. At the head of wholly British troops, he succeeded in gaining some victories over the barbarians and conferring the status of foederati on numerous barbarian hordes. He drove the remainder, in particular Vandals, Alans, and Suebi, toward Spain. Finally, he established his capital in Arles, in the south of Gaul, and proclaimed himself emperor of the West, in opposition to Honorius, who ruled in Ravenna.

Stilicho, loyal to his son-in-law Honorius, was preparing to reconquer Gaul at the head of an army of Visigoths when Honorius had him arrested and beheaded in 408 on a charge of treason. (Honorius may have feared that the general wanted to proclaim as augustus his son Flavius Eucherius, who, due to his mother, belonged by right to the Gens Flavia, and for whom Stilicho had asked for Honorius's sister, Galla Placidia, in marriage.) It was a tragic mistake. The Visigoth king Alaric, loyal to Stilicho, went down into Italy, had Honorius deposed, and placed on the imperial throne the prefect of the city of Rome, Attalus. In return, he demanded to be appointed *magister militum*— commander-in-chief—of the Roman army.

Attalus refused, so Alaric deposed him and reinstated Honorius, who, however, refused in turn to stand by the agreement. For this reason, Alaric retaliated in 410 by subjecting Rome to a sack that lasted three days. It was the first sack of the capital in eight centuries, therefore the impression it made throughout the Empire was immense—far greater, in fact, than the actual material damage suffered by the city and the Roman population. Shortly afterward, Alaric died in Cosenza and his successor, Ataulf, placed himself again at the service of Honorius, offering to reconquer Gaul, where in the meantime another Roman noble, Flavius Jovinus, had instated himself in Trier, proclaiming himself emperor in addition to Constantine III, who ruled in Arles.

The Visigoths were employed by the new commander of Honorius's army, Flavius Constantius, who was sent to Gaul to put an end to the secession. In 412, Constantius defeated and killed Constantine III and then unleashed Ataulf against Jovinus, who was also killed. Directly afterward, Constantius sent the Visigoths to Spain with the task of wiping out the Vandals, Alans, and Swabians who, having been driven out by Constantine III, had installed independent kingdoms there.

The Visigoths crossed the Pyrenees, wiped out the Silingi Vandals and the Alans, drove the Swabians into Galicia, and drove the Hasdingi Vandals into the extreme south of the peninsula, reconquering most of Spain. Here, in Narbonne, on January 1, 414, Ataulf married Honorius's sister, Galla Placidia, adopting Roman dress and surrounding himself with Roman functionaries. Far from constituting a destructive force, the Visigoths had by now become a pillar of the Roman Empire. The marriage to Galla Placidia conferred on Ataulf's son, born the following year, the rights of the Gens Flavia. In fact, Ataulf gave him the augural name of Flavius Theodosius, after his maternal grandfather, thus explicitly proposing him for an imperial future. Shortly afterward, however, the little Theodosius died, Ataulf was killed by his own people, and Galla Placidia was sent back to Honorius in Ravenna.

In 418, Constantius recalled the Visigoths to Gaul and installed them as foederati in Aquitaine. He assigned arable land to them as *hospites* (literally: guests) of the great landowners, who to that end placed at their disposal a part of their property. This allocation, which in fact tied the interests of the Visigoths to those of the great landowners, was almost certainly carried out to endow Aquitaine with a permanent garrison against the expansion of the Bagaudae revolt.[14] Taking advantage of the barbarian invasion of 406, the whole province of Armorica (later Brittany and Normandy) had risen up due to the Bagaudae, who had instituted an independent administration there. It was only in 418,[15] having covered himself in Aquitaine with the settlement of the Visigoths, that Constantius managed to crush the revolt and reestablish order in Armorica. Constantius also used barbarian populations to reinforce the defense of Gaul against possible new invasions from Germany. He confirmed the treaty of federation with the Salian Franks and the Ripuarian Franks, giving them arable land along the Rhine border.

Constantius then married Ataulf's widow, Galla Placidia, who bore him a son, the future Valentinian III. In 417, Constantius was named consul and in February 421 Honorius made him augustus, with the name of Constantius III. The Western Empire seemed to have regained its ancient greatness and security under a stable and valiant leadership. But it was an illusion that lasted only a few months. In September of the same year, Constantius died. Two years later, in 423, Honorius also died and was succeeded by his very young grandson Valentinian III, under the guardianship of his mother, Galla Placidia. An extremely pious woman, but energetic and resolute, she found a valid successor to Stilicho and Constantius in Flavius Aetius, the last of the great Roman generals. The son of the prefect of the Praetorian Guard, Jovius, Aetius had been led away from Rome as a hostage by Alaric, and had then lived for some time at the court of the king of the Huns, Rua. Indeed, until 450, Aetius employed large contingents of Huns in his army, as well as barbarians of various other Germanic ethnic groups. The Huns were valiant and trusted soldiers who also served in the Eastern army, to the extent that the bishop of Cyrene, Synesius, in order to defend his city from the incursions of desert raiders, had specifically asked Constantinople to send him a contingent of Huns.[16] (We should remember that the Huns had been installed in Pannonia in 409 as foederati—that is, allies of the Romans.)

For thirty years, from 424 to 455, Flavius Aetius was the real dominator of the West, but he concentrated his efforts almost exclusively in

Gaul and Italy, abandoning Britannia to itself and North Africa to the Vandals of Geiseric. Under pressure from the Visigoths, these Vandals had left Spain and invaded Africa in 429, laying siege to Hippona, the city of St. Augustine (who died during the siege), which fell in 430. Nine years later, they conquered Carthage and instituted an independent kingdom there.

Aetius was mainly committed on two fronts: First, he had to bring back to order the barbarian populations—mainly Visigoths and Franks—that had been settled in the territory as foederati by his predecessors and he had to repel massive invasions from outside, in particular Burgundians and Alamanni and his former friends, the Huns. Second, he was kept busy supressing a series of Bagaudae revolts that had again broken out in Armorica, Noricum, and in various other parts of Gaul. In 437, he inflicted a bloody defeat on the Burgundians (using troops mostly made up of Huns), who had invaded Gaul. In 443, he installed in Savoy—as foederati—what remained of their population, granting them arable land through the system of the hospitalitas, as had been done for the Visigoths with almost certainly the same goal: to build a permanent garrison against further Bagaudae revolts.[17]

He renewed the treaty of federation with the Salian Franks of King Merovech (founder of the Merovingians), who were installed in southern Belgium. He then negotiated with the Visigoths, recognizing their settlement of Narbonese Gaul, until, in 451, he found himself having to face a massive invasion of Gaul by the Huns, led by Attila, who had created a vast kingdom in the center of Europe. Attila was defeated at the Catalaunian Fields near Troyes in Champagne, by a Roman army consisting mainly of Visigoths (whose king, Theodoric, died in the battle), Burgundians, and Salian Franks (led by King Merovech), and he had to retreat. The following year, however, Attila invaded Italy, destroyed Aquileia, and sacked Milan and Pavia. He then withdrew* from the

---

*The Spanish bishop Hydatius, however, states in his chronicles that Attila's hurried withdrawal was due to the news that a Byzantine army had entered Hun territory, threatening his capital.

peninsula after a meeting near Mantua with Pope Leo, who implored him to grant an armistice, offering him an annuity.[18]

In the meantime, Aetius had fallen into disgrace, because he was accused of colluding with the Huns instead of exterminating them at the Catalaunian Fields. Valentinian III had Aetius's throat cut in Rome, in his presence, in 454. The following year, Valentinian too was assassinated, in revenge, by two of Aetius's loyal supporters. With him ended the Theodosian dynasty.

With the deaths of Aetius and Valentinian III, the imperial office in the West went into a coma. The subsequent events were a dramatic, at times grotesque, agony that would endure for another twenty years. During that time, the various barbarian ethnic groups contested the right to name the emperor. This was started by the Vandal king Geiseric, who, in 454, landed in Lazio and entered Rome without meeting resistance. Pope Leo persuaded him not to massacre or torture the inhabitants, but the pillage and systematic destruction went on for two whole weeks. When he withdrew from the peninsula, Geiseric took with him to Tunis an immense booty of gold and jewels and all the trophies of the Roman victories, including, it would seem, the furnishings of the Temple of Jerusalem, which Titus had brought to Rome three centuries earlier.

He also took as prisoner Empress Eudoxia, the wife of Valentinian III, and her two daughters, Eudocia, whom Geiseric gave in marriage to his son Huneric, and Placidia, the wife of the Roman senator Flavius Anicius Olybrius, who happened to be in Constantinople when his wife was taken. Geiseric thus felt entitled to interfere in the political vicissitudes of the Western Empire, and he proposed Olybrius as his candidate for the imperial purple. The aristocrats of Gaul, however, in agreement with the Visigoth Theodoric II, opposed him with their own candidate, the prefect of Gaul, Flavius Eparchius Avitus, a Roman noble from Auvergne. Avitus, however, was defeated and killed after just fifteen months of his reign by an ex-officer of Aetius, the Swabian Ricimer, who took the office of magister militum and instated in his place Flavius Julius Valerius Majorian (461), to replace him after a few months with another Roman noble, Libius Severus (461–465). The Franks, however, opposed him in Gaul with their candidate, an ex-officer of Majorian, the senator Flavius Aegidius, against whom Ricimer unleashed Theodoric, king of the Visigoths, who was, however, defeated in Orleans.

In agreement with the emperor of Constantinople, Leo I, Ricimer named as emperor the Greek Anthemius (a relative of Leo I), whose daughter he married. Geiseric reacted by devastating the Peloponnese and destroying a Byzantine fleet that Leo I had sent to Tunis. Ricimer was forced to recognize as emperor Geiseric's candidate, Olybrius, who, however, died shortly afterward, in 473.

The successor of Leo I, Zeno, then sent to Ravenna a new emperor for the West, Julius Nepos. This new emperor named as the commander of his troops a Roman noble from Pannonia by the name of Orestes, who had served Attila as a scribe. In that same year, Orestes rebelled and drove Julius Nepos out of Italy, instating as emperor, on October 23, 475, his adolescent son, Romulus Augustus (derisively called Augustulus—Little Augustus—by the Eastern emperor Zeno).

Orestes was killed the following year, the fateful 476, by his commander of the mercenaries, Odoacer, who was the son of General Edecon, one of Attila's closest collaborators and one of Orestes' own colleagues. Odoacer put together an army made up of barbarian soldiers from various ethnic groups—Sciri, Turcilingi, Heruli, and Rugi—with the promise, which he kept, of granting them arable land in Italy and he forced Romulus Augustus to resign, giving him a splendid villa in the Gulf of Naples. Then, through the Roman senate, he had himself assigned the title of patrician, charged with looking after Italy's political and military affairs on behalf of the emperor of Constantinople, Zeno, whose authority he recognized.

By then, however, it was a purely formal recognition. In practice, the West was a constellation of independent entities (they could not yet be defined as states) dominated by barbarian sovereigns and Roman nobles. These entities had emerged almost by the force of inertia from the breakup of central authority.

THE PRIESTLY FAMILY IS RESPONSIBLE FOR THE FALL OF THE WESTERN ROMAN EMPIRE

From these vicissitudes a reality emerges that is fundamentally important to our study: the primary responsibility for the collapse of the centralized imperial administration in the West fell entirely on the priestly family, which from this collapse was in no way weakened or diminished. In fact, if anything it gained in autonomy and security. This result was certainly not programmed from the beginning, but considering the premises created at the time of Constantine—the prohibition of the Roman emperors from residing in the capital and the situation that had been determined in the course of the fourth century by the massive employment of barbarian populations in the Western armies—it was inevitable that eventually the ruling classes that reported directly to Rome would decide that they could do without an emperor. In actuality, there was never a fall of the Western Empire; what happened was only a slow agony of the imperial office, which became ever more estranged from the interests of the Western ruling classes, clergy, and senate, until it had become an unsustainable burden for them. After the death of Valentinian III, the West was transformed into a battlefield for opposing barbarian armies that fought each other to impose their candidates for the imperial purple.

Traditionally, the emperor was the head of the army and his main task, at least in the West, was that of defending the state against external and internal aggression. In the course of the fifth century, the concentration of land in the hands of the clergy and the senatorial class, which enjoyed wide exemptions and privileges, had made the recruitment of soldiers from the Romanized populations extremely difficult, so the Western army came to be made up almost entirely of barbarian warriors installed as foederati by the generals Stilicho,

Constantius, and Aetius in Spain and Gaul. The army then had the task of safeguarding the autonomy and privileges of the clergy and the landed senatorial nobility. When these same armies began to be used against each other to impose short-lived emperors without effective power and incapable of imposing their authority on anyone, the ruling class that reported to the Roman senate decided to abolish the imperial office in the West, which by then had become a source of permanent instability and a cause of the enfeeblement of the military resources at its disposal.

The barbarian Odoacer was only the material executor of this decision, and he acted with the consensus and in fact the full support of the senate and the Roman clergy. This is proved by the fact that Romulus Augustus resigned in front of the senate. Directly afterward, the senate unanimously decided to send a letter to the Eastern emperor Zeno, declaring that it no longer intended to ratify the appointment of an emperor in the West. Indeed, it felt no need of an emperor in the West: to govern simultaneously both the East and the West, a single emperor was sufficient. The senate, therefore, solemnly declared in its own name and in that of all the people that it agreed to the seat of the universal Empire being transferred from Rome to Constantinople, renouncing its own right to choose the emperor. (Up until that time the appointment of a new emperor had always been ratified by the senate.) The letter continued by stating that the republic could count for its defense on the civil and military virtues of Odoacer, for whom it requested an official investiture as patrician.[19]

It was a very logical conclusion, if we consider the historical facts. We have already seen the convulsive spasms of the West in the two decades following the death of Valentinian. In the deposition of the last emperor, Odoacer performed a service not only for Italy, but also for the whole of the West, which gained from it in stability and prosperity. Further, the autonomy and privileges of the Roman ruling classes were guaranteed everywhere by the barbarian armies as they had never been under the Roman emperors.

Odoacer governed Italy with an army of barbarians of various ethnic groups, but he left the old offices and institutions intact and eventually made concessions to the Roman nobility and the Catholic clergy (although he was of Arian faith) that were far greater than the Christian emperors would ever have made, to the extent that he was acclaimed as "champion of the freedoms of the Roman senate." "The freedom of the Roman nobility," writes the historian Ernst Stein, "for which Brutus and Cassius had died at Philippi, was never so completely restored as it was by the first barbarian king to rule Italy." It is true that he handed out arable land to his own barbarian soldiers by taking it from the landowners, but the interests of the landowners were well safeguarded. No property had more than a third of its surface area expropriated, and to compensate, the landowners were indemnified with exemption from taxes, which came to the same amount.

For nearly twenty years Italy enjoyed a period of peace and economic rebirth. The peace was shattered by Theodoric's Goths, who took the place of Odoacer and his barbarians. The Roman clergy and aristocracy gave the appearance of remaining neutral in their opinions of the two contenders. Their status and privileges did not change under the new masters and neither did their autonomy with regard to the Western emperor. This might seem strange, given that the historians state that Theodoric was persuaded to invade Italy by the Eastern emperor Zeno. We cannot overlook, however, that Zeno's intervention had been agreed to or even solicited by the Roman ruling class. This even seems likely. Odoacer had initially been happy simply with the office of magister militum (head of the army) and with the honorific title of Roman patrician. He had, however, been quick to assume the name Flavius, thus claiming for himself the rights of the Gens Flavia and staking a claim for the imperial purple—not for himself, obviously, but for his son Flavius Telanus, whom he had named caesar, the precursor to the title augustus.

It was probably this move that brought about his death. The Roman priestly organization could not have been prepared to accept once again a Western emperor—and certainly not one of barbarian origin. In this its interests completely coincided with those of the Eastern emperor, who, in the absence of a fellow emperor, also remained nominally sovereign of the whole of the West. His authority was formally recognized by all the barbarian chiefs. From a formal point of view, therefore, the Roman Empire was again reunited under a single emperor. In practice, it was definitely divided into two parts, one subject to the secular branch of the family, the other to the religious branch, the church, which remained completely free from all influences and whose security was guaranteed by barbarian militias.

With the deposition of the last puppet emperor, Romulus Augustus, the division between civil and religious powers and their two different spheres of influence, which was brought about at the time of Constantine, was taken to its extreme and logical consequences. In the East the emperor was sovereign, but he formally recognized dependence on Rome in matters of religion. In the West the supreme authority of the emperor, from whom the various barbarian chiefs continued to receive confirmation of legitimacy, was formally recognized—and formally they governed in his name—but in practice, power was completely in the hands of the church and the senatorial ruling class.

In the other barbarian states into which the West had been subdivided, the situation was more or less the same as in Italy. In all of them, the Roman administrative system was maintained, the senatorial nobility kept their privileges and property, and the Catholic clergy saw their power and the ecclesiastical patrimony increase.

The old Western ruling class thus freed itself of its most onerous and difficult duty: providing for the recruitment and maintenance of an army to safeguard their security against foreign invasions and to safeguard their interests and privileges with regard to the subjugated population. These tasks were entirely transferred to the barbarians, who constituted a permanent warrior class and who performed them far more effectively than the Roman emperors and far more cheaply for the

Roman ruling class. Control over and administration of the subjugated Roman population, however, remained entirely in the hands of the old ruling classes.

Throughout the West, the barbarians became in practice (as they had always been) the champions and defenders of the independence of the senatorial class and the Catholic clergy. Independence from whom? Mainly from the emperor himself. This is not surprising, because, as we have seen, the fall of the Western Empire was the logical final consequence of that decision to safeguard the independence of the secret priestly organization against the centralized power by physically separating the seat of the imperial administration from Rome.

The historical facts therefore demonstrate that responsibility for the so-called fall of the Western Empire should be wholly attributed to the Western priestly family, and not to the barbarians. We should understand that neither the Visigoths nor any other barbarians who had settled in the Empire as foederati ever had the intention of bringing it down. In fact, the opposite was true. Ataulf, who succeeded Alaric in the same year as the sack of Rome, declared several times that he intended to gain glory for himself by bringing the name of Rome back to its past greatness. He would use the military power of the Visigoths, and he wanted to be remembered by posterity as "the author of the restoration of Rome."[20] Further, we must not forget, for example, that it was the Visigoths, Franks, Burgundians, and Alans who gave their lives at the Catalaunian Fields to save the Empire from invasion by Attila—one of the many episodes in which the barbarians fought in its defense. Stilicho, Constantius, and Aetius fought all their countless battles at the head of armies mainly made up of barbarians, whose deployment became ever more massive as the Roman population's civic sense weakened and it became more difficult to recruit soldiers from it. Yet the barbarians were not responsible for this. Responsibility fell entirely on the priestly family, which had never had a sense of loyalty to the state, but only a loyalty to the family, and had used the barbarians as the most efficient instrument for maintaining their dominion over Roman society and continuing to maintain their wealth and inordinate privileges.*

In the East, directly subject to imperial authority, things were completely different. In order to allow for the survival and governability of his state (to avoid political conditioning, to avoid social revolts by promoting well-being and the economy, and procuring the financial means to provide for defense and administration), the emperor had to revoke many of the privileges of the senatorial class and the clergy. He thus limited their powers and heavily taxed their property. In this way, the clergy and nobility were completely subjugated to the imperial authority and lost their autonomy. In return, the integrity and independence of the state were safeguarded.

In the West, however, the priestly family groups avoided this inevitable process by entrusting the defense of their autonomy, interests, and privileges to a class of professional warriors constituted from the barbarian populations. The price to be paid was the independence and unity of the state—a price, which as far as can be judged from the historical swings of that period, was paid deliberately and without hesitation. For that matter, it was in line with an ancient tradition. Under Persian domination, the Judaic priestly family had emerged as the dominant class in Judah on its return from the Babylonian exile and had continued to prosper under the dominion of the Tolomeans. Only when Antioch threatened its existence by prohibiting the Jewish religion did the family

---

*In this regard it is important to note that only the barbarians who had initially gone into the service of the Roman ruling classes as foederati—Visigoths, Goths, Burgundians, and Franks—could stay in the Western territories and form stable political units even after the fall of the Empire. All the other barbarians who had not placed themselves at the service of the Roman ruling classes had always and invariably been driven out or exterminated. The Alans, Swabians, and Silingi Vandals who had occupied Spain in 406 were wiped out by the Visigoths, on Flavius Constantius's behalf; the Hasdingi Vandals resisted in North Africa for almost a century, but were eventually swept away by Belisarius; the Alamanni, who had penetrated into Switzerland and Lorraine, were annihilated by Clovis's Franks; the Longobards, who had entered Italy in the seventh century, were completely vanquished by the Franks of Pepin the Short.

branches react, creating an independent state with, at its head, a king taken from its own ranks. As a whole, the period under the Hasmoneans, however, was not one of the happiest for the priestly family groups, which willingly accepted Roman dominion at least until it began to invade the sphere of religious autonomy. There was nothing strange or new, therefore, in the Western priestly family branches preferring the dominion of barbarian sovereigns to that of an emperor of their own lineage.

PART FOUR

The Judeo-Christian
Roots of European Aristocracy

14

THE EUROPEAN POSITION AFTER THE END OF THE EMPIRE

THE BARBARIANS AFTER THE FALL OF THE WESTERN EMPIRE

The Western Roman Empire vanished into indifference, or rather general relief, and from its ashes emerged a series of autonomous "states." They were not independent, because formally they continued to recognize the authority of the Western emperor and, in turn, were recognized by him. Each was ruled, as we have seen, by a barbarian sovereign at the head of a class of professional warriors—but the landowners, the civil service, and religion remained completely in the hands of the Roman senatorial families of priestly origin.

It is a fact that the barbarians respected the privileges and property of the Roman ruling class throughout Europe. The landowners who supplied food and soldiers to the troops of Visigoths, Franks, and Burgundians were the sons of those same landowners who had served under Aetius, placing at his disposal a part of their land to hand out to those same barbarians to whom they now gave their services. They had lost political independence to a barbarian military caste, but they had kept their properties and absolute control over Roman civil society thanks to that military caste.

Their powers and privileges had been assured by an instrument over which the priestly family groups had a monopoly and whose effectiveness had been demonstrated by the experience of a thousand years: religion. At the time of Rome, the priestly family lines had first taken control of the army and through this the imperial office, imposing the Christian religion on the whole Empire almost by force. Now that the army was in the hands of barbarians of various ethnic groups, it adopted the opposite strategy: it converted them to Christianity, thereby subjugating them on moral and cultural levels and subjecting them to the spiritual author-ity of the bishops and, through the bishops, to the authority of Rome. Thus in practice the West, although administratively divided, was more united than ever under the church of Rome. None of the new states saw themselves as independent political and territorial entities. Instead, they continued for centuries to consider themselves as autonomous entities within a single Christian empire.

The only exception was North Africa, which, having been con-quered half a century before the deposition of Romulus Augustus by the Hasdingi Vandals of Arian faith (who were not a federate of the Empire), was never again under Roman jurisdiction. When, in 533, the Vandals were finally cancelled from history by Belisarius, North Africa immediately became dependent on Constantinople. In Britannia too the priestly family branches must have suffered a momentary decline at the hands of the Saxons, to whom they abandoned the whole cen-tral part of the territory, immigrating to Brittany. They immediately counterattacked, however—this time with the weapon of religion—and completed the conquest of the archipelago that had never been accom-plished by the weapons of the Roman emperors. Subsequently, they even took back the territories occupied by the Anglo-Saxons. We will see in chapter 15 how, by the end of the sixth century, the whole archipelago recognized the authority of Rome and sent its money to the Vatican—actual tithes to the high priest who was in charge of the "Temple." The rest of Europe remained, without interruption, under the control of the priestly family groups, even though formally it was in the hands of barbarian kings.

The Visigoths had created a vast Romanized kingdom, which included most of the Iberian Peninsula, conquered by Flavius Constantius; the south of Gaul, with Aquitaine, where they had been installed as anti-Bagaudae by Constantius; and Provence as far as Arles, conquered in the course of the campaign against Emperor Constantine III, also ordered by Constantius. The Visigoth kingdom was the exact equivalent of that of Odoacer in Italy: the rights and privileges of the clergy and senatorial landowning aristocracy were completely safeguarded. Initially Arians (such as Odoacer himself), the Visigoths soon converted to Catholicism,* becoming its stout defenders.[1] Rome remained the constant point of reference for the bishops and, through them, for the whole population.

Even more Romanized than the Visigoth kingdom was the kingdom created by the Burgundians in the region where they had been installed as anti-Bagaudae in 443 by Aetius, from whom Burgundy took its name. Also initially Arians, they soon converted to Catholicism.

The most interesting developments for the priestly family branches took place in the northeast of Gaul, which (together with Pannonia and Italy) had always been a stronghold of the lines of the priestly family. It was also the seat of the last Western territory to be governed by a member of the Gens Flavia. Gaul had a long series of claimant augusti belonging to the Gens Flavia, but they had all been defeated and killed by whichever legitimate emperor was in power and residing in Ravenna. The only one who had managed to survive had been Flavius Aegidius,

---

*The Spanish Catholic church prospered under the Arian Visigoths, enjoying far closer relations with the Roman pope than they did after the Visigoths' conversion to Catholicism brought about by King Reccared (587). From that moment on, he saw himself as a new Roman-Christian emperor, and he quickly adopted the name Flavius after marrying a Roman noblewoman. (His father, Leovigild, had reversed the Roman prohibition against marriages between Romans and barbarians.)

of a senatorial family, who had proclaimed himself augustus in 462, with his capital in Soisson, in Champagne.

Ricimer, the barbarian who was governing Italy at the time and creating and discarding emperors at his pleasure, had unleashed the Visigoths of Theodoric II against Flavius Aegidus, but Aegidius, supported by the Franks, who were the backbone of his army, defeated them and consolidated his power over most of northern Gaul (Reims, Paris, and Metz, as far as Trier and Aachen). On his death, he was succeeded by his son Syagrius, who, however, had to make do with the more modest title of king of the Romans, because the senate, in the meantime, had abolished the imperial office in the West.

To the east of the Roman kingdom were settled the Franks—by then for more than a century. They were divided into the two main ethnic groups of the Ripuari and the Salii, led by King Childeric. For the fundamental role they would play in the history of Europe (and therefore of the priestly family groups), the Franks deserve a closer look.

THE KINGDOM OF THE FRANKS

The Franks constituted a group of Germanic tribes that occupied the upper Rhine Valley. Some had been part of the Roman Empire as foederati since the end of the third century. Emperor Probus had installed a tribe of Franks in Anatolia (Turkey) as far back as AD 278. A few decades later, other Franks were installed as foederati along the upper course of the Rhine and were charged with defending it. When the hordes of Germanic barbarians crossed the frozen Rhine in 406, the Roman garrisons they overran were largely made up of Frankish warriors. At the beginning of the fifth century, Constantius installed as foederati the Ripuarian Franks in the upper Rhine Valley, starting with Mainz, and the Salian Franks in Friesland and in Limburg, with Tournai as their capital.

In 451, these Salian Franks, led by King Merovech, founder of the dynasty that would govern for the next three centuries, had fought against Attila's Huns at the Catalaunian Fields, under Aetius. In 462, they had supported Flavius Aegidius's candidature to the imperial office, defeating the Visigoths unleashed against them by Ricimer. The Franks supported Aegidius and subsequently his son Syagrius until 476, when the Roman senate decreed the end of the imperial office in the West. On that occasion, Syagrius found himself in an unsustainable situation, no longer able to claim an office that was by then delegitimized. He had to make do with the more modest title of king of the Romans, which put him at the same level as other barbarian military chiefs, but without being able to use his own troops unless he resorted to forced conscription from among the Gallo-Roman population. By then, however, this was no longer feasible without damaging the privileges of the senatorial class and the clergy. He would inevitably have lost their support.

There is no documentary evidence that the bishops (and with them the whole senatorial class) under Syagrius solicited the intervention of the Franks against him, but it is certain that they did not support him and that they immediately sided with the Franks, who were militarily far stronger and incomparably more respectful of their privileges. Straight away, Childeric started invading the Roman "kingdom," occupying cities in the Loire Valley. In 482, he was succeeded by his son Clovis, an able and unscrupulous barbarian chief who was the real founder of the Frankish kingdom, reuniting under his dominion all the Frankish tribes on both sides of the Rhine. He went on the offensive against his former ally Syagrius, defeating him at Soisson.

Syagrius fled to his ex-enemy Alaric II, king of the Visigoths, and solicited his help. Alaric, however, handed him over to Clovis, who had him beheaded. Thus died the last Western sovereign belonging to the Gens Flavia. In the following years, Clovis devoted himself to eliminating systematically his internal rivals, real or potential, among the ranks of his own relatives and warriors. In practice, then, he became king of all the Salian Franks, even those who had remained on the far side of the Rhine and who were sent into Gaul. Impressed by these successes, the Ripuarian Franks also placed themselves under his command and moved toward the West, occupying Trier, Metz, Chalons, and Reims.

Ruthless and ferocious against his internal rivals, Clovis conversely followed a policy of moderation and conciliation with the Roman population, who constituted the vast majority in the territories he had subjugated. In 486, Remegius, the bishop of Reims, had written to him, urging him to spare the conquered cities from destruction and plunder and setting forth the advantages of maintaining good relations with the bishops who represented these cities.

All the bishops assured him of their full and loyal support, and they busied themselves with arranging the marriage of Clovis to Clotilde, daughter of the king of the Burgundians, who had converted from Arianism to the Roman orthodoxy. Clovis allowed himself to be easily persuaded by his wife, consenting to their children being baptized according to the Catholic rite. It was probably due to pressure from the Gallic bishops and landowners that Clovis turned on the Alamanni, who had given themselves over to violence against the Roman population in Switzerland and in Alsace-Lorraine. In 496, he inflicted a bloody defeat on them at Tolbiac. Following this, according to legend, he decided to convert to Christianity after a votive offering. The year of the conversion is uncertain: some say it was 506, others 498 (which seems more likely). In any case, Clovis was baptized on Christmas Day in Reims, along with three thousand of his warriors.* Bishops from all over Gaul† exulted at the news, greeting Clovis as "the light of the sun, already high in its path."

In 500, Clovis attacked Burgundy, succeeding in detaching it from its alliance with the Visigoths. Certain of being able to count on the

---

*It is significant that the baptism took place on Christmas Day, sacred to Sol Invictus, and that the bishops compared Clovis to the sun. For the Christians of the time, still under the influence of Sol Invictus, Christmas was an extremely significant holiday. It continued to be of fundamental importance and was chosen innumerable times for the most important occasions, such as baptisms and coronations of sovereigns.

†It is important to emphasize the fact that all the bishops without exception, according to modern studies, came at that time from the Roman senatorial class.

friendly attitude of the bishops in Aquitaine, whose Roman population was entirely Catholic, Clovis went on an expedition against the Visigoths, which he presented as a crusade against the Arian heretics. Beaten at Vouillé, near Poitiers (507), the Visigoths had to surrender all of Aquitaine and Toulouse to the Franks. With this battle, Clovis's Franks became masters of almost the whole of Gaul, from the North Sea to the Pyrenees. Only Marseilles and Provence remained in the hands of the Ostrogoth king Theodoric, while the kingdom of the Burgundians, in what is now Burgundy, maintained a nominal independence but in practice was no more than a low-ranking ally.

Emperor Anastasius from Constantinople sent Clovis the insignia that made him his representative in Gaul, thus legitimizing his power. The bishop Gregory of Tours writes that on this occasion Clovis received the diploma of the consulate, was invested with the purple tunic and the chlamys in St. Martin's basilica, and had his head girded with the diadem. Directly afterward, he established his capital in Paris, where he died in 511.

The dynasty founded by Clovis survived more than two centuries, a period rich in events that were among the liveliest and most interesting in the whole of European history. Mostly, they consisted of internecine struggles between members of the dynasty, but it is not within the sphere of this book to go into the details. What interests us here is being able to follow the vicissitudes and destiny of the branches of the priestly family that made up the aristocracy and clergy of Roman Gaul and being able to establish whether and how they emerged at the end of this period.

In Gaul, as in the rest of Europe, they had found the barbarian chief to be the most efficient defender of their privileges. Here too the civil service remained in the hands of the Gallo-Roman senatorial nobility and the bishops who were drawn from the ranks of this nobility. The senatorial class identified with the great landowners who controlled the country, while the bishops controlled the cities with virtually sovereign powers.

Compared to the other barbarian kingdoms, however, that of the

Franks had two peculiarities that were at the basis of its enduring success. The first was that the two ethnic groups fused almost immediately into a single people. As far as they were concerned, the Franks had been integrated in Roman society for more than a century, but the opposite was also true: the Romans, especially the higher classes, for a long time enjoyed privileged relations with the Franks. It is important to note, in this regard, that Syagrius (like his father) used troops of Franks and spoke their language perfectly. This is a sign that the process of reciprocal integration, which in a few years would make the Franks indistinguishable from the Gallo-Romans (at least for subsequent historians), had begun well before the official death of the Western Empire. The consciousness of belonging to a single people was already evident in Gregory, bishop of Tours (538–594), even though he belonged to the Roman senatorial aristocracy and had great classical knowledge. He is emblematic of the readiness of the Roman aristocracy to identify with the Frankish nation, to the extent that after a few generations it became impossible, or nearly so, to establish the true origin of the figures who determined the vicissitudes of the Franks in the service of the Merovingian dynasty.

In general, it can be said that the great landowners—who eventually constituted the emergent part of the Frankish aristocracy—were descendants of the owners of the great landed properties that had been formed in Gaul from the third century onward, thanks to the policy of open favoritism conducted by the Christian emperors. The Frankish sovereigns, in fact, never expropriated from the Roman landowners. They limited themselves to taking over imperial property and lands that had been disposed of freely. Court revenues, appointments in the army, and possession of cities and castles were the prizes for the aristocracy of Frankish origin, whose power was not based on the possession of land. The Merovingians personally had no landed properties—or had them only to a negligible degree—which was absolutely inadequate to their position to the extent that they were unable to compensate the services rendered to them with the consignment of land.

The second "peculiarity" of the Franks was their prompt conversion to Catholicism, unlike the other barbarians, who were mainly Arians. Clovis thus became the champion of Catholicism, greeted by bishop Gregory of Tours as a new Constantine, and he obtained the enthusiastic support of all the bishops both inside and outside his kingdom. The church had become the main pillar of Western Roman society, and its support was the decisive factor in Clovis's personal success, the rapid integration of the two ethnic groups, and the stability of the Frankish monarchy. Alliance with priestly family groups had turned a minor barbarian chief into the king of a great state. From that moment on, however, the dynasty he had founded became hostage to the priestly family lines, which sustained it only until they were in a position to replace it.

15

THE PRIESTLY FAMILY
IN GREAT BRITAIN

THE CONQUEST OF BRITANNIA

Before proceeding to an examination of the vicissitudes of the priestly family branches in Gaul, let us look at its fate in an area that was geographically and economically marginal in the history of the Roman Empire, but which had formidable importance in the history of the priestly family: Britannia. It was in Britannia that it established its first real power base, and it was from here that Constantine set out on his conquest of the whole Roman Empire. From then on, despite its historical highs and lows and moments of deep crisis, the island remained the family's undisputed fiefdom, which after more than a millennium of absolute loyalty to Rome, was able to detach itself and create a worldwide empire that rivaled that of Rome.

It is perhaps no coincidence that in England we find the first historical testimonies to the existence of modern Freemasonry, the organization that represents the primitive secret priestly organization.

We have seen that by the end of the third century there was a considerable number of high-ranking Christian officers in the Roman army. This presence must have been particularly strong in the legions stationed in Britannia. It was these legions that, on July 25, AD 306, proclaimed as augustus the son of Constans Chlorus, Flavius Valerius Constantine. In this way, they paved the way for the triumph of Christianity. We must presume (as testified by the legend of the Four Crowned Saints) that the Christian officers were members of the priestly family. The large number of officers in Britannia belonging to the Mosaic priestly organization is proved by the spread in that period of the cult of Mithras along the whole length of Hadrian's Wall—and particularly in York, seat of Constans Chlorus.

These officers brought their families with them, and of course they came to make up the elite of local society. In all likelihood, they were Christian families. This presupposes the presence of a Christian clergy, with priests and bishops who also came from branches of the priestly family.

The Roman world's first contact with Britannia had taken place in the years 53 and 54 BC, when Julius Caesar carried out two forays onto the island. The real conquest, however, was begun nearly a century later, in AD 43, and completed in 83 by Agricola. For the next three centuries and beyond, the island saw the constant presence of a Roman garrison. At the turn of the second century, Hadrian built the defensive wall that bears his name, and a few years later Antoninus Pius moved it by about a hundred kilometers to the north. By the end of the second century, Britannia had been completely romanized. Scotland and Ireland, however, remained outside Roman dominion, inhabited respectively by the barbarian tribes of the Picts and Scots. Considering its peripheral position far from the Roman floodlights and the rapid economic development that occurred at the beginning of its colonization, the island must have held a particular attraction for the lines of the priestly family, which were in search of opportunities to grow economically and socially, recycling themselves as genuine Roman citizens.

We must therefore conclude that they landed there quite early, even independently of the Christian officers in the army (who anyway might have served as an excellent vanguard). Actually, we have testimonies to a Christian presence in Britannia from as far back as the second half of the second century. The English historian Nennius, who at the turn of the ninth century compiled a *History of the Britons*[1] relates that around 167, Pope Eleuterus sent some missionaries on the request of a local dignitary, a certain Lucius, who is presented as an indigenous king despite his Roman name. He was probably an imperial functionary or Roman military chief, in any case an initiate of Sol Invictus. The missionaries sent must have been from a priestly family, and it is likely that other nonclerical members came with them.

The presence of Christians in Britannia is also confirmed by Tertullian, who in his book *Against the Judaeans,* written at the beginning of the third century, goes so far as to say that "a part of Britannia still inaccessible to the Romans had already been conquered by Christ." At the beginning of the third century, there were Christian martyrs in Britannia, which testifies to the presence of Christians on the island. One of them, St. Alban, put to death probably in 208 or 209, became famous and had an enduring cult in his land. He is cited in the biography of St. Germanus, bishop of Auxerre, who, on the occasion of his coming to Britannia in 429, apparently paid his respects to him in the sanctuary built in his honor near Verulamium. The monk and historian Gildas provides some interesting details with regard to Alban. He was in fact a Roman soldier who had given refuge to a priest fleeing Gaul.[2] This is confirmation of the ties that existed between the army and the priests in this first phase of Christian expansion.

Legends dated much later relate that in the second century was founded the monastery of Glastonbury—which then became central to the Arthurian saga—and even that the island was Christianized by Joseph of Arimathea, who landed there with the Holy Grail, the chalice used by Christ during the Last Supper. These are only legends, but they provide a further indication that Christianity was present in Britannia as far back as the second century.

In any case, the priestly family must have made the island one of its territorial strongholds starting in 297, when Constans Chlorus installed his headquarters in York, the main British city near Hadrian's Wall.

Very soon, the high ranks in the army were occupied by members of the family, many of whom came not from the usual Pannonia, but from the opposite part of the Empire: Spain. Testimonies to the total control over the local troops is provided by the wide diffusion in that area of Mithraic "lodges" and by the fact that Constantine the Great was proclaimed augustus on the same day that his father died. We have no information regarding the means and the times involved in the spreading of Christianity on the island, but we must conclude that from then on it was rather rapid and thorough.

We know for sure that just eight years later there were at least three bishops' sees in Britannia who covered three of the four provinces into which the territory was divided. We find these bishops, along with other prelates, in the list of the participants at the Council of Arles, held in 314 (only a year after Constantine's Edict of Tolerance). Eleven years later, at the Council of Nicaea, the Britons appear on Athanasius's list, which includes all those who had accepted the orthodox creed. In 359, three British bishops were honored in the chronicles for having convinced the emperor to agree to refund their travel expenses when they participated in a congress on the Continent.

In the course of the fourth century, Christianity not only completely conquered Roman Britannia, but also went beyond the territory administered by Rome in what appears to have been in actual fact a private policy of expansion on the part of the priestly family. When, in 368, supreme command of the troops in Britannia was entrusted to the Christian general Flavius Theodosius (father of the future Emperor Theodosius I), the island was entirely controlled, in practice, by the priestly family. Further, if some position of power—whether in the civil service, the army, or religion—was still to be occupied, the Spanish general must have taken care of completing the job in the five years he was absolute master of the island. Certainly, Theodosius favored the rise of the Spanish branch of the family. After him we find another Spanish general at the head of Britannia, Flavius Magnus Maximus, who was almost certainly from the same group of families belonging to the Gens Flavia.

In the ten years he spent on the island prior to his transfer to Trier as augustus, Magnus Maximus must have provided for the instatement of members of his own family or connected families at the head of all the provinces of Britannia, thus insuring a solid and enduring personal power base. (It is no coincidence that a certain number of ruling dynasties in post-Roman Britannia traced themselves back to Magnus Maximus.) Once he had set up the island in this way, he had himself proclaimed augustus by his troops in 381, after which he made himself recognized as such by the troops stationed in Gaul. In 383, he moved to Trier, taking with him most of the British troops, because he was sure of being able to maintain control over the island even though it remained undefended. Maximus died in 388, killed by Theodosius in his attempt to conquer the Eastern Empire. Britannia then found itself defenseless, exposed to raids by the Scots from Ireland (as demonstrated by the abduction of St. Patrick, which happened in those years), by the Picts from Scotland, and by the Saxons from Germany.

Around 397, Stilicho had to intervene in Britannia to repel the assaults of the Picts and the Saxons and to reinforce the defenses against them by restoring the forts along Hadrian's Wall. In addition, he built new fortifications along the coast to contain invasions from the sea.[3] The troops deployed in Britannia, however, were withdrawn in 401 to face the invasion of Italy by Alaric's Visigoths, and they never returned. Left completely to their own devices, the functionaries who had been installed at the head of the various provinces (or rather dioceses, as they were called at the time) of the island by Magnus Maximus had to take care of their own defense. To this end, as was by then the usual local practice, they appointed a commander-in-chief, an imperator, charged with enlisting troops on the island and commanding them. The title of augustus was conferred on him, in keeping with tradition.

Between 401 and 406, three augusti were appointed: Marcus, Gratian, and finally Flavius Claudius Constantine,[4] all rigorously Christian, of course, and all drawn from the ranks of the island's bureaucracy. Nothing is known of the first two, not even the circumstances of their deaths. The third, Constantine III, called to the aid of the Gauls in the winter of 406–407, when they had been invaded by a torrent of Germans, moved to the continent, thus beginning an adventure that would lead to his death a few years later. (He was beheaded in Arles in 411.)[5]

Britannia remained completely cut off from the rest of the Roman Empire and, we must presume, completely under the power of the priestly family, which from then on governed the island in total autonomy. The entire nobility and British clergy at the turn of the fifth century must have been made up of members of one or another branch of the priestly family, as in Israel at the time of Josephus Flavius—to the extent that the monk Gildas, who, around 550, wrote a history of the Britannia of this period,[6] compared it, significantly, to a "new Israel."

THE CONQUEST OF IRELAND, SCOTLAND, AND BRITANNIA

Some British historians sustain that after the withdrawal of Roman troops in 401, power stayed in the hands of local indigenous chiefs, and the population rapidly returned to paganism and the customs of pre-Roman times. Yet the little historical evidence we have shows a completely different situation: there is no doubt that Britannia remained firmly under the control of the ruling class instated by Magnus Maximus, at least for the subsequent fifty years, during which time Christianity, far from declining, became stronger and more aggressive than ever, so much so that it was in this period that it completed its conquest of the whole archipelago, including Ireland and Scotland. The withdrawal of the Roman troops coincided with a period of large expansion for Christianity and the priestly family, which began to operate in the archipelago in full political autonomy.

It crossed the Irish Sea and began on its own behalf, and with considerable success, the "colonization" of the Emerald Isle—not by force of arms (at least it does not appear so from the historical chronicles), but with the pacific instrument of religion. We can presume that there had already been a Christian presence in the country since the second century (this is what Tertullian apparently alludes to), arriving in the wake of commercial enterprises run by members of the branches of the priestly family. Otherwise, it would be impossible to explain the instant and total success of St. Patrick, the Roman bishop to whom the Christianization of the island is attributed. He was born in Banna, in Cumberland, in 372, and was the son of the deacon Calpurnius and grandson of the bishop Potitus—certainly of priestly origins, therefore, on the basis of our thesis. On the death of Magnus Maximus in 388, Britannia was the object of raids by Scots (from Ireland), Picts, and Saxons, and during one of these, Patrick was captured and taken as a slave to Ireland, where he came to know the language and customs.

Having returned to Britannia a few years later (in the meantime, order had been restored by Stilicho), he devoted himself to an ecclesiastical career and was ordained bishop in Gaul in about 425, after which he went back to Ireland. Through St. Patrick, who was certainly accompanied by other monks, the priestly family completely and profoundly conquered the whole of Ireland, which from then on would always be at the top of the list of countries devoted to the church of Rome. Patrick created a series of bishop's sees that covered the whole of the island at the head of which were instated bishops from Britannia and Gaul. We know for certain that one of them, Palladius, was sent as a bishop *ad Scottos in Christum credentes*[7] all the way from Rome in 431 by Pope Celestine I. In Scotland too Christianity had been preached among the Picts since the end of the fourth century by the bishop Ninian.[8] The total conversion of the Picts was completed only a half century later by a missionary from Ireland, St. Columbanus.

Other evidence shows that the rest of Britannia in the early decades of the fifth century was peacefully governed by bishops who do not seem at all threatened by a return of paganism. In the monastery of Monte Cassino, for example, there is a document written in about 425 by the British bishop Fastidius to a certain Fatalis,[9] who is exhorted to exercise modesty, contentment in his own status, and happiness, because Christ had been anointed with the oil of joy, love for the poor, and so on. There is nothing to suggest that the British Christians were being encircled by paganism.

In the same period, there were the preachings of the bishop Pelagius, one of the great figures of the church of his time. Born in Britannia around 380, he became a famous theologian who sustained the freedom and capacity of man to cooperate with Divine Grace. This thesis caused him bitter controversy with another great figure of that time, St. Augustine, who considered him a heretic. The heresy of Pelagius spread rapidly in the land of his birth, to the extent that it was necessary to call to Britannia the bishop of Auxerre, St. Germanus, together with the bishop of Troyes, Lupus, who in 428–429 preached against it effectively. St. Germanus's biographer, Constantius (who wrote in about 480, and was therefore very close in time to the events in question), maintains that the two bishops were called back to Wessex fourteen years later (in 442, forty years after the departure of the Roman legions), again to preach against the Pelagian heresy, which was completely uprooted. This is a clear demonstration that the British church in those years had other things to worry about than a return of paganism.

From both the civil and military viewpoints, the situation in the first half of the fifth century was far less dramatic than in the rest of the Western Empire and than what some British historians would have us believe. The withdrawal of Stilicho's troops in 401 caused no disruption on the island. The local notables limited themselves to electing new generals drawn from their own ranks to whom they entrusted the defense of the island by means of locally recruited troops. Their action was so effective that even Gaul, in 407, asked Britannia for help in stanching the Germanic tide that was engulfing them. The British troops led by Constantine III proved themselves to be very efficient—so much so as to make him think that the imperial dream, which would lead to his death in 411, could come true.

With the departure of Constantine, Britannia did not remain

defenseless. Others took his place. At this point, however, information becomes confused and imprecise, because it is related by historians who had a completely different and more limited vision of the world than that of their predecessors. The first among all of them was the monk Gildas, who described the events from the withdrawal of the Roman troops until the middle of the sixth century.

According to him, all the functionaries installed at the head of the various districts became kings. At a stroke, therefore, in his description and in those of subsequent historians, post-Roman Britannia was transformed into an agglomerate of many small independent kingdoms for whose defense, however, there was a common army commanded by a general with imperial powers. Evidently, the local authorities installed by the various generals and Christian emperors, starting with Constans Chlorus, and especially with Flavius Theodosius and Magnus Maximus, continued to administer their districts in complete autonomy, but they elected an imperator to provide for a common defense—a sort of *primus inter pares,* who commanded an army formed from locally recruited troops or mercenaries. The first British imperators of whom we have information were Marcus, Gratian, and Flavius Claudius Constantine.

This situation continued for at least another century after the withdrawal of Roman troops. We even know the names of some of these supreme commanders; they are cited in some of the few surviving documents relating to the history of this period. First on the list is a King Vortigern to whom the monk Gildas, for some reason, gives the appellation *superbus tiramnus* (arrogant tyrant). He started the ruination of Britannia by bringing in from the continent mercenary Saxon troops to fight against the Picts. The subsequent chronicles of Nennius and Bede and the *The British Historical Miscellany* always refer to him by the name Vortigern, a Gaelic word that means something very similar to "supreme commander."[10] It is therefore more likely to be a title than a name, because this Vortigern was certainly a general of Roman origin: his father's name was Agricola, son of a certain Triphun, which was almost certainly a corruption of the Latin

Tribunus.[11] It is also certain that he was related to Magnus Maximus, whose daughter he had married. (This can be seen from an inscription made at the turn of the ninth century on a memorial stone known as the Pillar of Eliphalet.)[12]

In the "Easter Annals," contained in *The British Historical Miscellany*, there is a very detailed reference to Vortigern and his role in Britannia: *"Guorthigirnus tenuit imperium in Britannia Theodosio & Valentinian consulibus & in quarto anno regni sui saxones ad Britanniam tenerunt"* (Vortigern was imperator in Britannia when Theodosius and Valentinian were consuls, and in the fourth year of his reign the Saxons came to Britannia). He was therefore made imperator in the year 425 and four years later enlisted Saxon mercenaries to fight against the Picts, who threatened Christian Britannia from Scotland. This is very clearly the same expedition of 429 that saw the participation of St. Germanus of Auxerre, who baptized the pagan mercenaries shortly before the battle.[13]

It was normal practice, consolidated for more than a century in the Roman Empire thanks to the Christian generals and emperors, to hire barbarian troops to fight against other barbarians. Thus, Vortigern did nothing unusual by enlisting the Saxons. It would appear that he settled them somewhere in the north of Britannia, granting them the status of foederati, as was the practice on the continent. Due to Britannia's isolation, however, his action was fraught with consequences. A few years later, the Saxons revolted against their masters and, allying themselves with their old enemies the Picts, set about sacking and conquering the Roman provinces.

The trigger for the Saxon revolt was probably a serious discord that broke out in 437 between Vortigern and the generals Vitolinus and Ambrose, of which we are again informed by the "Easter Annals" (which, however, do not enter into the merits of the dispute). What actually happened is not known. One likely hypothesis is that a dispute broke out among the Roman generals over possession of the imperial office and that Vortigern used his Saxon troops against his fellow countrymen, which would explain the title of superbus tiramnus and the cancellation of his real name from the annals. What is known is that from then on the Saxons set up on their own—they probably continued to serve under the command of Vortigern or one of his descendants, by then "Saxonized" (though we have no information about this). Other Saxons were called from the Continent, along with other Germans of the same ethnic group, Angles and Jutes, who conquered most of Britannia, starting with the territories originally assigned to the Saxons by Vortigern along Hadrian's Wall. Ten years later, in 446–447, they were already present in the far southeast of England, on the peninsula of Kent, where they instated their own king in Canterbury.

The rapid advance of the Saxons in the most fertile and richest lands of Britannia was probably favored by what was happening at the same time in Gaul. We have seen that in 435 a new Bagaudae revolt had removed Armorica from the control of the imperial administration in Ravenna. We have no precise information on what happened at the time, but we must conclude that this time the Bagaudae completely wiped out the ruling class, clergy, and landowning nobility that had been restored a few years earlier by Flavius Constantius. Certainly, Flavius Aetius's supression was ruthless, as was the Roman custom. It likely exceeded the excesses of the antirevolutionary supression in the Vendée fourteen centuries later. In 437, the Bagaudae revolt was crushed and the whole region of Armorica had to be virtually emptied. Aetius had to repopulate it by offering the "liberated" lands to the Roman notables who were then beginning to abandon Britannia under the pressure of the Saxons. The nobility of the provinces of Flavia Caesarensis and Maxima Caesarensis (which occupied the heart of England) had to abandon the country en masse and move to Armorica, which from then on took the name of New Britannia (the modern Brittany). The Saxons, therefore, must have found the whole country deserted from its ruling class, and they flooded south meeting little or no resistance.

They stopped, however, where the Britons did offer resistance. In Wales and Cornwall, the Britons had maintained the structure of the little autonomous kingdoms endowed with a common army and a supreme commander. We know for sure that after Vortigern the position was occupied by that Ambrose cited in the "Easter Annals." Gildas defines him as a Roman general, Ambrose Aurelian, commander of the army of the Britons, who fought various victorious battles against the Saxons, succeeding in containing their advance. Here too, if the name has any significance, we find ourselves dealing with a member of the priestly family. (Aurelian was the first Roman emperor openly adherent to the cult of Sol Invictus, as was Ambrose, right-hand man to Constantine, who made him prefect of Gaul. He was the father of Ambrose, bishop of Milan.)

The man who succeeded in blocking the Anglo-Saxon advance once and for all, inflicting a decisive defeat on them at Badon in 518, was another general of Roman origin whom the historian Nennius refers to as Artorius*—he who would go down in legend as King Arthur.[14] The "Annals of Cambria" for the year 518 record "the Battle of Badon, in which Arthur bore the cross of Our Lord Jesus Christ on his shoulders for three days and three nights and from which the Britons emerged victorious." The same annals report that Arthur was killed in 539 at the Battle of Camlann, and that in same year the plague broke out in Britannia and Ireland.

Artorius was perhaps the last imperator of Christian Britannia.[15] Later, numerous legends sprang up around him, which make him a key figure in the historical events of this period, but at the same time they contribute to shrouding those events in mystery. After him, the individual Christian kings began to act autonomously and the history of Britannia became ever more confused and chaotic.

---

*In his *History of the Britons,* Nennius states that "Arthur fought the Saxons in those days together with the kings of the Britons, but he was the supreme commander in the battles (*dux bellorum*)."

THE PRIESTLY ORIGIN OF THE ARISTOCRACY
IN THE BRITISH ARCHIPELAGO

In any case, it is not this history that interests us here. The events of this period have been briefly mentioned only to highlight the continuity and the ties that existed between the ruling class, both civil and religious, installed in Britannia by the Christian Roman emperors, and the ruling classes of the numerous Christian kingdoms that finally emerged with the passing of imperial authority. If, as has been said, the positions of power in Roman Britannia had all been occupied by members of the priestly family line, there is no doubt that the nobility and clergy of the subsequent British kingdoms (or at least the vast majority of them) descended from these same groups.

The ruling dynasties in particular, according to the genealogies provided by various sources, mostly descended directly from the Roman emperors, especially Magnus Maximus, who occupies a prominent place in British folktales and poetry, particularly in Wales. The Welsh poem "The Dream of Macsen Wledig" goes so far as to call him the greatest of the Roman emperors.[16] According to *The British Historical Miscellany,* there are various genealogical lists going back to the Roman emperors, and cited there are some kings directly instated by Magnus Maximus, including an Irish one. From a ninth-century inscription on the Eliseg Pillar, we can deduce that Vortigern had married one of Magnus Maximus's daughters and owed his position to him.[17]

Gildas lists five sovereigns who reigned in Wales in his time: Constantine (tyrannical offspring of the lioness Dumnonia); Aurelius Caninus (the lion's cub); Vortipor, king of Dyfed; Cuneglasus; and Maglocunus (dragon of the islands).* In addition to the kings with

---

*"Progeny of the lion and the lioness": this evidently refers to the standards or the characteristic symbols of the family. The lion is that of Judah. The dragon, which would become the symbol of Wales, was the symbol of a Roman legion. It was also the symbol of St. George and of the Archangel Raphael. All of this leads back to the branches of the priestly family. David L. Edwards says, "Latin names under Christian symbols appear on tombstones in Wales and Cornwall, or appear in the family trees of Welsh chieftains."[18]

clearly Roman names, *The British Historical Miscellany* also provides lineages for the other apparently indigenous kings, which go back directly to Roman families.[19]

Vortipor, for example, is commonly regarded as an indigenous king of Irish origin, but in his lineage in the *Miscellany* three Romans appear, including Magnus Maximus and a mysterious "Protector." Protector was a title given to a high-ranking officer in the imperial bodyguard. It is significant that this title is attributed to Vortipor himself on the memorial stone found not far from the court of Dyfed.[20] Cuneglasus and Maglocunus, too, have Roman origins, through their common ancestor Cunedda. This Cunedda, according to the text *The History of the Britons,* had been instated in Wales at the time of Magnus Maximus, in about 383, and he was undoubtedly Roman. From his family tree we learn that he was the son of a certain Aeternus, who in turn was the son of a certain Paternus of the red garment, and he of a certain Tacitus. The dynasty of Galloway, too, goes back in the *Miscellany* to Maxim Guletic—that is, Magnus Maximus—while others are linked to St. Germanus, Ambrose Aurelian, and so on.[21]

Many British scholars consider these lineages to be legends and tend toward an indigenous origin for these dynasties—which appears to be without any possible justification. Given the absolute historical continuity that characterizes this period, there is no doubt that the dynasties reigning in post-Roman Britannia emerged from the ruling class that were governing it at the time of the withdrawal of the Roman legions in 401. Further, this ruling class was definitely made up of Roman citizens—in fact, as we have seen, more precisely by members of the priestly family, because they were related in various ways to Emperors Constans Chlorus, Constantine, Theodosius, and Magnus Maximus.

The situation was different for the part of Britannia that, starting in the second half of the fifth century, had been conquered by the Anglo-Saxons. The Saxons were pagans (despite the hurried collective baptism imposed in 429 by St. Germanus on the first troops enlisted by Vortigern), and remained so for more than a century. Their conquest therefore effectively caused a temporary decline of Christianity in Britannia. Most of the ruling classes in the occupied regions, or those who were not massacred, retreated to the surviving Christian kingdoms in the south and west—especially to Gaul, in Armorica, where there was a massive influx of Britons toward the middle of the fifth century,* as we have seen.

It is certain that a substantial part of the previous Romanized and Christian population must have remained in Britannia to be subjected to the new invaders, and among them there were undoubtedly members of the clergy and landowning nobility,† as was the case in all the Roman regions conquered by the barbarians.[22] It is equally certain, however, that in the territories conquered by the Saxons, unlike on the Continent, the Roman administration had completely vanished, probably because the functionaries had migrated en masse to New Britannia, leaving behind them a political and administrative

---

*There is sufficient proof that there was a substantial migration of Britons to Brittany and Normandy starting in the middle of the fifth century (therefore coinciding with the beginning of the Saxon conquest). Many Breton and Norman names for saints and places are similar to Welsh names, and the Breton language is so similar to that of Cornwall that the fishermen from the opposite shores who met in the English Channel could converse with each other. Siconius, a bishop from Gaul, kept up a correspondence with the chief of a group of fugitives from Britannia, Riotamus, who had been sent to fight the Visigoths. In 461, the name of a British bishop, Mansuetus Episcopus Britannorum, appeared among the bishops who participated in a small conference in Tours. Because it was a local meeting, it seems likely that he administrated loyal supporters installed in New Britannia. It has been calculated that the number of people who migrated from Britannia to Brittany and Normandy was in the hundreds of thousands. It seems clear that the ruling classes and the rich had the most motivation and possibility to escape from the Saxon invasion.[23]

†While it is probable that many of the British fled to the west and became Welsh, those who stayed were not all slaughtered. A few personal names seem to be evidence of intermarriage between the triumphant Saxons and the remaining Britons. These include the famous names of Cerdic who was regarded as the founder of the royal house of Wessex, Caedwalla king of the West Saxons [from] 685–688, and the poet Caedmont.

vacuum.* These territories, therefore, were lost to the priestly family. Only Wales, Cornwall, and some other regions in south-central England (in addition to Ireland and Scotland) remained solidly in its hands.

Not for long, however. Once Saxon expansion had been blocked at Badon with the dazzling victory of the imperator Artorius, the priestly family went on the counterattack, wielding their most effective weapon: religion. The bridgeheads were the women belonging to the British dynasties of Roman origin who had remained on the island or who had fled to Gaul. Like all the barbarian sovereigns, the Saxons soon felt the need to legitimize their position (especially with regard to subjects of Roman origin), marrying princesses belonging to the previous ruling dynasties. Christian princesses, of course, wasted no time in persuading their consorts to adopt Roman customs and, especially, the Roman religion.

This process is particularly well documented in the chronicles of the Reverend Bede (*The Anglo-Saxon Chronicle*). Toward the end of the sixth century, Ethelbert, prince of Kent, married Princess Bertha, daughter of the Christian king of Paris, the Merovingian Charibert. Bertha was accompanied by (among others) her personal chaplain, Bishop Liudhard, and was in the habit of praying in a little Roman church to the east of Canterbury dedicated to St. Martin (a sure sign that the pagan Saxons had not destroyed the Christian churches, as is often stated). Ethelbert did not convert immediately to Christianity, but allowed it to be restored in all the territories under his control (he was *bretwalda*—chief—of the kings in the Anglo-Saxon heptarchy).[24] In

---

*Archaeology shows a sudden de-Romanization of the provinces conquered by the Saxons, and because of this it is often stated that the Saxons exterminated the Romanized British populations. They have therefore gained an infamy as bloodthirsty exterminators, which is probably wholly undeserved. Actually, it was Aetius who emptied central Britannia, dispatching the entire Romanized ruling class to New Britannia. It was a mass exodus that has its exact parallel in the displacement of the population of Noricum carried out half a century later by Odoacer to rescue it from the pressure of the Rugii barbarians.

596, Pope Gregory the Great sent Bishop Augustine (later proclaimed saint) from Rome with everything necessary for restoring the structure of the church in the territories from which it had been expelled a century and a half earlier. Augustine landed in Kent in 597, accompanied by forty monks (many of whom were probably priests), plus an unspecified entourage of relatives, scribes, and servants—a true army of faith. Ethelbert accepted baptism, along with thousands of his fellow countrymen (it was Whit Sunday) and persuaded other Saxon sovereigns to do the same. He then gave Augustine a free hand to carry out his work of reconstruction. Gregory immediately sent reinforcements—the bishops Mellitus, Justus, and others—with the task of founding two ecclesiastical provinces in the Saxon territories, each having twelve suffragan bishoprics (601). The metropolitan seats must have been the British bishoprics of York (for northern England) and Canterbury, capital of Kent, where Augustine had established his own seat.

In subsequent years other Saxon kingdoms also accepted the restoration of the church, in particular Essex, with its capital London (a see from 604 onward), and the kingdom of Northumbria, evangelized by the bishop of York, Paulinus. The definitive structure of the Anglo-Saxon church was brought to completion by Archbishop Theodore of Canterbury, a Greek sent by Pope Vitalyn in 669. At the end of the seventh century, England was once again entirely Christian, tied to Rome, in spite of the distance and the huge problems of communication, by a solid bond of subjugation. The Anglo-Saxon church actually became one of the most devoted and loyal to the Roman papacy, to which it began to pay the so-called Peter's Pence, a tithe instituted on the model of the one owed by the Jews to the Temple of Jerusalem.

In this way the priestly family regained possession of its ancient British domains, first through the clergy, which poured in en masse from Rome and from nearby Gaul, but also very soon by reoccupying the positions that had been lost on the nonclerical level. In this it followed various strategies. The first was a policy of alliance by marriage with the dominant Saxon families—with a series of crossed marriages and their substitution by hereditary rights as soon as the occasion presented itself.

To a lesser extent the presence of the bishops, together with the matrimonial policies, must have favored the reentry of the noble families that had emigrated during the initial phases of the invasion and the reemergence of the landowning nobility that had stayed behind. Moreover, the administration of church property and the collection of tithes favored the emergence of new families strictly tied to the church itself, which thus accumulated vast fortunes.

It was once again the matrimonial policy that bore the most fruit. By the ancient custom of the priestly family that had existed since Ezra's time, it was the mother—not the father—who transmitted priestly blood.* Athelstan, the first English king to unite the whole of England, was the illegitimate son of Edward the Elder (died 924), king of Wessex, of undoubted Saxon origin. His mother, Ecgwynn, however, was a Welsh noble (and therefore of an ancient priestly family). On succeeding his father in the kingdom of Wessex, despite understandable opposition, he quickly took control of the whole island, being recognized by the Saxon, Welsh, and Scottish kings alike. Eventually, he established himself in York, where he founded the first Masonic lodge for which we have historical information. It was a significant choice, because it was in York, in 306, that Constantine had been proclaimed emperor.

Athelstan died without fathering sons, so his kingdom went back to the purely Saxon dynastic line. The priestly family, however, always aimed to win absolute predominance and, given its strong links to the church and to the nobility of the same origins, it was inevitable that it

---

*Josephus proclaimed himself of royal blood on his mother's side. Still more significant is the fact, reported by Josephus Flavius, that the sons of Herod the Great and Mariamme considered themselves to be of royal blood not because they were sons of Herod, who was not even considered a noble, but because of their mother, who was the daughter of the last Hasmonean king, Alexander. Athelstan may well have inherited his priestly status from his mother.

would eventually succeed. It happened in France with the expulsion of the Merovingian sovereigns of Frankish origin (as we will see later). The same must have happened in England with the Saxon dynasties, even though they were by then completely Christian. This alone, however, was not enough to save the Saxons, just as it had not been enough for the Merovingians.

The right moment presented itself in the second half of the eleventh century. The king of England then, Aethelred II, had married Emma, the daughter of Richard I, duke of Normandy. Their sons, Edward and Alfred, were brought up in Normandy. Having become king of England, Edward the Confessor favored the rise of his relatives and Norman friends, and in 1051 he promised to leave the kingdom to his cousin William, duke of Normandy. At least this is what William said. On the death of Edward in 1066, he reclaimed the throne of England on the basis of that promise. Edward, however, in the meantime had left it to the Saxon Harold II, lord of Wessex. William, who had long been preparing for just this eventuality, assured himself of the full support of the church and landed in England at the head of a small army, raising the banner of Pope Alexander II. He defeated and killed Harold at Hastings, and immediately the English bishops hurried to crown him king of England in Westminster Abbey. It was sufficient to march through the rest of the kingdom from Wales to Scotland to take possession of it.

The duke of Normandy did not so much conquer as take back possession of the kingdom of England as if it were something that belonged to him and his family by right. But what was it based on? Edward the Confessor's promise, if there had ever been one, surely did not constitute an adequate basis. The fact that Edward was the son of a Norman princess is already more substantial. But there must have been more. In the fifth century, the northwest of France—Brittany and Normandy—had become a fiefdom of the British families fleeing the Saxon invasion. Most of the aristocracy of this region, therefore, must have belonged to groups descended from the families of priestly origin that had originally been installed in Britannia by Constans Chlorus, Constantine, Theodosius, and Magnus Maximus.

In the ninth century, what from then on would be called Normandy was conquered by a band of Vikings (men of the north, hence the name Normans) probably from the Orkneys, led by a certain Rollo,* the son of the Viking chief Rognvald I Eysteinsson. In 911, by the Treaty of St. Clair-sur-Epte, the Carolingian sovereign Charles the Simple recognized Rollo as his vassal, granting him as a fiefdom the duchy of Normandy. In return, Rollo converted to Christianity and married Poppa de Bayeux, the daughter of the count of Bayeux, a member of the local nobility.

Their son, William I Longsword married a woman from the same nobility, Sprota of Brittany, and all their descendants did likewise. Their son Richard I married Gunnora of Crepon, from whom was born Richard II, who married Judith of Brittany, from whom was born Robert I, father of William the Conquerer. William was also the son of a local woman, a certain Herleve de Falaise, who, legend has it, was the daughter of a leather tanner, and who was not even officially married. William, then, was a bastard, but his mother was surely not a woman of humble origins, because otherwise he could not have succeeded his father in 1035, while he was still a child, against the will of the aristocracy of Viking origin.

There was no doubt the *longa manus* of God, represented by the archbishop of Rouen (his father's brother), who protected and sustained him. It took fourteen years of hard struggle against the Viking aristocracy, which was virtually wiped out, before William succeeded in tak-

---

*During the second half of the ninth century, Normandy was frequently invaded by the Vikings, who began to establish themselves, initially temporarily, along the coasts. At the end of the century the settlements became permanent and began to threaten the kingdom of France. In 911, King Charles III was forced to accept as his vassal Rollo, who had taken over Rouen, and he gave Rollo the title of duke of Normandy. Rollo, converted to Christianity, organized a strong duchy, where the Norman conquerors fused with the local population.[25]

ing complete control of his duchy.[26] At the end of the struggle, we must presume that the Norman aristocracy was mainly made up of descendants of the ancient British lines of priestly origin and that William was regarded as belonging to them. Actually, he descended in a direct line from Rollo the Viking, but the blood that flowed in his veins was 95 percent Breton by female descent.

Through William the Conquerer, the priestly family regained total control over the British Isles and it never lost it again. A hundred and thirty years later, the Norman dynasty in turn was replaced by the Plantagenets, another family from the priestly pool, which had already been installed for centuries in the French region of Anjou. This is what we will see in the next chapter.

16

COUNTERATTACK!

THE RECONQUEST OF POLITICAL POWER

At Christmas in the year 800, Charlemagne, the king of the Franks, was crowned emperor—the first in the West since 476. The court poet Alcuin hailed him with the name Flavius Anicius Carolus.[1] In spite of the historians who insist on calling Charlemagne a barbarian descended from barbarian ancestors, this name is further confirmation that the Carolingians descended from one of those senatorial families of great landowners that had immediately integrated into Frankish society while keeping their property and privileges. We saw in chapter 13 that the family of the Anicis was one of the most eminent and richest in the Roman senate, and that one of its branches was among the greatest families in Gaul by the end of the third century. It belonged in some capacity to the Gens Flavia, because it was related to more than one emperor (including Carinus, Probus, and Anicius Olybrius).

We also saw conclusively that it was a family of Judaic priestly origin, as were all—or nearly all—of the families that made up the Gallic aristocracy from whose ranks came virtually the whole of the Catholic clergy, in particular the bishops. The Franks of barbarian origin held military power, but those of Gallo-Roman origin owned most of the land and controlled the economy and religion. They eventually also regained political and military power.

The Merovingian sovereigns had imposed themselves on Gaul thanks to the backing of the clergy and landed nobility, which continued as in the past to provide for the civil service and from whose ranks were drawn the functionaries who helped the sovereign to govern the kingdom. Inevitably, because they controlled the economy and religion, these functionaries, and especially those who held the office known as mayor of the palace, acquired more and more power. By the turn of the seventh century, all the power was already concentrated in the hands of the mayor of the palace and the king had become virtually a symbolic figurehead—albeit of fundamental importance, because he represented the unity of the Frankish state and it was in his name that the mayor of the palace governed. The Merovingians were called *roi fainéant* (do-nothing kings) for their ineptitude and lack of political initiative, and it was with this epithet that they went down in history.

The office of mayor of the palace was the prerogative of a restricted number of families of great landowners in a well-defined area centered on the ancient capital of the prefecture of Gaul, Trier. It was here, in the basin of the Moselle and the Rhine, and in Reims, Metz, Tours, Brabant, and Alsace-Lorraine, where the Roman legions had, from the second century onward, been infiltrated by members of the cult of Sol Invictus Mithras. The members of the line of the priestly family who would go on to conquer the Empire had installed themselves in this organization and made their fortunes. In addition, it was in this region that the first and most complete integration of the barbarian and Roman populations would take place, thanks to the actions of the branches of the priestly family, which for more than a century had been using barbarian militias for their defense, instilling in them respect for Roman law and culture.

Because the Franks (like the other European barbarians, for that matter) never expropriated the lands of the aristocracy or of the Gallo-Roman clergy, the great landowners who held and sustained the office of mayor of the palace were descendants of Gallo-Roman senatorial families. In all, there were about thirty families allied with each other, and subsequently, we find them at the head of all the European nations.

A characteristic of these family lines, which clearly betrays their priestly origins, was that of their being intimately linked to the church. Those who did not devote themselves to a political career were destined to become bishops or abbots, and all the branches founded large numbers of monasteries and abbeys in their respective domains. From the time of Pepin the Short onward, for example, the Carolingians controlled at least two hundred powerful abbeys, which they regarded as their personal property. To preside over them, they designated their own sons and daughters—legitimate or otherwise—wives and mothers, as well as close relatives and their most trusted supporters.

It was common practice to appoint to the head of the abbeys non-clerical people who had not taken religious orders. In fact, the line between nonclerical and clerical was practically nonexistent, and the respective roles were interchangeable. The nobles (those of Roman origin, that is) could be appointed as bishops overnight, sometimes at a very young age, and they could all become abbots without renouncing their civil appointments or family life. The mother of Pepin II, for example, was an abbess, and so were his wife and daughters. This was a common practice of all the great Carolingian landed nobility. The appointment of bishops and abbots was the prerogative of the king and the great local feudal lords, and the office was always conferred on their children or on their most loyal supporters in return for their services. Further, in their domains, the bishops had all the duties and prerogatives of nonclerical princes. The sole difference between their roles and that of actual princes was that their office was not hereditary. This is exactly as we would expect from a noble caste whose members considered themselves priests by birthright.

Clovis had created an immense kingdom that stretched from the North Sea to the Mediterranean. On his death, it was divided among his sons, and in this way there were created two Frankish kingdoms perennially struggling for supremacy: Austrasia in the northeast and Neustria in the west and central south. In the course of yet another

clash between the two kingdoms, in 613, two men distinguished themselves particularly: Arnulf and Pepin I.

Arnulf was born around 580 to a family that owned vast domains
on the plains of Woevre (a large tract of land between the Meuse and
the Moselle) and in the area around Worms. As a boy, as was the custom in the noble families of Roman origin, he received a good literary
education, with, of course, an accent on religion. As an adolescent, he
was sent to court under the guardianship of the then mayor of the palace, a certain Gandolf, a rich landowner from Metz who was apparently
from the same senatorial family as Bishop Gregory of Tours.

Despite his monastic tendencies, Arnulf married and had numerous
children. He acquired ever more influence at court and tied his interests to those of a noble in the same situation, Pepin, sealing an enduring alliance through the marriage of their children. Pepin came from
a family that owned immense tracts of land. The domains of his clan
extended to various parts around Metz, in Brabant, in Heysbaye, and
around Namur in the Meuse Basin, which had become the main road
for the economic traffic of northern Europe. Pepin had married a certain Itta, sister of the bishop of Trier, whose dowry included huge tracts
of land.

With the help of Arnulf and Pepin, the Merovingian king Chlothar
II reunited the kingdom of the Franks under his own dominion in 613.
As a show of gratitude, he offered Arnulf the vacant seat of bishop
of Metz, the capital of Austrasia. When Chlothar instated his son
Dagobert, just ten years old, at the head of the kingdom of Austrasia,
he entrusted him to the care of Arnulf, who also had the responsibility of government. To share this responsibility, he appointed Pepin as
mayor of the palace. Pepin soon remained alone in the government of
Austrasia, because Arnulf withdrew to one of the monasteries to which
he had disseminated his possessions in the area of Metz, in the foothills
of the Vosges Mountains.

The successor of Pepin I, his son Grimoald, thought the moment
had arrived to get rid of the Merovingian dynasty and instate himself

in its place. King Siegeberd II had no sons and despaired of ever having any, so he accepted Grimoald's proposal of adopting his son and giving him a typical Merovingian name, Childebert. Some time later, however, Siegeberd was presented with a son, Dagobert, by his legitimate queen, and he designated this son as his heir and entrusted him to Grimoald. On the death of the king, however, Grimoald refused to acknowledge the will of Siegeberd. He proclaimed his own son as the king's successor, locking up the legitimate heir in a convent. The reaction of the Frankish nobility, especially that of Neustria, was immediate: Grimoald and his son were killed and the Merovingian dynasty was restored. Evidently, it was not yet the right moment.

THE CAROLINGIANS

After a period of eclipse, Grimoald's son, Pepin II, known as Pepin the Short, regained control of the whole kingdom of the Franks, which he governed on behalf of the Merovingian sovereign Theodoric III. Pepin installed friends and relatives at the head of a large number of bishoprics and abbeys in France, and he distributed fiefdoms to his supporters. On his death, he was succeeded in the office of mayor of the palace by his son Charles, who would give his name to the following dynasty, because he was considered the first king in the family—though actually he never wore the crown and was never elected king. He was considered such in practice, however, especially by the pope and the bishops in France. On the death of the Merovingian sovereign Chlothar IV, who he had instated himself, he continued to govern alone, still with the title of mayor of the palace. On his death, the abbot Willibrord wrote a note in the official calendar of the abbey of St. Denis, where Charles was buried: "October 741, death of King Charles." In effect he had governed like a real sovereign, while never actually having that title.

Charles's most notable enterprise was the defeat he inflicted near Poitiers, on October 25, 732, on an Arab army that had invaded France. Charles was hailed as the savior of Christianity, and for this victory he was given the nickname of Martel (Hammer),[2] a deliberate parallel to Judas Maccabeus (Maccabeus means "hammer"), the founder of the Hasmonean dynasty. It was a significant parallel, because the Hasmoneans were kings and their descendants were of royal blood authorized to wear the crown. (We can remember that Josephus Flavius declares himself to be a descendant of the Hasmoneans on his mother's side.)

This crowning occurred formally with Charles the Hammer's son, Pepin III. Pepin conveniently provided himself with the cover of a Merovingian king appointed by him, the young Childeric III, but he prepared his own accession to the throne with care, first ensuring for himself the backing of Pope Zachary. As far as the Frankish church was concerned, it was not necessary for him to get its backing, because in effect it had been completely under the control of the Pippinid clan and the families allied with it since they had first appeared on the historical scene. This, in fact, had been the main reason for their irresistible rise.

Pepin directly controlled—or controlled through the families that were his allies—most of the bishop's sees in the Frankish kingdom and more than two hundred monasteries and abbeys, and he was careful to put them in the charge of relatives and supporters. In particular, he put his friend Fulrad in charge of the abbey of St. Denis, where Charles the Hammer was buried, and he instated another close ally, Chrodegang, as bishop of Metz. Before finally attempting his coup d'etat, he made sure of the backing of the pope through the abbot Fulrad. Having obtained it, he locked up the young Merovingian king, Childeric III, in the monastery of St. Bertin (where he died a few years later), assembled the nobles of the kingdom in Soisson, and had himself named king. It was November 751.

To crown his triumph and prevent a return of the Merovingians, a few months later Pepin had himself anointed king by the bishops in France, probably at the hands of Boniface, the pope's representative in Gaul, thereby reviving the ancient anointment ritual of the kings of

Israel and Judah. In this way, he was raised to the level of the biblical kings. The anointment was repeated at St. Denis three years later, on Christmas Day, by Pope Stephen II himself, who had come to France just for this purpose, and on this occasion Pepin's two sons, Charles and Carloman, were also anointed. In anointing the new royal family, Pope Stephen "forbade anyone, on penalty of excommunication, to dare in the future to choose a king outside the lineage of these princes, who were raised to the royal rank by Divine mercy through the intercession of the apostles and consecrated by the hand of the Pontiff, their vicar."[3]

Charles and Carloman were adopted as sons of the papacy, and the pope also became godfather to Giselle, Pepin's daughter. In return, Pepin went to Italy to defend the pope from the excessive power of the Longobards and granted to the papacy those territories, which would later form the church state. It was probably on this occasion that the so-called Donation of Constantine document was drawn up.

The visit to France of Pope Stephen II also heralded the end of any relationship of dependence of the papacy on the emperor of Constantinople.[4] Pepin and his sons were appointed Roman patricians, and with this title, Pepin took on the task of protecting the Holy See.

JUDAIC ASPECTS OF THE CAROLINGIAN KINGDOM

It seems clear that the Carolingians and the whole clerical and non-clerical nobility behind them strived to reproduce in every detail the reality of the Jerusalem of the Hasmoneans. One of the first acts of Pepin the Short, after his anointment, was introducing to his kingdom the practice of paying tithes to the Temple, which had been in force in Israel: from then on, the tenth part of all the products of the land were destined for the church, and it was the king's functionaries who took care of the collection. The practice of paying tithes to the church was emulated and extended to the whole of the West under Charlemagne and would remain in force for almost a millennium.

The references to Israel were continuous. We have already seen the appellation Maccabeus conferred on Charles I. It is also significant that Pope Stephen II and his brother and successor Paul I wrote numerous letters to Pepin in which they compare him to a "new Moses."[5] Charlemagne liked to call himself "chief of the new chosen people,"[6] and he compared himself to King Josiah, the sovereign of Judah who, at the end of the reign of the ungodly Manasseh, spared no efforts in "restoring to the service of God the kingdom that God had entrusted to him."[7] He took seriously the priestly status—so much so that he considered himself a king and priest at the same time and assumed for himself the right to legislate in the religious field and to receive the tribute of obedience from all the clergy, including the pope.

Another title he welcomed was that of "new David, triumphant over the enemies of Israel." As such, he regarded his mission as that of leading the "new chosen people" to their salvation and imposing the Christian faith on all the pagan peoples. Germans, Slavs, Scandinavians, Magyars, and so on, were conquered by force and converted to Christianity by any means—even at the price of atrocities and mass extermination. The Carolingian army grew to be similar to an army from the Hebrew Scriptures: soldiers fasted before battle and threw themselves into attack singing the Kyrie eleison.

Charlemagne fought wherever there was heresy, even outside the confines of his kingdom. Significantly, however, the Jews were never persecuted in this period; in fact, they enjoyed respect and protection as well as free access to the royal courts, including the papal one. In 812, Louis the Pious, son and successor to Charlemagne, promulgated a decree in favor of the merchants, in particular the Jewish ones, who attended the court, establishing that "they must be able to enter our palace freely. And if they wish to increase their means of transportation within the kingdom, so as to be able to trade more profitably for themselves and for us, let them be left in peace. The seizing of their goods must be neither tolerated nor inflicted . . ."[8] To meet the demands of the Jewish merchants, Louis went so far as to move market day from Saturday to another day of the week.[9]

Conspicuous in its absence is any reference to the Roman world, despite the fact that Charlemagne had revived its empire. Yet it was not the empire of Rome that he had brought back to life, but that of the church inaugurated by Constantine. Actually, the only parallel to the Roman world was the one drawn by Pope Leo III between Charlemagne and Constantine: in a mosaic he had made in the Lateran in 795, one side depicted Christ handing a standard to Constantine, and the other side showed St. Peter handing a banner to Leo III and a standard to King Charles.[10] The allusion to Charles as the new Constantine is clear. It is a very pertinent and significant parallel in the context of the priestly "theory": Constantine had conquered the Roman Empire for the priestly family, and Charlemagne had reconquered the whole of Europe.*

The mentality of Charlemagne and the noble class that supported him was also perfectly analogous to that of the Judaic priestly class at the time of the kingdom of Judah and the Western Roman aristocracy in the fifth century. Any sense of the state was dominated by the logic of the family and the religion it controlled. The "state" consisted of Christianity as a whole at whose summit sat the high priest, who from Rome was the guarantor of the state's unity. The territorial, ethnic, political, and administrative subdivisions had no relevance and varied continuously without in any way damaging the united nature of the Christian world. Charlemagne parceled out his kingdom to his sons and vassals without consideration of nationality. The only inviolable criterion was that power, with its connected property and privileges,

---

*Charlemagne forged Europe and imposed on it, to its farthest frontiers, a noble class entirely made up from the priestly caste. It was he too who revitalized and reestablished the rules of the secret organization—the heir of Sol Invictus—that grouped together these family groups and which, for convenience, I have called Freemasonry. The Cooke Manuscript says expressly that it was the king of the Franks Charles II (i.e., Charlemagne; the first was Charles the Hammer) who established Freemasonry in Europe and regulated its meetings. In fact, every year, at the beginning of the summer, Charlemagne convened a general meeting of his great nobles, ecclesiastics, military chiefs, and functionaries (a few hundred people, all belonging to families of priestly origin) to discuss matters of state.[11]

must be assigned to members of the families of priestly origin.

Charlemagne imposed on all inherited and conquered territories vassals that he selected exclusively from among members of the restricted group of families that had helped the Carolingians in their accession to the throne. The ethnic groups of people living in those territories had not the slightest relevance in his assignment of fiefdoms to vassals. In addition, linguistic differences were completely ignored, for Latin remained the official language of the clergy and the educated class everywhere.

Each vassal, of course, immediately adopted the vernacular spoken by the population subjugated to him, which makes it extremely difficult to establish the true origins of his family. At one time, for example, historians believed the various princes, dukes, marquises, and barons who governed Germany came from the local populations, which is not at all true. Today, even the most nationalistic historians acknowledge that the whole German nobility derives from a class of military officers and royal functionaries installed by the Carolingians and often tied to them by bonds of blood. Further, they have descended from the same restricted group.

A school of German historians, headed by Gerd Tallenbach,[12] has studied the evolution of this state aristocracy and has demonstrated how Charlemagne instated this group of nobles in the whole of Carolingian Europe. We find them in Italy as counts, abbots, and bishops not only in the conquered Lombard kingdom, but also in the duchy of Spoleto. The duchy was given as a fiefdom to a member of the Lambertini family, who in addition to its primitive Breton domains (Brittany was always an inexhaustible source of members of the priestly family) had obtained important fiefdoms in various parts of the Carolingian empire, including Alsace.

Another important branch in this group was that of the Unruochings. Its founder, Unruoch, was sent by Charlemagne to Denmark. His brother was made a count in Alamannia, while his son, Duke Eberhard of Friuli, started an important dynasty in Italy—and so on. The whole of the European aristocracy, which instated itself in the course of the ninth century, derived from these restricted family branches. Many of these evidently emphasized that their priestly ancestral origins were equivalent to those of the Carolingians, and they did not hesitate at the first favorable opportunity to raise themselves to royal status.

THE CAPETIANS

It is only in this context that it becomes possible to understand the change of dynasty that occurred toward the end of the tenth century, when the Carolingians were replaced by the Capetians. Of the first member of this family to emerge into history—a certain Robert—we know only that he belonged to the same family as Chrodegang, bishop of Metz, a native of the same region as the Carolingians and always their ally.

We meet Robert Capet for the first time as the favorite of King Charles the Bald. He married a noblewoman who was closely related to the Carolingian royal family. In 852, we meet him again as both the count and abbot of Marmoutier, near Tours. In 853, he became *missus dominicus* (envoy of the ruler) for various counties in Maine, Touraine, and Anjou. In 861, he received the title of duke of Neustria and was charged with defending the lands between the Loire and the Seine against the Bretons. He died in battle near Angers in 866, fighting victoriously against the Norman mercenaries that he himself had hired to fight the Bretons, but who had revolted against him.

Thus ended his career as condottiere, which does not seem to have been particularly grandiose or glorious. Yet in the *Annals of Fulda* he merits the title of "Maccabeus of our times."[13] Here, too, we have indications of his priestly status, because, though nonclerical and married, he was the abbot of various abbeys and controlled various bishop's sees. At the same time, then, he was both a military and civil chief and a man of the church in the tradition of the Mosaic priestly family. He is also linked precisely to the Hasmonean dynasty, a status that authorized his family to aspire to a royal crown—which they obtained little more than a century later. Robert's descendant Hugh Capet,* who in the meantime had become duke of Burgundy, was elected king of the Franks on June 1, 987, and on July 3, he was anointed in Reims Cathedral by Archbishop Adalbero. Thus emerged a new dynasty known as the third race because it came after those of the Merovingians and the Carolingians, which would reign over France for eight centuries, both directly and through the secondary branches of the Valois, the Orleans, and finally the Bourbons.

THE ANGEVINS

Another family of priestly origin that suddenly burst forth from obscurity as one of the greatest in Europe was that of the Angevins. We meet them for the first time in the historical chronicles around 800, when members begin to be instated as counts of Angers, the capital of a small region, Anjou, on the eastern border of Brittany. They must have either been lords in the area since ancient times (because they were one of the noble British families that had fled the Saxons) or been instated in the fiefdom of Anjou by the Carolingians. One situation does not exclude the other, because the Carolingians confirmed as their feudal lords those local lords who placed themselves at their service, especially if they belonged to the priestly caste. In the case of the Angevins, descent from a family of Roman-British origin is confirmed by one of the first counts mentioned in the medieval historical chronicles, Fulk Richin, the son of a certain Fulk Martel (Hammer). Richin expressly declares himself to have descended from an ancestor called Inghelgarius, who was in turn said to be a descendant of an illustrious Roman-British family.[14] Because there is evidence that

---

*The name Capet derives from the word "cape," and it seems to allude to the abbatial cape, a short mantel that was worn by abbots.

he came from the province of Flavia Caesarnsis Maxima, abandoned en masse in the wake of the Saxon advance by the Anglo-Roman nobility instated by Theodosius and Magnus Maximus, it is likely that Inghelgarius was related to the latter.

The Angevins must also have been a very important branch, on the same level as the Carolingians, because they too had descended from the Gens Flavia. This was evidently unknown to the masses, but was well known in priestly circles.

In the early centuries of this family group's known history, nothing important seems to have distinguished it from the various other similar noble families in the French province. A certain Fulk III acquired fame by participating in the early pilgrimages[15] to Palestine. His son Geoffrey the Hammer (a recurrent and very significant nickname in the family, because it recalls the Maccabees and was already linked to the Carolingians and the Capetians) enlarged his father's domains by incorporating various nearby fiefdoms in the Loire Valley, which, however, were almost lost again shortly afterward. Finally, in 1106, a certain Fulk V became count of Anjou, and he suddenly raised the branch to a status that was among the highest in Europe. The most remarkable and revealing aspect of this dizzying rise is that it was accomplished without force of arms.

In fact, the only military actions of Fulk V were limited to the reconquest of the city of Le Mans, which temporarily put him at odds with the neighboring duke of Normandy, Henry I, who was also king of England. He carried out his masterstroke in 1128, when he married his fifteen-year-old son, Geoffrey, to the twenty-six-year-old Matilda, who was the daughter of Henry I and the widow of the emperor of the Holy Roman Empire, the German Henry V, who had died in 1125. After the death of his firstborn son, William, in a shipwreck in the English Channel, Henry I had named his daughter Matilda as his successor to the throne of England and the duchy of Normandy. He also decided to place at her side a husband who would help her govern. He chose the very young son of Fulk V.

Geoffrey of Anjou, known as the Plantagenet, held no noble or any other kind of title at the time he was chosen, yet he suddenly became heir to the throne of England and the duchy of Normandy. The following year, his father, Fulk V, now a widower, also left him the county of Anjou and went to Palestine to marry Melisende, the eldest daughter of Baldwin II, the king of Jerusalem. Fulk V thus became heir to the throne of Jerusalem, which he took possession of two years later, in 1131.[16] In this way, in very short order, father and son found themselves respectively kings of Jerusalem and England.

A few years later, the young son of Geoffrey and Matilda, Henry II, by then solidly instated on the throne of England and master of the duchy of Normandy and the county of Anjou, further widened the family domains to the border of Spain by marrying a woman eleven years his senior, Eleanor of Aquitaine. Divorced from the king of France, Louis VII, Eleanor brought him in her dowry the kingdom of Aquitaine. A second branch of the Angevin family then laid claim to the Norman possessions in the south of Italy, taking the crown of the kingdom of the two Sicilies and subsequently also those of Hungary and Poland.

In just two generations, therefore, these provincial petty noblemen burst onto the Mediterranean scene from Scotland to the Pyrenees and from the Atlantic to the Dead Sea, with various royal crowns on their heads in addition to ducal and other less important ones. This prodigious rise cannot be explained only by the luck and ability of Fulk V, as historians seem to believe. Royal crowns were not won in the lottery.

The marriage of the fifteen-year-old Geoffrey to the mature Empress Matilda was surely not due to coincidence or simply to Fulk's diplomatic ability or to the fact that Henry I was short of suitable candidates to marry the future queen of England. The choice of husband for a widowed queen was a matter that involved all the great ruling families and, first and foremost, the church—because in effect it was a question of choosing a new king. We have no precise information on the reasons that determined the choice of Geoffrey of Anjou as the future king of England or who took part in the choice, apart from the parents of the couple. Yet we know who made the choice and how it was made the following year, when Geoffrey's father Fulk married Melisende, heiress to the throne of Jerusalem. Her father, Baldwin II, lacking sons and wishing to arrange for a successor to himself, had sent a delegation to the king of France, Louis VI (a Capet, the highest civil authority of the priestly organization in Europe), to ask him to choose a suitable candidate from among the French nobility to succeed him to the throne of Jerusalem. The king had chosen Fulk, but not before making certain of the consent of the pope, Honorius II. Fulk of Anjou, therefore, was designated king of Jerusalem by both the king of France and the pope.

The situation must have gone no differently with his son, Geoffrey the Plantagenet, and the Empress Matilda. On the death of the last of the Norman kings, who was without direct male heirs, the opportunity presented itself for a change of dynasty in England. The land could finally return to a dynastic line of 100 percent royal and priestly blood, by direct descent from the family of the Hasmoneans.

Whoever married the widowed empress would automatically become king of England and duke of Normandy. The matter surely could not be left to the initiative of individual claimants or to the tastes of the queen. We do not know the details of this choice (which was far more important than the choice of the distant king of Jerusalem), but it is certain that a choice was made by someone—no doubt, apart from Henry I, Louis the VI of France and Pope Honorius II.

The chosen house was that of the counts of Anjou. Theirs was a second-rate noble title, definitely inferior to that of the nobility over which they would find themselves ruling. The chosen ruler, besides, was just fifteen years old, had no experience, and was not yet bestowed with any noble title. This rise in fortunes seems an inexplicable miracle if we do not consider the fact that the hierarchy of the secret organization did not necessarily mirror the public hierarchy. Instead, the hierarchy must have been based on rights of precedence that were known within the family of priestly descent. These rights were sooner or later made to count.

Evidently, the family of Anjou could claim direct descent from a priestly family of royal blood; in this, they were equal to the Carolingians and the Capetians. It is no coincidence that the nickname the Hammer (i.e., Maccabeus) was recurrent among the ancestors and relatives of Fulk V[17]—the same nickname of Judas Maccabeus, the priest who founded the Hasmonean Judaic dynasty. Whoever descended from that dynasty had royal blood in his veins and sooner or later managed to assert his rights to the crown, with the support of the whole priestly family and, first and foremost, of the church of Rome. Thus not one but two royal crowns fell at a stroke to the family of the counts of Anjou—and more fell subsequently.

THE OTTONIDS

Other crowns rained down on the various branches of the same group of families—such as the crown of Bavaria, which went to the family of the Agilolfings. This line had started in competition with the Pippinid clan for the office of mayor of the palace to the Merovingians and had been installed as feudal lords by Charlemagne after the conquest of Bavaria.

Another line that had an enormous influence on the destiny of Europe are the Ottonids. They too belonged to the group of great landowners in the northeast of Gaul that was trying to raise its fortunes at the court of the Merovingians. We meet the first member of the line around 640. He was in the position of mayor of the palace to King Dagobert and guardian to his son Sigebert III. He came from Wissembourgs, in Alsace. The family was installed in Saxony by Charlemagne together with other Frankish families at the time of Charlemagne's bloody conquest[18] of Saxony.*

---

*The conquest of Saxony by Charlemagne was carried out in three successive military campaigns that saw the massacre of the local nobility, deportations of the population, and the instatement of nobility and clergy of Frankish origin.

In the course of yet another Saxon revolt at the time of Louis the Pious, the Ottonid Liudolf of Saxony distinguished himself in his supression of the revolt and was rewarded with the duchy of Saxony.[19] The family's fortunes were consolidated by the marriage of Liudolf's daughter, Liutgarda, to the son of Emperor Louis the German, Charlemagne's son. In 912, Liudolf's grandson, Henry, transformed the duchy of Saxony into a kingdom and Henry's son Otto I became emperor.

In just two generations, then, the family went from being dukes to being kings and then emperors. The family also provided bishops, abbots, and abbesses throughout Saxony and, in 999, even a pope, Gregory V.

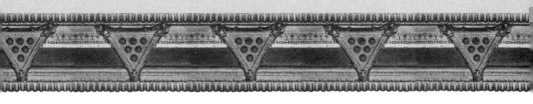

17

THE PERPETUATION
OF POWER BY THE
PRIESTLY FAMILY

THE PRIESTLY ORGANIZATION AT THE TIME
OF THE CAROLINGIANS

With the advent of the Carolingians, the priestly family regained control in Western Europe in an even more complete manner than had been the case under the Christian emperors following Constantine. Western Europe became the exact parallel of what the reign of Judah had been at the time of the Hasmoneans: it was a theocratic state where the ruling class of nobles, from the emperor and the great feudal lords to the last of the knights, was composed of descendants of the Mosaic priestly family—and the ecclesiastical hierarchies were drawn exclusively from this class.

The concept of the family existed in lieu of the concept of the state. Large kingdoms were formed and then divided, only to reform and redivide quite independently of the ethnic substrate of the populations governed. The Middle Ages seemed like a period when there was a perpetual instability of borders amid a permanent political chaos. In actual fact, this was not so. The whole of the Christian world was considered to be the undivided property of the priestly family. The borders of the New Israel were those of Christianity. The movements of the internal borders reflected only the changing fortunes of single branches of the family, and not of the priestly organization as a whole.

We are led to believe that this organization was still active at the time of Charlemagne. Its traditional ritual contents and its way of operating must have been derived largely from that organization created by Ezra at the time of the return from the Babylonian exile and reestablished in Rome by Josephus Flavius. Yet it is certain that at this time it no longer possessed a centralized structure and had no autonomous power to make decisions. Further, its aim was no longer to infiltrate the offices of the public administration.

Sol Invictus Mithras had maintained the character of a united, autonomous organization, at least up to the end of the fourth century. The various mithraea were spread throughout the Empire, and each of them brought together the local members of priestly origin, probably with a certain differentiation depending on whether they were mainly military or civil officials. At the local level, each mithraeum was completely autonomous in its decisions (especially given the distances and the time required for communication). Yet the aims were common to all of them, and every mithraeum was accountable to a central authority, the pater patrum situated in Rome, from whom they received instructions.

Because he was the head of the priestly organization, the pater patrum must have been the equivalent of the high priest of the Jewish tradition, and it is likely that he was chosen on the basis of his genetic seniority. We know for certain that he was not the same person as the bishop of Rome. One of the regular policies of this period was to maintain a clear distinction between the Mithraic organization and the church. We are thus led to conclude that even if the men directly and publicly involved in the Christian religion—the local presbyters and bishops—were chosen from among the members of branches of the priestly family, they were not active members of the organization.

Furthermore, none of the public figures who belonged to Sol Invictus were ever technically members of the church, because none of them were baptized, even when they openly professed their Christian faith. Christianity was the religion that was favored by Sol Invictus and was the undisputed domain of the priestly family, but those who followed a political career were never baptized. Baptism meant giving up any kind of public position once and for all and starting an exclusively ecclesiastical career. One example may suffice: St. Ambrose. All the members of Sol Invictus, however, were priests, and we have seen that during the course of the third and fourth centuries, they had also infiltrated the traditional pagan religions, arriving at the top of the Roman priestly castes. For this purpose, we have seen that they had developed a syncretistic philosophy that allowed them to reconcile the monotheism professed by the priests of Jewish origins and the multiplicity of pagan divinities. These multiple gods were considered to be expressions or aspects of a unique superior divinity represented by the sun.

This created a strange and paradoxical situation. For more than a half-century after Constantine, three leading positions—or rather, institutions—coexisted in the Roman Empire. They were formally independent of each other, but their spheres of authority were closely connected with wide areas of overlap, which inevitably ended up creating situations of conflict. Two of these positions were public and possessed a bureaucratic organization that extended all over the state: There was the emperor, who held civil and military power, but who was, at the same time, the high priest—the supreme head of all religions—in his capacity as pontifex maximus. There was also the bishop of Rome, who was head only of the Christian religion. Christianity had authority over all the churches in the Empire and was considered the only legitimate religion of the priestly family, with spiritual and moral authority over all its members, including the emperor. Finally, there was a third institution: Sol Invictus Mithras. It had no public office or bureaucratic structure, it operated in conditions of the utmost secrecy, it included the heads of the branches of the priestly family, and thus it presumed or attempted to control and influence the decisions of both of the other two authorities. At the head of Sol Invictus Mithras was the pater patrum, who, from the fourth century on, was usually a leading member of the Roman senate.

The new organization of the Empire adopted in Milan in 313 aimed to avoid conflict between these three authorities by limiting the responsibilities and the spheres of influence of each of them. Judging by the behavior of the Christian emperors, it is clear that they believed that Christianity, like all the traditional pagan religions, came under their authority as pontifices. (To cite one of the many possible examples, the epoch-making Council of Nicaea was convened and presided over by Constantine, technically a pagan at that time, who gave rise to the so-called Caesaro-papism.)

The situation is less clear with regard to the relationships between the emperor and the Mithraic organization, because the latter founded its power not on the occupation of public positions, but only on the loyalty of its members. It is perfectly evident that Sol Invictus Mithras maintained an autonomous, sovereign role at least until the time of Constantine. During the whole of the third century, it was capable of creating and destroying emperors at will, and its power was undoubtedly greater than that of the emperor. It acted as a shadow government of the Roman Empire to the point that for several decades it could afford to designate expendable emperors, who could be controlled and eliminated on the first occasion of disobedience.

Diocletian's attempt to free the emperor's power from the control of Sol Invictus, which terminated in a slaughter of Christians, determined a radical change in the policy of the secret organization, which from then on chose the Christian religion as a means to control society. This led to the imposition of Christianity all over the Empire, and consequently to a radical change in Roman society.

Inevitably, the Mithraic organization itself was also forced to adapt. First of all, it must have lost the role of shadow government that it had had before Diocletian. The emperor and the head of the Christian church, the two leading public authorities of the Christianized Empire, which were both emanations of the same secret organization, were by nature incapable of accepting any limitations to their authority in their respective fields of responsibility. The secret priestly organization thus came to be squashed between these two poles, which it had itself created. Sooner or later it was bound to lose its autonomy and its decision-making power. At first, this foreseeable outcome was avoided by the decision to move the strongest element of the triad, the emperor, away from Rome (the seat of the head of the Mithraic organization) and to form an alliance with the bishop of Rome, who was the weaker element at that time and appeared to be subordinate to Sol Invictus (because he had no political power and his followers in the Empire were still a minority).

As we have seen, this decision marked the beginning of the process that eventually led to the division of the Roman Empire into two separate parts with two different destinies. It did not succeed, however, in guaranteeing a permanent autonomy for the Mithraic organization. From the moment in 324 when Constantine declared that Christianity was the state religion, the fate of Sol Invictus appeared to be sealed. Within fifty years, Christianity spread throughout the Empire, gaining such influence and power that the balance of power with the secret priestly organization was overturned, making the latter subaltern and without any real autonomy.

The social base of the followers of Sol Invictus had undergone a radical change during the third century. Most of them belonged to the equestrian order, which was the backbone of the imperial administration, the army, and the praetorium. Thanks to imperial policies, which actively encouraged this process, practically all the members of the equestrian order became senators during the third and fourth centuries, completely replacing the families of the original aristocracy. Halfway through the fourth century, as we have seen, all the members of the Roman senate professed to be followers of Christianity or Sol Invictus. We have also seen that during the fourth century, the pater patrum, the

Mithraic pope, was always a member of the Roman senate. It is beyond doubt, therefore, that in the end the Mithraic organization was controlled at the central level by the Roman senate.*

The bishop of Rome controlled the Christian churches all over the Empire, but in Rome itself, he was undoubtedly subordinate to the senate, on which his appointment and his security depended. We should not forget that Pope Damasus was imposed as head of the church and acquitted from the charge of murder, thanks to the pater patrum Agorius Praetextatus, who drove his rival, Ursinus, out of Rome.

THE PRIMACY OF THE BISHOP OF ROME

The balance of power was overturned at the end of the fourth century. In 383, in confirmation of an edict of Gratianus, the Roman senate had prohibited public manifestations of a paganlike character in all the Western Empire. From that moment on, Sol Invictus Mithras lost control over the religions of the Empire, because the only religion permitted (with the exception of Judaism) was Christianity. The following year, 384, saw the death of Agorius Praetextatus, the last of the senators indicated as Mithras's pope. The appointment passed by default to the Roman Catholic bishop. On December 11, 384, Pope Damasus died and Syricius was elected. His importance in the history of the church is considerable: he was the first bishop of Rome to assume the title of "papa" (pope), acronym of pater patrum.

Syricius not only took on the title of the head of the Mithraic organization, but he also assumed his political prerogatives. His pontificate represents a milestone in the affirmation of the primacy of the Roman church, and he is remembered in history as the initiator of the so-called *decretales*—that is, pontifical documents drawn up in the form of letters, which had the authority of laws and were, from then on, the

---

*Archaeological excavations show that most senatorial families of the fourth century possessed a private mithraeum.

instrument of papal power.[1] With Syricius, the secret priestly organization completely lost its operative autonomy and became subordinate to the church. Practically overnight, the Roman senate, which had been supposed to be the stronghold of paganism, was discovered to be totally Christian, and the head of the church, the new pater patrum, became the leading authority in the Western Empire—obviously together with the Roman senate, with whom he governed from then on in perfect harmony.

The worship of Sol Invictus Mithras was formally declared illegal immediately afterward, in 396,[2] but its official abolition undoubtedly did not mean that the organization was dismantled. It underwent only a change of identity, for the open worship of the sun was no longer acceptable in a Christianized world. Even if the organization continued to maintain its solar attributes, Sol Invictus assumed the more religiously correct name of Great Architect of the Universe, borrowed from the Pythagoreans, and Mithras disappeared from the scene, at least as far as Rome was concerned. Outside the capital, in certain secluded areas of the Alps and in particular in the Vosges (the area that was to see the rise of the mayors of the palace of the Merovingians and of those families allied with them), Sol Invictus continued to survive, in accordance with the ancient customs, for the whole of the fifth century.

Yet it was no longer and could no longer be the organization that had enabled the priestly family to gain control of the Roman Empire. Now that stage was over, and having accomplished its main function, the organization continued to survive only as a means to defend the interests of the Roman senatorial class and the Catholic clergy, which was an expression of this class.

In the Eastern Empire, under a sovereign who could not accept any conditioning by a secret organization that was beyond his control, it soon became useless and eventually disappeared. In the Western Empire, on the contrary, it was the emperor's position that was eliminated, and real power remained in the hands of the senatorial caste and the clergy. Yet they had placed military power in the hands of a series of barbarian leaders who could not govern without the mediation of the senators and clergy, although they possessed an enormous power, which somehow had to be kept under control. Thus the need for a secret organization in which the members of the priestly family could recognize themselves and through which they could defend the interests of their category. We can therefore conclude that it survived all through the period of the so-called barbarian kingdoms.

We do not lack evidence to confirm this. For example, those who held public offices continued for some decades not to be baptized and to celebrate Mithraic rituals in private. When Alaric besieged Rome in 410, Pope Innocentius I authorized the senate to return to pagan rituals in the illusion that this might avert the danger. (Symmachus had defended the tradition, arguing that it had served the capital admirably. The adversity that was tormenting Rome was attributed to the fact that the emperor had abolished the ancient syncretistic customs of Sol Invictus.) Then there is the testimony of Pope Leo the Great, who observed in 460, fifty years later, that many Christians turned toward the sun before entering St. Peter's and bowed in its honor.[3]

This means that the organization continued to operate with its traditional contents and forms. The name Mithras had been definitively cancelled, but the sun continued to be omnipresent in the Catholic religion, and all its feast days continued to be celebrated with the greatest solemnity. The "day of the sun" became "the day of the Lord" and Christmas became the most important festivity of the year and the date regularly chosen for the most significant ceremonies of a nonreligious character. Clodoveus, for example, was baptized on Christmas Day; Pepin the Short was anointed king on Christmas Day; and on Christmas Day, Charlemagne received the imperial crown.

Historians carefully avoid underlining this fact, but there is no doubt that in the eighth century the nobility that emerged as sovereign and master in Europe was composed almost entirely of descendants of the senatorial nobility who had come to power in the Roman world during the fourth and fifth centuries. This miracle could not have occurred without a constant, well-organized policy defending the interests of that class—and without the fact that this policy was pursued by an organization promoting solidarity among its members and acting as an organ of decision-making and coordination.

After the year 396, mithraea were very gradually abandoned as meeting places for the secret organization, although some were still built in Rome after this date.[4] In contrast with the affirmations of some historians, the mithraea were not destroyed by Christians:* as we have seen, churches were erected over many of them, and it is possible that they continued to be used as reserved meeting places. The ritual practices that were carried out there must have continued for a long time, albeit in a private form, purged of their more openly pagan elements. It is through these rituals that the senatorial class of the Western Empire must have maintained its mutual solidarity and class-consciousness during the subsequent two centuries of barbarian domination.

Starting from the fifth century, hundreds of abbeys and monasteries sprang up all over Europe. They were built by the great landowners, who used them as a source of livelihood and a retreat for themselves and their families.[5] Churches and monasteries must have been places where meetings of members of the priestly family continued to be held, and rituals there must have gone back to the tradition of Sol Invictus. As medieval copiers closed in monasteries preserved the great classical culture, so also they must have maintained the esoteric traditions of the priestly organization, which had created these centers. Mithras had disappeared, substituted by the Great Architect of the Universe (in this period, references to God as the Great Architect are very frequent),[7] but the priestly organization was far from disappearing.

---

*The only documented destruction of a mithraeum by Christians[6] is narrated by Jerome, and refers to the destruction of a Mithraic grotto in Rome in the period of the prefect Gracchus, in 376–377, and thus long before the worship was declared illegal. This is clearly an isolated episode due almost certainly to questions of a personal character, because at that time Sol Invictus was at the height of its power in the capital.

THE REGIUS AND COOKE MANUSCRIPTS

One document that allows us to give a name to this nameless organization, the heir of Sol Invictus, is the so-called Regius Manuscript, also known as the Halliwell Manuscript, the most ancient known document that speaks of Freemasonry. It dates back to 1390 and was copied by an English priest, certainly from an older document. The manuscript shrouds the origins of Freemasonry in an air of legend, but also contains some information of great interest for our thesis.

It defines Masonry as a craft, a kind of universal guild set up by "great gentlemen and ladies" in order to provide for their sons and descendants "a way to support life better, without great illnesses, troubles or strife." It was an organization, therefore, to which only the members of clearly identified noble families had access (it was written from ancient times that apprentices must be of lawful blood). Their aim was to insure an adequate livelihood for them forever.

Similar content can be found in another document, the Cooke Manuscript, written between 1410 and 1440 and a transcript of a still older document.*

This manuscript begins by going back over the history of the first few chapters of Genesis, narrating that the two sons of Lamech—a descendant of Adam—named Jubal and Tubalcain, were the inventors of all the arts, in particular geometry, the one that includes all of them and that is symbolized by the compass and square. Having learned that God would destroy the earth with a flood, they engraved the sciences

---

*The *Poema Regius,* donated by George I, was traced in 1830 in the British Museum, and it had previously been a part of the Royal Library—thus the name Regius Manuscript. It was published by James Halliwell in 1840—thus the name Halliwell Manuscript. It is a complete poem of 794 rhyming verses written in an archaic English. It was written by an English cleric around 1390, but it is the transcription of a more ancient text. The Cooke Manuscript was produced slightly later (written between 1410 and 1440, though at least a part is dated to 1388), and it was published for the first time in 1861. The two manuscripts contain regulations, legends, and instructions for the fulfilment of the duties of Masonry, which they situate in a period that was very ancient already at that time.[8]

they had invented on two pillars made of materials that could not be destroyed by water or by fire.* After the flood, the pillars were found by two wise men, Pythagoras and Hermes Trismegistus, who deciphered them and taught the sciences that had been engraved on them. The manuscript goes on in its narration of biblical history, together with some considerations about the world of Babylon and Greece, from where the teachings of geometry derive by way of Euclid. Finally, however, it comes to the point: "While the children of Israel were living in Egypt, they learnt the Art of Masonry. And subsequently, when they were led out of Egypt, they arrived in the land of Behest, which is now called Jerusalem. And King David began the construction of Solomon's Temple. King David loved masons, and gave them the rights that they still have nowadays . . ."

Subsequently, it is said:

> Solomon confirmed the instructions that David, his father, had given to the masons. And Solomon himself taught them in a way that is not very different from the methods used nowadays. And from there this important science was taken to France. . . . Once there was a worthy King of France called Carolus Secundus, that is to say Charles II (Charlemagne), and this Charles was elected King of France by the Grace of God and by descent. And this same King Charles was a mason before becoming King, and when he became King, he loved the masons and held them in great esteem, and gave

---

*A precise connection to Josephus Flavius is contained in the theme of the two pillars, which the descendants of Adam erected out of fear that the wrath of God, in the form of a flood, would cancel the human race and the original wisdom. The source of this legend is Josephus Flavius, who narrates of the sons of Seth:

> *They were the inventors of that particular branch of wisdom, which regards the heavenly bodies and their order. And so that their inventions would not be lost before they were sufficiently well known, on the basis of the prediction of Adam that the world would be destroyed a first time by fire and a second time by a mass of waters, they built two pillars: one of bricks and the other of stone. They engraved their discoveries on both of these, so that if the pillar of bricks was destroyed by the flood, the stone one would remain.*[9]

them positions and regulations in accordance with his plan, some of which are still in use in France; and he himself established that they should meet in an assembly once a year to discuss together.

Obviously, the Regius and Cooke Manuscripts cannot be taken as true historical texts, but they are significant for various reasons. First of all, they speak of Masonry, thus proving beyond all possible doubt that this institution existed, with the same name, at least three centuries before its official birth. They also show the continuity between the Masonic institution as it was known in the fourteenth century and the modern one, which presents the same legendary contents. Second, the manuscripts show that the term *mason* has no connection to the building art, as is intended by modern historians. It identifies the Masons as Jewish priests to whom the secrets of all sciences had been entrusted since the time of David and Solomon. That is to say, they show that the term *masonry* defines the priestly organization whose traces we are seeking here in this text.

Judging by the manuscripts, Masonry was a craft connected to geometry and astronomical and mathematical sciences in general, and not to construction alone. Only nobles, starting from the king, had access to it. Charlemagne himself was a Mason. It is only in the eighteenth century that the word *mason* is made to derive from the French term *maçon* or the English *mason,* which mean a "builder." Yet for an organization based on secrecy and that gives every word meanings that are different from the etymological ones, it would be unlikely that only in its official definition of itself, it uses a term (Masonry) devoid of any hidden meanings. Almost certainly, the word mason has a cryptic meaning linked to the Hebrew custom of writing consonants but not vowels. In all likelihood it derives from the name Moses and stands for the descendants, or sons, of Moses. Is this a forced interpretation? No more than the present-day one. Indeed, it is perfectly consistent with what has been said so far about the origins of the priestly family and its relationship to Freemasonry.

Undoubtedly, the writers of the manuscripts could not mean that Charlemagne and the sons of the noble families who made up Masonry were "builders"; but that they were Moses's sons was quite right if they truly descended from Jewish priests. Also, the fact that in the same period, we find the word *massoni* used in Italy to refer to great noble families* would lead us to exclude the meaning of builders, because there is no etymological connection in Italian between the term *massone* and the one used for defining the builders.

In any case, the manuscript refers to well-known historical events when it states that the Mason Charlemagne convened the Masons every year in an assembly to discuss the affairs of the kingdom. Continuing a custom established by his father, Pepin, this king convened an assembly of the bishops and the great nobles of his kingdom every year.[10] The meetings were public in the sense that everyone knew where and when they were held,† but the discussions and the decisions were reserved. Along with the annual meetings he personally convened, Charlemagne ordered similar meetings to be held at the local level by all the magnates of the kingdom.

These manuscripts, therefore, confirm our hypothesis about the survival of the priestly organization, its way of operating, its meeting places, its members, the aims it intended to achieve, its territorial organization, and its character as a caste organization grouping together the descendants of Moses. This last fact was undoubtedly known only to a few select members at the top of the hierarchical scale, but we are led

---

*There is a road that runs down from Fiesole—the seat of the splendid villas of Lorenzo the Magnificent, Pico della Mirandola, and Poliziano—to Careggi, to the Platonic Academy of Marsilio Ficino. This thoroughfare is now—as it was then—via dei Massoni.[11] A derivation from the word *masso* (large stone) has been hypothesized, but the fact that *massone* refers to the Medici family and the leading Neoplatonic figures of their court, makes it far more likely that the term had been coined to define the descendants of Moses in a cryptic manner.

†In the *Annales Regni Francorum,* the meetings convened by the Carolingians are mentioned every year, and are practically the only mentioned events, together with the military campaigns and the dynastic questions—a sign of their great importance.

to believe that it was a precise choice of theirs that every descendant of Moses should be identified forever by the term *mason,* which derived from their ancestor's name. Yet the word was disguised by the definition "builder," which was perfectly in line with the new name attributed to the Supreme Being: Great Architect of the Universe.

18

THE CRUSADES

THE RECONQUERING OF JERUSALEM

During the Middle Ages, branches of the family of priestly origin occupied all the political, religious, economic, and cultural niches in European society, and they were organized in associations of mutual solidarity and support that had spread to an extent unequalled either previously or since. At that time, European society was penetrated and controlled in a complete way by the descendants of those Jewish priests taken to Rome by Titus after the destruction of Jerusalem.

They must have been filled with such a delirium of omnipotence that they believed it was at last possible to make a dream come true—one that they had been harboring for a thousand years in the secret of their "lodges": to regain possession of Jerusalem from which they had been driven out, first by the Roman legions, then by the hordes of Muhammad. This was deliberately and consciously conceived as a family project.

Countless pages have been written to try to explain the phenomenon of the Crusades, but no convincing explanation has been found for the real motivations that prompted all the European nobility to embark on an extremely costly and risky adventure, turning their back on positions of absolute supremacy at home, in order to take possession of a strip of land that was half desert. What prompted them to do this?

The host that stormed from Europe to the Middle East was not a class of disinherited nobles, of cadets without a future, like the *hidalgos* who were later to seek fortune in America. It was made up of the crème de la crème of nobility: dukes, counts, barons, and at least six kings and two emperors put their kingdoms and their own lives at stake in order to conquer Jerusalem and insure its possession not for themselves, but for the whole of the Christian world. It was a collective venture of all the European nobility and clergy, because Jerusalem was always considered a common possession whose sovereign was chosen by the church together with the great leaders of Europe and whose defense was equally of interest to the whole European class of nobles.

Yet it was of interest not for religious reasons. The center of Christianity, starting from the end of the first century, had always been Rome. Since then, Jerusalem had not played any significant role in the history of the church. With the triumph of Christianity under Constantine, Jerusalem had started to be the destination of pilgrimages for believers who wanted to visit the places where Jesus had lived and died. The mother of Constantine, Helena, was the first pilgrim to visit the place and to seek out relics of the life and Passion of Christ (which were almost all sent to Rome and Constantinople) and to identify the most significant sites of those events, starting with the site where the most sacred monument of all Christianity was built: the Holy Sepulchre.

Yet the patriarch of Jerusalem had no authority over other churches and was subject to Rome, like all the other bishops of the Empire, without any special privilege, apart from that of managing the holy places and collecting the proceeds that came from the pilgrims. With the Arab conquest of Jerusalem, this situation remained practically unchanged. When Caliph Omar entered Jerusalem in February AD 638, the patriarch Sophronius was at his side in his capacity as the most important magistrate in the city, which had surrendered without fighting. Muhammad in person had ordered that the "people of the Bible"—that is, the Christians and the Jews—should be granted the right to keep their places of worship and to use them without any restrictions.

The Christian community in Palestine was allowed to continue to practice its faith undisturbed. The ecclesiastical hierarchies maintained their structure and all their previous prerogatives and dependencies intact, and the management of the holy places remained entirely in their hands, including the proceeds of the Christian pilgrims, who continued to have free access to Palestine (apart from suffering sporadic episodes of banditry). From a strictly religious point of view, there was no reason to free the holy places, because they had always remained fully the possession of the church of Jerusalem, governed by a patriarch who enjoyed complete religious freedom, and they were freely accessible to all Christians. The religious motivation, therefore, was only a pretext, officially proclaimed before the population in order to mask motivations of a quite different nature.

It is impossible to understand the phenomenon of the Crusades if we do not take into consideration the profound motivations of the members of the priestly family. Jerusalem had been the cradle of their origins, a family possession by divine right, which must have been perennially present in their rituals, for it is still present today in the rituals and traditions of Freemasonry. All this finds a perfect explanation if we consider that the European nobility descended from the priests who had to leave Jerusalem a thousand years earlier and adopt Rome as their new homeland. Yet they had never forgotten their original homeland. How could they have done so? All the Masonic rituals are set in Jerusalem—as we have said, they must be the reproduction of rituals practiced in the priestly family from the beginning. For one thousand years, generation after generation, the members of all branches of the priestly family had grown up secretly reciting the role of priests and princes of Jerusalem. The idea that it was a Holy City that belonged to the priestly family by divine right was drummed into them from the first moment they entered a Masonic lodge and was repeated continually as they gradually advanced in the hierarchy of the organization.

When a Prince of Jerusalem visits a lodge, and it is known that he is a prince, the Master sends a delegation to find out if he desires to be received with all the honors that are due to his royal condition . . . he sends four of his senior masters to receive him with their swords unsheathed. The prince enters with his sword in his hand, and with his lance and shield, he stops between the guards and salutes the master without taking his helmet off. . . . [W]hen he advances toward the Master, all the brethren form an arch with their swords, under which he passes. . . . [A] prince of Jerusalem does not receive these honors if a brother of a higher degree is present . . .[1]

Jerusalem was present everywhere in the family traditions and in their secret rituals, and the desire to reconquer it must have grown as the overall power of the family grew.

If a thousand years seems a long time to maintain a claim of this kind, it is sufficient to consider that the Jews, as a people, have maintained for almost two thousand years their hope of returning to their original homeland. "Next year in Jerusalem" has been the closing wish of the festivities for the New Year during all this time—and this wish was put into effect as soon as conditions were favorable. How can we imagine that a priestly caste could forget their claims to that city? Their origins were indissolubly linked to it, over it they had exercised undisputed control for centuries, and they therefore had far greater motivations than those of the Jewish people.

When Jerusalem fell under the heel of Islam, the priestly family was too worried about its own survival to be able to think of the Holy City. It was one of them, Charles the Hammer, alias Charles Maccabee, who stopped the tide of Islam at the heart of Europe. The following three centuries were spent both on the defensive and recapturing ancient positions. Also in this period, however, the thought of Jerusalem and their rights to the city never passed from the minds of the family. Pepin the Short and Charlemagne cultivated close relationships with the Abassides sultans who governed the city. Further, when Charlemagne arrived in Rome in the year 800 to be crowned emperor, he was met by a delegation from the patriarch of Jerusalem, who handed to him the keys of the Holy Sepulchre and the standard of the city. Now why should the patriarch of Jerusalem have handed over to a Frankish king the symbols of the possession of the Holy City and the keys of the Holy Sepulchre if Charlemagne had no ancestral rights over Jerusalem? The patriarch could not have hoped to receive any political advantage from Charlemagne. Instead, it can be explained as an act of dutiful homage to the man who had become the leading exponent of the Jewish priestly family to whom the city belonged by right.

It was inevitable that they would try to reconquer it as soon as conditions became favorable. In 1066, the priestly family had regained complete control over Great Britain through the Angevin dynasty; the Normans* under Robert Guiscard had seized southern Italy from the Longobards (who were historically enemies of the church), together with Sicily, pushing the Muslims out of Italy; the family had also launched an offensive in Spain, reconquering part of the Iberian Peninsula and definitively blocking any possibility of Muslim expansion.

At this point, the family was in a condition to reconquer its original possessions. It was sufficient for a pope of minor stature such as Urban II to launch a simple appeal, without particular conviction, in order to spark a race to the Middle East. The fact that it was not religious piety that prompted the Crusaders is proved by the infinite atrocities and indiscriminate massacres, partly of Christian populations, that were perpetrated by those who claimed to be fighting in the name of Christ. An example is very significant: besides being an agnostic from the religious point of

---

*The Normans who conquered southern Italy in the eleventh century, seizing it from the dominion of the Muslims and the Longobards, are usually thought to be descendants of the ancient Vikings. This might be true of some of the knights, but not of their leader, Robert Guiscard. He was the son of Tancredi of Hautville and Fredesinde, the daughter of the duke of Normandy. Tancredi was a local noble of whom nothing is known. Almost certainly, he descended from an ancient British family of priestly origins who had settled in Normandy during the Saxon invasion.

view, the emperor Henry II, who succeeded in recapturing Jerusalem by diplomatic means, was actually excommunicated when he set out on his Crusade.

Religion was the official pretext, but the real reason—the only one that could justify the determination with which the European nobility threw themselves into the venture—was to regain possession of their ancient country of origin, which was permanently present in all their rituals. It was truly a collective venture of the European nobility and clergy, just as the loss of Jerusalem little more than a century later was also a collective tragedy.

THE LOST WORD

It is likely that another element, somewhat less ideal, was important to attracting hosts of members of the priestly family to Palestine. If Masonry is in some way the image of the organization of that time, we must conclude that the rituals that are recited today derive from those of that period. Among these, a position of absolute centrality is occupied by the ritual regarding the Royal Arch—the secret crypt where the most sacred treasures of the priestly family were hidden. The information about its location had been lost on the occasion of the destruction of Jerusalem by Nebuchadnezzar* and the deportation of the priests to Babylon.

Since the return from exile, they had not ceased to look for it. It was the *lost word,* the secret lost on that occasion and never recovered. David had entrusted the possession of this crypt to the high priest Zadok (1 Chronicles 16:39), and it had remained in the possession of his descendants for four hundred years, until the Babylonian exile. Then the secret of its location had been definitively lost, but what was

---

*On that occasion, Nebuchadnezzar put to death at the same time all the leaders of the Temple (Jeremiah 52:26). The secret of the crypt must have been held within this group.

not lost was knowledge of its existence. It was a crypt of exceptional importance to the family, which from then on did not cease to mourn its loss and to search for it. This subject still occupies an important part of Masonic rituals nowadays, and did so all the more then. The fascination of these rituals—which, we must remember, were then considered to be indisputable historical truth and not simple legends or ceremonies with a symbolic meaning, as they are today—must have exerted an irresistible attraction for those who knew about these secrets. No king or emperor was able to resist.

The first to search for the crypt were probably the Templars, who, as far as we know, spent the first ten years of their activity in Palestine not defending pilgrims along the roads that led from the sea to the city, but carrying out archaeological research on Mount Moriah, on the ground around the Temple. Historians and mystery hunters still wonder whether they succeeded and what they found. Perhaps they found nothing, or perhaps they located something hidden underground by their predecessors, the Omayyadi, who had built the so-called Mosque of Omar and had undoubtedly examined closely the underground passages of the mountain during the four centuries of their occupation. Yet the Templars certainly did not find what they were looking for: the crypt with the Ark of the Covenant and the most sacred treasures of the priestly family. If they had, it would undoubtedly have been made known. It is confirmed by the Masonic rituals, however, that they are still searching for it:

> Brethren, all our temples have been destroyed, our working tools have been broken, our pillars have been knocked down and shattered.* In spite of all our precautions, the Holy Word† has again been lost. We work night and day, but in vain, because we do not know how to recover the Word. . . . [I]f you desire to assist us in

---

*The reference is to the destruction of Jerusalem by Nebuchadnezzar.
†That is to say, the secret of the location of the crypt.

this emergency, and to help us to recover the Lost Word, you must follow me . . .

The flaming star is no longer visible, the cubic stone exudes blood and water, and the Holy Word is again lost. . . . [W]e shall try with all our might to recover the Word, so that the light may shine again, and Masonry may return to life. Do you want to help me in this?

My brother, you have pledged to help me in the search for the Holy Word. Return to the West, and prepare to follow me . . .

A brother, a knight of the East and of the West, who has traveled through darkness and the most formidable places in search of the Lost Word . . . hopes, with your help and your instructions, to attain this desired prize of his toils . . .[2]

A thousand years ago, these same dialogues were repeated in a completely different atmosphere compared to that of today. Then, the adepts knew exactly what they were talking about, and they believed firmly in what they were saying. Those secret meetings were arranged by men who held the destiny of the world in their hands, and in those meetings that destiny was decided.

Meetings of the kind must have been the order of the day in Europe, involving men from simple knights to the highest levels of the feudal hierarchy, including the emperor, as is indicated in the Regius and Cooke Manuscripts and confirmed by historical chronicles. Further, the promises to search for the lost Word—that is, the secret of the crypt—were not empty or meaningless. How much did this promise count in prompting hosts of young nobles to set off for the adventure in Palestine? No one will ever know, just as no one will ever know the story of the research carried out in the course of the century during which the family maintained control in Palestine first by the Templars, who seem to have been the most deeply involved in this research from the earliest phases of their stay in the Holy Land. This is a secret story of which we can find only hints in the contents of the Masonic rituals.

THE KNIGHTLY ORDERS

The Crusades were a great collective venture of the Western branches of the priestly family. The fall of Jerusalem in 1187 and, perhaps even more so, the 1291 fall of Acri, the last possession of the Crusaders in Palestine, were a traumatic shock for the whole European nobility. They were not so much a material loss, because from this point of view, Jerusalem had always been a heavy liability for the West, but rather a moral loss of incalculable importance. The entire ruling class in Europe saw severed all links to the city that had been its cradle of origin.

It is difficult to judge whether and to what extent this trauma contributed to the decline of the priestly family as such, to the degeneration of the secret organization and to the progressive loss of awareness of their origins, at least at the level of the general majority.

As we have seen, however, not everyone was aware of the priestly origins of the noble class, because only a minority of these organizations must have maintained its original initiatory character and the traditional contents of the highest degrees. Among these, we must include abbeys and various monastic orders, who must have preserved the memories of the past on behalf of the clergy and the great nobility—and probably also some associations of nobles in which the most authentic spirit of the original institution of Sol Invictus could have survived.

In any event, these were organizations without any autonomy or capacity for private political initiative, because they were subject to political and religious authority and were closely controlled by them. The Crusades offered a historical circumstance that allowed some of the smaller and medium-level nobility to break free from the tutelage of the great magnates and to try to reconstruct an autonomous and sovereign esoteric priestly organization.

Jerusalem was outside the sovereignty of the European reigning dynasties. It had returned to being the common property of the priestly family to which the whole of the European nobility recognized itself. This nature as a common possession is demonstrated by the fact that nobles coming from all over Europe spontaneously united, forming monastic military orders whose aim was to defend Palestine using not the cross, but the sword. Historically, the first knightly order was that of the Hospitallers, which was founded in about 1070 as a religious order of Benedictine obedience when a hospital dedicated to St. John the Baptist was set up in Jerusalem to cure pilgrims visiting the Holy City, which was still in Muslim hands. In 1113, it was recognized by the pope as a religious order dedicated to the care of the poor and the sick. It was only in 1128, however, in the wake of the example of the Knights Templar, that it was transformed into a true military order while maintaining the mission and the name of Hospitallers of St. John.*

The first Christian monastic order with essentially military characteristics and functions was founded in 1118 in Jerusalem by Hughes de Payens and Geoffroy de St. Omer, together with seven other French knights, with the declared aim of protecting pilgrims who went to the Holy Land. The knights took monastic vows and assumed the name of Poor Knights of Christ. The king of Jerusalem at the time, Baldwin II, granted them as their residence the building that was believed to have been the ancient stables of King Solomon (today the Mosque of Al Aqsa), on the Temple Mount. From this location, they subsequently received the name Knights of the Temple, or Templars. The order was officially recognized in 1128, at the Council of Troyes, by Pope Honorius II.

Last, the Teutonic Order was created in 1198 by German knights who had followed Emperor Frederick I Barbarossa in his tragic adventure of the Third Crusade.

These were real monastic orders whose followers took a vow of chastity and poverty and spent many hours of the day and night in

---

*This order of Benedictine obedience arose to run the hospital dedicated to St. John the Baptist, which appears to be significant, because it links the order directly to Sol Invictus and to modern-day Masonry: St. John's feast day is still linked to the summer solstice, which at the time of the reform of the Julian calendar fell on June 24, and the solstice was among the most important celebrations of Sol Invictus and is the most important of all for Masonry.

prayer. The reason for their existence, however, was the defense of the Holy Land, and for this reason they wore a cuirass and a sword instead of a cowl and a crucifix. To all effects, they were professional warriors dedicated to war, which always appeared to be a striking anomaly in the Catholic religion, in flagrant contrast to the pacifism preached by Christ. In reality, this was no anomaly, but was instead a perfect continuation of the traditions of the priestly family. Josephus Flavius was a priest but also a warrior and a military leader. The followers of Sol Invictus had taken control of the Roman army and were, first of all, military men.

During the fifth century, military functions in the West had been entrusted to the barbarians, but immediately afterward, the priestly elite had started to take back control of the army. With the Carolingians, they had returned to being completely dedicated to arms as well as to religion. Further, there was no distinction between warriors and religious figures: bishops and abbots in the eighth and ninth centuries were more skilled in the use of the sword than the crucifix.

The monastic condition of their members ensured that the knightly orders would never fall under the control of a hereditary dynasty. At the same time, it insured total independence from any civil authority and submission exclusively to the religious authority. The orders were governed by a grand master elected from among their members, and he recognized exclusively the authority of the Roman pope—but only formally, at least with regard to operative matters. It does not appear that the pope ever gave any instructions of a military or operative character regarding the scene of operations in Palestine. In this field, they formed a totally autonomous, sovereign militia, which had undertaken the task of defending the common property, independently of the incumbent seated on the throne in Jerusalem and frequently in opposition to him.

The knightly orders came to combine in themselves the characteristics of monastic orders and those of noble guilds. The truly original traditions of Sol Invictus must have been revived in their secret rituals. Let us consider, for example, the Templars, perhaps the best-known order and the most popular. The order was founded by nine knights—all belonging to the medium-level nobility—under the patronage of Bernard of Clairvaux, who composed the rule and interceded with the pope in order to obtain his blessing. This birth certificate is no coincidence: Bernard was the prior of the Cistercian monastic order, the most esoteric branch of Christian monasticism, and his heraldic symbol was a chessboard with black and white squares, exactly like the one that occupies the center of the floor of every Masonic temple around the world.

The organization of the Templars (the other orders were structured in the same way) was made up of at least three completely distinct components. At the top were the knights, who had to be nobles. From among them they elected the grand master, the supreme head of the order with absolute powers. The second level was made up of free men who were not nobles, the so-called sergeants, who carried out functions of grooms and attendants. They might fight, if need be, but they were excluded from the rank of the knights. After that, there were administrators, artisan workers, professionals of various kinds (including the seamen who served in the fleets of the order), servants, farmers, and so on, who were particularly numerous in the European seats. They recruited new followers and sought financing for the war effort in the Holy Land. The churchmen and chaplains who carried out functions of an essentially religious nature were a category apart.

The knights were true priest-warriors, and they met for secret rituals, which, we are forced to believe, derived not only from the guilds of nobles from which they came, but also from the monastic order of the Cistercians. We know for certain of the existence of these rituals, because we have knights' confessions extorted by means of the Holy Inquisition's torture. As far as we can judge, the inquisitors were not in the slightest disturbed by the existence of secret rituals, which were accepted as normal and were to be expected, but they searched for blasphemous elements in them that did not show respect for religion.

Apart from these aspects, nothing is made public regarding the rituals, whose roots, we are led to believe, lay in the tradition of Sol

Invictus. For the Templars in particular, there is a curious element that links them to Sol Invictus Mithras: one of the most peculiar characteristics of the funeral monuments of the order is that the knights were represented with their legs crossed. Nobody knows the reason why, but we cannot imagine that it is a simple coincidence that in all the mithraea there are always two characters with their legs crossed in the same way.

Thus the Templars came to combine the characteristics of a profoundly initiatory monastic organization like that of the Cistercians and those of the guilds of nobles, which were widespread at that time, especially in France and Germany. In Europe, both of these were subject to the control of the religious authorities (the monastic orders were directly accountable to the pope) and to the civil authorities (the guilds of nobles were always local in character, and were subject to the control of the authority that was responsible for the territory).

The Templar organization in Palestine, on the contrary, was free from any control of superiors, because it was autonomous and sovereign apart from the formal tribute of obedience to the pope. The same was true of the other knightly orders. This lack of control allowed them to preserve the ancient rituals and traditions that the European monarchies and the Roman church tended to cause to disappear. It is therefore because of the Templars and of the other knightly orders that the rituals and secrets of Sol Invictus survived unaltered, or almost so, until our age.

Though they were born as a monastic order, the Templars were soon transformed into a real transnational state, with a dense network of property and seats distributed in a capillary fashion in all the countries of Europe. They even had their own civil population centers, which were subtracted from the local authority. These commanderies soon assumed such a great military and economic importance that they made the Templars a world power. In particular, the order created the first truly international banking system, thus becoming the leading financial power of the time.

As long as the headquarters of the order remained in Palestine and the reason for its existence remained the defense of the common possession of the Holy Land, the Templars were able to prosper undisturbed in Europe. The fall of Acri in 1291, with the massacre of hundreds of knights, was a severe blow to the order, whose military and economic power in Europe, however, was not affected. The new grand master, Jacques de Molay, established his headquarters in Paris, where the most important and the richest of the Templar commanderies was situated. It was a tragic mistake.

The presence of an independent militia of a supranational character, which was the expression of an intermediate noble class who in this way regained autonomous sovereign prerogatives, the order's network of forts covering all Europe, and its unlimited financial resources could not be tolerated in a Europe that was already organizing itself into well-defined national entities. These lands were under the control of dynasties, which, it is true, were of priestly origin, but were extremely jealous of their own political autonomy. A military order in Palestine, devoted to its defense, could be tolerated, even if it was not accountable to anybody except itself and the pope. But an autonomous sovereign order on European territory, with enormous resources and the right to extraterritoriality, was a destabilizing threat that had to be placed under control or eliminated.

As far as we know, the king of France, Philip the Handsome, first tried the solution of control, asking to be allowed to join the order. Legend says that it was his resentment for the refusal of his request that prompted him to react violently against the order; but the historical evidence demonstrates that more than feelings were involved. Political reasons decided the fate of the Templars. Grand Master Jacques de Molay had evidently misjudged the position in which the order had come to find itself after the loss of Palestine and had not realized the need to find an arrangement that did not upset the European civil authorities.

The other orders immediately realized this. The Teutonic knights moved to the periphery of Europe, on the coasts of the Baltic, to lands that they themselves took care of Christianizing, thus creating their own autonomous kingdom in Prussia, which did not upset anybody. The Hospitallers created their own independent state at Rhodes (leading to the name Knights of Rhodes). Subsequently, in 1530, after the island fell into the hands of the Turks in 1522, Charles V made them a gift of the island of Malta, transforming them into the sovereign Order of the Knights of Malta, who still exist in Rome, where they moved in 1834 after being driven out of Malta by Napoleon Bonaparte in 1798.

De Molay's lack of foresight marked the condemnation of the Templar order. His refusal to submit was equivalent to a declaration of war against the French monarchy and practically all the Christian national states. The outcome of the clash was far from being a foregone conclusion, which was demonstrated by the care and secrecy with which Philip the Handsome prepared the mortal blow to be inflicted on his enemy.

Even the pope, the supreme head of the order, though sick at heart* and well aware that the Templars were innocent of the charges of which they were accused,[3] had to accept the political reason and decree the dissolution of the order. It was a decision taken unanimously by the leading exponents of the priestly family under the control of the pope and the king of France. The Templars were small fry compared to the great nobility that by now occupied (in a stable way) the thrones of Europe. They could be sacrificed without excessive damage. It was a painful sacrifice for the family, but was necessary in order to avoid greater problems.

The order was officially dissolved in 1312 by the pope. Jacques de Molay went to the stake, with a few other exponents in France and Italy. The property of the order was assigned to the Hospitallers, into whose ranks the surviving Templars were invited to pass. In some countries

---

*A document found recently in the Vatican, the so-called Chinon Parchment (copies can be seen at www.osmtj.com/CHINON.htm), shows that the pope had fully absolved the Templars from the charge of heresy.

such as Portugal, the order continued to survive undisturbed, thanks to the simple expedient of changing its name, returning to the original name of Poor Knights of Christ. In the British Isles the order did not survive as such, but the Templars individually did not undergo any persecution. The English king Edward II claimed for himself the property and the belongings of the Temple, but he allowed most of the knights to join the Hospitallers or to take refuge in Scotland, where they were made welcome. It is common opinion that here they were admitted to the local Masonic organizations, thus giving rise to the modern-day Masonic traditions.

AMERICA, A ROUTE OF THE TEMPLARS[4]

The dissolution of the Templar order was probably at the origin of another event, which had epoch-making consequences for Western civilization. There are indications and valid reasons to believe that it contributed decisively to the beginning of the great geographical explorations and eventually to the discovery of America, which officially took place two centuries later. The Templars possessed a fleet of sixteen vessels anchored in the port of la Rochelle, on the Atlantic coast. When Philip the Handsome unleashed his repression, this fleet put out to sea with hundreds of knights and was never heard of again.*

Some say that the Templar fleet took refuge in Scotland, where it was welcomed with open arms by the local noble, Bruce (the ancestor of a dynasty of Freemasons), to whom the knights gave decisive support in the Battle of Bannockburn, which sanctioned the independence of Scotland from England. Various indications lead us to believe, however,

---

*The Templar seafaring tradition may find a descendant in the piracy that arose a few centuries later. Everybody knows the emblem of the pirates (or rather, corsairs): a black flag with the skull and crossbones. Yet not everybody knows that the skull and crossbones appeared on the flag carried by Templar ships and on the flag that preceded the hosts of knights on the battlefield. The reappearance of this Templar symbol on corsair ships in the Renaissance might not be a simple coincidence.

that at least a part of the fleet continued their voyage in a northwesterly direction, arriving in Iceland, and from there, in America. This story is not so improbable. Centuries earlier, the Vikings had already arrived as far as Iceland and nearby Greenland, colonizing them, and they had undoubtedly reached the coasts of Canada. The presence of lands to the West was thus well known among the populations gravitating around the North Sea.

Circumstantial evidence has been found in America of the presence of Templars, but there are also clues that some of them returned to Europe. For example, some representations of Masonic symbols in the chapel of Rosslyn, constructed south of Edinburgh between 1446 and 1450 by Earl William of St. Clair,* seem to confirm a knowledge of America before Columbus. These decorations include cobs of corn.

One or more of the Templar ships may have returned to Europe, landing eventually in Portugal, where the order had continued to survive undisturbed. (King Denis, 1279–1325, the initiator of the epic period of the Portuguese navy, was a Templar and had refused to apply the papal bull of suppression.) Their venture remained secret but not without consequences. Besides confirming the existence of lands to the West, they must have brought with them nautical charts with details of these lands, and these remained a jealous secret of the crown (or rather, of the Templar order, which was in his service). Christopher Columbus, who was a cartographer in Portugal, must have come to know of them at the Portuguese court; he was related to the royal family through his wife. This is a story that remains to be explored.[5]

However things went, the discovery of America opened up a new frontier of conquest for the priestly family, making them forget the bitterness of the setbacks they had suffered in the Holy Land. (Attempts to reconquer it continued, with little success or veritable catastrophes,

---

*The St. Clair family has an important place in the history of the Templars: a count St. Clair took part in the First Crusade, during which the order was formed. In 1101, Catherine of St. Clair married the founder of the order, Hughes de Payens, and subsequently many members of the family became Knights Templar.

until 1366, but the dream of a Crusade was not given up until the end of the fifteenth century.) The new continent was considered to be a possession of the family by right, and the head of the family, the pope, was called in to arbitrate its division. In this way, the family arrogated to itself the possession of the whole world that remained to be discovered and legitimized the colonial policy that was to characterize subsequent centuries.

above: The treasure of Jerusalem's Temple paraded in Rome (from the triumphal arch of Titus). It was handed over to the Romans by Jewish priests.

right: (Detail) The Menorah paraded in Rome during the triumph of Vespasian and Titus.

below left: Hypothetical model of the Temple built by Herod in Jerusalem and destroyed by Titus Flavius.

below right: The Temple platform at the time of the Templar knights. Their seat was in the building on the left, thought to be the ancient stables of King Solomon. At the center is the mosque built by Caliph Omar. Its octagonal plan inspired many buildings of the Templar knights.

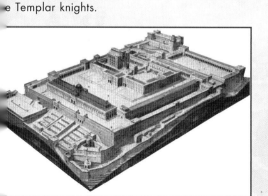

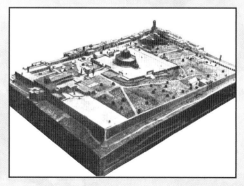

Sol Invictus Mithras

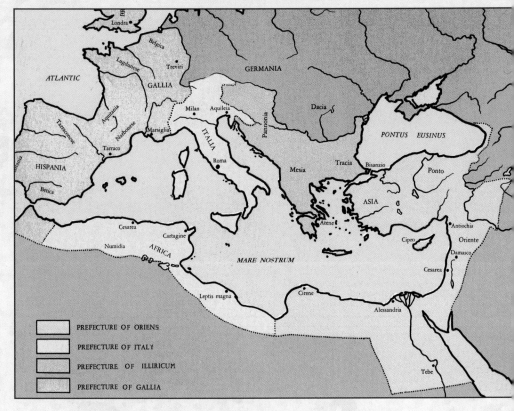

The Roman Empire at the time of Diocletian, divided into four Prefectures. The two "augusti,"
Diocletian and Maximian, governed respectively the Illiricum and Italy's Prefectures;
the two "cesars," Constans Chlorus and Galerius, Gallia and Oriens' Prefectures.

Coin of emperor Aurelianus with a radiated crown,
symbol of Sol Invictus Mithras (ca. 275).

Coin of emperor Probus, with Sol Invictus Mithras
(ca. 280).

Coin of emperor Constantine, with a representation of the
Sol Invictus and the inscription "SOLI INVICTO COMITI"
(To [Constantine's] comrade the Invincible Sun).

Jesus Christ represented as the Sol Invictus, leading the solar chariot. Mosaic from the third century, in the Vatican grottos under St. Peter's basilica, on the floor of the tomb of Pope Julius I.

Emblem of the Sol Invictus

Above: Monuments of Templars' tombs in the Church of the Temple, London. They are always represented with their legs crossed—nobody knows why.

Left: Cautopathes in a mithraeum with their legs crossed.

Rendering of a Templar tomb.

Sol Invictus Mithras Never Set

The sun is the most widespread symbol in the Catholic religion. It is always represented at the back of God and whoever is related to God, including the Madonna, angels, and saints. It always stands out in the churches, above the altar and the entrance, and it marks the most sacred objects, like the cross, the monstrance, the papal chair, ceremonial vestments, decorations, and so forth.

Top left: Giotto di Bondonne, *Kiss of Judas*, 1306. Fresco painting. Arena Chapel, Padua, Italy.
Top right: Pietro Lorenzetti, *The Virgin with Child and Saints*, 1330. Fresco painting. Basilica of Saint Francis of Assisi, Assisi, Italy.
Bottom: Diego Velázquez, *The Coronation of the Virgin*, 1644. Oil on canvas. Museo de Prado, Madrid, Spain.

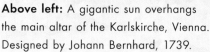

Above left: A gigantic sun overhangs the main altar of the Karlskirche, Vienna. Designed by Johann Bernhard, 1739.

Above right: The sun dominates the chair of St. Peter, St. Peter's Basilica, Rome.

Right: The sun is represented on the facade of all gothic cathedrals. The rose window of Notre Dame of Rouen.

Right middle: When a rose window is not present, the sun is usually represented as a picture or a sculpture above the entrance of the church. St. Anthony's Basilica, Padua, Italy.

Right bottom: The entrance of Palazzo Vecchio, one of the most important buildings in Florence, Italy. A large ornament stands out, with the sun in the middle, surrounded by lions, lilies, and other priestly symbols.

Above left top: The symbol of the sun, together here with Christian acronyms, appears on many Italian houses. Camaiore Lucca, Tuscany, Italy.

Above left bottom: Detail of a window, Duomo Cathedral, Milan.

Above middle and far right: The sun is always represented on reliquaries and monstrances and quite frequently on the back of the cross.

The Sun represents the Great Architect of the Universe in Masonic traditions and it is always dominant in their symbols.

Left: Example of a Masonic apron.

Below left: The Masonic apron of George Washington with a sun dominating a number of priestly symbols.

Below middle: The Declaration of the Rights of Man under the patronage of the Sun.

Below right: The Grand Orient of Italy's logo. Like most Masonic emblems, the sun is the main element.

Ancient Judaic Coins and Seals with the Main Symbols of European Heraldry

Above top left: Hasmonean coin with eagle and lily.
Above top right: Judaic seal, second century BC.
Above bottom left: Five-pointed star or David's seal in Jerusalem.
Above bottom right: Seal with a cock (tell en-Nasbeh).

Modern Israeli coins (half, one, five, and ten shekel) reproduce symbols that were in use among Judaic priestly families at the time of the Hasmoneans, and that were subsequently adopted by European heraldry.

Coats of Arms of Jewish Families

In the emblems of Jewish families throughout Europe there are symbols that appear on the coats of arms of European royals and nobles: lions, eagles, lilies, towers, columns, five- and six-pointed stars, mountains, sun, moon, harps, cocks, bees, and so forth. It appears that the main symbols of European heraldry derive from symbols of Judaic priestly family groups.

Anguillara

Alatri

De Rossi

Soave

Di Mosé

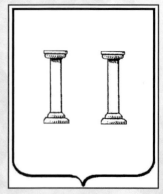

Salmon

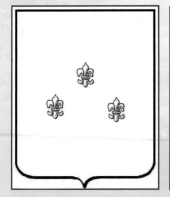

Zarfatti

Di Castro

Finzi

Pappo

Cohen

Ghershom

Corcos

Castelli

Perez

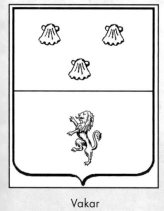

Vakar

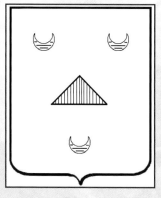

Treves

Amburgo

Jewish Symbols on Tombstones (Jewish Cemetery, Venice)

On the tombstones of Jewish cemeteries we find the same symbols used by high nobility and royals throughout Europe.

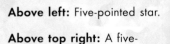

Above left: Five-pointed star.

Above top right: A five-pointed star with the lily on top.

Above bottom right: Blessing hands, tower, and five-pointed star.

Upper left: Lion with star.

Upper right: Lions and palm tree.

Lower left: Lions and tower.

Lower right: Lion with a lily-like scepter.

Upper left: Blessing hands and tower.

Upper right: Harp.

Lower left: Eagle with two crowned heads.

Lower right: Dragon with head and feet of a chicken.

Below top left: Sun and tower.

Below bottom left: Sun in a circle.

Below right: Sun in the center of four lilies.

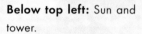

Coats of Arms of Early Popes

Emblems of popes from the fifth to tenth centuries, as they appear on personal seals. They are not recognized as real coats of arms, as heraldry had not yet begun. The symbols are the same that we find in Jewish tombstones: lions, towers, lilies, roses, eagles.

St. Felix (483–492)

Pelagius I (556–561)

Benedict I (575–579)

Sabinianus (604–606)

Boniface III (607)

Formosus (891–896)

Sergius III (904–911)

Coats of Arms of Popes from the Twelfth to the Seventeenth Centuries

Often they reproduce the coat of arms of the family to which they belonged. Lions, lilies, roses, eagles, towers, dragons, and so on are the symbols that appear on them, clearly derived from the Judaic tradition.

Innocent III (1198–1216)

Celestine IV (1241–1243)

Urban IV (1261–1264)

Clement IV (1265–1268)

John XXI (1276–1277)

John XXII (1316–1334)

Urban VI (1378–1389)

Martin V (1417–1431)

Paul III (1534–1549)

Sixtus V (1585–1590)

Leo XI (1605)

Paul V (1605–1621)

Coats of Arms of Modern Popes

A coat of arms is chosen by the pope himself when installed on the Holy See. The preferred symbols are still those of the Judaic priestly tradition.

Pius IX (1846–1878)

Pius XI (1922–1939)

John XXIII (1958–1963)

Paul VI (1963–1978)

John Paul I (1978)

Shields of Arms of English Knights at the Battle of Agincourt (1415)

(from S. Friar & J. Fergusen, *Basic Heraldry*, a catalog of Judaic priestly symbols)

King Henry V
of England

Edward
Duke of York

Humphrey
Duke of Gloucester

Holand

de Vere

Mowbray

Mortimer

Montagu

de la Pole

Clifford

Clinton

Botreaux

Gamme

de Thorpe

Codrington

Lions, lilies, and eagles are the most common symbol in the coats of arms of royal houses, high nobility, nations, and towns.

Albrecht Dürer, *Emperor Charlemagne and Emperor Sigismund,* 1513. Oil and tempera on panel. Germanisches National Museum, Nuremberg, Germany. The eagle and lilies are his emblems, the sword and the cross his instruments.

Right: Bust of Charlemagne (treasure of Aachen Cathedral), decorated with eagles and lilies, the two symbols that he employed in his seals and official documents.

Below: Mantle of Queen Anne Stuart embroidered with harps, lions, and lilies, the most common priestly symbols.

Coats of Arms of European Royals, Nobles, Countries, and Towns

LIONS

Flag of the British royal family

Flanders

Lion and lilies in the
Royal Arms of Scotland

Royal Arms of Norway

Early Arms of Habsburg

Finland

England

Luxembourg

Sweden

Estonia

The Netherlands

Spain

LILIES

Capetian Kings of France

France

Arms of the Farnese
Family of Italy

Royal Arms of England
in 1405

The Lily of Florence

Richard III of England

Flag of Acadiana showing lilies,
castle, and five-pointed star, all
priestly symbols

Flag of Quebec

EAGLES

Germany

Poland

Arms of the Habsburg
Monarchy (Austria)

Russian Federation

Teutonic Order

Arms of the Hohenstaufen
Dynasty of Germany

Arms of Charles I of Spain

Arms of Napoleon I

Distribution of Heraldic Symbols throughout Europe

The Medici Family and Freemasonry

Left: Portrait of Cosimo Medici I (1537–1574) in the Palazzo Vecchio. In his left hand he holds Masonic symbols.

Below: The Medici coat of arms depicted by Vasari in Palazzo Vecchio. The Medici's balls are arranged in a triangle, a priestly symbol as well as a Masonic one.

Above: The classical coat of arms of the Medici family, with six balls arranged 1, 2, 2, 1, to form a six-pointed star.

Right: Tomb of Cosimo Medici I, where the family's coat of arms is represented with the balls arranged in a triangle.

PART FIVE

The Mosaic Origins of Modern Secret Societies

19

THE ROLE OF JUDAISM
IN THE CHRISTIAN
WORLD

The first part of this book has been dedicated to the demonstration that the Jewish priestly family, the one that, according to Josephus Flavius, represented the totality of the noble class of the Jewish people, descended not from Aaron, but from Moses. The following parts give a synthetic narration of the historical events of the first few centuries of the Christian era, with the aim of demonstrating, if nothing else, the plausibility that the entire aristocratic class of developing Europe was composed of descendants of that same family, and therefore of Moses.

The central argument of this hypothesis is that the descendants of the branches of the priestly family that survived the massacre of Jerusalem in AD 70 took possession of power in the Roman Empire and replaced the ancient noble families—to such a point that by the end of the fourth century, they represented practically the totality of the senatorial aristocracy of the Western Roman Empire. By that date, the small landowners had practically disappeared. Thus, if we exclude the areas of imperial property, almost all the remaining lands belonged to the church and to the great senatorial landowners from whose ranks the Catholic clergy came. The barbarian populations who divided the spoils of the Western Empire did not expropriate this landowning aristocracy of its possessions and privileges, and consequently it eventually reemerged as the noble class in the various states that formed on European soil.

In Rome and in Italy in general, the senatorial families continued to remain at the top of society, with a partial, temporary regression only on the advent of the rule of the Longobards. In Britain, they continued to maintain power in all the territories not included in those surrendered to the Saxons (which, however, were reconquered after a couple of centuries). In Spain, the Visigoths continued to rely on the support of the clergy and the Roman senatorial aristocracy, which maintained their positions. In Gaul, the Burgundians and the Franks continued to respect the rights and the property of the clergy and of the Roman aristocracy, and we have seen that the Carolingians eventually imposed on all Europe a great nobility coming entirely from a group of no more than thirty families, all of whom supposedly descended from the ancient Roman senatorial aristocracy.

At this point, therefore, continuing any historical analysis becomes superfluous for the purposes of the demonstration of the hypothesis presented in this book. If the analysis performed so far is correct, the whole of the European aristocracy descends directly from the family of Jewish priestly origin or families closely related to it. Consequently, the history of the Jewish priestly family coincides with the history of Europe. In this part of the text, then, rather than analyzing historical events, we will study specific aspects that confirm or reinforce the notion of the priestly origin of European aristocracy (and of the Catholic clergy, of course, which derived from it). In this way, we will clarify, in light of the priestly hypothesis, certain historical details that have never been fully understood.

Before moving on to an examination of these details, however, it is useful to discuss briefly a group that appears to be crucial in the history of the priestly family: the Jews.

From the time of the Carolingians on, European society was rigidly stratified, and moving from one social class to another was rare and difficult. Furthermore, it was practically impossible for anyone who was not highborn to gain access to the noble class. There were some important exceptions, however, which are highly significant in connection with the priestly hypothesis. Even if the Jews were theoretically on the fringe of Christian society and veritable untouchables, they continued to maintain close relationships to popes, bishops, and civil rulers, and if they accepted baptism, they were admitted directly to the ranks of the nobility and had immediate access to the highest religious positions. An exemplary case is that of the Jewish Pierleoni family, who converted to Christianity halfway through the tenth century and immediately became one of the leading and most influential families in Rome. (Soon after converting, a member of the family became pope.)[1]

Yet how is it possible to explain this anomalous and unusual fact—as well as the fact that the church has always had an extremely ambiguous relationship to the Jewish world? In order to understand this, we must go back to the period of the institution of the Mithraic organization. As we have seen, Sol Invictus Mithras was not a religion, but an esoteric organization, like modern-day Freemasonry. So what kind of relationship did it have with the religions of its followers? In other words: Was there a religious creed that its followers were obliged to accept? In modern-day Freemasonry (which, as we have said, represents the fossil image of the Mithraic organization), membership in a particular religion is not required: aspirants for admission are required only to believe in the existence of a Superior Being, whatever name or form it may take. By statute, avowed atheists cannot be accepted in the organization.

This superior being is given the generic name of the Great Architect of the Universe (G.A.O.T.U.), which, as we have discovered, is the same name that the Pythagoreans attributed to the sun, whose symbol always appears in the east of Masonic temples along with the images of pagan divinities such as Saturn, Minerva, and Hercules. The same symbolism is found in Roman mithraea: the sun was represented in the east, with Mithras and the bull (which also, we should remember, was the symbol of Yahweh in the Jewish world), while all around were arranged images of the principal divinities of the pagan world, in particular Jupiter, Hercules, Saturn, Venus, and Minerva. We can deduce from this that in order to gain access to the Mithraic organization, no profession of a particular creed was required, but recognition of a Superior Being was necessary.

According to the hypothesis presented here, which is backed up by significant archaeological findings, the founders of the Mithraic organization were Jewish priests. Further, we have concluded that they took control first of the church of Rome, and then imposed Christianity in the whole of the Roman world. Yet we cannot consider that all the followers of the Mithraic organization were Christians. Christianity was, at least initially, a particular sect of Judaism that was open to proselytism in the pagan world, but it was definitely distinct from the Mithraic organization, as it was from the Jewish religion and other religions whose symbols had found hospitality in the mithraea. At least at the initial levels of the organization, this soon made it possible also to affiliate people coming from the pagan world, such as, for example, the emperor Commodus.

We are forced to presume that the higher degrees of the organization were reserved for people of priestly origin, who, as far as we can judge on the basis of archaeological, historical, and literary evidence, professed a sort of syncretistic monotheism in which every divinity was an expression of a single Superior Being. They considered themselves to be priests not of one divinity in particular, but of the whole divinity as such, in whatever form it was presented. The emperor Elagabalus, for example, was a priest of the sun, but in his palace, he erected altars to Jewish, Christian, and Samaritan divinities, and he continued to occupy the position of pontifex maximus—that is, the supreme priest of all pagan religions. The other emperors who were followers of Sol Invictus, and subsequently Christian emperors from Philip the Arab to Constantine to Gratianus, continued to occupy the role of pontifex maximus without finding in this any contradiction with their individual profession of faith. Julianus represents the maximum expression of the syncretistic mentality of the followers of Sol Invictus. He was called the Apostate because he tried to push the syncretistic creed to its extreme consequences, unifying all religions and creating a single class of priests with the same characteristics and the same rules of behavior independent of the name of the divinity to whose worship the single priests were dedicated. It was thanks to this vision that he tried to reconstruct the Temple of Jerusalem.

This particular philosophy reconciling polytheism and Jewish monotheism had allowed the Roman senate, whose members in the fourth century were largely followers of Sol Invictus Mithras, to take control of all traditional pagan religions. Obviously, the senate was reluctant to relinquish this control, as demonstrated by the passionate defense of traditional pagan institutions presented by Symmachus to the fervently Christian emperor Valentinianus, who remained uncertain about what to do for a long time. Only the authoritative contribution of the supreme Christian authority of the period, Ambrose, the bishop of Milan, succeeded in convincing Valentinianus that the time had come to abandon every form of pagan tradition and to impose definitively over all the Empire the creature of the secret priestly organization: Christianity. This takeover took place with an extraordinary facility and a speed, given that Sol Invictus controlled the totality of religions.

Within very little time, the pagan religions disappeared like snow in midsummer, together with all their symbols—except those linked to the most genuine tradition of Sol Invictus, starting with the sun, which today is still dominant in all representations of Christianity. Only in the case of Judaism was a particular status recognized. It was legitimized as the font of Christianity, and thus was guaranteed its survival. Clearly and obviously, no Christian priest could forget his Jewish origins or repudiate his membership of that family to which the Jewish priests belonged.

The Mosaic family could not deny its origins; the Jewish religion was a creation of Moses and has always been identified with his family. It is legitimate to think that a large percentage of descendants who became members of the organization of Josephus Flavius were sooner or later entirely Christianized, abandoning Mosaic Law. Others, however (we should remember that there were as many as two hundred fifty members of the priestly family saved by Josephus Flavius), must have remained faithful to Judaism. Still others, perhaps, chose a compromise, continuing to follow the Mosaic Law even as they accepted Christian principles.[2] (Members of this particular sect were called Ebionites, and their presence is testified until the fifth century.*)

We may consider that the descendants of the priestly family coexisted in the Mithraic organization independently of whether their families had remained Jews or had become Christian. Sol Invictus emperors, from Elagabalus to Gallienus to Julianus the Apostate, were extremely favorable to Judaism. The crunch came when triumphant Christianity imposed the abolition of the Mithraic organization and absorbed its members. Those who were Jewish must have found themselves in a marginal position, a kind of limbo where they were protected physically and economically, but at the same time were excluded from the benefits of their Christian colleagues.

A clear trace of this situation can be found, as always, in modern-day Freemasonry. Here, we find a very special category of people, called *cowan* or *cohan* (*couan* in French), who are considered to be excluded brothers—that is, in possession of all the requisites to belong to Freemasonry, but excluded from it for reasons that are not specified. Now Cohen, Cohan, Khan, and the like are surnames that distinguish Jews of priestly origin, who are known as *cohanim* (the Hebrew plural of *cohen*).

The members of the priestly family who had remained Jews, the cohanim, must have continued to maintain a privileged relationship with their Christian brothers and must have enjoyed their protection. Of

---

*We should not forget Symmachus the Ebionite, who lived at the time of the Severans and was a possible ancestor of the senatorial family of the same name.

course, this protection was also extended to the population that insured their survival: the Jews. This remained the case until relatively recently, when the two religions entered a practically irreversible collision course and the Catholic church assumed an attitude of concrete ostracism and true persecution toward the Jews. Until this point, however, the Jews were always tolerated and openly protected by the ecclesiastical hierarchies, unlike all the other religions and the heretical Christian sects.

The subject of the Jews and their relationships to the Christian community is of the greatest interest for our hypothesis, and is full of surprises. The relationship between Christianity and Judaism was imposed from a doctrinal point of view as soon as Christianity triumphed over paganism, conquering all the levers of power and gaining the right to decree the life or death of other religions. While the condemnation of all other religions—in particular, the deviations from orthodox Christianity—was firm and unreserved, the Jewish religion was permitted according to the pretext that it served as a testimony to the authenticity of what was written in the Hebrew Scriptures. In practice, it was considered the elder brother of Christianity—a brother who was somewhat stubborn, who still had not realized that the Messiah had come and had thus lost his rights as the firstborn son, but who did not deserve to be eliminated as a result. The Jews were therefore allowed to survive as such, but with limitations that confirmed their separation with respect to Christians.

On the legislative level, this discrimination began with Constantine. One of his first decrees was to forbid anyone to be converted to Judaism, under penalty of the confiscation of all his possessions. Besides this, the Jews were subjected to various limitations, such as the ban on possessing Christian slaves, the prohibition of mixed marriages, and so forth. Our modern-day sensitivity would judge these to be intolerable discriminations; but seen in the context of that period, they assume a value that is exactly the opposite. Judaism was officially recognized as the predecessor of Christianity—practically complementary to it—and as such was not a religion to be fought, but to be protected, albeit on a different level. From then on, at least in the West, the Jews lived under Christian protection, without suffering the persecution, often extremely ferocious, to which the other religions and the various heretical sects were subjected.

For all the Middle Ages, Jews were a "protected species" in Western Europe, with the only exception being Visigoth Spain, where Jews were forced either to abjure or emigrate. Many were converted, giving rise to a class of crypto-Jews who were subsequently called Marranos: they pretended to be Christians, but fundamentally they were Jews. The others emigrated to Gaul and Rome, where they were well accepted. It is true that they suffered discrimination and limitations, but they were never persecuted (a mere gust of wind would have been enough to blow them away). Indeed, on the contrary, the civil and ecclesiastical authorities always granted them a series of privileges that guaranteed a sort of monopoly for them in certain economic sectors. The first laws, which expressly dealt with the protection of Jewish traders, guaranteeing their free access to the court, were promulgated by the Carolingians.

Popes and bishops were no less tolerant, and Jews could freely frequent their courts as personal doctors, artisan workers, and, of course, bankers. Clearly, the church did not give up in its attempt to convert them, but incredibly and surprisingly for that period (and highly significant for our hypothesis) is the fact that converted Jews very often moved straight into the high spheres of the Christian nobility and almost immediately had access to the highest religious positions. We can find outstanding examples, as we have seen, in the Roman Pierleoni family, who started to make and unmake popes immediately after their conversion from Judaism in the tenth century, and in other popes such as Innocentius VIII, who came from a Cypriot Jewish family called Cybo.

The favor shown to the Jews by the nobles and the high members of the clergy, however, was not shared by the populace, who more often than not blamed their recurring misfortunes on this privileged minority. They were considered a population apart, whose contact with the ruling classes was a source of envy and suspicion. Popular hatred was incited by a series of shameful accusations (such as that of ritual infanticide), and above all by the preaching of the minor friars (Franciscans and Dominicans), who were often incredibly acrimonious and violent toward the Jews. This gave rise now and then to cases of pogroms, which were generally condemned and punished by both civil and religious authorities.

The first great massacres of Jewish communities were carried out in the eleventh century by German crusaders led by the infamous Emich, Volkmar, and Gottschalk, who systematically wiped out the Jewish enclaves of Rhineland. It is significant that the Jews took refuge in churches and in bishoprics in an attempt to escape the massacre, and that the German crusaders were not stopped by the Muslims, but instead were annihilated by the Christian king of Hungary, Coloman.

These were isolated episodes, however, because elsewhere, especially in Italy, the Jewish communities continued to prosper without great difficulties until the end of the fifteenth century. The dramatic change of fortunes came about with the fall of the kingdom of Granada (financed, incidentally, by Sicilian Jews), in 1492. Three months later, the Aragonese sovereigns, prompted by political reasons and, above all, by an implacable enemy of the Jews, the Dominican Torquemada, signed a decree expelling the Jews from Spain. Shortly afterward, they were expelled from Sicily and Sardinia. Meanwhile, in the place of the formerly Jewish Innocentius VIII, the papal throne was occupied by a member of the Spanish Borgia family, Alexander VI.

Unlike the kings of Spain and the Spaniards surrounding him in Rome, however, Alexander continued to maintain an attitude of great favor toward the Jews, and he welcomed fugitives from all over the Mediterranean to the point that the Jewish community in Rome more than doubled under his pontificate.

The tolerant attitude of the pope toward the Jews was also adopted by his successors. It underwent a radical, irreversible change only after the Lutheran Reformation. This provoked a series of changes and more rigid positions in the church, which led to the Counter-Reformation, of which the Jews were the main victims. Up to then, they had been protected as living witnesses of the truth of Christianity. From then on, however, they became the witnesses of the punishment that Catholicism reserved on this earth for anybody who showed signs of dissidence.

The first step toward the ostracism of the Jews was taken by Pope Paul III Farnese, even though he was personally well disposed toward them. In 1540, he recognized the order of the Jesuits, and two years later, he introduced in Rome the Inquisition, with the name of the Holy Office. These instruments were conceived in order to moralize the church, rather than with an anti-Jewish function, but they soon turned into the worst enemies of the Jews. The real turning point, however, was reached under his successor, Julius III del Monte. He was not personally unsympathetic to the Jews—even some of his doctors were Jews—but he allowed himself to get involved in a dispute between Christian editors, which came to an end in 1533 with a bull condemning the Talmud and the order to burn all existing copies of it, together with the relevant rabbinic literature. A Franciscan friar accused of having converted to Judaism was also burned at the stake.

This bull marked the breakdown of the thousand-year-old acquiescence between the two religions. This breakdown was made final and irreversible two years later by the bull "Cum nimis absurdum," issued in 1555 by Paul IV Carafa, who came from the ranks of the Inquisition and was animated by an implacable hatred for the Jews.[3] This bull begins with the words "As it is absurd and highly unfitting that the Jews, who have been condemned for their sins by God to eternal slavery . . ." and it closes with a series of obligations and prohibitions, which reduced the Jews to a subhuman level, depriving them of all freedom and rights. All this was sealed by burning some Marranos at the stake in Ancona.

This bull officially supplied the anti-Jewish set of tools, which were to be used with varying levels of ignominy in the following centuries, culminating in the Nazi Holocaust. In conclusion, Judaism and the church of Rome entered an irreversible collision course only between

1553 and 1555, with the anti-Jewish bulls of Julius III del Monte and Paul IV Carafa. Thus the church's animosity is a relatively recent event. Until 1553, the two religions had coexisted in relative harmony, and in the history of the West, there had been a continual transfer of great personalities from the Jewish world to the Christian one, in accordance with the hypothesis presented here.

20

HERALDRY

THE ORIGINS AND MEANING OF HERALDRY

The consistency of an historical reconstruction carried out in the light of the priestly hypothesis is in itself a significant indication of its validity. In fact, many indications have emerged to support it, and a host of others may be discovered by means of targeted research among the pages of ancient and medieval texts and in the archives of the Vatican and various monasteries. Without hunting in the archives, however, we can simply look around us and discover much to prove that this thesis is coherent. A formidable array of proof can be found in heraldry, which is, in fact, an inexhaustible source of information about the origins and the history of noble family lines.

In the ancient world—like today—graphic symbols were used in order to represent authority and affiliation with particular societies. The territorial districts of ancient Egypt, for example, possessed emblems that distinguished the civil and military authorities. In addition, the primitive Roman standards bore religious or warlike symbols, such as the eagle, which were subsequently adopted as emblems of the Roman legions. In these well-ordered societies, emblems were used to recognize civil or military authorities immediately.

Yet it is in the Hebrew Scriptures that we find the first mention of the existence of symbols associated with single individuals and their families: "Every man of the children of Israel shall pitch by his own standard, with the ensign of their father's house . . . and the children of Israel pitched by their standards, and so they set forward, every one after their families, according to the house of their fathers" (Numbers 2:2, 34). Every family in Israel, from the time of Moses, had its own standard.

It may be considered certain, therefore, that on their return from Babylonian exile, each of the twenty-four branches of the priestly family, who was party to the agreement arranged by Ezra, possessed its own standard. It may be considered equally certain that each group of descendants that entered into the secret organization formed in Rome by Josephus Flavius had in turn some symbols that distinguished it. The Jews are very conservative people, therefore, these symbols must have always remained in use among the priestly families. By showing its symbol each member of a priestly family could be recognized by another throughout the Empire, and the rank occupied in the hierarchy of the Mithraic organization was immediately understood. These same symbols were later certainly used in the heraldic coats of arms of those families.

Heraldic symbols started to distinguish publicly the various European noble families from the eleventh century on. They are the most significant and perhaps most striking circumstantial evidence at the disposal of the common researcher—who does not have access to more or less secret archives—about the origin of those families.

Heraldic symbols are found everywhere in Europe: on public and private buildings, churches, monasteries, cemeteries, manuscripts, official documents, seals, and all sorts of monuments. Heraldry was the public and immediate means to show feudal authority and the rank of single nobles. Heraldic symbols were a sort of calling card, which proclaimed to the world a man's position and influence, the place his house occupied in society, the great families to which he was related, his possessions (houses, castles, landed property, fiefs, cities, or even nations), and his realizations (churches, cathedrals, palaces), which were marked with those symbols. It goes without saying that these were exclusively noble symbols, and nobody would have dreamed of using emblems to which he was not entitled. (For example, the usurpation of papal insignia was once considered a crime that carried the death penalty.[1])

This is why the almost meteoric spread of the use of heraldic symbols among the noble families of all Europe in the twelfth century is dumbfounding: it is incomprehensible and inexplicable unless we contend that every noble family in Europe already knew—and had used since time immemorial—the heraldic symbols to which it was entitled. The Internet did not exist at that time, and there were no official publications containing lists of symbols that were available or already used by other families. Further, communication from one end of the Continent to the other was slow. Yet almost all the European noble houses raised their coats of arms practically in unison. Though this should have given rise to an endless series of claims and disputes over the improper use of the symbols in the various coats of arms, this did not happen, except to a very limited extent, and the disputes that did arise were settled by recourse to the arbitration of higher authorities. Everyone knew exactly what rights he had—and was able to recognize the rank and the origin of any European house, however distant and little known, from its coat of arms.

This may seem incredible until we consider that those symbols had been the hallmark of members of the priestly family for at least fifteen centuries. According to the traditional theory, which is presented in most textbooks on heraldry, the use of heraldic coats of arms originated from the need of medieval knights, who were covered with armor from head to foot, to recognize each other on the battlefield. Without doubt, this was one of the advantages (even if several authors have their doubts) of the custom of publicly displaying heraldic symbols, but it certainly does not explain their origin. The use of heraldic coats of arms was also adopted at the same time by churchmen, popes, bishops, abbots, entire monastic orders, traders, and other categories of people who did not normally frequent battlefields.

Above all, this theory does not explain the origin of the symbols that appear in those coats of arms. Among other things, it has been historically established[2] that the use of heraldic symbols, even if not of true coats of arms, goes back at least to the time of Charlemagne. The families that made up the administrative backbone of the Carolingian empire used dynastic and territorial emblems on seals, coins, customs stamps, flags, standards, and on every other occasion when it was necessary to identify themselves officially, both in times of peace and in war.[3] Further, there is evidence that these symbols belonged to single families, or groups of interrelated families, and they were exclusive and hereditary.

In the church, the use of symbols that may be defined as heraldic was documented since the beginnings of the seventh century: Pope Sabinianus (604–606) had as his symbol an eagle with its wings spread; Boniface III (607) a tower; Boniface IV (608) and Honorius I (625) a cross; Gregory II (731) two lions facing each other, carrying a rose in their paws. In the tenth century, there was a series of seven popes represented by an eagle with wings spread, and so on. These symbols, like those used by Charlemagne, are exactly those we find later reproduced in the coats of arms that distinguished the European nobility.

Because the great European nobility derives, as we have said, from senatorial families—who, on the basis of our hypothesis, must have been of priestly origin—the symbols adopted by them must have been in use in the Jewish family groups from which they descended. The Bible tells us that every Jewish family had its own emblem, but we do not know which symbols were used by the branches of the priestly family that came to Rome with Titus and Josephus Flavius, because they are not recorded in historical chronicles. We have two criteria, however, that allow us at least to imagine what they might be or to recognize them as such when we come across them.

First, they must be symbols that we find described in the Bible or else that we find in use in Jerusalem in the time after the return from the Babylonian exile up to the city's destruction. Second, we must note that many of the descendants of the priestly families who immigrated to Rome with Titus were not converted to Christianity, even if they continued to be members of the secret organization (the cohanim). Given the conservative spirit that characterizes these descendants, they must have maintained their original family emblems unaltered through successive generations. The symbols used by the branches of the Jewish family of priestly origin that arrived in Rome at the time of Titus should coincide with those used by the lines of those same groups that became Christian and that eventually made up the European nobility. If the priestly hypothesis is correct, therefore, we should find many similarities—and some exact correspondences—between the symbols of modern Jewish familiesy and the heraldic symbols of European nobility.

Heraldry should—and does—thus offer further support of the priestly hypothesis. We will see that all European and papal nobility used symbols that we can consider indicative of their priestly status.

THE SYMBOLS OF JEWISH FAMILY BRANCHES

We can begin to explore the mine of Jewish family symbols first by trying to establish, on the basis of biblical and historical testimonies, those main symbols that were in use at the time of the reign of Judah. We can then check them against a sample of European Jewish family symbols.

The first Jewish symbol is clearly that of the lion. "Judah is a lion's whelp . . . he stooped down, he couched as a lion, and as an old lion; who shall rouse him up?" (Genesis 49:9): Jacob uses these words to bless his third son, Judah, when he confers on him primogeniture. Since that time, the lion has always been the symbol of the family of Judah and of the kings who descended from it—those who governed the kingdom of Judah from Jerusalem, starting with David. The lion, therefore, is the first and most certain symbol of Jewish origin, and could be used only by priestly groups who composed the aristocratic class of that kingdom. We frequently find it on coins and seals of that period.

Other symbols that go back to David and that are somehow connected to the worship conducted in the Temple of Jerusalem include harps, psalteries, and cymbals, the instruments that the king ordered to be played in front of the Lord (Chronicles 25). Ezra revived the custom of having "David's musical instruments" (Nehemiah 12:27–43) played by specialized groups of priests. It is likely, therefore, that some priestly groups may have adopted as their symbols the musical instruments they played.

Another well-known Jewish symbol is the so-called Star of David, also known as Solomon's Seal. It is made up of two isosceles triangles superimposed on each other to form a six-pointed star. In spite of the name, this symbol appears in Jerusalem for the first time in the sixth century BC, after the return from the Babylonian exile, and it was connected to the worship of Yahweh.[4] Rather than the symbol of a single family, therefore, it seems that it was a religious symbol representing the Divinity and was common to all those dedicated to God's worship. This symbol is also found in Christian churches and cathedrals. In the eighteenth century, it started to be used by Jewish revival movements, and subsequently it spread with Zionism, finally becoming the symbol of the state of Israel and being represented on its national flag. Yet there are also examples of its use by individual Jewish family groups: in 1822, for example, the Rothschilds included it in their coat of arms.

More than the six-pointed star, however, during the priestly rule of Jerusalem, the most common symbol was that of a flower: the lily. Its name in Hebrew is *shoshan,* which derives from the number six (*shesh*). It represents the six-pointed star. The Israelites considered the lily to be the most noble of all flowers, the symbol of the Divinity. The lily decorated the capitals of the two pillars, Jachin and Boaz, placed at the entrance to Solomon's Temple (1 Kings 7:19) and the Molten Sea (1 Kings 7:26), and it often appeared on the capitals of Jewish pillars from the tenth to the seventh centuries BC.

The prophet Hosea (eighth century BC) describes the lily as the flower that is the symbol of Israel: "I will be as the dew to Israel; he shall grow as the lily . . ." (Hosea 14:6). After the Babylonian captivity, the lily became an extremely popular motif in Jewish art. Together with the inscription "YeHuD" (which means Judaea), it appears as a national symbol on various coins minted in Jerusalem at the time of the Hasmoneans. It is still represented on modern Israel's coins.

Another symbol that is clearly of Jewish derivation is the *pentalpha*, or five-pointed star. It appeared on the fronton of the Temple in Jerusalem and very often on ancient Jewish tombs in Jerusalem. In addition, the five-pointed star finds a precise floral correspondence in the wild rose with five petals, a symbol that often takes its place or is superimposed on it.

One symbol that is clearly of Jewish priestly origin is that of the eagle with its wings spread and claws splayed. It appears on coins minted in Jerusalem during the period of the Hasmonean monarchy and is therefore probably linked to some branch of this family. For this reason, it is here referred to as the Hasmonean eagle—to distinguish it from the Roman eagle, which usually preceded the Roman legions. Unlike the Jewish eagle, the Roman eagle had its wings semi-closed and its claws closed over a bundle of rods and thunderbolts, because it was the bird sacred to Jupiter, the lord of the thunderbolt. (A perfect reproduction of it was included by Napoleon I in his coat of arms.[5])

Other symbols that we may expect to distinguish a priestly family are those that allude to the Temple of Jerusalem, such as, for example, the holy mountain on which it was built, the pillars that stood at its entrance, the decorations on the floor of the Holy of Holies, and so on. All of these symbols would have been used by branches of the priestly family of Jerusalem at the time of Josephus Flavius, and we should therefore expect to find them in later times among Jewish family groups and among the Christian ones that descended from them.

Let's see, then, the symbols used by Jewish families in modern times. Out of a sample of one hundred fifty emblems of Jewish families, traced in various documents of the Museum of the Jewish Community in Rome, the symbols most frequently represented are the following (see parentheticals for the number of appearances noted):

- Rampant lions, single or in couples, against a palm tree (23), against a tower (9), and against a pillar (6); (total 38)
- lions, single or in couples, in various postures and with various objects (menorahs, stars, crowns, etc.) (27); (total 65)
- palm tree (symbol of the sun), alone or with other elements (30)
- tower, alone or with other elements (18)
- sun and crescent moon, together (5) or separate with other elements (12); (total 17)
- cock, generally with a stalk of wheat or a branch in its beak (12), sometimes on a mountain with three peaks (6); (total 18)
- crown (10)
- pillar, isolated (2) or with lions (6); (total 8)
- five-pointed star (15) or six-pointed star (7); (total 22)
- Hasmonean eagle, crowned or two-headed, with wings and claws open (3)
- mountain with three peaks (7) or six peaks (2), arranged to form a triangle; (total 9)
- lily (5)
- menorah (4)
- triangle with hands (3), elements arranged in a triangle (2); (total 5)
- goose (3)
- harp (2), rose (2), heart (2); (total 6)
- bees, tree with serpent, peacock, jug with water (1 each)

The symbols most frequently used are that of the lion, as was to be expected of Jews, and the palm tree, a plant unknown in the Western world but full of sacred meanings in Palestine at the time of Jesus (we have only to think of Palm Sunday) and before. Palm trees were represented on the door of Solomon's temple (1 Kings 6:32) and on its bronze basins (1 Kings 7:36). These symbols are surprisingly followed in frequency by the tower and the cock, which we do not know how to fit into Jewish tradition, because they do not appear generally; the sun and the crescent moon (a symbol, according to a Renaissance tradition, of the Israelite tribe of Issachar); and other symbols that refer to elements of the Temple of Jerusalem (which, incidentally, we also find in Masonic temples), such as pillars, checkered floors, elements arranged in a triangle or of a triangular shape (including mountains with three or six peaks), stars with five or six points, the lily, the rose, the menorah, and the harp, which are clearly of Jewish priestly origin. From this list it also appears that symbols such as geese, bees, trees, and so forth, which often appear in Christian noble coats of arms, are of Jewish origin. Of course this list is not exhaustive of all Jewish symbols; many others can be found in synagogues, cemeteries, and documents of other Jewish localities, in Venice, Prague, Paris, and so on. One of the most common symbols to be found there is the dragon.

It is important to notice that these are not noble coats of arms, which were not permitted for the Jews, but distinctive family symbols found in private documents, on tombstones and benches, in prayer books, or on other objects that were always of a private nature. Given the great attachment to tradition of the Jewish families, it is legitimate to assume that these symbols were derived from an ancient family tradition, and were not copied from analogous symbols in use in the heraldry of Christian nobility.

In many cases, the symbols of Jewish family groups are exactly identical to those that appear in the heraldic coats of arms of great Christian noble family groups that were closely linked to the church. These groups could not have authorized Jewish family branches to use their own crests, and we cannot imagine that these Christian family groups copied them from the Jews. The most plausible explanation is that these Christian and Jewish groups had in common a distant ancestor who came from Judaea, whence most of these symbols seem to have originated.

It is important to point out that some of these symbols have been revived in the modern state of Israel and are present in its insignia and on its coins—in particular, the Star of David, the pillar, the lily, and the harp. It is clearly not possible to assume that they were taken from European nobility's symbolism; their roots undoubtedly lie in the most ancient Jewish traditions. It is from these traditions that the European nobility, which had the same origin, drew its heraldic symbols, and not vice versa.

THE ORIGIN OF THE COATS OF ARMS OF EUROPEAN NOBILITY

Each of the priestly branches that had been a party to Ezra's agreement had to have its own particular symbol, which identified it immediately as a family of Mosaic origin and at the same time characterized it with respect to the other branches in the group. These symbols were probably used only among the families themselves—on tombs, seals, and in other strictly private ways—and they served as secret signs of recognition among the various family groups.

With the strengthening of the priestly organization and the exponential growth of its members, the need for public identification must have developed along with the possibility to trace the origins of each family group. Eventually, with the assumption of public positions that involved the issue of official documents, the family symbols began to be used as seals, confirming the identity of the issuer of the document and its authenticity. This use is attested in the Roman church from the sixth century on and among the Carolingian nobility from the time of Charlemagne.

It is only in the twelfth century, however, with the beginning of the Crusades, that the symbols of identification of nobility became used universally and heraldry as we know it today was born. Along with providing a veritable mine of consistent evidence in favor of the priestly hypothesis, heraldry represents a powerful tool to identify the origins of European noble family groups. Interestingly, the majority of them can be traced back to the Jewish priestly family, for their coats of arms include both symbols that can be traced back to Jewish use and symbols that reveal a priestly status.

SYMBOLS OF MEMBERSHIP IN A FAMILY CLAN

We have seen that the most important symbols that characterize individual Jewish family groups are the lion, the dragon, the eagle, the harp, and the tower. These are all present in the coats of arms of most of the reigning houses and regions of Europe, and their origin can be traced back to the times of the Roman Empire. They therefore offer highly significant evidence in favor of the priestly theory.

The Lion

The emblem that can most clearly be connected to Jewish tradition is that of the lion, the symbol of Judah, the son of Jacob and ancestor of the Davidic dynasty. The lion was obviously the symbol of the kingdom of Judah itself, of which the Jewish priests represented the noble class. In particular, the lion must have been the symbol of royalty in Judah, and therefore one of the symbols used by the Hasmoneans in order to demonstrate their royal status.

The Christian descendants of the priestly family were to underline forcefully their right to wear the royal crown. In fact, the first kings of a priestly line of which we have historical evidence had the lion as their emblem. It is not necessary to reach the Middle Ages to find lion symbols; they appeared in Britannia immediately after the departure of Stilicho from the island, at the beginning of the fifth century. The monk Gildas tells us about it in his chronicle, *De excidio Britanniae*. He informs us that immediately after the departure of the Roman legions, a certain number of kings were anointed in Britannia (in accordance with the Jewish custom). The first of these was Vortigern, the son of the tribune Agricola and son-in-law of Magnus Maximus, who enrolled the Saxons as auxiliary troops, thus determining the ruin of the island. Gildas names five other Britannic kings, and at least two of these had the lion as their emblem. The first is a certain Constantine, the son of the "lioness Damnonia," who reigned over Cornwall and Devon; the other is Aurelius Caninus, who is defined as the "whelp of the lion" and who had established his kingdom slightly to the north, in Wales. We can note that Aurelius Caninus was almost certainly the son, or at least a relative, of Ambrosius Aurelianus,[6] whom Gildas defines as "a man . . . whose parents had been clothed in imperial purple on the basis of their merits." We meet him as the opponent of Vortigern for control of the island and as the victorious general against the Saxons.

The lion, therefore, was the emblem of some of the first reigning houses established in Britannia—and it must have been the lion of Judah, for it was not an emblem in use among the Roman troops. Nor can we imagine that it was a symbol taken from the local fauna, given that there have never been lions in northern Europe. The lion emblem had probably been brought to Britannia by the Spanish branch of the Gens Flavia, first by the general Flavius Theodosius and immediately afterward by his relative from the same region, Flavius Magnus Maximus. They came from a region of Spain that was undoubtedly their undisputed fief, because its capital was called Aquae Flaviae. The symbol of the family must have been a lion, because subsequently the area took the name León, which it still has—and its heraldic symbol is the lion. Theodosius and Magnus Maximus took personal possession of vast territories in Britannia and appointed members of their own family and relatives as heads of the various Britannic provinces.

We have seen that various kings who emerged after the withdrawal of the troops of Stilicho were related in a number of ways to Magnus Maximus, and clearly, their symbol must have been the lion, as is confirmed by the chronicle of Gildas. In addition, many of the family groups who left Britannia under the threat of the Saxons and moved to Brittany and Normandy must have been related to Theodosius and Magnus Maximus and must therefore have had the lion as their symbol.

In fact, we find it in the coats of arms of Breton and Norman family groups, and from Normandy it returned to England.

One of the first English royal seals with a heraldic meaning is that of the Norman William I, the Conqueror, who had two lions as his emblem. William was a descendant of the Viking Rollo, but, as we have seen, had 95 percent Breton blood in his veins. In addition, the Plantagenets, a branch of the Angevin dynasty that later replaced the Norman dynasty, had the lion as their symbol. This could be expected, because their ancestor Ingelgarius was related to Theodosius and Magnus Maximus. The Norman Richard I (1195), called Lionheart, had three lions as his emblem, and from then on, these creatures always appear in the coats of arms of English reigning houses and appear in many coats of arms of English noble family groups and cities. Together with the lily, they became the symbol of the monarchy.

In his capacity as emperor, Magnus Maximus sojourned for a long time at Trier, the capital of the province of Gaul, and as such, the seat of the imperial administration. In the region around this town we find another of the main centers involved in the dissemination of the lion as a heraldic symbol. It had become the symbol of two regions, Flanders and Brabant, as well as the symbol of a large number of local noble family groups. Two centuries after Magnus Maximus, these same groups helped the Carolingians in their ascent to the throne and were rewarded with fiefs and royal crowns, above all in northern Europe. Thus we find the lion of Judah in Belgium, Germany, Bohemia, and Czechoslovakia as the symbol of the nobility that was installed in that period by Charlemagne. Subsequently, we find it among the nobility and the reigning houses of Denmark, Norway, Sweden, and even Finland.

The lion is without doubt the symbol that takes, literally, the lion's share in the coats of arms of the northern European reigning houses and nobility, and it indicates their membership in the priestly pool, both by direct origin and also due to the matrimonial policy typical of the family. From what we have discovered, the use of the lion as symbol in central and northern Europe can be linked to the Spanish branch of the

Gens Flavia, which, with Theodosius and Magnus Maximus, imposed itself in Britannia and in Gaul. Yet the origin of this symbol in the southern parts of Europe, in particular in Italy, is quite different.

As we have seen, we find the lion among the symbols of Roman Jewish family groups and in the Christian world in coats of arms of noble family groups in central Italy. In these cases, two origins are possible: first, the family groups may have descended from Jewish converted to Christianity in the Middle Ages. This is the case of the Pierleoni family, one of the greatest Roman noble families from the tenth century on.

Another possibility is that they belonged to Roman senatorial families who had inherited the right to the symbol directly from the first Jewish priests who emigrated to Rome. This group includes not only individual people such as Pope Gregory II (715), but also regions and cities. Among the latter, Venice deserves special consideration.

The Lion of Venice

The lion of Venice is not linked to the Spanish Gens Flavia, but has a more ancient origin, probably deriving from some Italic ancestor of that Gens. The first symbol of Venice had been the dragon of St. Theodorus, also of Jewish origin, which we will shortly discuss. In 828, the dragon symbol for the city was changed to the lion of St. Mark, whose corpse had been stolen from Alexandria in Egypt. (In that same year, two Venetian merchants, Buono da Malamocco and Rustico da Torcello, came back from Egypt with a body, which they claimed was that of the evangelist. It had been taken from Alexandria and hidden in a basket under some pig's meat to avoid the control of the Muslim customs officers.[7]) It was universally known that the lion was the distinctive emblem of St. Mark, which is not surprising, considering its widespread use among Jewish family groups.

Mark is first mentioned in the Acts of the Apostles (12:12) as the companion of St. Peter escaping from Herod's prison. Shortly afterward (Acts 12:25), we find him as the helper of Barnabas and Paul at Antioch, and then at Salamis (Cyprus) (Acts 13:5). Some time later, he returned to Jerusalem (Acts 13:13), evidently after a misunderstanding with Paul, for in the end, Barnabas and Paul separated because of him (Acts 15: 36–41): Barnabas wanted to take him with them again, but Paul did not agree. For this reason, each went his own way. They evidently eventually made peace, however, because, writing to the Colossians (4:10) from prison, Paul says: "Aristarchus, my fellow prisoner, saluteth you, and Marcus, sister's son to Barnabas (touching whom ye received commandments: if he comes unto you, receive him)." In his second letter to Timothy (4:11), he tells him: "Take Mark, and bring him with thee: for he is profitable to me for the ministry."

Last, Mark is mentioned in another letter that Paul writes from prison, the one to Philemon (24). It is the same prison from which he wrote the letter to the Colossians, because his companions—Aristarchus and Epaphras—are still the same, as are his collaborators: Mark, Demas, and Luke. It is undoubtedly the prison where Paul was held in Rome, pending trial by the emperor, because in it he declares that he is "aged and now also a prisoner because of Jesus Christ, (9)"[8] and he is free to receive visits and to carry out his apostolic ministry. Paul, Aristarchus, and Epaphras are evidently the priests freed by the intercession of Josephus Flavius in AD 66.

Thus, Mark was a Jewish priest (as is also shown by his education) and a disciple of Paul, and after Paul's death, he must have played an important role in the church in Rome. Legend has it that Mark was the founder of the church of Aquileia and that one day, passing by the lagoon on his way to Rome, an angel indicated the island of Rialto, prophesying that his tomb would be there. This is only a legend, but it undoubtedly stemmed from a nucleus of historical truth with regard to the church of Aquileia, if nothing else, which became the seat of one of the most important patriarchates in the Empire. We should not forget that Aquileia was one of the first cities where the members of Sol Invictus Mithras settled at the beginning of the second century, and from then on, it became their fief. It is highly probable that the founders of the church of Aquileia were if not Mark himself, then at least members of his family or of a priestly family related to him. This would also explain why the Venetians, who mostly came originally from Aquileia, went to search for St. Mark's corpse and always demonstrated veneration and love for him, which are not found in any other town for any other patron saint.

What is certain is that Mark ended his life as the bishop of Alexandria in Egypt, where he was initially buried until his body was taken away by the Venetians. When and why did he leave Rome (or Aquileia) for Alexandria, and how did he become a bishop? We have seen from the letter of Pope Clement that during the period of the Flavians, the church of Rome imposed its leadership on the other churches in the East, sending bishops of its own choice there. Alexandria was the second city of the Empire, after Rome, and could not be left to itself. Evidently, Pope Clement sent the most prestigious priest he had at that time to govern it—Paul's faithful disciple, the evangelist Mark.

Everything adds up, then—including the spread of the symbol of the lion of Judah, which is what interests us at the moment. Immediately after Rome, Pannonia was the first area colonized by the priestly family, who took over the customs office at Poetovium and began to infiltrate the army at Carnuntum at the beginning of the second century. At the end of the third century, the family of priestly origin occupied all the centers of the economy and power in this area, and as a result, all the emperors from Aurelianus on come from here, like many of the great personalities of the church, starting with St. Jerome. Aquileia, the border town between central Europe and Italy, was undoubtedly the undisputed fief of the family of priestly origin and was one of the greatest centers of Christianity.

At the end of the fourth century, all the lands that did not belong to the imperial catasto were the property either of the church or of nobles of priestly origin. No small landowners existed. Those who worked on the land were serfs in the service of the great landowners. The islands of the Venetian lagoon were also undoubtedly the property of either members of the church or of the nobility who lived in cities on the terra firma, in particular Aquileia, Padua, Altino, and Oderzo. They almost certainly possessed farms in the lagoon and salt works, which were run by their servants, and these farms supplied them with fish and, above all, salt. In 402, the Goths, under the command of Alaric, attacked Aquileia and started sacking Istria and Veneto, causing a wave of refugees to arrive on the islands of the lagoons of Grado and Venice. All the nobles who owned property took refuge there, together with their servants. After the danger had passed, many returned to their houses on the mainland, but they did not abandon the islands, which in the meantime had been populated. According to the Venetian tradition, they set up the initial skeleton of an autonomous administration of the lagoon on March 25, 421. In this way, the families who were the owners of the islands in the lagoon not only developed the economy of the lagoon for their own profit, but also prepared an escape route in the event of new invasions, which were increasingly likely in those uncertain times.

The occasion for relocation presented itself just thirty years later, in 452, when Attila, the "scourge of God," reduced Aquileia to a heap of rubble and with it, a large part of the hinterland of Veneto. A second, definitive wave of refugees occupied the lagoon. Because they had nothing to which to return, the refugees settled there and created an autonomous government, first at Grado (in 466), which was raised to the level of a patriarchal see in place of Aquileia. Later, in 742, the seat of the government of the lagoon was transferred to Malamocco, and the glorious history of the Republic of Venice began. This history cannot be separated from that of its noble class, which governed the city for more than a thousand years. This class was certainly composed of members of the priestly family. Confirmation of this is found in a letter of Cassiodorus, the minister of Theodoricus, addressed to the maritime tribunes in 523, just seventy years after Attila. In this letter, he affirms that the Venetian lagoon was inhabited in that period by many family groups who were reduced to poverty because they were forced to live on the meager resources offered by the lagoon—but were undoubtedly of "noble origins."[9] The history of Venice, then, is the history of a city that, from the beginning, was the exclusive property of a group of direct descendants of Moses.

The Eagle

The eagle is usually associated with imperial power, and in fact, all the European imperial family groups have an eagle in their coat of arms. According to common perception, its use is traced back to the Roman eagle, which was the symbol of the father of the gods, Jupiter, and was often used as an emblem of the Roman legions. The eagle that appears in European coats of arms, however, is not the Roman one, but the Hasmonean eagle, which was engraved on the coins of the kingdom of Judah at the time of the Hasmoneans.

The Hasmonean eagle appears for the first time with Charlemagne. As we will see, he used the symbol of the lily in his seals and other personal objects, and he used that of the Hasmonean eagle as well. The lily was used to underline his priestly condition (he considered himself to be a king-priest), and the eagle was very probably an individual emblem to show that he belonged to a particular family clan.

It is possible that this also underlined in some way his imperial state—that is, it was a symbol adopted by the priestly family groups, which included among their ancestors at least one Sol Invictus emperor. The symbol of the eagle was frequently used among noble family groups that came from a stretch of territory extending from Savoy to ancient Pannonia, through Noricum, Illyria, and Aquileia (which took its name from the eagle), and from there, northward along the Rhine valley.[10] This is the area from which came all Sol Invictus and Christian emperors of the third and fourth centuries. Undoubtedly, they possessed vast landed properties in these regions, where their descendants subsequently made up the backbone of the senatorial nobility.

We have seen, for example, that Charlemagne was connected to the Anicis, a Gallo-Roman senatorial family that possessed large properties of land also around Aquileia at the time of Diocletian and was related to the emperors Carus and Carinus. Some of these families, such as the Savoy (Italy's royal family), substituted the symbol of the eagle in their coats of arms with another one, specifically the cross. On the contrary, others, such as the Hapsburgs, whose known ancestors came from a castle in the village of Hapsburg, in western Switzerland, maintained the symbol, raising it to the level of imperial dignity.

Another imperial family that had as its symbol the Hasmonean eagle are the Othonids, who derived from and were almost certainly related to the group of families that had helped the Carolingians in their ascent. All the European imperial houses had the eagle as their symbol, which suggests that this was indicative of a sort of ancestral right to the title, deriving from the Roman emperors of Pannonian origin.

The Hasmonean eagle, however, is also the symbol of family groups of central and northern Italy (for example, that of Pope Sabinianus [604–606]) who never advanced any imperial claims, and also of some Jewish family groups. We are forced to conclude, then, that it was a characteristic of one branch of the priestly family that came to Rome in the entourage of Titus. These members later moved to Pannonia, among the followers of Sol Invictus, and became the dominant class there. Most probably it was a family of the Gens Flavia, strictly related to Josephus Flavius.

The Dragon

Among the heraldic symbols that characterize family groups with royal blood, there is the symbol of the dragon. Indeed, together with the lion, it is one of the first to appear in historical chronicles referring to a family of priestly origin. Among the kings mentioned by the Britannic monk, Gildas, there is a certain Maglocunnus, who is defined with the title of Dragon of the Islands—clearly a moniker from his emblem. The dragon was the emblem of a Roman cohort stationed in Britannia, and it was probably the emblem of its commander, who was doubtless a follower of Sol Invictus, like all the senior officers of that period. He probably was the founder (or was a close relation of the founder) of the royal family of Maglocunnus, a certain Cunedda, a Roman official appointed in Wales by Magnus Maximus. The dragon must have been the family emblem of Cunedda, from whom another of the Welsh kings mentioned by Gildas, Cuneglasus, also descended. The dragon was also the symbol of Artorius, who defeated the Saxons at Badon, giving rise to the legend of King Arthur. Artorius was also known by the name Pendragon, evidently from the symbol on his insignia. The dragon later became the symbol of Wales, and even today it appears in the coat of arms of the Prince of Wales.

It is extremely likely that this was a symbol with Jewish priestly origins. The dragon was the symbol of the tribe of Dan.[11] According to the Bible a cadet branch of the Mosaic priestly family had settled in Dan (see chapter 2), and it must have entered into the pact decided among the twenty-four branches of the priestly family at the time of Ezra, maintaining the symbol of the tribe from which it came. A dragon is represented on the base of the menorah on Titus's triumphal arch. The dragon is omnipresent in Jewish, Essenian, and proto-Christian literature. In Revelation, for example, two chapters—12 and 13—are dedicated to the dragon, which also plays a key role in the outcome of the events. It is the symbol not only of the archangel Raphael, but also of saints such as George, Theodorus, and Michael. Because the saints had always belonged to the priestly caste, the dragon must have been the symbol of the family group to which they belonged.

Further, this family had settled not only in Britannia. In exactly the same period, the emblem of the dragon was flying over an emerging city situated thousands of miles from Wales: Venice. It was the emblem of its first patron saint, Theodorus.[12] (A statue of St. Theodorus from Amasia, with the dragon, can still be seen in Venice on the western column of the square next to St. Mark's.)

It also appears in the coats of arms of other royal and noble families, especially in northern Europe—in Denmark, Norway, and other countries around the Baltic Sea, where it was adopted by the Teutonic knights. It is the first priestly emblem (indeed, the very first heraldic emblem) that appears in the coat of arms of the Russian reigning dynasty, thanks to the marriage of the prince of Moscow, Basil I, and a Lithuanian princess (of Teutonic origins) who brought to him, as part of her dowry, the right to use a priestly coat of arms.[13] And thanks to their subsequent matrimonial policy, this dynasty, too, became an integral part of the priestly environment. As a result, other priestly symbols—the harp, the lily, the lion, and the two-headed Hasmonean eagle—became part of the Russian imperial coat of arms.

The Harp

The Davidic harp is another symbol that is not of minor importance in the heraldry of family groups of royal and noble blood, especially in the British Isles. It is the symbol of Ireland, and it therefore almost certainly dates back to the period of the conversion to Christianity of this island. It was presumably the emblem of the family of St. Patrick or at least of some member of the priestly family in his entourage who assumed a ruling position on the island. From Ireland, the symbol of the harp was later taken to Scotland, and became an integral part of the royal insignia of that country. Through Scotland, it also entered the royal coat of arms of England. Obviously, we are not talking about the migration of only the symbol, because it invariably accompanies the movement of a particular person who is the bearer of that symbol—a movement either by marriage or conquest or for any other reason.

The harp is present in the coats of arms of many noble family groups of the British archipelago whom we must consider to be of priestly descent. It is beyond doubt that this is a symbol of Jewish origin because it is also present on the coins of modern Israel.

The Tower

The tower is an extremely widespread symbol in heraldry, especially in Italy and Spain. In fact, together with the lion, it is one of the symbols of the Spanish monarchy, which has incorporated the emblems of two Christian kingdoms that survived in the Iberian Peninsula after the Arab conquest: León and Castile. Like that of the lion, its use would appear to be very ancient, because Castile took its name from the symbol for a castle. The tower was probably the distinctive symbol of the family (or group of families) who possessed most of the lands in this region at the time when it started to become an autonomous entity. Its origin, therefore, probably goes back to the landowning senatorial class of the fifth century, which must have had close connections to the Gens Flavia of the neighboring León.

The symbol of the tower does not have a clear relationship to the ancient Jewish tradition. Yet it very frequently appears in the emblems of modern Jewish families (see the list at the beginning of this chapter). Consequently, we can consider it more than likely that it was the emblem of one of the branches of the Jewish priestly family that came to Rome in the entourage of Titus Flavius.

In Italy, it is the symbol of powerful noble family groups, such as the Torrigiani family, who have provided the church with various popes and bishops. An origin from the senatorial families of Rome appears to be probable, because the tower already appears in 607 as the symbol of Pope Boniface III, who belonged to the Roman senatorial nobility.

Yet given the large number of Roman Jewish family groups that used the symbol of the tower, we must consider another possible origin: this was symbol of Jews who lived in Castile and were forced to conversion at the time of the Visigoths, and it was brought (or brought back) to Italy by those who preferred to emigrate rather than abjure. Some of these branches of the priestly family may have subsequently been converted in Rome. The Jewish origin of the Torrigiani family, for example, appears to be suggested by the name itself (Torrigiani means "residents of the tower"), which derives from the family symbol (and not vice versa). This frequently occurs among Jews.

SYMBOLS REFERRING TO THE TEMPLE
IN JERUSALEM

Among the symbols that we may consider to be family emblems are some that suggest the priestly condition of the family group because they appear to refer to the Temple of Jerusalem. Consequently, these symbols identified families who must have originally served in that Temple. The most explicit in this sense are the pillar, the mountain, and the checkered floor.

The Pillar

One of the most striking elements characterizing the Temple built by Solomon in Jerusalem were the two pillars, Jachin and Boaz, standing at its entrance. Today, these pillars still maintain a great symbolic importance in relation to the Temple. Therefore, it was natural and likely that the pillar would be taken as the emblem of a group of the priestly family that had originally served in that Temple. The Jewish origin appears to be confirmed by the large number of Jewish family groups who have a pillar as their family symbol and by the fact that the pillar is also depicted on coins in modern Israel.

In the world of Christian nobles, the pillar is a symbol that was almost exclusively found among the Roman nobility linked to the church, whose main representatives are the great and well-known Colonna family. The origin of this family, as for many others of the Roman aristocracy, is obscure. The fact that they bear the same name as their emblem* leads us to believe that the Colonnas were likely a Jewish family converted to Christianity and immediately ascended into the higher Roman aristocracy.

The Mountain

The mountain, like the pillar, is a symbol that appears almost exclusively in central Italy, in connection with the church. The symbol of

---

*[*Colonna* means "column" in Italian. —*Editor*]

the mountain was an indirect reference to the Temple of Jerusalem built at the top of Mount Moriah, which plays an important role in Jewish tradition. Membership in the priestly class of those who used this symbol is confirmed by the fact that the mountain is always depicted in groups of three or six, and the groups are arranged to form a triangle. This is an extremely transparent symbolism, which, as we will shortly see, alludes to the Divinity to whom the Temple of Jerusalem was dedicated.

Various great family groups closely linked to the church have these mountains as their symbol. It is no coincidence that the same symbol characterizes a large number of Jewish family groups and also one of the greatest Italian banks—undoubtedly the oldest one—which took its name from this emblem.*

Checkered Floor

Another priestly symbol is the checkered floor. Its origin is traced back to the floor of the Holy of Holies in Jerusalem. It was presumably adopted by high priests to demonstrate their right of entry into the Holy of Holies. This, too, is a symbol originally limited to central Italy, and is closely connected to the church. We find the checkers superimposed on other heraldic figures of priestly derivation, such as the Hasmonean eagles of as many as five popes of the tenth century.

The checkerboard was the symbol of the Di Segni family of counts, who provided the church with popes. It is no coincidence that the Di Segni family is also a cohen family, and the present chief rabbi of Rome is named Di Segni.

Checkers are also a symbol of the Cistercian monastic order created by Bernard of Clairvaux (religious orders adopted the heraldic symbol of their founder), the originator of the order of the Knights Templar. From the Cistercians, the checkers were evidently transferred to the

---

*The "Monte dei Paschi" of Siena. In its emblem there are three mountains arranged to form a triangle.

Templars, and eventually, either directly or through the Templars, they entered into European heraldry.

SYMBOLS OF MEMBERSHIP IN THE PRIESTLY CLASS

Undoubtedly, the most widely used and widespread symbols in European heraldry are those that indicate not membership of a particular clan of Jewish origin, like those seen so far, but membership in the priestly order itself. These are symbols that represent the Divinity that was worshipped in the Temple of Jerusalem. They include the triangle; two triangles superimposed (also called the Star of David or Solomon's Seal); and the five-pointed star. These symbols are very often suggested by the floral representations of the lily (hexagram) and the rose with five petals (pentagram). Furthermore, in a striking number of coats of arms, they are indicated only by the arrangement of the heraldic elements, which are repeated three times (forming an isosceles triangle), or six times (arranged to form a simple triangle—3, 2, 1—or a double one—1, 2, 2, 1).

In addition, the cross, which began to be used from the time of Constantine, can be considered a symbol of membership in the Catholic church. Very often, the cross, as with triangles, is only suggested by the position of five repeated elements arranged in a cross.

Five-Pointed Star

Let us start with the greatest of the presumed descendants of Josephus Flavius: the emperor Flavius Constantine. Did he possess a distinctive family emblem? We do not know. We know that at the beginning of his reign, he made widespread use—on coins and monuments—of symbols connected to Sol Invictus. After the battle of Milvian Bridge, he had the Christian Chi Rho symbol drawn on certain standards. We do not know what symbols were designed on imperial seals.

We do know from a Christian source, however, what symbol he

had erected over his tomb. For his burial, Constantine saw to the construction of a grand basilica in Constantinople dedicated to the twelve apostles. This was also to be used as a tomb by his successors. On the top of this basilica he had placed not a cross, as normally appears on all churches, but rather a five-pointed star. This is the same star that stood on the facade of the second Temple in Jerusalem and that appears on many Jewish tombs of that period (like the cross on Christian tombs). The pentagram is not of Jewish origin; it already appeared as a powerful symbol linked to the Divinity in ancient Egypt. Evidently, however, it had been adopted by the Jewish priestly elite, who had made it the symbol of their organization and used it to indicate members and also the property of the organization.

The five-pointed star, or pentagram, both explicitly and in the form of a rose with five petals (as we will shortly see), is the symbol that most frequently appears in places dedicated to Christian worship in the first millennium. Yet it is also one of the symbols that appears most frequently not only in the coats of arms of Jewish and noble family groups linked to the church, but also in the heraldry of the church up to today. The last pope to include the five-pointed star in his coat of arms was Pope John Paul I, who had three of them added over six mountains arranged in a triangle (that came from the coat of arms of his predecessor Paul VI).[14]

Five-pointed stars also distinguish objects dedicated to Christian worship, such as images of the Madonna, and even territorial and state-owned entities where Christian worship is, or originally was, prevalent. We must recall that Italy itself is under the aegis of the pentagram, which marks all of its documents and all who are dedicated to its service. As we can expect, Italy is not the only country that is marked by the sign of the pentagram. In addition, the European Union and the United States of America are so marked. The stars that appear on their flags all have five points. This was not just a question of aesthetics; it was a precise choice with a deep symbolic meaning. It is no coincidence that the church registered a vehement protest because its request to include in the European Union's constitution an explicit reference to its "Judeo-Christian origins" was not accepted. The European Parliament turned down the request in order to be sensitive to the lay world and Muslims, but it allowed the evidence of Judaeo-Christian roots to be depicted forever in the symbolism of its flag.

The Rose with Five Petals

The pentagram appears in a multiplicity of contexts, but no less frequent is the use, in its place, of the symbol that clearly represents it: the rose with five petals. Often, the rose is superimposed on five points, called thorns in heraldic language, which can be seen between the petals. While this suggestion is enough to transmit meaning, the pentagram is sometimes explicitly superimposed on the rose.

The rose is the symbol that recurs most frequently in Romanesque churches, convents, and monasteries. It is also the symbol of the so-called Comacini Masters, a brotherhood of architects who, starting from the period of the Longobards, took part for several centuries in the construction of churches and cathedrals in Italy and in northern Europe. Many consider them the precursors of the modern-day Masons.

The rose with five petals, either white or red, single or multiple, also appears in the coats of arms of many noble family groups. It was included among the symbols of royalty when it was adopted by the English houses of York and Lancaster, who long contended the throne of England during what were called the Wars of the Roses. Its introduction in England dates back to Henry III, who adopted it when he married Eleanor of Provence, and since then it has remained associated with the royal house of York. Subsequently, as a result of marriages, it was also adopted by the house of Lancaster and then gradually by a significant portion of English nobility.

The Single and Double Triangle (Six-Pointed Star)

Though the pentagram is a priestly symbol, the triangle and double triangle, or hexagram, are undoubtedly symbols that represent the Divinity.

In Christianity in particular, the triangle has become the symbol of the Trinity, and above or behind the altar in practically all churches, it represents God. There is no doubt, however, that Christianity borrowed this from Jewish tradition, even if its most distant origin as a symbol of the Supreme Divinity can be found in ancient Egypt. The triangle, formed by hands or other elements (e.g., mountains), often appears in the coats of arms of cohen Jewish family groups, to underline their priestly status.

The highest expression of the Divinity in the Jewish world, however, was represented by two triangles superimposed to form a six-pointed star, also called the Star of David or Solomon's Seal. The fact that it is a symbol of Jewish origin is proved not only by its name and by historical evidence, but also by the fact that it flies over the newly reconstituted state of Judah: Israel. In popular perception, the six-pointed star is essentially a Jewish symbol. Many might be surprised, therefore, to learn that it very frequently appears in Christian churches and cathedrals on floors and in friezes and in decorations of frontons and walls.

The six-pointed star appears not only in many Jewish family symbols, but also in a very large number of coats of arms of the church—from those of popes, cardinals, and bishops, to underline their priestly status, to those of dioceses and religious institutions.

Less frequent is the explicit use of triangles, either double or single, in the heraldry of lay noble families. Yet the triangle remains the most universally used symbol in heraldry, and it appears in the vast majority of noble coats of arms, suggested by the geometric divisions of the coats of arms, and above all by the number and the arrangement of the heraldic elements in the coat of arms itself.

A great variety of symbols are used in heraldry besides those mentioned here—for example, balls, shells, and animals—which do not necessarily have a clear priestly meaning and are probably linked to some historical fact or even linked to the original profession of the family group. The priestly status is suggested by the fact that these symbols are mostly repeated in groups of three and arranged to form a triangle. Typically, the three elements are arranged at the vertices of a triangle, as in, for example, the three bees in the Barberini coat of arms. Other times, they are arranged in such a way as to form a triangle, like the three mountains in the coat of arms of the Monte dei Paschi bank. Often the triangle is represented by three dots that are repeated several times in the coat of arms, completing the figures represented in it. We can see this arrangement in the crest of Pisa, made up of a cross with three dots at the end of each arm, or in Anglo-Saxon noble coats of arms, which have the ermine repeatedly appearing.

The elements are very often six in number, arranged to form a simple triangle (in superimposed rows of 3, 2, 1) or a double triangle (1, 2, 2, 1). In the case of the double triangle, if the vertices are united to the opposite two intermediate elements, the result is a Star of David. Examples of the simple triangle include the coat of arms of the great Farnese family, composed of six lilies arranged in rows of 3, 2, 1. An example of the double triangle is the Medici coat of arms, composed of six balls arranged in rows of 1, 2, 2, 1.

That the arrangement of the elements or dots is intentional and means to represent a triangle is proved by the fact that Lorenzo de Medicis (the Magnificent) himself drew a different version of his coat of arms in which the six balls are arranged in rows of 3, 2, 1 and are inserted in a geometric triangle. However it is represented, the triangle is the dominant geometric shape in the coats of arms of the European nobility and in those that were linked to the church. For those who used it, it indicated, immediately and directly, membership in the priestly order.

The Lily

One of the most widespread symbols in European heraldry is the lily, which, as we have seen, was the flower that symbolized ancient Israel, and thus appears today on the coins of the modern state of Israel. As the rose is the symbol that substitutes for the pentagram, so the lily represents the Star of David. It is formed by six petals arranged in two groups of three superimposed in such a way as to create a perfect six-pointed star, and it is used in place of the Star of David and is meant to share its meaning. It reveals membership in the Jewish priestly family.

It seems to have been used mainly by the descendants of the Pannonian branch of the Gens Flavia as a symbol of their divine right to govern. This branch had settled in central Europe in the second century. From the beginning, the lily imposes itself as the symbol of royalty. Its earliest documented use is by Flavius Anicius Carolus—Charlemagne—who included it on his clothes, scepter, crown, and seals (preserved in Rome). Lilies also appear repeatedly in the manuscripts of the Carolingians.[15] That it was a symbol of priestly status rather than an emblem of a family clan is proved by the fact that, as we have seen, Charlemagne also used the symbol of the Hasmonean eagle, which was a family emblem.

Before Charlemagne, the symbol of the lily appears on certain Byzantine coins minted between 610 and 685 and representing the emperors Heraclius, Constantine II, and Justinian II—which is perfectly understandable, given their priestly status. There is no evidence, on the contrary, that the lily was used by the Merovingians, in spite of the fact that artists of the fourteenth century, who identified the lily with royalty, painted the Merovingians with their clothes covered with lilies. The only lilies linked to a member of the Merovingian dynasty are those that appear on the crown and scepter of Queen Fredegond, consort of king Chilpèeric I, on her tomb at Saint Germain des Près.[16]

Charlemagne and his successors granted the privilege of using the symbol of the lily to dozens of cities in France (or perhaps it would be more appropriate to say that they attached their property stamp on those cities), including Paris, Lille, Brest, Caen, Poitiers, Niort, Tours, Blois, Bordeaux, Angers, Orléans, Reims, Fréjus, Le Havre, Laon, and Versailles.[17] This privilege was also granted to some Italian cities. The most significant example is the city of Florence. Charlemagne allowed it to use the symbol of the lily, which he defined as the "illustrious flower of royalty." On the occasion when it was adopted, the original name of the city was changed from Fluentia to Florentia.[18]

The Capetians, who succeeded the Carolingians on the throne of

France (and subsequently on the throne of half of Europe), also adopted the lily as their symbol. The lily became the symbol of France (a kingdom dedicated to God), and appears as the symbol of the French monarchy in all the coats of arms of the royal family groups. From France its use extended into England and into all the countries whose reigning houses and nobles became related to the French dynasty.

Ultimately, the Angevins, whose family symbol was the lion, as we have seen, eventually adopted the lily, probably in homage to the prevailing French custom of associating it with royal status. They clearly had a perfect right to use this symbol, given their imperial pedigree. Carolingians, Capetians, and Angevins must all have considered themselves to be direct descendants of the Hasmoneans, for the nickname Hammer (Maccabee) appears among the ancestors of all three dynasties.

Elsewhere, however—for example in Italy—the lily was to remain only an indication of membership in the priestly class, without any connection to royalty. It was included on the coats of arms of noble families who had no aspiration to royalty—such as, for example, the Farnese family—and also on the coats of arms of many popes. (The last, in chronological order, was Pope Paul VI Montini.)

Crosses

A symbol that is frequently found among the European nobility and various religious institutes and orders is that of the cross, with all its forms and variants. Indeed, it could not be otherwise in a Europe that was formed under the aegis of Christianity—above all, if we consider the fact that heraldry developed in and was imposed on all Europe at the same time as the Crusades in which the symbol of the cross distinguished the Christian warriors who were opposed to the infidels. Many noble family groups adopted the symbol of the cross in order to testify to being champions of the faith, militant followers under the banner of Christ—even if they could just as well have laid claim to other symbols.

The cross is not in itself a symbol that indicates membership in the family of Jewish priestly origins and never appears as a symbol of Jewish families. In the twelfth century, when heraldry developed, the European nobility had been stable for at least three centuries. As a result, a certain number of great family groups may have felt the need to demonstrate their militancy under the banner of Christ, rather than their membership in the priestly order. For example, this was the case with the Savoy family, whose original symbol, the Hasmonean eagle, was replaced by the cross, and with the Lorraine family, who led the First Crusade to its victorious conclusion and then adopted as their symbol the double cross that bears their name.

Those who adopted the cross were probably family groups who could not boast ancestral rights to royalty and therefore did not have any interest in maintaining their original symbols. None of the early royal dynasties have the cross among their symbols. The Savoy and Lorraine family groups were dukes who rose to royalty only in a later time. In fact, the Lorraines maintained the title of duke until the conclusion of the First Crusade, when the royal crown of Jerusalem was offered to Godfrey of Bouillon, the duke of lower Lorraine (as second choice, after the refusal of Boemond), who, however, refused it. It was the brother of Godfrey, Baldwin, who assumed the title of king of Jerusalem—and he was the first and last representative of the Lorraine family who wore a royal crown. On his death, the throne of Jerusalem passed to the Angevin Fulk V, who had married Baldwin's first daughter, Melisende.

The Savoy family rose to royal status much later, perhaps in the wake of the Portuguese royal family, who were related to the house of Savoy. Portugal was formed only in the eleventh century by the unification of territories of León and others wrested from the Moors in a fief granted by the king of Castile to a Provençal noble (whose coat of arms was the lion). The latter's son, Alfonso I, was elevated to the rank of king by the pope in 1139, and on that occasion he adopted the Savoy cross as his own emblem and that of his kingdom. The cross had been brought as part of her dowry by his wife, Matilda, the daughter of Amedeo III of Savoy.[19]

The Portuguese cross, however, is only suggested by five shields arranged in a cross, with each shield in turn containing a cross made up of five dots. Crosses made up of five dots or composed of five elements are frequent in heraldry—expecially in Great Britain. Much more frequent is the use of the cross in its many varied forms—above all in the heraldic symbols of cities or nations.

The cross clearly indicated militancy in the Christian faith and subjection, at least initially, to the Roman pope. It was not, however, as we have seen, a symbol of membership in the priestly order. On the contrary, this was often indicated by other elements combined with the cross itself, such as the four lilies that sometimes flower at their extremities (as in the emblem of Edward the Confessor). Other crosses suggest the triangle by dividing the extremities into two separate points or by limiting the cross to only three arms (a happy compromise between triangle and cross).

SYMBOLS DERIVING FROM SOL INVICTUS

Sol Invictus Mithras was an esoteric institution created, according to our analysis, by the Jewish priestly family. Rituals and symbolism, therefore, must have had their origin in the Jewish esoteric traditions (albeit with overlaps that must have been an external homage to the Roman pagan world). These traditions in turn had their roots in the kingdom of the Mitannis (the country of origin of Abraham, as well as of Mithras) and in the Egypt of the pharaohs.

The symbol most linked to Sol Invictus is the sun, which is omnipresent in the symbolism of the church, appearing almost always behind the crucifix, behind the eye of God at the center of the triangle that represents the Trinity, and in a multitude of other contexts. In addition, it very frequently appears in heraldry not as a real symbol, but as the background on which the heraldic symbols themselves are placed, which is similar to how the image is used in much Christian symbolism. The sun is often represented on the great honors awarded by sovereigns, and it has a great relevance in the Renaissance Neoplatonic revival. *The City of the Sun* by Campanella, which had an enormous influence at that time, is an outstanding example of this. It rarely appears alone in coats of arms, except in those of Freemasons and in Jewish family symbols, where it is usually combined with the symbol of the moon.

The moon, too, occupied a place of honor in Mithraic symbolism, and it still maintains this place in modern Masonic symbolism—in fact, it, in combination with the sun, is represented in all Masonic temples. Equally important, albeit unknown to the majority of people, is the role of the moon in the Jewish religion. The lunar origin of the god Yahweh is beyond doubt. Yahweh is the god of the revelation to Moses during the period in which the Jews were in Egypt, and Jah is the name of the moon in ancient Egyptian. The revelation was given on Mount Sinai, the mountain sacred to Sin, the god of the moon in Mesopotamia. It seems that the moon, together with the sun, was the distinctive symbol of the tribe of Issachar, and it appears as a symbol in various Jewish coats of arms. We must therefore consider as probable its use as the distinctive emblem of a Jewish priestly family that emigrated to Rome—and from this it reemerged in Christian heraldry.

The moon appears in a long series of coats of arms of noble family groups. Their priestly status is also indicated by the fact that it usually appears in the company of other symbols, such as five- or six-pointed stars, or it is repeated three or six times in order to form a triangle. In some coats of arms, it is repeated five times, forming a cross.

Other Mithraic symbols do not find expression in coats of arms, but were instead adopted by particular groups of people to indicate their status. For example, in mithraea there is always the presence of two figures, called torch bearers, who characteristically are represented with their legs crossed—much like, as we have seen, the statues placed on the tombs of Knights Templar.

THE PRIESTLY ORIGIN OF EUROPEAN HERALDRY

Only from the twelfth century did heraldry impose itself as a system to identify the European noble family groups. We have seen, however, that the use of distinctive family symbols was much more ancient and was employed not only on the seals placed on documents and various objects of personal use—such as clothes, arms, crowns, and so forth—but also on tombs, churches, and other civil or religious constructions as well as on villages, cities, and even buildings over which the family group that owned the symbol boasted rights of property or that had been built at the care and expense of the family.

From the twelfth century on, every noble family group, without exception, publicly adopted its own heraldic symbol. No nobility existed without a coat of arms, and the use extended to every public institution and association and religious order (which took the symbols of their founder, protector, and owner), monasteries, abbeys, convents, trade associations, and public offices.

All of the heraldic symbols of the twelfth century contain emblems that, in one way or another, reveal membership in the priestly order. In the great European nobility, as we have seen, lilies, lions, eagles, dragons, towers, and various kinds of crosses are the dominant elements. Among the minor nobility, we find a completely different set of symbols, but the priestly condition is usually indicated by the number and the arrangement of these symbols, which are generally three or six in number and are arranged in a triangle or double triangle, or are five in number and are arranged in a cross. This provides significant confirmation of the validity of our priestly hypothesis and at the same time supplies a criterion to evaluate the origins of European noble family groups and, within certain limits, their position in the priestly hierarchy.

With the passing of time and the extension of heraldry, we find the appearance of coats of arms in which the priestly symbols are absent, replaced by symbols such as the horse, the deer, the wild pig, and so on. This is probably an indication that they belong to families of the new nobility or foreigners who do not have any priestly origin.

Many families that are not of priestly origin, such as the Russian reigning dynasties and their great nobility, adopted coats of arms as a result of marriages to women of the upper European nobility. The usual policy held that priestly status and rights were acquired through women in a family group. We have seen this with the son of Herod (an Idumaean, and therefore not a Jew) and Mariamme (a Hasmonean), and it was confirmed at the time of the emperors belonging to the Gens Flavia and, subsequently, by the Viking Rollo, the Normans, and others.

In the church, priestly symbols began to be used by popes as seals and as personal symbols in the early Middle Ages. The list begins with the successor of Gregory the Great, Pope Sabinianus (604–606), who set up as his symbol an eagle with its wings spread. After him came Boniface III, who used a tower as his distinctive symbol. The following popes adopted more strictly Christian symbols, such as the cross or the Chi Rho (the same one used by Constantine on his standards and coins). In 715, Gregory II, a Roman, returned to using the symbol of two lions facing each other, holding a rose in their paws. In 904, Sergius III inaugurated a series of five Roman popes who had as their symbol a Hasmonean eagle with gold and black checkers.

The second millennium started with Pope Silvester II, who chose as his symbol a gilded lily. His successor, Sergius IV, had six stars arranged in a triangle (1, 2, 3). They are followed by Benedict VIII, John XIX, and Benedict IX, who used the checkered eagle. In 1045, Gregory VI returned to the two lions facing each other, holding a bezant in their paws. It was a coat of arms to be expected for this pope, who belonged to the once-Jewish Pierleoni family. Subsequently, more lions were used by Victor II, Nicolò II, Gregory VII, Gregory VIII, Anastasius IV, and so on. The two-headed Hasmonean eagle was employed by Honorius II and Gregory VII. Celestine II used three lilies arranged in a triangle. Urban II, Callistus II, and Clement III used a checkered coat of arms, and Eugene III used the crescent moon.

These are all symbols that we have already seen: the lion of Judah, the Hasmonean eagle, the lilies of Israel, the crescent moon, the rose, the checkered figures, the elements arranged in a triangle—all are frequently depicted in Jewish coats of arms. Is this just coincidence? Until recent times, almost all the papal coats of arms contained symbols that are clearly priestly in one way or another. Pius XII, for example, had as his coat of arms three mountains arranged in a triangle with the dove of peace; John XXIII adopted the lion of Venice above a tower with two lilies at its sides. Above three mountains arranged in a triangle, which composed the coat of arms of his family (Montini), Paul VI placed three lilies in a triangle; Pope John Paul I, Luciani, adopted as his coat of arms six mountains arranged in a triangle, surmounted by three five-pointed stars and the lion of Venice. Pope John Paul II, Woytila, was the first to break with this tradition, placing in his coat of arms a banal cross, not in the center, and a letter of the alphabet M (for Mary). His successor, Pope Benedict XVI, placed in his coat of arms symbols that are not priestly, but he arranged them in a triangle.

The nobility of Rome (and the surrounding area—that is, central Italy) was linked from the fourth century on to the Catholic church, for which it has provided most of the popes. It derives directly, without significant changes, from the senatorial nobility of the fourth century. Some families can easily be traced back to that century and have provided popes and churchmen of high rank as well as noblemen of the province. Other families who become protagonists in Rome are clearly of Jewish origin. Particularly in Rome (more than in barbaric Europe, where what counted was the possession of land), the cohanim were recognized as members of the Mosaic priestly family, and the inclusion of converted cohanim in the local nobility was easier and more immediate.

It is therefore plausible that various noble families who appeared on the Roman scene starting from the new millennium, without being able to trace their precise origin, derived from converted Jews. An indication of Jewish descent might be the name, which refers to the symbol of the family or to the profession indicated by that symbol. For example, this might be the origin of the Italian noble families of Colonna and Monti (their names derive from the symbols of the column and of the mountains that appear in their coat of arms) or the Medici family (the name means "doctor" and the balls, which appear in their coat of arms, was the symbol of this professional category).

Heraldry, then, offers formidable support to the priestly hypothesis. We find that the whole of European and papal nobility made use of symbols, which were indicative of either Jewish priestly family groups or priestly status. Furthermore, all heraldry is characterized by the omnipresence of the sun. The use of symbols can always be traced back to families who were linked to Sol Invictus. The chance that it is all a coincidence must be considered remote.

PRIESTLY SYMBOLS IN THE MASONIC TRADITION

In the previous chapters, among the sources of information about the secret organization and the affairs of the Jewish priestly family, Freemasonry has been mentioned several times as an insitution that has preserved the forms and the contents of the primitive secret priestly organization as well as traces of its subsequent evolution.

Confirmation of the link existing between the priestly family and Freemasonry can be found in the important and significant symbols that appear in Freemasonry. The symbol of this organization that stands out in relief to the east in all the Masonic lodges in the world is the usual triangle with the eye in the center, the symbol of the Divinity, the Great Architect of the Universe (G.A.O.T.U). Behind the triangle, the sun is almost always depicted. In correspondence and writing of various kinds, however, this symbol is rarely represented. In its place there appear three dots arranged in a triangle, which became the emblem of Freemasonry and identifies any document in which it appears as Masonic. There are also three candlelights in the middle of the temple, arranged in a triangle.

The Masonic symbols of the square and the compass are connected to the double triangle: in the course of Masonic rituals, they are placed one on top of the other, on the Bible, to form a sort of six-pointed star. The five-pointed star is also a fundamental symbol in Masonic rituals and is called the Flaming Star—that is, the pentalpha superimposed on the sun.

In Masonic temples, the sun and the crescent moon are depicted respectively to the right and to the left of the triangle, which represents the Great Architect of the Universe, the signs of the zodiac are designed on the side walls, and the starry sky is depicted on the ceiling. Other elements always present in these temples include the two pillars, Jachin and Boaz, placed at the sides of the entrance, and a rectangle with black and white checkers placed at the center of the temple, in front of the chair of the venerable master. The sun is present in the Masonic rituals and celebrations, which are linked to the summer and winter solstices (the two St. Johns—a link that undoubtedly dates back to the Roman period—because it was only then that the solstices were celebrated on those dates*). These are clearly all symbols of Jewish priestly origin, which can be found in the coats of arms of Jewish families, noble families linked to the Church, and religious orders.

There is no way of knowing whether this symbolism was present in Freemasonry at its origins or if it was introduced at some subsequent stage of its evolution—but in either case, it offers further evidence that Freemasonry is in some way directly connected to the priestly family. In many ways it appears to derive from the Mithraic organization, and consequently Freemasonry is in itself a sort of bridge connecting Sol Invictus and the Jewish priestly family.

GREAT FAMILIES OF JEWISH ORIGIN:
THE MEDICIS

At this point, we possess all the elements to try to explain the rise in many cities—especially in Italy—of great families whose origins remain impenetrably obscure, such as the Medici, Colonna, and Orsini families, which head a long list of many others that have played a decisive role in

---

*In the Julian calendar the solstices fell on 24 June and 25 December, days dedicated to the god Janus, later replaced respectively by St. John the Baptist and the Evangelist. The latter moved to 27 December when 25 December became the Sun's birthday.

Italian history. The possibility that they originated from Jewish cohanim family groups appears to be far from unlikely. We have already seen examples of converted Jews who directly entered the nobility and were admitted to the highest religious positions, such as the Pierleoni family, who converted in the tenth century and were immediately catapulted to the top of the Roman aristocracy. Yet there must have been many other less well-known cases that passed the notice of historians of the period.

Traditionally, since the time of Constantine, Jews were not allowed to possess land, and consequently there was no way in which they could enter into the great land-owning aristocracy. Certain professions, however, were open to them: medicine, trading, and above all, money lending, which was forbidden for Christians, because it was considered to be a form of usury. We have already seen that the Carolingians had promulgated a series of laws whose aim was specifically to favor the exercise of these professions by Jews. In this way, many Jewish families must have accumulated vast fortunes, which could not be transformed into landed property unless their owners converted to Christianity. Thus it happened that toward the end of the first millennium, many rich Jewish families must have followed the example of the Pierleoni family, converting to Christianity and thereby becoming part of the aristocracy and the corporations of city trades.

The history of the Medici family appears to be emblematic in this sense, for it represents the whole range of possible conditions of families that descended from the Jewish priests who had come to Rome under Titus. According to one of the traditions that the Medici family itself allowed to circulate, the family members were originally simple coal traders at Campiano, a little village in the Mugello area, on the hilltops overlooking Cafaggiolo, where Cosimo the Elder had a large villa with towers built by the architect Michelozzo.[20] In reality, their origins are shrouded in mystery. The only certainty is that they did not come from the countryside. The first member of the Medici family of whom we have historical information, Chiarissimo, was mentioned in 1201 in the registers of the important Woolworkers Guild in Florence and was a member of the General Council of the Republic. We know only the name of Chiarissimo's father, Giambono, and the fact that at that time, the Medici family was already rich and powerful and had without doubt been citizens of Florence since time immemorial. In the area of the Old Market, of which they were the undisputed lords, they possessed houses, and they lent money to the Camaldolite Abbey of Coltibono, as well as to Count Guido Guerra, who is mentioned by Dante as a hero of the Battle of Benevento (1265).

From then on, the Medici family was always one of the leading families in Florence. A certain Francesco Medici commanded a company of knights against the emperor Arrigo VII. Ardingo Medici was a prior in 1291, and subsequently master of the mint. Guccio Medici was gonfalonier of justice in 1296. A certain Giovanni de Medici was a commissary in the war against Lucca and was subsequently beheaded for events connected to that role. Salvestro de Medici was a prior and eventually gonfalonier in 1378. In 1393, the lordship of the city was offered to Vieri de Medici, who refused.

At the beginning of the fifteenth century, the family was among the richest in the world, and on his death in 1429, Giovanni di Bicci said to his sons: "I leave you amid infinite riches" in spite of enormous sums paid out to support the anti-pope John XXIII. His son Cosimo, called the Elder, inaugurated the actual lordship of the family over the city of Florence. Cosimo immediately demonstrated his ties to the church, giving hospitality in Florence to Pope Eugene IV and the council in 1439 that for a short time solved the question of the schism of the church of Constantinople.

It is unthinkable that the Medicis did not know the true origin of their family. If they tolerated or even favored the rise of legends that could not be verified, this is an indication that they preferred to maintain this subject's privacy. To understand the priestly origin of the family, it is sufficient to examine the coat of arms that characterized it: It is extremely simple, but has unmistakable meaning. It is composed of six balls arranged to form an intertwined double triangle, or Star of David. Lorenzo the

Magnificent designed other versions in which the isosceles triangle explicitly appeared. Both of these emblems are unequivocally priestly.

The family's origin as simple coal merchants is implausible. Balls were a symbol that distinguished those who exercised the medical profession in the Middle Ages. The family's surname itself leads us to believe that their original profession was that of doctors. This is also confirmed by the fact that the family had chosen as their patron saints two brothers who were doctors, Cosmas and Damianus, martyred under Diocletian. It was Cosimo the Elder who made this choice and had their story painted by Beato Angelico, a sign that he attributed great importance to it.

In antiquity, the medical arts had something sacred about them, and it was usually the priests who exercised the profession of doctor. In the Middle Ages and the period directly following them, the profession was preferably, if not exclusively, exercised by Jews. On the basis of these elements, therefore, it appears highly probable that the Medici family descended from a Jewish priestly family group whose members were converted to Christianity around the end of the first millennium or at the beginning of the second. This would also explain the fact that they came to the forefront of their world as bankers, which is a profession traditionally reserved for Jewish families, and that from the beginning, they appeared to be closely tied to the church of Rome not only from a financial point of view, but also on the purely priestly level, for they provided as many as three popes and four cardinals.

In addition, the connection between the Medici family and Freemasonry is highly significant, centuries before the foundation of the Grand Lodge in London. Examples include the Neoplatonic school founded by Lorenzo the Magnificent and the Academy of Design, created by Cosimo I, which are veritable proto-Masonic organizations. There are also paintings—such as those of Cosimo at the Palazzo Vecchio (Old Palace) in Florence—in which Medici family members are represented with the undoubtedly Masonic symbols of a square and a compass in their hands.

21

MODERN MASONRY

THE SECRET OF THE MOSAIC ORIGIN

On the basis of the historical reconstruction we have carried out (and of the genetic evidence, as we shall see in chapter 22), a large percentage of the European population has priestly origins. According to the hypothesis presented in this book, the great majority of European noble families, both of the upper and the lower nobility with all their secondary branches, must have descended more or less directly from the group of Jewish priests who came to Rome in the entourage of Titus. The question we may ask now: How did this information come to be lost by almost all of them?

Josephus Flavius was well aware of and proud of his origins, and the same may be said of the other priests who followed him to Rome. Even today, after two thousand years, the cohanim, who are descendants of the priests who remained faithful to Judaism, are well aware and proud of their priestly origins. Yet the same cannot be said of the descendants of the group of priests who became Christians and conquered the Roman world. As far as we know, they seem to have completely lost this information about their origins. This requires a credible justification. It is, after all, the kind of information that ought to be unforgettable within a family—and the kind that would be impossible to keep secret if it were known to all the members and descendants of the family.

One fundamental consideration to help us understand how the Christian branch of the priestly family lost the information about its priestly origins is the composition of Sol Invictus Mithras—that is, the membership of the organization. Women were excluded from the beginning, and perhaps they did not even know about its existence. With regard to men, all the adults of the branches of the priestly family were probably affiliated at the beginning, starting at the first level. Subsequently, depending on the family rank, social position, and personal gifts, they rose in the hierarchy of the organization, gradually passing to the higher levels.

One of the cornerstones on which the ambitious plan of Sol Invictus Mithras was founded—the plan to infiltrate the Roman world and conquer it—was undoubtedly secrecy. Further, among the most jealously guarded secrets of the initiatory organization was undoubtedly that of the priestly origin of its members. If their Jewish origins were common knowledge, the possibilities of infiltration into the army and administrative apparatus would have been compromised. Because it was a lodge secret, it was likely a forbidden topic in the family, and as a result, the memory at the family level must have been lost within a very few generations.

It has been said that the Mithraic organization was divided into two levels, and that only at the second level—that is, starting from the fourth degree—did members have any decision-making power and come to know of the secrets of its origin and priestly status. Anyone who did not enter into the organization or did not reach a certain level within it never came to know of the existence of priestly status. (Interestingly, one of the strictest rules in modern Masonry is that members at a certain initiatory level should not in any way reveal the secrets of that degree to members of lower degrees.)

As the number of priestly families gradually grew and the Mithraic organization expanded, access to the higher levels necessarily had to be limited. One of the requirements for the maintenance of any secret is that the number of those allowed to share it is as small as possible. Thus the higher operative level had to be limited; knowledge was reserved to heads of families, firstborn sons, and those members of the priestly family who proved to be particularly active and gifted. These were the only ones who knew the family secrets. All the others must have been unaware even of the fact that they belonged to a priestly line. Undoubtedly, they were aware that they belonged to the aristocratic class and possessed exclusive privileges, though they did not know the reason why.

The secrets of the priestly family, therefore, must have been handed down only within the higher level of the initiatory organization. We are led to believe that all the members of the Roman senatorial class had knowledge of it (all the senators of Sol Invictus of the fourth century held the highest degree—pater) and at least all the heads of families of the great nobility, which had settled in Europe at the time of the Carolingians, who came directly from that class. In addition, the ecclesiastic hierarchies must have known about these secrets. From an analysis carried out by medievalist scholars on the social origin of bishops all over Europe in the fifth, sixth, and seventh centuries, it seems that almost all of them belonged to the senatorial class.[1]

The continual references and the restoration of uses and customs of the period of the kings of Judah, together with the use of names of Maccabean origin among the upper Carolingian nobility, are a clear indication that this nobility was aware of its Jewish priestly origins. Yet what about today? Is it possible that the Christian branch of the family has completely lost this information at all levels? We can conclude that it is unlikely. Even today, there must be a nucleus that is aware of their priestly origins.

None of the cohanim—the Jewish branch of the priestly family—has lost the notion of its origins. The cohanims' ancestors must have been members of the same group of Romanized priests that started the ascent to imperial power, and some of them must have been, at least initially, members of Sol Invictus. Obviously, the obligation to secrecy held for them too, but because the status of rabbi passes hereditarily from father to son, and a rabbi must necessarily be of priestly origin, this knowledge has been handed down uninterruptedly within rabbinic families, and obviously in the Jewish communities in which they operated.

There is at least one secret, however, which has not been handed down, even among the cohanim: the secret of their Mosaic origin. Without exception, they all follow the genealogy officially established by Ezra: they believe that they descend from Aaron. Starting from Ezra, therefore, the secret of Mosaic origin must have been handed down exclusively within the secret initiatory organization, from which the cohanim were excluded after the triumph of Christianity. If the hypothesis is correct that the term *mason,* coined in the Middle Ages to indicate people of priestly origin (see chapter 17), is only a cryptic way to indicate the sons of Moses, then in that period there were still initiatory associations that maintained the secrets of the higher levels of Sol Invictus.

We can exclude the fact that at the time of the Carolingians, secret initiatory societies existed that were beyond the control of the civil or religious hierarchies. All the great nobility and the bishops belonged to the higher Masonic level—the one that, according to the Regius Manuscript and historical chronicles, was convened by the king annually to discuss the affairs of the kingdom. Below this assembly of magnates there existed a plethora of local Masonic organizations of a lower level, and these operated under the supervision of the authorities.

The rituals of the priestly family must necessarily have been handed down within this generalized Masonic system—but the more delicate and important secrets must have been the prerogative of the higher level. For the most part, they were transmitted orally, and consequently, we may presume that this took place mainly in stable structures that were particularly suitable for maintaining traditions and rituals in a reserved manner. In addition to bishops, abbots were members of the priestly elite, because they usually came from the great noble families. We should remember that the Carolingians and the families associated with them founded hundreds of monasteries all over the territory they controlled and where they disposed the goods of the church, which were a form of wealth collectively usufructed by the lay aristocracy for their supernumerary sons.[2] Parallel to this, starting from the sixth century, various monastic orders sprang up all over Europe, and these attracted the cream of the aristocracy. First among these orders was the Benedictine.

It is likely that in these religious structures, where the line between layperson and ecclesiastic was often somewhat indistinct, the secrets, traditions, and rituals of the primitive priestly organization were handed down (just as it was in these structures that the texts of classical antiquity were preserved). Yet in addition, the organizations of noblemen, the direct heirs of Sol Invictus, have never died out. As a result, we must presume that through them the more markedly secular and organizational elements of the original tradition were handed down—especially those concerning the genetic origin of the various noble groups, which was the main basis of their rights to supremacy.

Given the proximity and the close connection between the religious institutions and the nobility, these two traditional currents, while diversifying, likely never have diverged substantially. Furthermore, in the period of the Crusades, these two traditions must have combined in the military monastic orders. The Hospitallers, for example, were an offshoot of the Benedictine order, and the Templars were of Cistercian obedience. Both were composed of knights coming from the low- and medium-level European nobility who took the monastic vows, but were part of an organization of a secular and military nature. Both knightly orders held initiatory ceremonies and rituals of an esoteric nature, and these probably sprang from the union of the traditions of the founding monastic orders and those of the guilds of nobles from which the knights came.

Overall, these traditions must have reproduced in some way the original traditions of Sol Invictus, even if, given the vagaries of oral transmission, there must have been significant variants between one knightly order and another. Traditions and rituals of the knightly orders were likely also transferred to the guilds of nobles that multiplied all over Europe starting from the thirteenth century, after the definitive loss of the Holy Land.[3] The Crusades, with the blossoming of autonomous and sovereign knightly orders and the opposition between the empire and the papacy, had led to the end of the Masonic system monolithically controlled by the empire and the church. The city corporations had opened the way to municipal liberties—above all in Italy—while in the territories controlled by the empire (Franconia, Swabia, the Rhine basin) numerous societies of nobles had sprung up. These were composed of an aristocracy, which, by playing one prince against another, succeeded in maintaining a certain degree of autonomy and freedom of action.

These societies were spontaneous, free associations of nobles who recognized each other as equals (despite differences in titles and material riches). Each possessed a statute that members swore to respect, and they had given themselves rules and rituals derived from those of the knightly orders of the Holy Land. The influence of the Teutonic Order on the guilds of nobles of northern Europe was particularly important. After the fall of Acri in 1291, the order had taken refuge in Prussia, where it had created its own autonomous kingdom. From there, it organized regular expeditions against the pagan Baltic countries, and nobles from all over Europe took part in these. The so-called journey to Prussia had become a compulsory step in the training of the low- and medium-level nobility. One of the customary ways of honoring the best fighters was the "table of honor," a ritual banquet that took place at a round table, following the Arthurian model.[4]

These journeys contributed decisively to the integration of the European aristocracy and to the homogenization and fraternization of the guilds of nobles in their various parts. As a result, in the course of the Hundred Years War between France and England, French and English nobles who had met in Prussia honored each other and saved each other's lives. The guilds of nobles, more than the city trade corporations, seem to be at the origin of what later became modern-day

Masonry. This is so not only with regard to the structure, contents, and social rank of the noble guilds' members, but also for a temporal reason: their existence is well documented during all the period from the end of the Crusades to the eve of the official institution of Masonry.

Even if there were no such official confirming documents, we are led to consider it practically certain that these guilds of nobles were organized into levels or degrees, like Sol Invictus and, in turn, the Carolingian Masonry and our modern-day Masonry. We know for certain that the emperor and the great electors of Germany were members of these guilds, which often met under their presidency. In their case, however, they must have been part of an exclusive level reserved only for the uppermost aristocracy of the empire and who met regularly in exclusive diets. The most important and jealously guarded secrets—such as that of Mosaic and priestly origin—must by now have been reserved only for this level. Among the general mass of noble families of a lower level, an awareness of their priestly origin must have rapidly died out.

THE HISTORICAL ORIGINS OF MASONRY

By almost universal agreement, modern Masonry is an institution of English origin, which started in London in 1717. On June 24 of that year, on the feast of St. John the Baptist (the date is important, because it coincides with the summer solstice at the time of the institution of the Julian calendar and is thus a direct connection to Sol Invictus), four Masonic lodges in London united to form the Grand Lodge of England. Six years later, in 1723, the Protestant pastor James Anderson wrote the constitution of the order (the constitution of the Free Masons, containing the history, charges, regulations, and so forth of the most ancient and right worshipful fraternity), which is still in force in its original form.

It is all too evident, however, that Masonry did not begin on that date. The Grand Lodge of London simply brought together preexisting lodges, creating a coordinating organism capable of adopting other lodges under its own jurisdiction. Several professedly Masonic lodges existed at the time in various English towns and in Scotland and Ireland. The same was no less true on the Continent. The clearest historical proof that Masonry existed long before its official foundation and that it was widespread not only in England, but in all Europe, is offered by the bull of condemnation issued by Pope Clement XII just twenty years later.[5] In it, he affirms that for a "long time" this society had been condemned in most countries as dangerous to the safety of the state. This is a clear reference to the guilds of nobles, which, in a sense, were in conflict with the absolute authority of the princes. They sought to safeguard their autonomy and freedom of action, which must have been the object of repression in the most centralized monarchies and particularly in the state of the church.

There is a substantial quantity of literature about Masonry that has not succeeded so far in throwing light on its origins. Quite the contrary: the deeper we delve into this literature, the more confused we become and the more we realize that it is impossible to arrive at any sensible conclusion on the basis of historical documents. All that happened before 1717 completely escapes any historical research carried out by traditional means. We know for certain that something existed before that date, but in three centuries of research, nobody has been able—or perhaps nobody has wanted—to find out what it was.

The prehistory of Masonry is lost in a darkness that is all the more profound because its official founders did not trouble to illuminate it with the slightest ray of light.* The first person who wrote an extensive report about its origins was the author of the constitution, James

---

*According to certain historians of the nineteenth century, a large number of historical documents referring to Masonry were destroyed in 1720 by the founders of the Grand Lodge themselves, for fear that their publication might produce negative effects.[6]

Anderson. Yet he limited himself to repeating what is said on the subject in the Cooke Manuscript, without troubling to give any information about what had happened in the three centuries that separate him from this document, and without troubling to lend a minimum of historical credibility to what it says about the origins of the organization. He traces Masonry all the way back to Adam.*[7] The result has been that his report is considered pure legend.

On the same level, we find a host of works, mainly written by Freemasons, who claim extremely ancient origins, but in a vague and confused manner. What we know for certain is that the Masonic phenomenon was already ancient in 1390,[8] the period to which dates the first historical document confirming its existence, the Regius Manuscript. Of a slightly later date is the construction of Rosslyn Chapel, near Edinburgh, Scotland, whose sculptures recall Masonic rituals still in use today. These sculptures seem to confirm a close relationship between the Knights Templar and Masonry.[9]

Kilwinning is one of the first avowedly Masonic Scottish lodges we know of, and its existence is confirmed already in 1314 (four centuries before the Grand Lodge of London was founded), when the Scottish king Robert Bruce is said to have admitted the Templar exiles who had escaped the persecution of Philip the Handsome.[10] Even more ancient is the origin of the first Masonic lodge in York, which, according to the tradition mentioned in the Halliwell Manuscript, is said to have been founded in 926 by King Athelstan.

The existence of Masonic lodges on the European continent is also documented long before 1717—and these are lodges that were formed

---

*From a historical point of view, this is senseless, unless we imagine that the document was written for initiates who possessed a particular key to read it, which would restore an intelligible and plausible historical meaning. For example, in the apocryphal text *The Apocalypse of Moses,* the "treasure cavern" in which all the patriarchs were buried, undoubtedly refers to the same secret crypt of the Masonic Royal Arch's ritual, and the first patriarch, Adam, is a clear allusion to Moses. If we take this text as one of the keys to interpret Anderson's historiography, the origins of Masonry must go back to Moses, which is decidedly less improbable and wholly in line with our thesis in this book.

independently of the English ones. The Dutch lodge of The Hague called Het Vreedendall, for example, is supposed to have been founded in 1519. Destroyed in 1601 and rebuilt in 1637, it preserved among its documents the so-called Charter of Cologne, the alleged 1535 record of a meeting of the "elect masters" of the lodges founded in the cities of London, Edinburgh, Vienna, Amsterdam, Paris, Lyon, Frankfurt, Hamburg, Antwerp, Rotterdam, Madrid, Venice, Ghent, Königsberg, Brussels, Gdansk, Middelburg, Bremen, and Cologne.[11] A congress of "stonemasons" was held at Regensburg in 1459, where nineteen "masters" from Swabia, Franconia, Bavaria, Upper Rhine, Switzerland, and Austria took part. (Some scholars see this congress as the real birth date of Freemasonry.)[12] A few years later, in 1464, an analogous congress was held in Speyer.

The theory that receives most support today among orthodox scholars, and which is also shared by the vast majority of members, is that Masonry originated from corporations of artisan builders (or stonemasons) in the Middle Ages. Curiously, this hypothesis was not even mentioned in the works of the early historians of the confraternity or in the first documents that refer to this organization, the Regius and Cooke Manuscripts. In fact, it was introduced only halfway through the eighteenth century, by a non-Mason, Abbot Grandidier,[13] in a book about the cathedral of Strasbourg. The hypothesis was subsequently developed and studied by various authors, especially Masons, who trace the organization back as far as alleged confraternities of builders of republican Rome or even earlier. Yet there is no document or historical testimony that makes it possible to establish a direct link between the corporations of medieval builders and modern Masonry.

The most significant elements of proof for this theory are offered by certain building-related elements included in the vast symbolism of the order and the name of its members: Free Masons. Yet for an organization that was born in secrecy and that has a particular tendency to use substitute words to mask the real meaning of certain terms, the public use of this name is not particularly significant.* Further, the building-related symbols used in the Masonic order have a purely allegorical meaning, and are outnumbered by a mass of symbols and traditions that refer directly to Mithraic symbolism and to the traditions of the priestly family. The building-related elements are the square and the compass (normally superimposed on one another to form a Star of David) and a number of references linked to the working of stone. This is perfectly natural, for the priestly organization revolved around the construction of the first and second Temples in Jerusalem. Furthermore, at the time of the reconstruction of the Temple, Herod the Great instituted a special body of mason-priests, who were the only ones authorized to go into the Holy of Holies for the execution of work inside there. This body of mason-priests continued to operate for the following duration of the Temple, charged with carrying out periodic maintenance. It is natural, therefore, if Masonry derives from the priestly family of Jerusalem, that it should preserve building elements in its symbolism and traditions.

OPERATIVE AND SPECULATIVE MASONRY

Among the arguments that various scholars present to support the building origin of Masonry,[14] one of the most important is the fact that modern Masonry defines itself as speculative in contrast with the original masonry, which tradition defines as operative. The following explanation of these terms is given by Masonry itself: Operative masonry was the organization whose members materially worked with stone,

---

*It is not doubtful that *mason* refers to builder—this meaning is declared in all the documents, writings, and rituals of the Freemasons. The problem is that this is the name by which the members designate themselves, above all with respect to the profane world. The tendency of this organization to play with words, to encode them or disguise them, however ingenuously or transparently, is well known. It is likely that the word *mason* was deliberately adopted by members to express their descent from Moses, but that this was hidden under a different meaning chosen in view of the assonance of the name and the building connections present in the symbolism of the Masonic order.

squaring it off into blocks that could be used for the construction of temples—that is, stonemasons and builders. Speculative Masonry refers to the organization whose members work on the stone of their own souls. This image is undoubtedly poetic, but it does not find any correspondence in reality, because it is not possible to determine a period in which the organization was composed only of builders or the transition stage when they were replaced by members from the nobility.

The classic example of operative masonry, which is quoted by all Italian historians, is that of the Comacine Masters.[15] Some historians actually indicate these masters as the true founders of Masonry. Tradition has it that they were involved for centuries in the construction of the Romanesque churches of half of Europe and, subsequently, of the Gothic cathedrals. That they were Masons—in the sense indicated in the Regius Manuscript, that is descendants of the priestly family associated in the defense of their interests—has already been said (the term "master" by which they are defined indicates an origin that is far from menial). Confirmation in this sense is provided by the coat of arms of the confraternity: a compass above a rose with five petals. The compass is the most classic of the Masonic symbols, and the rose with five petals is a common priestly symbol, which very frequently appears in Romanesque churches starting from the eighth and ninth centuries and is present in the coats of arms of some of the leading European noble families.

Yet we must question the hypothesis that the Comacine Masters were the originators of the Masonic institution. Analogous claims with the same kind of proof and arguments have been advanced for English and German confraternities that define themselves as stonemasons. Some historians also include among the ancestors of Freemasonry alleged confraternities of stonemasons made up of Cistercian, Benedictine, and Oblate monks, who from the beginning were masters of the science of construction and the keepers of the art of building used for erecting the great medieval abbeys. All these builders had to be considered freemasons, but certainly they were not the originators of Masonry.

In the Middle Ages, the big business that moved the economy of states, the equivalent of the great public works today, was the construction of cathedrals. A large number of priestly symbols are to be found on them. This is perfectly natural, because, according to our analysis here, customers and financers usually belonged to the priestly elite. In addition, those responsible for the planning and execution of the work must have also belonged to this elite, because they came from the best educated class of society and possessed architectural knowledge and notions that are still capable of surprising us today. On the contrary, the manpower to build the cathedrals was undoubtedly supplied by workers of the menial, illiterate class who had to carry out the most tiring and humble jobs.

The term *stonemasons,* which is used at times to define the members of Masonic organizations, cannot be interpreted literally. (The Four Crowned Saints are also defined as stonemasons, even though they were centurions.) The people belonging to these organizations were never simple workers, as a certain kind of populist rhetoric tries to show. Rather, they always belong to the noble class or to the high clergy or to the group of great personalities of the period. For example, Emperor Maximilian took part in the congress of stonemasons held at Regensburg in 1459 and in the following one held at Speyer (1464)—not as an observer, but as a member of the confraternity. He personally authenticated the brotherhood book in which the results of the decisions of the congress were recorded. His workshop partner was the great artist Albrecht Dürer, who carved in the wood of the arch of triumph the effigy of the emperor dressed as a master builder. Tradition has it that Emperor Rudolph IV was also a member of the building yard of St. Stephen's Cathedral.[16]

The Regius Manuscript mentions among the members of the lodge of York only "dukes, earls, and barons also, knights, squires, and many more, and the great burgesses of that city."* Among Masonry members,

---

*"King Athelstan proclaimed in the whole country, to all the Masons of art, to go to him immediately . . . He held an assembly of various lords, in accordance with their status: dukes, earls, and also barons, knights, gentlemen, and many others, and the leading citizens of that city; they were all there, in accordance with their degree. They were there, according to their resources to establish the condition of these Masons."

it mentions Charlemagne, King Athelstan (924), and his brother, Prince Edwin. While these testimonies are considered to be legend by orthodox scholars, other such testimonies do have a true historical value. The signatories of the Charter of Cologne of 1535, for example, include the sovereign archbishop elector of the empire, Wied; a churchman from Antwerp, Van Noot; the philosopher Van Uttenhove; Jacobus Praepositus, a collaborator of Luther; a member of the noble Genoese Doria family; and Philip Melantone, a jurist, politician, and philosopher who was a doctor at various German universities.

All these, according to present-day orthodox theories, belong to what should have been operative masonry, made up essentially of artisans and building workers. Yet there is no trace of this in any document. All the historical evidence indicates that members of the Masonic confraternities were always and exclusively members of the ecclesiastical world, the nobility—including sovereigns—and the cultural elite. There is never the slightest mention of simple workers. Furthermore, it is inconceivable that kings, princes, ministers, bishops, and abbots—the ruling class of a society where social divisions were absolute and insuperable—should have desired to sit side by side with real stonemasons and builders—traditionally at the bottom of the social scale—and call them brothers.

Historical evidence demonstrates that the members of so-called operative masonry all belonged to noble families (and were thus of priestly origin). In addition, the Masons who were members of the first Grand Lodge in London were all gentlemen—that is, members of the noble class. Anderson's constitution, however, declares explicitly and officially that the newborn organization was no longer "operative" but only "speculative." Was this a factual consideration or rather a limitation imposed on the new organization?

Evidently, the terms *operative* and *speculative* are not to be interpreted with their literal, dictionary meaning. (This kind of literal interpretation rarely happens in Masonic terminology.) It is beyond doubt that these terms should indicate either two different moments, or two substantially different levels of the organization. If we exclude the officially sponsored interpretation, only two possible hypotheses are left: the first is suggested by the Masonic ritual regarding the construction of the "spiritual temple" in place of the material one destroyed by Titus.[17] The operative priests would have been those in the service of the Temple in Jerusalem, the speculative ones those in the service of the spiritual temple. The transformation from operative into speculative Masonry, therefore, would have taken place at the same time as the institution of Sol Invictus Mithras. This hypothesis is attractive but not at all convincing, because it looks rather strained for many reasons.

The second hypothesis refers to two different levels of the Masonic organization, and it is the more plausible notion. We have seen that in the first three degrees of Sol Invictus Mithras, it was possible to affiliate people who were external to the priestly family, who were not introduced to the secrets of the family. These degrees, therefore, must have had a function that was purely formative—that is, speculative. The higher degrees, on the contrary, must have been reserved exclusively to ascertained descendants of the priestly family, and all the truly operative functions—that is, the political decisions and the consequent adoption of action—were reserved for them.

The first few degrees, therefore, must have made up the speculative level of the organization, the level where members of any origin could be accepted (even boys, judging by what Porphyrius says), because they were not initiated into the true mysteries of the organization. The higher degrees made up the operative level reserved for members by birthright who had access to the institution and who proceeded on its hierarchic scale on the basis of genetic requisites (a categorical imperative in the Jewish priestly world). They were the only ones entitled to access to the secrets of the family. This distinction never elapsed, because there has always been a level in European nobility that we can define as operative—the level at which all the decisions of a political nature were made—which was above a speculative level made up of those proto-Masonic organizations that the Regius Manuscript describes as subject to the supervision and control of civil and religious authorities.

The Grand Lodge in London was defined as speculative because it was composed of lodges of the first three levels (apprentice, companion, master), into which the members were "accepted" independent of any consideration of their genetic character, and which could not take decisions on matters of religion and politics. The Grand Lodge remained speculative even when higher levels were introduced—the various ritual bodies, mainly the Scottish Rite and the Rite of York. These levels had no genetic connotations and no operative tasks—and they have none today, always remaining subordinate to the Grand Lodge. We do not know whether there exists today an operative Masonic level reserved for the descendants of priestly families, or for somebody else, where decisions of political nature are made and actions are taken. If it exists, however, it certainly is not a part of the regular Masonic system established in London in 1717.

Starting from this date, Masonry has remained essentially speculative. Membership in the family of priestly origin is not a requisite and is not even known to members of the institution. Further, it certainly is not included among the secrets that are communicated to them during the various initiations. It is equally certain that the institution is in no way in the service of interests of the priestly family or of its individual members, even if traditionally, at the top of the Grand Lodge in London, there has always been an English prince of royal blood who, on the basis of the hypothesis presented here, is among the most eminent members of that family.

The fact remains, however, that initially, and for at least all of the eighteenth century, the vast majority of Masonry affiliates were represented by churchmen and members of the nobility. In 1723, the grand master of the unified lodge in London was Duke Philip of Wharton, and the English nobility was present in large numbers in the lodges. The same occurred in the Grand Lodge of York, set up in 1725 in competition with that of London:* it was joined by several peers of England,

---

*The Grand Lodge of York, which claimed to have been founded in 926 by Prince Edwin, designated itself and its followers as Ancients, in opposition to the Moderns, as the members of the Grand Lodge of London were called.

including members of the royal family. One particularly active member was the duke of Atholl, who held the position of grand master. In 1813, when they eventually united, the two Grand Lodges were led by two members of the royal house: the duke of Kent for the Moderns (the Grand Lodge of London) and for the Ancients (a Grand Lodge that referred back to the ancient Masonic tradition of York), the duke of Sussex, who had succeeded his brother, the prince regent, later George IV, in this position.

No less illustrious were the members of Masonry on the Continent, which appears in the official historical records immediately after the constitution of the Grand Lodge in London, as if it were a direct derivation even if its existence came from long before. In particular, German and Austrian Masonry included among their members Emperor Franz I, the husband of Maria Theresa of Austria; King Frederick of Prussia; the prince-bishop Count Schaffgotsch of Wroclaw; and a long list of names of the great nobility and middle-European senior clergy.

Modern-day Masonry, therefore, was initially an institution composed almost totally of members of the aristocracy in the wake of the tradition described by the Regius Manuscript. After the French Revolution, the noble component was progressively diluted by access of members of the middle class, and today, no limitations of a social nature exist. The structure of the organization and its traditional contents and rituals, however, are practically the same as those of the Masonry of the eighteenth century and have now been frozen for more than two centuries.

Modern-day Masonry is no longer an institution that is reserved for or controlled by the priestly family, but this does not exclude the existence of a direct, continuous link between it and the organization created in Jerusalem by Ezra and recreated in Rome by Josephus Flavius. The initial hypothesis that it reproduces the organization of Sol Invictus Mithras, as a fossil reproduces the forms of a living being, appears to be legitimate and allows us to obtain reliable information about the original organization and its subsequent evolution. We can therefore legitimately and confidently affirm that Masonry presents the underlying theme of the history of the Jewish priestly family from the time of its origins, and it allows us to look at even the family's most intimate and secret affairs. It is a story with many shady areas, and these gradually become more blurred as we draw closer to the present day—but for the period before the eighteenth century, this history offers a sufficiently clear, consistent, and complete view to appear reliable, at least in its essential outlines.

THE PRIESTLY FAMILY IN THE WORLD OF TODAY

With regard to today, we have a sufficiently detailed knowledge of the history of the various national organizations of Masonry and of individual Masons to realize that it is strictly intertwined with the history of the Western world. At the popular level, in particular in schoolbooks, there is a tendency to ignore completely the role played by Masonry in the formation of modern-day Western society; but it is beyond doubt that most of the protagonists of the history of the West in the eighteenth and nineteenth centuries were Freemasons. The founders of the English Royal Society, which pioneered the modern scientific revolution, were Freemasons, as were the originators of the French Revolution, whose motto of freedom, equality, and fraternity has been universally adopted by Masonry. Many of the members of the first American Congress were Freemasons, starting with George Washington and those who wrote the Constitution of the United States. Likewise, the protagonists of the Italian Risorgimento, from Mazzini to Garibaldi, were Freemasons. Ultimately, the creators of the democratic system were Freemasons.

It is true that this fact is purely accidental: they were Freemasons because they belonged to a particular social class, but their actions were not dictated by the Masonic institution, because it was, as it is now, devoid of any operative functions. In fact, the majority of their adversaries and opponents also belonged to the same institution. The fact is that the members of the Masonic institution belonged to a social class that historically had always been characterized by continuous internal struggles to conquer positions of supremacy. These struggles have become more intense and radical in a period of profound economic and social change such as the modern age, and have caused the reemergence of fringes of the priestly family once secondary or marginalized. This latest emergence is due to the rapid increase of their economic power.

They have not, however, denied their origins, and indeed, they have continued to apply their hallmark to their most significant achievements. Washington, for example, is built in accordance with a planimetry that is clearly Masonic in its derivation; the gardens opposite the Royal Palace in Brussels have the layout of a Masonic temple; the one-dollar banknote created by the Founding Fathers of the United States of America is literally crammed with Masonic symbols; and on the flag of the United States, as on that of the European Union, there is a series of five-pointed stars. These are the equivalents of the marks on medieval cathedrals, houses, cities, and nations of Europe—marks that did not refer to the creators of those works, but to their owners who had commissioned them and had them built: members of the priestly family.

Even if there is no certainty on the subject (and there could not be), it is legitimate to presume that, at least at the beginning, there was a higher level in Masonry reserved for members who were well aware of their priestly origin and knew about the secrets of the family. There is one indication, in particular, which seems to confirm this. The Grand Lodge of London has always declared that it does not know anything about the origins of Masonry before 1717, and it favors any theory or hypothesis, however nonsensical, that does not make any reference to the ritual contents and the solar elements that could connect it to the Jewish priestly family and to Sol Invictus. In particular, the theory of an origin from the corporations of stonemasons is practically a dogma, in spite of the fact that it is manifestly groundless and not backed by any historical evidence.* It seems to be more than justified that this origin story is a deliberate attempt to lead people off the track.

There appears to be a clear effort to distract attention from what seems to be the only explanation that is consistent with the contents of Masonry and to divert it—seemingly successfully—in another direction. Masons themselves—at least the vast majority of members—are unaware of the origin of their traditions and their rituals. They limit themselves to repeating them, generation after generation, exactly as they have been handed down, without wondering where they came from, and who set them up and why. They recognize that these traditions and rituals are wholly tied to the Jewish priestly reality and revolve around the Temple of Jerusalem, but they do not draw any conclusions from this fact, and they continue to endorse with conviction the fable that Masonry started from medieval builders' confraternities.

It is unlikely, however, that information, which is, after all, of secondary importance for members, should have been handed down for centuries with limited alterations in the rituals and traditions, and that the most essential and fundamental information for the priestly elite—information about their origins—should have been completely lost. Someone must have continued to possess it. In effect, there is a widespread conviction that at the heart of Freemasonry there is an important secret. Given the continual and probably deliberate attempt to divert attention from the true origins of Masonry, we are led to believe that this is exactly what the secret is about—and that there is a level, at

---

*This theory is accepted as undisputable truth by the majority of modern-day Freemasonry historians, but it is far from being proved. For example, the French Mason Paul Naudon, in his book *Les origines de la Franc-Maçonnerie* (Paris: Ed. Dervy, 1991), starts by saying: "In order to search for the origins of Freemasonry, it is necessary first of all to recognize its original characteristics, those that we must find in the institutions from which it seems to have originated." According to Naudon, these institutions could only be corporations of builders. All the rest of his work is reduced to the search for traces of builders' organizations throughout history, taking for granted that they were the predecessor of Freemasonry.

the top of Freemasonry, at which this secret is known. This should be an operative level.

We don't know if it really exists. What looks certain is that since the Grand Lodge of London was created, Masonry has been an essentially speculative organism, which no longer has the slightest genetic connotation and is accessible to everyone up to the highest degrees in the organization. A minimum of knowledge about its structure, its regulations, and its ways of operating leads us to exclude that Masonry might represent an organism at the service of some hidden forces. Clearly, it is an organization subject to plagiarism, divisions, and deviations that may easily degenerate it and transform it into an organization of a completely different nature. In the three centuries of its history, there have been numerous examples of this. Not least of all is the so-called P2 Lodge, an Italian organization, which, under an apparently Masonic guise, pursued the aim of infiltrating the power system on behalf of single individuals. Yet these are deviations that have always been disowned by the Masonic body. With regard to the priestly family, modern-day Masonry seems to have become an inert fossil. It is clearly not an instrument of its power.

When the present characteristics of this institution were fixed in 1717, Europe was governed by absolute monarchs flanked by an omnipotent nobility and clergy, who for the most part had descended from the priestly family and held all the power and all the resources. The world belonged completely to them. Masonry, however, was mainly composed of members of the medium and lower nobility. The reason to fit them into an officially recognized organization, controlled from the top, could be only to prevent possible threats to the power of the upper levels of the aristocracy from the lower levels. We should not forget that one of the most solemn and binding acts required, then as now, from those accepted into the organization is the oath of faithfulness to the institutions and the authorities of the initiate's country.

Members of the aristocratic class had always been united in the defense of their privileges before the rest of the population, but engaged in a permanent struggle among themselves to achieve supremacy. The dynamics of history and the evolution of society are largely a product of these internal struggles. Today, the power of the nobility as such has declined, like that of many other branches of the family, starting with the Gens Flavia of Roman memory and continuing with the Carolingians, and so on. The instruments and the means of exercising power have changed radically as a result of the revolutionary modifications of the last few centuries. The industrial and scientific revolutions have radically changed the social and economic structure that had allowed the aristocracy to prevail.

New forces have gained the upper hand, taking control of the economy and political power. Nothing, however, leads us to suppose that their origin is different. The Star of David, the pentalpha, and a countless series of priestly and Masonic symbols appear in the flags, the coats of arms, and the logos of most international organizations and most of the Western states. It is a discreet but unequivocal presence—and behind all this, there still seems to be the priestly family.

In order to realize this, we need only look at the list of the components of the organizations that unite the "magnates" of the world and who seem to exercise a decisive influence on the decisions of Western national governments. There is no conspiracy, no secret organization, no big brother plotting in the shadows to destabilize democratic societies by means of the corruption and the degradation of the masses (a theory dear to the old Nazi libellers). The members of these organizations are well-known public figures subject to public control.

The grandees of the world meet nowadays to discuss the problems of the world, just as the grandees of the kingdom met at the time of Charlemagne to discuss the problems of Christianity and to propose solutions and policies. They meet in broad daylight, for all the world to see, even if in a reserved manner. Their names are known and are published every year, together with the agenda of the main problems under discussion. It is sufficient to type the word Bilderberg in an Internet search engine for anyone to have access to this information.

The so-called Bilderberg Group takes its name from the locality where, for the first time in 1954, some of the leading figures in the Western world met together. Since then, the group has continued to meet every year, each time in a different locality, for a conference that lasts for three days. A glance at the list of those who are invited to these meetings is illuminating. They include the last European monarchs, together with bankers, business leaders, political advisors, university professors, ministers, and high-ranking bureaucrats of international organizations such as the United Nations, NATO, and the European Community: Rockfeller, Rothschild, Lazard, Ford, Agnelli, Elkann, Kissinger, Monti, Barroso, Tremonti, along with monarchs and princes such as Juan Carlos of Spain, Bernard and Beatrix of Holland, Charles of England, Philippe of Belgium, and so on.

These are by definition the powerful of this world, and the world's destiny is decided in the course of their meetings. What is striking about this group, however, is the apparent lack of homogeneity of the members. If we consider their substances, their social position, and the roles they play in their respective countries, it is difficult to understand what may be the common denominator that links them. Yet if we analyze their names and their origins, we realize that what unites most of these people is their genetic basis—that is, the majority of them belong to the stock of those family groups, which, in the course of this book, have been identified as descendants of the Mosaic priestly family.* Today, as yesterday, the world belongs to them.

---

*One example is the young Elkann, heir to the Agnelli dynasty, whose name represents the quintessence of the priestly line, because it is composed of El (God) and Kann, which identifies the cohanim: priest of God.

22

THE ULTIMATE EVIDENCE

GENETIC PROOF

Up to this point, the evidence accumulated to support this text's priestly hypothesis is circumstantial, even if it is consistent. Taken individually, the pieces of evidence mean little and can be subject to a thousand different interpretations. Taken together, they form a highly consistent argument, and they trace the course of a long story that is perfectly plausible and coherent. What's more, they offer the advantage of clarifying convincingly a long series of mysteries and inexplicable coincidences. In a court of law called to judge the historical truth of the hypothesis sustained in this book, however, the jury would probably bring in a negative verdict for lack of evidence. Almost certainly, even the presentation of original documents proving that historical figures were members of the secret priestly organization would not succeed in changing the verdict. One of the rules of science is that exceptional discoveries, which revolutionize an entire scientific vision, must be supported by proof of an exceptional nature in order to be taken into consideration. Unless an actual history of the priestly organization popped out of some authoritative archive that was above suspicion—such as the Vatican Library, for example—which is highly unlikely, it is not clear what kind of exceptional evidence might emerge from an examination of the historical archives.

There is, however, a kind of evidence that is accepted as conclusive in all the courtrooms of the world: genetics. In this case, genetics should be able to provide irrefutable confirmation of the historical reality of this hypothesis.

According to the account of Josephus Flavius, at least two hundred fifty people belonging to the Jewish priestly family were saved by him and restored to their prior economic conditions. Many of these were women and children, but doubtless there were also some adult males. Josephus Flavius mentions about fifteen men of a high priestly rank, including himself. It may be presumed that entire family nuclei were saved. How many? It is difficult to make an estimate. Probably somewhere on the order of at least fifty family nuclei of the priestly class followed Titus to Rome.

All the members of these families had a common genetic basis, because they all descended from the group of twenty-four branches that had created the priestly organization of Jerusalem under the auspices of Ezra in the fifth century BC. The priestly origin of each of these groups had been personally controlled by Ezra, who had excluded from the priesthood anyone who did not have his credentials in order. Ezra had compelled the priests who had married women not of priestly origin to repudiate these wives, under penalty of exclusion from the priesthood, and had imposed extremely strict laws of marriage for the future.[1] From a genetic point of view, therefore, the priestly family of Jerusalem composed an extremely homogeneous, "certified" set, and consequently, the group of two hundred fifty people saved by Josephus Flavius must have had a homogeneous genetic basis.

Probably not all of them moved to Rome, but we may presume that the members of the families of the adult priests most seriously compromised with the Romans—those mentioned by Josephus Flavius—did indeed immigrate to Rome. At least fifteen family groups, for a total of about one hundred people, settled in Rome, starting from AD 70.

They were all groups who possessed considerable financial resources, and tended, by tradition and for religious reasons, to have as many children as possible. Josephus Flavius, for example, had five sons after his arrival in Rome, three of whom—Hircanus, Justus, and Agrippa[2]—outlived him and must have created in turn three independent family groups, even if we do not have any further information about them. This initial pool of family groups must then have multiplied rapidly. A conservative estimate leads us to presume that at the end of the second century, the male adults belonging to the pool of the priestly families numbered no less than five hundred and at least five thousand toward the end of the third century, when the family had complete control of all the levers of power of the Roman Empire through the lodges of Sol Invictus Mithras.

Clearly, this was a minority compared to the great mass of the population,[*] but it was expanding exponentially. With the conquest of the imperial purple robe, all the families belonging to the priestly clan received lands and noble titles. During the course of the fifth century, most of the arable land of the West ended up in the hands of great landowners belonging to that family group and to the church. During that century, but especially during the sixth century, the population of the Roman Empire dropped dramatically, due to the worsening of economic conditions, the barbarian invasions, wars, and a series of natural disasters and pestilences. Under the reign of Justinian, for example, it is calculated that the Oriental population fell by 50 percent.

Only one family group must have continued to increase in number, for, due to their economic resources and their mutual support, they were affected to a much lesser extent by those limiting factors. The members of this group undoubtedly had greater possibilities of surviving and multiplying than the others, and this was true for all the subsequent

---

[*]Many scholars have calculated the population of the Roman Empire in its various phases, and their estimates vary wildly. It seems, however, that at the end of the third century, the overall population of the Empire was not lower than fifty million.

centuries, up to today. It is therefore logical and intuitive that their percentage, compared to the total population, has grown constantly and has reached a far-from-negligible value. Almost all of their descendants must be unaware of their origins, but modern genetic techniques are sufficiently well developed to be able to establish with certainty whether they belong to the priestly clan.

There are two methods that are used at present in the field of genetics to establish the origin of populations. The first is based on an examination of the mutations that have taken place in mitochondrial DNA (mtDNA), and the second is based on variations in the so-called Y chromosome. Every human being inherits two copies of nuclear genes, one from each parent. The two copies together form new genes, which combine the characteristics of both. There is, however, one particular area of the cell, called the mitochondrion, where we find fragments of DNA transmitted exclusively by the mother. The reason is simple: the paternal genes are transmitted by the sperm that fertilizes the female egg and combines with the corresponding genes of its nucleus. Thus the DNA in the mitochondrion of the egg cell is not involved in the recombination of genes and is transmitted unchanged to the baby—except, of course, for accidental mutations. The mitochondrial DNA of every person therefore descends directly from his or her female ancestors, without any contribution from the male side. On the contrary, the Y chromosome, which is that particular chromosome that determines the sex of the baby, is transmitted exclusively by the father, without any contribution from the mother.

In its transmission from mother to daughter, mtDNA may undergo small mutations that have no effect on the person, but are in turn transmitted to their descendants. Through the examination of these small differences in mtDNA, therefore, it is possible to establish whether two individuals have a common female ancestor in the family tree. With the passing of centuries, groups of people who live in the same area and who intermarry accumulate quite distinct sequences of mutations. All the individuals whose mtDNA presents the same mutations with respect to a reference sequence have in common the same female ancestor, and based on the frequency of mutations with respect to the reference sequence, it is possible to make an approximate calculation of the period when this common ancestor lived.

The same is true for the Y chromosome, with the difference that the groups that present the same sequences of variations have a male ancestor in common, no matter which mtDNA group they belong to. Usually, there is no relation between the group that we belong to by maternal descent and the one determined by paternal descent, unless a certain population descends from a single couple or from a very limited group of couples whose descendants continued to intermarry.

This, of course, is the case with the Jewish priestly family, whose members should descend (apart from accidental intrusions of external elements into the line of descent) from Moses himself, on the male side, and from his wife Zipporah, or at least from a limited group of Midianite women, on the female side. It is presumed that the sons of Moses married women chosen from among their Midianite relations, and that from then on, the marriages took place mainly within the priestly caste, as the Bible confirms. This should make it particularly easy to determine the identity of the Mosaic priestly descendants, whatever religion or population they presently belong to.

THE COHANIM CHROMOSOME

The particular sequence of variations of the Y chromosome that distinguishes the Jewish priestly caste has been identified and is known by the name of the Cohanim Chromosome. As we have seen, *cohanim* is the plural of the Hebrew word *cohen,* which means "priest." All the Cohens or members of families whose surname derives from this (Kohen, Cahan, Kahn, Kogen, etc.) are considered by Jews to be direct descendants—by the male line—of the priestly clan of Jerusalem and, consequently, of Aaron. (As we have seen, however, this attribution to Aaron was imposed by Ezra only in the fifth century BC; the true ancestor of the priests was Moses himself.) In any case, these groups descend directly from those priests who survived the massacre of Jerusalem (either because they were among the group of two hundred fifty saved by Josephus Flavius or because they lived elsewhere), who remained faithful to the Jewish religion, and who were later excluded from the secret organization recomposed by Josephus Flavius. They were therefore excluded from the Christian priesthood, but they continued to act as rabbis in the Jewish communities.*

In 1995, it was one of them, the Canadian cohen Karl Skorecki, who had the idea of verifying whether there existed a sequence of variations in the Y chromosome that was specific for cohanim. Like all the cohanim, Skorecki had no proof of his own priesthood other than the word of his father and of his father's father before him, and so on for centuries. He wondered if, apart from oral tradition, any other proof existed of his special status. The answer, he realized, might lie in his DNA. His reasoning was simple: the Y chromosome is transmitted from father to son, like the status of priest among the Jews. Because all cohanim believe that they descend from a single ancestor, this claim should find confirmation in their Y chromosomes.

In 1996, Skorecki contacted Michael F. Hammer of the University of Arizona at Tucson, who had used the Y chromosome to investigate the origin of the Japanese population. Working with colleagues of University College, London, Skorecki and Hammer obtained samples of DNA from 188 Jews who hailed from Israel, Canada, and England, 68 of whom declared that they were cohanim.

The scientists initially concentrated on two genetic markers of the Y chromosome, arriving at the conclusion that effectively the Y chromosome of cohanim is different from that of other Jews, thus confirming the

---

*Their existence and their priestly status, as we have seen, were also recognized by members of the Christian priestly organization. In Masonry, the term *cohan,* or *cowan,* was used to define those who possessed the requisites for membership—clearly genetic requisites—but were not accepted as members for some reason. That is, they were recognized as having priestly origins, but did not possess all the requisites to assume positions of power in Christian society.

oral tradition, which says that priestly status is transmitted on a genetic basis.* In order to have definitive confirmation of these results, however, it was necessary to use a larger number of genetic markers. Skorecki and his collaborator, Neil Bradman, requested the collaboration of Professor David B. Goldstein of the University of Oxford, and they carried out a second study, collecting samples of DNA from 306 Jews, 106 of whom said that they were cohanim, and expanding the selection from two to twelve genetic markers.

Results confirmed the hypothesis that the Y chromosome of the Jewish priests had a common origin: 97 of the 106 cohanim possessed the same sequence of six genetic markers. On the contrary, only 109 of the remaining 200 Jews displayed the same sequence. Once they had determined what from then on was defined as the Cohanim Modal Haplotype (CMH)—that is, the chromosome common to all cohanim, defined by the sequence of six genetic markers—the scientists went on to evaluate the period when the common male ancestor should have lived.[3] On the basis of microvariations in the sequences within the six markers, they arrived at the conclusion that the common ancestor of the group of cohanim examined should have lived between 84 and 130 generations ago—that is, between 2,100 and 3,250 years ago. This result agrees with the reconstruction of the history of the Mosaic priestly family presented in this text.[4]

Confirmation that the Cohanim Chromosome is able to determine the direct descendants of Jewish priests, even if they are unaware of their origin, was obtained in a surprising manner: by examining the DNA of a Negro Bantu-speaking tribe, the Lembas, who live between South Africa and Zimbabwe. Today, the Lembas are mostly Christians, but according to their oral traditions, they descended from Jewish ancestors. These traditions were never taken seriously, starting from the ethnologist Tudor Parfitt, who published a study on the population in 1992.

---

*The study, published in the journal *Nature*,[5] also confirms the common origin of Ashkenazic and Sephardic priests, who separated about two thousand years ago.

Having been informed of the results of Skorecki and Goldstein, Parfitt returned to the Lembas to verify among them the presence of the genes typical of priests. The result was amazing: 9 percent of the Lembas analyzed possessed the cohanim Y chromosome, and this percentage went as high as 53 percent in one particular clan, who were indicated by their traditions as direct descendants of the founder of the tribe, evidently a Jewish priest who had arrived in that area (who knows how or when?). All this was in perfect agreement with their oral tradition.[6]

Here was all the more reason why the majority of the descendants of the groups who became members of the secret organization recomposed in Rome by Josephus Flavius should possess the genetic markers characteristic of cohanim. They were all priests of proven priestly descent, and, as the words of St. Jerome testify, possession of priestly status depended exclusively on genetic factors. The only difference lies in the fact that while the cohanim and the Lembas can be identified as such a priori, due to their oral traditions, the same cannot be said for the modern-day descendants of the priestly groups that emigrated to Rome with Josephus Flavius.

No known traditions exist that link the Christian families who emerged in a dominant position in Roman society to the Jewish priestly family. This link has been established for the first time by the hypothesis presented in this book. Such a link makes it possible to determine the families that should be bearers of the priestly gene. Targeted research would thus easily be able to verify the correctness of this hypothesis.

Yet it is not necessary to await the results of such studies in order to obtain immediately positive answers in this sense. Instead, we can rely on early genetic research that aimed to know the origin of the various European populations and the relationships existing between them. The Cohanim Chromosome has been identified in a high percentage of the Christian European population, which, on the basis of the existing historical documents, do not appear to have any relationship to the Jews and even less to their priests.

One of the first wide-spectrum studies, carried out by analyzing the Y chromosome of the European population, was conducted by the greatest living geneticist, Cavalli Sforza. He identified ten male ancestors from whom the entire European population descends. Two of these ancestors gave rise to two distinct population groups, now identified in all genetic studies by the abbreviations EU9 and EU10, which are both characterized by the cohanim marker. They make up about 20 percent of the sample on which Cavalli Sforza carried out his research, which was composed of 1,007 individuals—a fairly representative sample of the European population, but unfortunately too small to give a precise idea of the distribution of each of the ten groups, and in particular of the two groups mentioned. The important aspect, as we will shortly see in connection with mtDNA, is that the EU9 and EU10 groups, unlike all the others, whose ancestors date back to the Palaeolithic age, have a relatively recent origin and undoubtedly come from the area of Mesopotamia, where these groups, especially in Kurdistan, reach numbers higher than 50 percent of the entire population.

Cavalli Sforza was not aware of the work of Skorecki, and consequently he hypothesized that these groups represented the wave of populations who were responsible for the spread of agriculture in Europe in the late Neolithic age. They came from Mesopotamia, where, the consensus of scientific opinion believes, agriculture was born. It was only after the studies of Almut Nebel, Dvora Filon, Bernd Brinkmann, Partha P. Majumder, Marina Faerman, and Ariella Oppenheim[7] that the EU9 and EU10 groups were connected to the Cohanim Chromosome, because they present the same sequences of genetic markers.

This obviously surprised the scholars who discovered the CMH, because though they found no difficulty in explaining such a high percentage of bearers of that gene in Mesopotamia, where a large number of Jews had been deported first by the Assyrians and later by the Babylonians under Nebuchadnezzar (and from where the ancestor of the Jewish people, Abraham, came), they found enormous difficulties in explaining the presence of the Cohanim Chromosome in such a high percentage of the European Christian population. What's more, this percentage is extremely high in certain areas of Europe, where the chromosome is found in the majority of the population yet no important presence of any Jewish population has ever been historically demonstrated.

No extensive study or targeted research has been carried out in this field, but there are health organizations, such as hospitals, blood banks, and so on, that systematically carry out genetic analyses on the different kinds of material they collect. They possess an imposing mass of data, which is at the disposal of anyone who desires to carry out targeted research. After examining the genetic data collected by these organizations in Hungary, Iraq, and Italy, a German researcher, Avshalom Zoossmann-Diskin,[8] published an article challenging the conclusions of Skorecki and Goldstein about the CMH and denying that the marker discovered by them was exclusive to cohanim.

Zoossmann-Diskin criticizes the validity of their conclusions mainly because, on the basis of the data collected by the health organizations, the CMH is the most common haplotype among southern and central Italians, Hungarians, and Iraqi Kurds, and is also found among many Armenians and South African Lembas. According to Zoossmann-Diskin, this excludes that cohanim have their own gene. Otherwise, how would it be possible to explain the presence of the same gene in such a large part of the Christian population of Italy and Hungary?

In light of the priestly hypothesis, however, we know that a large number of people, particularly in central Italy and in Hungary (the heart of the ancient Pannonia), must be descendants of groups belonging to Sol Invictus Mithras and therefore the family groups of Josephus Flavius and the other priests who came to Rome with him. It is not a coincidence, then, that the cohanim gene should be the most widespread among the Italian and Pannonian populations; this is a fact that we should necessarily expect, if the hypothesis is correct.

With regard to Iraq, this too is not a coincidence. It has been said that Abraham and his tribe came from Nahor, which is situated in Ur of the Chaldees—that is, in Kurdistan, in north Iraq. There is nothing strange, then, in the fact that Moses, the ancestor of all the cohanim, should bear the genes of an ancestor coming from the area from which Abraham came, Kurdistan. Further, the explanation that the CMH stems from the Jews deported to Mesopotamia long ago (in the Middle Ages, they represented the majority of the Babylonian population), has a certain validity.

Thus what Zoossmann-Diskin considers to be evidence against the CMH becomes striking proof in favor of the priestly hypothesis. Pannonia, the homeland of Constantius Chlorus, Constantine, Valentinianus, Justinian, St. Jerome, and a long list of other figures identified in the preceding pages as descendants of the Jewish priestly family, was the region that first fell under the domination of their secret organization at the beginning of the second century. With regard to central Italy, where Rome is situated, nothing must be explained: the priestly descendants must have been concentrated here in particular, in the countless priestly groups that converged on the city, thus creating the Roman nobility. The same may be said of southern Italy, which was always a dominion of the priestly family, starting from when Titus stationed in Apulia a large number of Jewish family groups deported from Jerusalem, to the division of its territory among the Roman and Byzantine nobility, and to its conquest by the Norman Robert Guiscard, who, as we have seen, was of ancient Britannic priestly origins.

Cavalli Sforza's study shows that the CMH is widespread all over Europe, but the sample used for genetic analysis is too small to give any significant indications about the real distribution of the various groups and their percentage in the various regions of Europe. (For example, the German sample is composed only of 23 individuals who represent three of the ten European genetic groups, whereas there are as many as 80 Basques, 50 Sardinians, 45 Calabrians, and a total of 200 Syrians, Kurds, and Lebanese.) Therefore, this study does not contradict the priestly family theory, because it demonstrates the presence of the cohanim gene in a high percentage of the European Christian population. Yet it is not able to prove this in a statistically valid manner, because it does not provide a geographical distribution or a division among social classes for this gene. On the contrary, when very large genetic samples are taken into consideration, as Zoossmann-Diskin did in the former Pannonia and in central and southern Italy, results are in perfect agreement with the priestly hypothesis.

This is another powerful argument in its favor, but in order to obtain absolute certainty, it is necessary to carry out targeted research among the populations of certain areas (Rome, Venice, the area of the Danube, Brittany, Cornwall, etc.), and especially in certain social classes and family groups identified as descendants of the priestly family. Targeted research could start from the lists of the noble families kept by the Vatican. The church has always been an elitist organization. It is sufficient to surf the Internet, for example, to find a list of more than six hundred Italian families, with their noble coats of arms, who were alone allowed by a decree of Pope Honorius III to provide nuns for the Carmelite Order.[9] We may presume that most of these family groups owed this privilege to the fact that they belonged to the pool of groups representing the priestly family. Genetic research carried out on a significant sample of people who bear the surnames of these houses today (the surname is usually transmitted by the male line) should make it possible to verify whether the percentage of those who bear the Cohanim Chromosome is significantly higher than that of the rest of the population, thus confirming the priestly hypothesis with certainty.*

THE FEMALE GENETIC MARKER

Definitive confirmation could come only from a crossed mitochondrial DNA control, because this is transmitted exclusively by the female line.

---

*A study based on surnames (in particular his own) was carried out by the famous geneticist Brian Sykes (the author of *The Seven Daughters of Eve*), showing that a close genetic relationship exists between people who have the same surname, even if the memory of a family connection has been lost for centuries.

For example, a high percentage of CMH was also found, understandably, among the Kurds, because, as unequivocally indicated by the Bible (see Genesis 24:4–10), Abraham was born at Nahor, in the heart of modern-day Kurdistan, and this was the area of origin of the Jewish population who followed him to Palestine. Moses, therefore, in all probability descended from a male who came from the north of Mesopotamia. Yet he married the Midianite Zipporah, a Bedouin girl from Sinai, and we can assume that his sons, Gershom and Eliezer, married women of the same Midianite tribe. The priestly line, therefore, descends on the female side from a different stock compared to the rest of the Jewish population, whose female ancestors came from Mesopotamia.

This gives us the possibility of tracing the direct descendants of the initial couple, Moses and Zipporah. A large percentage of Jewish cohanim who are undoubtedly descendants of Moses should have mitochondrial DNA belonging to a group that is common in more than 50 percent of Bedouin women (but not in Kurdish women). The same should be true of the branches of the priestly family that have become Christian. We do not know whether and how long the rule of marriages within the group was respected, but we have the historical proof that in this group, the female line of descent was sometimes more important than or at least as important as the male one. The percentage of people with mtDNA similar to that of the Bedouins of Sinai should be remarkably close to that of Jewish cohanim and clearly higher than the rest of the Jewish population.

It does not appear that any mtDNA investigations were carried out parallel to the Y chromosome tests with regard to cohanim, and consequently we do not know whether there is a mtDNA that is typical of cohanim in the same way that there is a specific identifying Y chromosome. Yet the analysis of historical circumstances leads us to believe that it should exist, because men were cohanim only if their mothers also belonged to a priestly family. Skorecki did not think of integrating his research with an analysis of mtDNA, or if he did, he has not made the results known.

We possess, however, some extremely significant results in this sense, obtained from a highly authoritative source who carried out an analysis of mtDNA on a very large sample of the European population, leading to the identification of the female equivalent of the Y chromosome of cohanim—that is, the mtDNA of the female descendants of the women who followed to Rome the priests of the group led by Josephus Flavius and who must, therefore, be related somehow to Zipporah, the wife of Moses. This vast, detailed research on mtDNA was carried out by the English scientist Brian Sykes, and was made known to the general public in the book *The Seven Daughters of Eve.*

Mitochondrial DNA, it has been said, is transmitted exclusively from mother to daughter. This circumstance makes it particularly easy to trace the priestly family. According to the doctrine established by Ezra, it was the woman who transmitted priestly status to her male children. Frequently, in the history of this family, above all in the early Middle Ages, we can see that great family groups were added to the priestly clan by means of marriages. Important examples include that of Athelstan, the first Saxon Christian monarch. He was the son of a woman of the Welsh nobility (undoubtedly of priestly origin) and the Viking dynasty of Normandy, whose sovereigns (starting from the Viking ancestor, Rollo) always married women of the local Breton nobility, likewise of priestly origin.

While the members of the priestly family had a greater chance of survival within the overall population, within the priestly family it was the women who had greater probabilities of survival compared to the males. Unlike other societies, which practiced female infanticide, in these family groups women were a value to be protected and exploited by means of shrewd marriages. According to the law imposed by Ezra, the purity of the priestly race depended on them. Consequently, the direct descendants of the women who followed the group of priests to Rome with Josephus Flavius must necessarily be carriers of their mtDNA, which must differ in some way from that of other European women.

Among the groups of mtDNA present in Europe, therefore, there must necessarily be one that is clearly recognizable as the priestly mtDNA, and its percentage compared to the rest of the population must be fairly high—and quite close to that of the carriers of the male Cohanim Chromosome.

Through an examination of thousands of samples of DNA, Sykes established that the entire European population descends from seven women: six extremely ancient, born in the distant Palaeolithic period, from seventeen thousand to forty-five thousand years ago. Yet the seventh (whom he decided to call Jasmine) is recent and was born somewhere in the Middle East no more than ten thousand years ago. He bases this deduction on the fact that more than 50 percent of the Bedouin population of Arabia and the West Bank belongs to the Jasmine clan with the same mtDNA. Thus the wife of Moses, Zipporah, and her Midianite relations, of whom the women of the Jewish priestly caste are descendants, must have belonged to the Jasmine clan. In Europe, as many as 17 percent of the population belongs to this clan, which is similar to the number of carriers of the EU9 and EU10 markers.

What is even more significant, however, is the distribution throughout Europe of the individuals belonging to the Jasmine clan. The other six more ancient clans have extremely varied percentages—from approximately 50 percent of the clan that comes from a female ancestor called Tara by Sykes, to the 5 percent who derive from an ancestor called Velda, but they are all distributed fairly uniformly over European territory, which is a sign that the population was well mixed in the course of the past millennia. On the contrary, the Jasmine clan is distributed in patches, indicative of a relatively recent colonization that has not allowed the population time to mix homogeneously.

Sykes tries to explain this anomaly by arguing that the first six groups are the descendants of the Palaeolithic inhabitants who settled in European territory between fifty thousand and ten thousand years ago, whereas the Jasmine clan was composed of those Mesopotamian populations who, according to him, introduced agriculture into Europe in the Neolithic and following periods. He hypothesizes that they penetrated into the European continent starting from seven or eight thousand years ago, moving in two directions: from the Balkans through central Europe and along the coasts of the Mediterranean and the Atlantic, as far as the British Isles. These conclusions are somewhat improbable, but he is forced to draw them on the basis of his initial presupposition—that agriculture was a product of the Jasmine clan, imported from Mesopotamia. Sykes, however, is unable to explain this distribution concentrated in confined areas, isolated from one another, which presupposes a much more recent origin and above all a way of spreading that is different from what he hypothesized.

The Jasmine clan is concentrated in the area of ancient Pannonia and in central Europe in the valleys of the Rhine, the Meuse, and the Loire. It can also be found in central Italy, in limited areas of Spain and Portugal, and along the Atlantic coasts of Brittany, Cornwall, and Wales. By an extraordinary coincidence, these are exactly the areas where the priestly family took root and multiplied, according to our analysis, starting from the second century AD.

Is this a simple coincidence? Perhaps, but the coincidences begin to be a bit too frequent. The Jasmine clan must be made up of descendants of the priestly family who settled in Rome after the destruction of the Temple. To prove it definitively, we need only verify whether in this clan, the presence of the priestly Y chromosome is dominant. (At the same time, it would be interesting to check the mtDNA of Jewish cohanim.) Those who combine the Y chromosome of cohanim and the mitochondrial marker of Jasmine in their genetic patrimony have an excellent chance of descending directly from Moses and Zipporah.

The genetic approach is extremely encouraging, and is capable of providing the definitive proof of the priestly family theory that historical documents so far seem to be unable to supply. The male priestly chromosome that characterizes cohanim seems to have been identified. Its percentage should be particularly high among the members of the European nobility together with the mtDNA of Jasmine's clan. It would not be difficult or too costly to carry out this simple check. If the result was positive, then even the most skeptical of historians would have to agree that the time has come to start thinking about rewriting the history of the last two thousand years.

NOTES

INTRODUCTION. THE JUDAIC PRIESTLY LINE

1. Moses A. Shulvass, *The History of the Jewish People,* vol. 1 (Chicago: Regnery Gateway, 1982), 79–84.

CHAPTER 1.
CENSORSHIP IN THE BIBLE REGARDING
MOSES AND HIS DESCENDANTS

1. Deuteronomy 34:1–6.
2. Ibid., 10–12.
3. Exodus 18:2–6.
4. Erich Weidinger, *Gli Apocrifi—L'altra Bibbia che non fu scritta da Dio* [The Apocrypha—The Other Bible That Was Not Written by God] (Alessandria: PIEMME, 1997); Ephrem Syrus, *The Cave of the Treasure,* New Testament Apocrypha, 34:5–89.

CHAPTER 2.
THE DISAPPEARANCE OF MOSES'S SONS
IN THE BOOKS OF JOSHUA AND JUDGES

1. Joshua 21:10–18.
2. Judges 3:8–11.
3. Weidinger, *Gli Apocrifi—L'altra Bibbia che non fu scritta da Dio,* 34:12–89.
4. 1 Samuel 2:12.

CHAPTER 3. THE MOSAIC PRIESTLY FAMILY

1. 1 Samuel 2:27.
2. 1 Chronicles 24.
3. 1 Chronicles 24:1–6.
4. The Fourth Book of Ezra 14.
5. Exodus 6:20, Numbers 26:59.
6. Benjamin of Tudela, *The Itinerary of Benjamin of Tudela: Travels in the Middle Ages,* trans. by Marcus Nathan Adler (Oxford: Oxford University Press, 1907).
7. Samuel 6:12.

CHAPTER 4. THE DESCENDANTS OF MOSES TAKE OVER AS THE HEADS OF ISRAEL

1. Genesis 11:27.
2. Flavio Barbiero, *La Bibbia senza Segreti* [The Bible without Secrets] (Milan: Rusconi, 1988), part 4, chapter 14.
3. Josephus Flavius, *Autobiography,* 1:1.
4. Barbiero, *La Bibbia senza Segreti,* part 4, chapter 9.
5. 1 Samuel 8:5.
6. Ibid., 10:1.
7. Ibid., 15:11.
8. Ibid., 26:5.
9. Ibid., 24:7.
10. Ibid., 14:20.
11. 1 Kings 11:40.
12. David M. Rohl, *Pharaohs and Kings—A Biblical Quest* (New York: Three Rivers Press, 1995), 121.
13. 1 Kings 14:25.
14. Ibid., 12:21.
15. 2 Kings 8:22.
16. M. Baratta et al., *Atlante Storico* [Historical Atlas] (Novara: De Agostani, 1979), 4.
17. Jeremiah 1:6–10.

CHAPTER 5.
RECONSTITUTION OF THE KINGDOM OF JUDAH

1. Ezra 4:4.

CHAPTER 6. JOSEPHUS FLAVIUS

1. Suetonius, *Lives of the Caesars,* Book VIII, chapter V, XVI.
2. Shulvass, *The History of the Jewish People,* vol. 1, 139.
3. Norman Golb, *Who Wrote the Dead Sea Scrolls?* (New York: Touchstone Books, 1995), 123.
4. Josephus Flavius, *The Jewish War,* VII, 5, 7, 161.
5. Ibid., VI, 8, 3.
6. Shulvass, *The History of the Jewish People,* vol. 1, 139.

CHAPTER 7.
THE DESTINIES OF THE PRIESTLY FAMILY

1. Acts 23:6–10.
2. Josephus Flavius, *Life,* 3.13.
3. Gabriel Peters, *I Padri della Chiesa* [The Fathers of the Church], vol. 1 (Rome: Borla, 1984), 59.
4. K. Bihlmeyer and H. Tuechle, *Storia della Chiesa* [The History of the Church], vol. 1, *L'antichità cristiana* [The Christian Antiquities] (Brescia: Morcelliana, 1994), section 10.
5. Peters, *I Padri della Chiesa,* 59.4. 61.
6. Bihlmeyer and Tuechle, *Storia della Chiesa* [The History of the Church], section 15.2.
7. Flavius, *Autobiography,* 7–12.
8. Josephus Flavius, *Jewish Antiquities,* Book XVIII, 3.3.
9. Acts 10–11.

CHAPTER 8. BUILDING THE SPIRITUAL TEMPLE

1. Bihlmeyer and Tuechle, *Storia della Chiesa,* vol. 1, section 19.5.

CHAPTER 9. SOL INVICTUS MITHRAS

1. Peters, *I Padri della Chiesa,* vol. 2, 210.
2. Bihlmeyer and Tuechle, *Storia della Chiesa,* vol. 1, section 41.2.

3. Peters, *I Padri della Chiesa,* vol. 2, 213.

4. H. George Pflaum, *L'impero romano* [The Roman Empire], vol. 4 (Mondatori: Propilei Grande Storia Universale, 1967), 480.

5. Reinhold Merkelbach, *Mithras il Signore delle grotte* [Mitra: The Master of the Caves] (Genoa: ECIG, 1988), 149.

6. Barbiero, *La Bibbia senza Segreti,* part 1.

7. Franz Cumont, *The Mysteries of Mithras* (White Fish, Mont.: Kessinger, 1910), 152.

8. Harry Kenison, *The Mystery of Mithras* (White Fish, Mont.: Kessinger, 1961).

9. Cumont, *The Mysteries of Mithras,* 155.

10. Merkelbach, *Mithras il Signore delle grotte* [Mitra: The Master of the Caves], 149.

11. Ibid., 181.

12. Ibid., 169.

13. Ludovico Gatto, *Storia di Roma nel Medioevo* [The History of Medieval Rome] (Rome: Newton and Compton, 1999), 23, 32–33.

14. Bihlmeyer and Tuechle, *Storia della Chiesa,* vol. 1, section 75.7.

15. Cumont, *The Mysteries of Mithras,* 192.

16. J. Gelmi, *I Papi, da Pietro a Giovanni Paolo II* [The Popes, from Peter to John Paul II] (Milan: Bur, 1986), 22.

17. Lucio De Giovanni, *L'imperatore Costantino e il mondo pagano* [The Emperor Constantine and the Pagan World] (Naples: D'Auria, 2003), 143.

18. Gatto, *Storia di Roma nel Medioevo* [The History of Medieval Rome], 38.

19. Merkelbach, *Mithras il Signore delle grotte,* 112.

20. Henry Andrew Franken, *Franken Manuscript* (White Fish, Mont.: Kessinger, 1783).

CHAPTER 10. THE STRATEGY OF THE PRIESTLY FAMILY TO CONQUER THE ROMAN EMPIRE

1. Merkelbach, *Mithras il Signore delle grotte* [Mitra: The Master of the Caves], 149.

2. Ibid., 174.

3. Ibid.

4. Ibid., 149.

5. Bihlmeyer and Tuechle, *Storia della Chiesa,* section 16.4.

CHAPTER 11. THE TAKEOVER OF THE IMPERIAL OFFICE

1. Bihlmeyer and Tuechle, *Storia della Chiesa,* vol. 1, 87.

2. Merkelbach, *Mithras il Signore delle grotte,* 113.

3. Marta Sordi, *I cristiani e l'impero romano* [The Christians and the Roman Empire] (Milan: Jaca, 1983), 105.

4. Ibid., 106.

5. Ibid., 121.

6. Ibid., 126.

7. H. B. Workman, *Persecution in the Early Church* (Oxford: Oxford University Press, 1980), 102.

8. Merkelbach, *Mithras il Signore delle grotte,* 183.

9. Sordi, *I cristiani e l'impero romano,* 119.

10. W. Seston, "The Decline of the Western Roman Empire," in *Propilei,* vol. 4, 565.

11. Merkelbach, *Mithras il Signore delle grotte,* 110–14.

12. Seston, *Propilei,* vol. 4, 601.

13. Merkelbach, *Mithras il Signore delle grotte,* 184.

14. Seston, *Propilei,* vol. 4, 565.

15. Michael Grant, *The Emperor Constantine* (London: Weidenfeld and Nicolson, 1993), 17.

16. Sordi, *I cristiani e l'impero romano,* 136.

17. Workman, *Persecution in the Early Church,* 107.

18. George Pflaum, "The Roman Empire," in *Propilei,* vol. 4, 456.

19. Sordi, *I cristiani e l'impero romano,* 134.

20. Seston, *Propilei,* vol. 4, 569.

21. Sordi, *I cristiani e l'impero romano,* 137, note 13.

22. Ibid., 137.

23. Ibid., 136.

CHAPTER 12. THE CONSOLIDATION OF POWER OVER ROMAN SOCIETY

1. Bihlmeyer and Tuechle, *Storia della Chiesa,* vol. 1, section 41.1.

2. Ibid., section 41.2.

3. Aurelius Victor, *De Caesaribus,* 28 (Liverpool: Liverpool University Press, 1994).

4. Edward Gibbon, *The History of the Decline and Fall of the Roman Empire,* vol. 2 (New York: Simon and Schuster, 1974), chapter 28, note 12.

5. Ibid., 74.

6. S. Mazzarino, *Aspetti sociali del IV secolo* [Social Aspects of the Fourth Century] (Milan: RCS, 2002), 305.

7. Ibid., 305.

8. Seston, *Propilei,* vol. 4, map page 628.

9. E. A. Thompson, *Romans and Barbarians—The Decline of the Western Empire* (Madison: University of Wisconsin Press, 1982), 41.

10. Ibid., 71.

11. Ibid., 46.

12. Bihlmeyer and Tuechle, *Storia della Chiesa,* section 14.4.

13. Seston, *Propilei,* vol. 4, 607.

14. Gibbon, *The History of the Decline and Fall of the Roman Empire,* vol. 2, 52.

15. Josef Gelmi, *I Papi* [The Popes] (Milan: Rizzoli, 1987), 22.

16. Seston, *Propilei,* vol. 4, 579.

17. Ibid., 385.

18. Ibid., 388.

19. Gibbon, *The History of the Decline and Fall of the Roman Empire,* chapter 23, 255.

20. Seston, *Propilei,* vol. 4, 591.

21. Pierre Maraval, *Le Christianisme de Constantine à la conquete arabe* [Christianity from Constantine to the Arab Conquest] (Paris: Presse Universitaire de France, 1997), 16.

22. Seston, *Propilei,* vol. 4, 592.

23. Ibid., 601.

24. Ibid., 608.

CHAPTER 13. THE PRIESTLY FAMILY AND THE SO-CALLED FALL OF THE ROMAN EMPIRE

1. Richard Krautheimer, *Rome—Profile of a City, 312–1308* (Princeton: Princeton University Press, 2000), 3–31.

2. Ludovico Gatto, *Storia di Roma nel Medioevo* (Rome: Bulzoni, 1999), 38.

3. Seston, *Propilei,* vol. 4, 601.

4. Codex Theodosianus XI, 7, 13.

5. Gibbon, *The History of the Decline and Fall of the Roman Empire,* chapter 28, note 12.

6. A. B. Griffith, *The Archaeological Evidence for Mithraism in Imperial Rome* (Ann Arbor: University of Michigan, 1993).

7. Codex Theodosianus XVI, 10, 10.

8. The saints Cantius, Cantianius, and Cantianella, venerated on May 31.

9. Tacitus, *Annals,* XV, 74.

10. Gibbon, *The History of the Decline and Fall of the Roman Empire,* chapter 31, 169.

11. Ibid., 170.

12. Thompson, *Romans and Barbarians—The Decline of the Western Empire.*

13. Seston, *Propilei,* vol. 4, 633.

14. Thompson, *Romans and Barbarians—The Decline of the Western Empire,* 31.

15. Ibid., 32.

16. Seston, *Propilei,* vol. 4, 604.

17. Thompson, *Romans and Barbarians—The Decline of the Western Empire,* 33.

18. Ibid., 150.

19. Gibbon, *The History of the Decline and Fall of the Roman Empire,* chapter 36.

20. Thompson, *Romans and Barbarians—The Decline of the Western Empire,* 45.

CHAPTER 14. THE EUROPEAN POSITION AFTER THE END OF THE EMPIRE

1. J. M. Fallace-Hadrill, *The Barbarian West, 400–1000* (Cambridge, Mass.: Blackwell, 1988), 121–22.

CHAPTER 15. THE PRIESTLY FAMILY IN GREAT BRITAIN

1. David Edwards, *Christian England* (London: Fount Paperbacks, 1989), 20.

2. Ibid., 21.

3. Seston, *Propilei,* vol. 4, 633.

4. Leslie Alcock, *Arthur's Britain* (London: Penguin, 1971), 98.

5. Seston, *Propilei,* vol. 4, 636.

6. Gildas, *De excidio et conquestu Britanniae,* ed. J. A. Giles (London: Henry G. Bohn, 1848).

7. Bihlmeyer and Tuechle, *Storia della Chiesa,* vol. 1, section 44.2.

8. Ibid., section 44.3.

9. Edwards, *Christian England,* 22.

10. Alcock, *Arthur's Britain,* 103.

11. Ibid., 124.

12. Ibid., 98.

13. Edwards, *Christian England,* 24.

14. Ibid., 33–35.

15. Ibid., 34.

16. Alcock, *Arthur's Britain,* 96.

17. Ibid., 98.

18. Edwards, *Christian England,* 28.

19. Ibid., 121.

20. Ibid., 122.

21. Ibid., 126–29.

22. Ibid., 40.

23. Ibid., 28–29.

24. Bihlmeyer and Tuechle, *Storia della Chiesa,* vol. 1, 288.

25. Pierre Riché, *The Carolingians* (Philadelphia: University of Pennsylvania, 1993), 248.

26. Edwards, *Christian England,* 115.

CHAPTER 16. COUNTERATTACK!

1. Krautheimer, *Rome—Profile of a City, 321–1308,* 117.

2. Riché, *The Carolingians,* 44.

3. Ibid., 69.

4. Ibid., 71.

5. Ibid., 73.

6. Ibid., 118.

7. Ibid., 117.

8. Ibid., 318.

9. Ibid., 117.

10. Ibid., 119.

11. Ibid., 125.

12. Ibid., 117.

13. Ibid., 196.

14. Anne J. Duggan, *Nobles and Nobility in Medieval Europe: Concepts, Origins, Transformation* (Woodbridge: Boydell Press, 2000), 104.

15. Steven Runciman, *Storia delle Crociate* [History of the Crusades] (Turin: Einaudi, 1966), vol. 1, 42.

16. Ibid., 280.

17. John Harvey, *The Plantagenets* (London: Wheaton and Company, 1969), 18.

18. Riché, *The Carolingians,* 104–7.

19. Ibid., 186.

CHAPTER 17. THE PERPETUATION OF POWER BY THE PRIESTLY FAMILY

1. Gelmi, *I Papi* [The Popes], 22.

2. Codex Theodosianus XVII.10.14.; A. B. Griffith, *The Archaeological Evidence for Mithraism in Imperial Rome.*

3. Grant, *The Emperor Constantine,* 136.

4. Griffith, *The Archaeological Evidence for Mithraism in Imperial Rome,* 241.

5. Merkelbach, *Mithras,* 241.

6. J. Morsel, *L'Aristocratie Médiéval, V°–XV siècle* [The Medieval Aristocracy, 5th–15th Century] (Paris: Publications of the Sorbonne, 2004), 137.

7. D. Iogna-Prat, *La Maison Dieu—Une histoire monumentale de l'Eglise au Moyen Age* [The House of God—A Monumental History of the Church of the Middle Ages] (Paris: Éditions du Seuil, 2006), 125.

8. Eugen Lennhoff, *Il libero muratore* [The Freemason] (Livorno: Bastoni, 1972), 39; Eugenio Bonvicini, *Massoneria Antica—Dalla carta di Bologna del 1248 agli antichi doveri del 1723* [Ancient Masonry—from the Bologna Charter of 1248 to Ancient Duties of 1723] (Rome: Atanor, 1989), 144.

9. Josephus Flavius, *Jewish Antiquities,* I, 2, 8.

10. B. W. Sholz and B. Rogers, *Carolingian Chronicles* (Ann Arbor: University of Michigan Press, 1972), 35.

11. Bargellini and Guarnirei, *Strade di Firenze* [The Streets of Florence] (Florence: Vallecchi, 1977); Umberto Bartocci, *America, una rotta templare—sentieri segreti della storia* [America: A Templar Course—Secret Paths of History] (Arezzo: Edizioni della Lisca, 1995), 69.

CHAPTER 18. THE CRUSADES

1. Henry Andrew Francken, *Francken Manuscript,* initiation to the 16th degree: Prince of Jerusalem.

2. Albert Pike, *The Magnum Opus,* 1857 (Whitefish, Mont.: Kessinger, 2004), the ritual of the XVIII degree: Knight or Sovereign Prince of the Rose-Cross.

3. Barbara Frale, *Il Papato ed il processo ai Templari—L'inedita assoluzione di Chinon alla luce della diplomatica pontificia* [The Papacy and the Process of the Templars—The Acquittal of Chinon in the Light of the Papal Diplomatica] (Florence: Giunti, 2001).

4. Umberto Bartocci, *America una rotta templare—sentieri segreti della storia* [America: A Templar Course—The Secret Paths of History].

5. Ruggero Marino, *Christopher Columbus, the Last Templar* (Rochester, Vt.: Destiny Books, 2007).

CHAPTER 19. THE ROLE OF JUDAISM IN THE CHRISTIAN WORLD

1. Gatto, *Storia di Roma nel Medioevo* [The History of Medieval Rome], 325.

2. Attilio Milano, *Storia degli ebrei in Italia* [The History of the Jews in Italy] (Torino: Einaudi, 1992), 245.

3. Ibid.

CHAPTER 20. HERALDRY

1. B. B. Heim, *L'Araldica nella Chiesa Cattolica* [Heraldry of the Catholic Church] (Vatican City: 1981), 93.

2. Stephen Friar and John Ferguson, *Basic Heraldry* (London: Herbert Press, 1993), 10.

3. Beryl Platts, *The Origin of Heraldry* (London: Proctor Press, 1980); Ottfried

Neubecker, *Heraldry—Sources, Symbols and Meaning* (London: Macdonald and Jane's, 1977), 5.

4. Richard Siegel, *The Jewish Almanac* (New York: Bantam, 1980).

5. Stephen Slater, *The Complete Book of Heraldry* (London: Lorenz Books, 2002), 197.

6. Alcock, *Arthur's Britain,* 124.

7. J. J. Norwich, *Storia di Venezia* [The History of Venice] (Milan: Mursia, 1981), 46.

8. Ibid.

9. Cassiodorus, *Epistle 24,* cited in Gibbon, *The History of the Decline and Fall of the Roman Empire,* chapter 35.

10. Ibid., 110.

11. Neubecker, *Heraldry,* 224.

12. Norwich, *Storia di Venezia,* 48.

13. M. Maclagan, *Lines of Succession, Heraldry of the Royal Families of Europe* (London: Grange Books, 2002), 199.

14. Heim, *L'Araldica nella Chiesa Cattolica,* 154.

15. A. De Beaumont, *Recherche sur l'origine du blason et en particulier sur la fleur de lis* [Search for the Origin of Heraldry and in Particularly for the Fleur de Lis] (Paris: Puiseaux, 1996), 88–119.

16. Ibid., IX.

17. Ibid., XXI.

18. Ibid., 125.

19. Maclagan, *Lines of Succession,* 181.

20. Piero Bargellini, *Storia di una grande famiglia, i Medici* [The History of a Great Family: The Medici] (Florence: Vallecchi, 1980), 12.

CHAPTER 21. MODERN MASONRY

1. Joseph Morsel, *L'Aristocratie Médiéval* [The Medieval Aristocracy], 30.

2. Ibid., 274.

3. Ibid., 276.

4. Eugen Lennhof, *Il libero muratore* [The Freemason], 29–30.

5. Papal Encyclical, "In eminenti apostolatus specula," April 28, 1738.

6. John Sheville and James L. Gould, *Guide to the Royal Arch Chapter* (White Fish, Mont.: Kessinger, 1867), 11.

7. F. J. Speidel, *The York Rite of Freemasonry—A History and Handbook* (Oxford: Press of Oxford Orphanage, 1978), 8.

8. Christopher Knight and Robert Lomas, *The Second Messiah* (London: Century Books, 1977), 20–49; M. Baigent and R. Leigh, *The Temple and the Lodge* (London: Corgi Books, 1998), 158.

9. Eugenio Bonvicini, *I Riti massonici,* Orientamenti—Rivista di vita muratoria [Masonic Rituals, Orientamenti—Review of Masonry] (Naples: Libreria Editrice Redenzione, 1992), 12.

10. Eugenio Bonvicini, *L'ordine dei Fratelli di Giovanni o framassoni,* Rivista massonica, vol. LXX, maggio/giugno [The Order of the Brotherhood of St John, Review of Masonry] (Milan: Bonpiani, 1979).

11. Lenhoff, *Il libero muratore,* 36.

12. Ibid., 32.

13. Paul Naudon, *Les origines de la Franc-Maçonnerie* [The Origins of French Masonry] (Paris: Éditions Loubatieres, 1991).

14. Latino Bonci, *I maestri Comacini,* Rivista massonica [The Comacini Masters, Review of Masonry], vol. XIV, Ott. 79, 421.

15. Lennhoff, *Il libero muratore,* 38.

16. Knight and Lomas, *The Second Messiah,* 209.

17. Ibid., 49.

CHAPTER 22. THE ULTIMATE EVIDENCE

1. Josephus Flavius, *Life,* 1.5; 426–27.

2. *Nature: International Weekly Journal of Science* (January 2, 1997).

3. N. Bradman, M. Thomas, D. G. Goldstein, "The Genetic Origins of Old Testament Priests"; C. Renfrew, *Population-specific Polymorphisms* (Cambridge, England: Cambridge University Press, 1998).

4. A. B. Spurdle, T. Jenkins, "The origins of the Lemba 'black Jews' of southern Africa: Evidence from p12F2 and other Y-chromosome markers," in *American Journal of Human Genetics* 59 (1996): 1126—33.

5. K. Skorecki, S. Selig, S. Blazer, R. Bradman, N. Bradman, P. J. Warburton, M. Ismajlowicz, et. al., "Y chromosomes of Jewish priests," in *Nature: International Weekly Journal of Science* 385 (1997): 32; M. G. Thomas, K. Skorecki, H. Ben-Ami, T. Parfitt, N. Bradman, D. B. Goldstein, "Origins of

Old Testament priests," in *Nature: International Weekly Journal of Science* 394 (1998): 138.

6. "The Y Chromosome Pool of Jews as Part of the Genetic Landscape of the Middle East" (Jerusalem: Department of Haematology, Hadassah Medical School, Hadassah University Hospital; Hebrew University, Laboratory of Biological Anthropology and Ancient DNA; Hebrew University, Hadassah School of Dental Medicine, 2001).

7. Avshalom Zoossmann-Diskin, "Are today's Jewish priests descended from the old ones?" in *HOMO: Journal of Comparative Human Biology* 51, no. 2–3 (2000): 156–62.

8. See www.araldicavaticana.com/index.htm.

9. Barbiero, *La Bibbia senza Segreti,* 15.

SELECTED
BIBLIOGRAPHY

Alcock, Leslie. *Arthur's Britain—History and Archaeology AD 367–634*. London: Penguin, 1971.

Altheim, F. *Storia della religione romana*. Rome: Settimo Sigillo, 1996.

Apocrypha—The Other Bible That Was Not Written by God. Alessandria: PIEMME, 1997.

Arcella, S. *I Misteri del sole*. Naples: Controcorrente, 2002.

Aurelius, Victor. *De Caesaribus*. Liverpool: Liverpool University Press, 1994.

Baigent, M., and R. Leigh. *The Temple and the Lodge*. London: Corgi Books, 1998.

Baratta, M., et al. *Atlante Storico*. Novara: De Agostani, 1979.

Barbiero, Flavio. *La Bibbia senza Segreti*. Milan: Rusconi, 1988.

Bargellini, Piero. *Storia di una grande famiglia, i Medici*. Florence: Vallecchi, 1980.

Bargellini, Piero, and Guarnirei. *Strade di Firenze*. Florence: Vallecchi, 1977.

Bartocci, Umberto. *America una rotta templare—sentieri segreti della storia*. Arezzo: Edizioni della Lisca, 1995.

Bihlmeyer, K., and H. Tuechle. *Storia della Chiesa*. Brescia: Morcelliana, 1994.

Bonvicini, Eugenio. *Massoneria Antica—Dalla carta di Bologna del 1248 agli antichi doveri del 1723*. Rome: Atanor, 1989.

Bradman, N., M. Thomas, and M. Goldstein. "The Genetic Origins of Old Testament Priests." *Nature: International Weekly Journal of Science*.

Cannon, John, and Ralph Griffits. *The Oxford Illustrated History of the British Monarchy.* Oxford: Oxford University Press, 2000.

Crouch, David. *The Birth of Nobility: Constructing Aristocracy in England and France 900–1300.* Edinburgh: Pearson, 2005.

Cumont, Franz. *Le religioni orientali nel paganesimo romano.* Bari: Laterza, 1967.

———. *Textes et Monuments figures relatifs aux Mystères de Mithra.* Bruselles: H. Lamertin, 1896, 1899.

———. *The Mysteries of Mithras.* White Fish, Mont.: Kessinger, 1910.

De Beaumont, A. *Recherche sur l'origine du blason et en particulier sur la fleur de lis.* Paris: Puiseaux, 1996.

De Giovanni, Lucio. *L'imperatore Costantino e il mondo pagano.* Naples: D'Auria, 2003.

Duggan, Anne J. *Nobles and Nobility in Medieval Europe: Concepts, Origins, Transformations.* Woodbridge: Boydell Press, 2000.

Edwards, David L. *Christian England.* London: Fount Paperbacks, 1989.

Fallace-Hadrill, J. M. *The Barbarian West, 400–1000.* Cambridge, Mass.: Blackwell, 1988.

Faulkner, Neil. *The Decline and Fall of Roman Britain.* Stroud and Charleston, England: Tempus, 2004.

Finberg, H. P. R. *The Formation of England, 550–1042.* London: Paladin, 1974.

Finley, M. I. *The Ancient Economy.* Los Angeles: University of California Press, 1973.

Flavius, Josephus. *Autobiography.*

———. *Jewish Antiquities.*

———. *Life.*

———. *The Jewish War.*

Frale, Barbara. *Il Papato ed il processo ai Templari—L'inedita assoluzione di Chinon alla luce della diplomatica pontificia.* Florence: Giunti, 2001.

Francken, Henry Andrew. *Francken Manuscript,* 1783. Whitefish, Mont.: Kessinger, 1997.

Friar, Stephen, and John Ferguson. *Basic Heraldry.* London: Herbert Press, 1993.

Gatto, Ludovico. *Storia di Roma nel Medioevo.* Rome: Newton and Compton, 1999.

Gavin, F. *The Jewish Antecedent of the Christian Sacraments.* London: Macmillan, 1928.

Gelmi, Josef. *I Papi, da Pietro a Giovanni Paolo II.* Milan: Bur, 1986.

Gibbon, Edward. *The History of the Decline and Fall of the Roman Empire.* London: Penguin, 1994.

Gildas. *De excidio et conquestu Britanniae.* London: Henry G. Bohn, 1848.

Golb, Norman. *Who Wrote the Dead Sea Scrolls?* New York: Touchstone Books, 1995.

Grant, Michael. *The Emperor Constantine.* London: Weidenfeld and Nicolson, 1993.

Griffith, A. B. *The Archaeological Evidence for Mithraism in Imperial Rome.* Ann Arbor: University of Michigan, 1993.

Hallam, Elisabeth. *The Plantagenet Chronicles.* London: Greenewich, 2002.

Harvey, John. *The Plantagenets.* London: Wheaton and Company, 1969.

Heim, B. B. *L'Araldica nella Chiesa Cattolica.* Vatican City: 1981.

Holy Bible, King James Version. New York: Free Press, 1973.

Iogna-Prat, D. *La Maison Dieu—Une histoire monumentale de l'Eglise au Moyen Age.* Paris: Éditions du Seuil, 2006.

Knight, Christopher, and Robert Lomas. *The Second Messiah.* London: Century Books, 1977.

Krautheimer, Richard. *Rome—Profile of a City, 312–1308.* Princeton: Princeton University Press, 2000.

Lennhoff, Eugen. *Il libero muratore.* Livorno: Bastoni, 1972.

Leon, H. J. *The Jews of Ancient Rome.* Philadelphia: Jewish Publication Society, 1960.

Lilie, Ralph-Johannes. *Bisanzio la seconda Roma.* Rome: Newton and Compton, 2005.

Logan, F. Donald. *A History of the Church in the Middle Ages.* New York: Routledge, 2002.

Maclagan, M. *Lines of Succession: Heraldry of the Royal Families of Europe.* London: Grange Books, 2002.

Maier, Paul L. *Eusebius—The Church History.* Grand Rapids: Kregel, 1999.

Maraval, Pierre. *Le Christianisme de Constantine à la conquête arabe.* Paris: Presse Universitaire de France, 1997.

Marino, Ruggero. *Christopher Columbus, the Last Templar.* Rochester, Vt.: Destiny Books, 2007.

Mazzarino, Santo. *Aspetti sociali del IV secolo—Ricerche di Storia tardo Romana.* Milan: RCS, 2002.

Merkelbach, Reinhold. *Mithras il Signore delle grotte.* Genoa: ECIG, 1988.

Milano, Attilio. *Storia degli ebrei in Italia.* Turin: Einaudi, 1992.

Morsel, J. *L'Aristocratie Médiéval, V°–XV siècle.* Paris: Publications of the Sorbonne, 2004.

Naudon, Paul. *The Secret History of Freemasonry.* Rochester, Vt.: Inner Traditions, 2005.

Neubecker, Ottfried. *Heraldry—Sources, Symbols and Meaning.* London: Macdonald and Jane's, 1977.

Norwich, J. J. *Storia di Venezia.* Milan: Mursia, 1981.

Peters, Gabriel. *I Padri della Chiesa.* Rome: Borla, 1984.

Pflaum, H. George. *L'impero romano.* Mondatori: Propilei Grande Storia Universale, 1967.

Pike, Albert. *The Magnum Opus,* 1857. Whitefish, Mont.: Kessinger, 2004.

Read, Piers Paul. *The Templars.* London: Phoenix Press, 1999.

Renfrew, C. *Population-Specific Polymorphisms.* Cambridge, England: Cambridge University Press, 1996.

Riché, Pierre. *The Carolingians.* Philadelphia: University of Pennsylvania, 1993.

Rigon, R. *Il culto di Mithra tra mito e storia.* Saluzzo: Ed. Barbarossa, 1983.

Rohl, David M. *Pharaohs and Kings—A Biblical Quest.* New York: Three Rivers Press, 1995.

Roth, Cecil. *The Jews in the Renaissance.* Philadelphia: Jewish Publication Society, 1959.

Runciman, Steven. *Storia delle Crociate.* Turin: Einaudi, 1966.

Salway, Peter. *A History of Roman Britain.* Oxford: Oxford University Press, 1993.

———. *Roman Britain.* Oxford: Clarendon Press, 1981.

Savage, Anne. *The Anglo-Saxon Chronicles.* London: Greenewich Ed., 2002.

Seston, W. *The Decline of the Western Roman Empire.* Mondatori: Propilei Grande Storia Universale, 1967.

Sheville, John, and James L. Gould. *Guide to the Royal Arch Chapter.* Whitefish, Mont.: Kessinger, 1867.

Sholz, B. W., and B. Rogers. *Carolingian Chronicles.* Ann Arbor: University of Michigan Press, 1972.

Shulvass, Moses A. *The History of the Jewish People,* 3 vols. Chicago: Regnery Gateway, 1982.

Slater, Stephen. *The Complete Book of Heraldry.* London: Lorenz Books, 2002.

Skorecki, K., et al. "Y chromosomes of Jewish priests." In *Nature: International Weekly Journal of Science* 385 (1997): 32.

Sordi, Marta. *I cristiani e l'impero romano.* Milan: Jaca, 1983.

Speidel, F. J. *The York Rite of Freemasonry—A History and Handbook.* Oxford: Press of Oxford Orphanage, 1978.

Spurdle, A. B., and T. Jenkins. (1996) "The origins of the Lemba 'black Jews' of southern Africa: Evidence from p12F2 and other Y-chromosome markers." *American Journal of Human Genetics* 59 (1996): 1126–33.

Stenton, Frank. *Anglo-Saxon England c. 550–1087.* Oxford: Clarendon Press, 1971.

Suetonius. *Lives of the Caesars.* N.p., N.d.

Sykes, Bryan. *The Seven Daughters of Eve.* London: Bantam Press, 2001.

Thomas, M. G., et. al. "Origins of Old Testament priests." In *Nature: International Weekly Journal of Science* 394 (1998): 138.

Thompson, E. A. *Romans and Barbarians—The Decline of the Western Empire.* Madison: University of Wisconsin Press, 1982.

Weidinger, Herich. *Gli Apocrifi—L'altra Bibbia che non fu scritta da Dio.* Alessandria: PIEMME, 1997.

Workman, H. B. *Persecution in the Early Church.* Oxford: Oxford University Press, 1980.

"The Y Chromosome Pool of Jews as Part of the Genetic Landscape of the Middle East." Jerusalem: Department of Haematology, Hadassah Medical School; Hadassah University Hospital, Hebrew University, Laboratory of Biological Anthropology and Ancient DNA; Hebrew University, Hadassah School of Dental Medicine, 2001.

Zoossmann-Diskin, Avshalom. "Are today's Jewish priests descended from the old ones?" In *HOMO: Journal of Comparative Human Biology* 51, no. 2–3 (2000): 156–62.

INDEX

Page numbers preceded by CP refer to color insert page.

BOOKS OF RELATED INTEREST

Secret Societies
Their Influence and Power from Antiquity to the Present Day
by Michael Howard

Moses and Akhenaten
The Secret History of Egypt at the Time of the Exodus
by Ahmed Osman

Secret Societies and the Hermetic Code
The Rosicrucian, Masonic, and Esoteric Transmission in the Arts
by Ernesto Frers

The Secrets of Masonic Washington
A Guidebook to Signs, Symbols, and Ceremonies at the
Origin of America's Capital
by James Wasserman

Founding Fathers, Secret Societies
Freemasons, Illuminati, Rosicrucians, and the
Decoding of the Great Seal
by Robert Hieronimus, Ph.D. with Laura Cortner

Secret Societies of America's Elite
From the Knights Templar to Skull and Bones
by Steven Sora

Christianity: An Ancient Egyptian Religion
by Ahmed Osman

The Invisible History of the Rosicrucians
The World's Most Mysterious Secret Society
by Tobias Churton

INNER TRADITIONS • BEAR & COMPANY
P.O. Box 388
Rochester, VT 05767
1-800-246-8648
www.InnerTraditions.com

Or contact your local bookseller